Almost a Boffin
The memoirs of Group Captain
E.E.Vielle, OBE, RAF (Rtd)

E.E. Vielle

First published in 2013 by Dolman Scott Ltd

Almost a Boffin©2013 by E.E.Vielle

ISBN 978-1-909204-15-7

Dolman Scott Ltd
www.dolmanscott.com

Acknowledgement

I would like to express my thanks to the Museum Managing Director of the Farnborough Airsciences Trust and his staff for the photographs of the former scientists who served at RAE.

Dedication

I humbly dedicate this book to all those courageous aircrew in Bomber Command during the Second World War. In particular, this Dedication is to those who lost their lives – many needlessly – through the treachery of a few scientists who had misplaced loyalties and aspirations, whilst trusted by their colleagues at the Royal Aircraft Establishment, Farnborough, which I have revealed in the pages that follow.

Chapter

Almost a Boffin
The memoirs of Group Captain E.E.Vielle, OBE, RAF (Rtd)

Preface

I started writing this in 1962 – relatively soon after I left the RAF. But the contents regarding the communist activities of certain highly placed officials, and my miraculous escape from their attempt to kill me in December 1949, has influenced me to delay publication until they (and their likeminded comrades) were less likely to cause me any trouble as a result.

If, however, I should now suddenly die or be seriously injured, you may guess the reason.

E.E.Vielle.

Chapter 1

Introduction

I was born in London in April 1913 – 100 years ago. Now, to my 15 great grandchildren I am a relic of a bygone age. They regard me rather like an ancient monument – Nelson's Column in Trafalgar Square, for example – except that, when prodded, I can still talk. They (bless them) regard the world in which I grew up to be almost as remote to them as the Ice Age does to me. Nevertheless, they (and their parents) express interest in my life. So, rather than relating the same things to each of them, I have decided to write it out just once for all of them. Hence these memoirs.

But my memoirs also have another purpose – to explain that, but for the activities of three communist British scientists, the Germans would probably not have started the Second World War. They certainly would not have been able to invade France in 1940 and would probably have lost the war that year.

Starting in the 1920s, those three scientists deliberately sabotaged the ability of the RAF to operate efficiently. They prevented Bomber Command, in particular, from being properly equipped to do their job. Furthermore, I am probably the last person alive with detailed knowledge of that fact.

Everyone lives an interesting life. But some, by sheer chance, are more varied or unusual than others. Most are affected by big events. In my case, the Great Depression of 1929-1931 resulted in me joining the Royal Air Force instead of going to university. The Italian invasion of Abyssinia caused me to get married when I was 21 – long before I had intended. The fall of France in 1940 decided me to evacuate my wife and daughter to Canada. Many families have experienced similar upheavals due to big national, or international, events.

But it is often quite a tiny thing that results in big changes and makes life so much more interesting. And I have had far more than my fair share of these. For example, it was mainly the result of me

1

inheriting a telescope and sextant from my grandfather that the RAF transferred me to the "Special Duty List" on three separate occasions (totalling nearly 7 years) to work with scientists on various Top Secret projects. That partly resulted from my various inventions – including one which led to the development of the Cruise Missile. Another (later) invention resulted in me being offered twice the salary of an Air Marshal to leave the RAF at age 43 to become managing director of a company set up to exploit it. A flying incident in 1935 resulted in me becoming privy to a matter of historical interest (affecting the Princess Diana drama), which the "Establishment" has tried to deny ever occurred. The loss of a fishing rod in the St. Lawrence River in Canada led to my involvement in a search for the Rommel Treasure in the Mediterranean. The escape of a Russian count from the firing squad in Moscow in 1917 affected my life during the last war. In 1956, a flying incident gave me the idea for a novel for which Hitchcock later bought the film rights – which in turn caused me to take up residence in Switzerland and write more novels. A chance remark in 1960 led to my association with a Swiss bank and my development of a system of investment that turned £32,000 in 1974 into £7,000,000 ten years later. And so it goes on. Tiny events have led me into what I believe has been an unusually interesting life.

I was privileged to meet and work with many wonderful people – particularly some of the top scientists in the UK and USA (including, for example, Albert Einstein), and I made many delightful friends. But I have also met some really awful people. Four in particular, each of whom I trusted, have tried to swindle me. It is uncanny, and quite frightening, that in two cases their only sons met tragic deaths and the other two died of cancer soon afterwards.

At the outbreak of the Second World War, and later during the "Cold War", I was in a unique position to observe the tremendous (and little realised) damage done to our national interest by some communists in our civil service.

During my lifetime I have witnessed – and experienced – vast changes. When I joined the RAF I was taught to fly on a type of biplane that was designed in 1912 (just 9 years after the Wright brothers' first flight) and was used throughout the First World War. Its top speed was normally 70mph and, even in a vertical dive with the engine at full power, it had a terminal velocity of only about 120 mph – considerably less than the 155mph speed at which I later used to cruise my Mercedes on German autobahns. During my 25 years' RAF service, I flew 150 different types of aircraft, including, shortly before I retired, a fighter at supersonic speeds, which resulted in a terrifying discovery of great importance to other pilots. Needless to say, I have been extremely lucky in surviving that incident and numerous other "near misses" as a pilot, and then had another miraculous one while out walking at age 96!

After leaving the RAF, my life became even more varied, just as exciting, and – as my age increased – in many ways more enjoyable. I can now look back and relate any interesting events without enduring the awful tensions, stress and emotions that I experienced at the time. Instead, until recently, as I relived any event by describing it, or recorded it on my computer, I used merely to ask my loving partner to refill my glass with: "Another Black Label please, darling." But two years ago an accident to her forced me into a retirement home, where I am now completing these memoirs and wondering what the contents of the final chapter will be.

Being a resident in this Retirement Village (Chantry Court in Westbury, Wiltshire) is quite like living in a suite of rooms in a luxury hotel – except that we all carry a press button alarm which summons help if urgently needed. One evening recently, I was downstairs chatting to the duty receptionist when her buzzer rang. She quickly phoned to check that it was not a false alarm and then got up to go quickly to the assistance of a charming old retired Army General and his wife.

"This is a REAL emergency!" she exclaimed, causing me to visualise a serious accident, with broken bones and blood everywhere.

She then explained: "He can't get the cork out of his wine bottle!"

Happily, although I am 15 years older than the General, I still do not yet contemplate experiencing an emergency of that magnitude.

Chapter 2

Early days
(1913-1931)

The first memory of my life is a feeling of fear. Intense fear.

It must have been transmitted to me by my frightened mother, who was cradling me in her arms and clasping me to her breast.

I remember hearing bangs. Then more bangs – and feeling my mother clasping me more closely. She was probably trembling. My brother remained silent. My sister was whimpering. I began crying.

We were sheltering in the cupboard under the stairs. My father, a Naval Officer on leave, who had been outside, opened the door of our cupboard and said something to my mother. He took my brother and sister by their hands and led them out through the front door into the street. My mother, with me in her arms, followed. The bangs seemed much louder.

My father shouted over the noise to me to look up into the sky.

I stopped crying and opened my eyes. My father was pointing along the road to the sky above the houses on our right. The sight I then saw was imprinted as a vivid picture in my memory which remains indelible to this day. Whenever I think back to my childhood that scene always reappears. It is the first event in my life that I remember with clarity. It still remains the most awesome spectacle I have ever witnessed.

Beams from the searchlights were angling across the night sky in all directions. Bangs and flashes from the guns and bursting shells were almost incessant. Some of the searchlights had converged on a large object which was on fire, way above the housetops. It quickly became an enormous furnace in the night sky, with flames rising to a great height above it.

It was as though the sun had suddenly exploded into a giant fireball. It lit up the whole area and almost hurt my eyes to look at it. I then watched the skeleton framework, outlined against the brilliant background, begin to descend. It fell slowly at first, but with gathering speed, until it finally disappeared below the housetops, leaving no more than a glow in the sky.

The bangs had ceased and were replaced by an eerie silence, soon to be followed by the steady screech of the "all clear" sirens. With fear no longer being transmitted to me from my mother, I probably fell contentedly asleep.

But that picture of the German Zeppelin in flames over London in the First World War (I think in 1915) is as clear to me today as it was at the time. And the memory of it, suddenly flashing in front of me many years later, caused me to react quickly enough to save my own life and that of a friend in the far-away South Island of New Zealand. It seems to me now that I also saw people falling, or jumping, from the gondola beneath the Zeppelin; but this may be because I have since watched people jumping to their deaths in another conflagration.

The other main incident indelibly imprinted in my memory occurred when my parents were giving a lunch party for about a dozen people. I was seated in my highchair to the right of my mother at the end of the table. For dessert she had prepared trifle and had instructed me to wait until she had served all the others first. I loved trifle and had waited anxiously, fearing that there might be none left for me. So when at last my mother turned to me and asked: "Would you like a little?", I gave my logical reply, hammering on the tray of my chair with my spoon to emphasise it, and making what I was later told was my first ever sentence:

"No!" I shouted. "Not a little – only much."

To my astonishment the whole company burst into loud laughter. To this day I can remember the surprise I felt. I could not understand this outburst. I felt deeply hurt and began crying.

That small incident left me with a complex for life – a fear of doing, saying or writing, something perfectly logical but which might lead to criticism or ridicule. That fear was later largely responsible for me arranging my first two novels (both of which became world-wide best sellers and were translated into more than 20 languages) to be published only under pen names.

My mother later claimed that that first sentence of mine was also an accurate indication of my whole attitude to life. My acquisition of the nickname "Tubby" tends to justify that view.

In 1917, aged four, I happened to be at the top end of our road (probably playing with a ball, as there was not much space for that in our garden) when I heard aircraft and saw in the distance a formation of quite large ones approaching. I watched them with interest. I had never before seen so many aircraft together, nor such big ones. They were coming from the direction in which I had

My last day with long hair

seen the Zeppelin. I continued watching them, quite fascinated, with no sense of fear, even though shells were bursting in the sky. My mother came screaming to me to come back quickly and managed to get me into our shelter in the cupboard under the stairs before the louder bangs reached our area. Afterwards, my collection of shrapnel became bigger. That was the daylight Gotha raid on London that June which caused over 600 casualties.

In the autumn of the following year there came a day when I was given a small stick with a coloured flag on it and was told there would be no more bangs. We were going out into the street at 11 o'clock with all our neighbours to wave our Union Jacks and cheer. My parents seemed so excited and happy that I was infected with their obvious joy – in spite of being told there would now be no more shrapnel for me to add to my collection.

Being part of the crowd in the street, waving my little flag, singing the National Anthem and Rule Britannia and clapping with all the rest gave me a sense of pride that has stayed with me always.

Standing beside my father, wearing his RNVR officer's uniform and medal ribbons, added to that great feeling. I sensed that something terribly important had happened. Without understanding it, I somehow got the impression that our lives were to be dramatically changed for ever. I waved my flag even harder. That was Armistice Day – 11th November 1918.

"That was the end of the war to end all wars," I was told. At the time I did not have the faintest inkling of what that really meant. I still don't!

Quite a few other events stand out in my memory of the First World War. The lovely taste of dripping on hot toast (which remains a great treat); being bathed in a copper bath in front of the kitchen range; whooping cough (twice); the pain of ingrowing toenails; roasting chestnuts on the kitchen range; the different cries of the street-traders (coalman, milkman, rag and bone man, etc) as they passed down our street (Dalmore Road, West Dulwich) on their horse-drawn carts; listening in particular for the "All-realm" call when we ran short of coal for the kitchen range; holding out the jug for the milkman to use his different- sized ladles to measure the amount he put into it from his large urn; stroking the cats that waited expectantly for him to spill some onto the pavement; going with a shovel and pail to collect horse droppings from the road as manure for our vegetable garden; helping my mother count the number of sacks of coal that the coalman tipped down the chute into our cellar and making sure the sack was really empty when he folded it to put it back on the cart; searching our road for pieces of shrapnel after an air-raid; and, while on holiday in Herne Bay, watching an aircraft which had landed at low tide on the sands being swamped by the rising tide.

I lived in a completely different world from children today, with that enormous difference being basically explained in two words. The first is MOBILITY – whether of people, information (instantly), sounds of music, and things. This resulted from the almost complete absence of motor cars, telephones or, until I was at Dulwich College Prep School, any radio communication, except by Morse Code.

Anywhere more than about three miles from a railway station was rarely visited by anyone without a horse or pony to take them. Nearly everyone lived in a small, compact community, knowing each other – but rarely even knowledgeable about what went on in other areas, although the use of bicycles was gradually beginning to remedy that.

The second word is AVAILABILITY – for example of lighting, which doubles (on average) the time that people can be active, of heating (including hot water from a tap), and generally of ample food supplies.

Another big difference, for example, is that we effectively produced no refuse. That was because practically everything was used (often re-used – like the newspapers which were cut into 4-inch square pieces to provide the toilet paper) or buried in the garden, where it quickly rotted away. The vegetables mainly came either from our garden or the local allotments in a basket with no wrapping and were usually eaten the day they were picked. Dustmen were unknown and the "rag and bone" man who periodically came down our street shouting "ragabone" collected only unwanted garments and the clean bones from the stew with every scrap of food already extracted.

Also, although we had a piano which my sister played quite well, we rarely heard any other music – except from the carol singers at Christmas and on the relatively rare occasions when we went to church. My parents occasionally went to a concert or to the opera, but it was not until we had a Pathe gramophone (which was when I was about 8 years old in 1921) that I first heard the magical sounds of an orchestra. The films were silent (although some cinemas had a piano) and were, of course, only black and white until the 1940s. It is difficult for children today to visualise a world without music!

Sometimes, on frosty nights – and particularly if I had developed a cold – my mother would light a fire in my bedroom. Also, she would hum a tune to help me go to sleep. I would lie there contentedly in bed watching the flickering flames casting shadows round the room and sometimes seeing the full moon moving across the window and silhouetting a branch of our cherry tree. Getting up in the morning in the freezing cold was a different matter.

My Grandmother born 1827

Quite often I would walk up the road and round the corner to 39 Carson Road, where I would listen to my maternal grandmother's descriptions of her earlier life. She had been born in 1827 (two reigns before Victoria became Queen) and had been present at a ceremony connected with Queen Victoria's coronation. I spent many happy hours listening to the stories she told me about life in those days. She laughed as she told me about the strange clothes people wore when she had been a child – not at all like the modern world in which she was then living in 1917. Yet there she was, wearing a flimsy lace bonnet and voluminous black skirt down to her ankles (as was the fashion early last century). Why do I now think that funny?

Unfortunately, I did not have a tape recorder, but regard it as a privilege to have had direct contact with someone living in that era. If any of my great-grandchildren (the fifteenth has recently arrived) should live to my age, then my personal live contacts will together have spanned nearly 300 years! Viewed like that, it does not seem so long since the Romans were here in England!

I soon learned to look forward to each different season, not so much because of the temperature or weather, but for the different treats which each seemed to bring. My favourites were asparagus, then strawberries, and so on – each being available for only just a short period – through to the raspberries and plums, then finally to the apples stored in the loft three inches apart on newspaper, which sometimes kept them edible until Christmas. Each new vegetable, fruit or nut, as it came into season, was a big landmark in the year – looked forward to with great excitement and thoroughly enjoyed during its brief appearance – but then unattainable until it came into season the following year. We even waited for the Brussels sprouts to have a winter frost to bring them to their most tasty condition. We could almost tell the date by the fruits and vegetables which were on display at the greengrocers. Pots of jam, made from the fruits, were very popular – as were the tins of some foods that gradually became more available after the First World War.

West Dulwich, at that time, still had open fields and some had been turned into allotments. Sometimes (at first in my pram, then in a pushchair, then walking) I would accompany my mother to the ones nearby, where we could often get vegetables fresher and cheaper than at the greengrocers. Other times she would take me with her up our road and round to where there was a row of half a dozen shops. They, and the street traders who called out their wares as they passed down our road on their horse-drawn carts, provided everything we really needed to live.

That little row of shops made it rarely necessary for the inhabitants of that area to venture further away. Some with bicycles did make longer trips and for an outing others walked to one of the nearby parks – particularly Dulwich Park, which Queen Mary visited each spring to see the famous blossoms there. The omnibus (with solid rubber tyres) coming from London stopped at nearby Thurlow Road on its way up to the Crystal Palace at the top of Sydenham Hill. That was how, I think in 1918, I was taken to see Charlie Chaplin in "Shoulder Arms" there – the first film I ever saw.

If anyone wanted something that was outside the scope of our local shops to provide – an unusual occurrence – then a bus or train to Brixton, where there were much bigger shops like the Bon Marche, was the probable answer. Otherwise, people rarely ventured outside the district.

For holidays, only those resorts with a train service could normally be considered and my parents chose Herne Bay and Margate in Kent. We used a horse-drawn cab to take our baggage and us to West Dulwich station. At Victoria Station (where we had to change trains) the stench of the dung and urine from the many horses waiting stationary with their cabs outside the station entrance made a notable – but quite friendly – impression on me because it was associated with travelling and holidays by the sea.

Few people on holiday normally ventured more than walking distance from the railway station. Apart from the main holiday resorts which had a railway station, practically all the rest of the British countryside, and coastline, were unspoiled and almost completely free of visitors. Gypsies in their slow-moving horse-drawn caravans had almost a monopoly of that privilege.

In our garden we had a large cherry tree that attracted blackbirds. Food was always in short supply and my father used to shoot some of them with a .177 smooth-bore gun that I later learnt to use. My mother boiled them first in their feathers before cooking them in a pie.

Sometimes, on Sunday mornings, I was allowed to get into bed with my parents and enjoy the cosy feeling of cuddling up to my mother. When they got up to dress, I was told to put my hands over my eyes and not look, but of course I took a peep. I remember seeing my father, with his knee pressed hard against the middle of my mother's back to increase leverage, as he strained to tighten the strings in her whalebone corsets. She was very proud of her wasp waist, but even at that age I thought that women who used such artificial practices must be very stupid – a view reinforced when I learnt about what the Japanese did to their daughter's feet. In spite of not keeping my eyes hidden, it was not until I was 11 years old that I realised there was any real difference between the male and female bodies. Before that there had been nothing that aroused my interest in any such trivial matters.

Soon after the First World War ended my father returned to his business activities in London, only to discover that his partner (whom he had trusted) had taken advantage of my father's absence to swindle him. My father's main failing – which I and my daughter Pat have both inherited – was to be a bad judge of character and far too trusting. Nevertheless, he soon picked up the pieces and we moved in 1919 to a bigger house (81 Alleyn

Park) – just opposite Dulwich College, where my brother and then I were later educated.

The Southern Railway line from London to the Brighton area of the South Coast ran across the bridge in front of the house going uphill and disappearing behind the Post Office a hundred yards up the road in the direction of the Penge tunnel. My brother, who was six years my senior, was always fascinated by trains and kept a log of the times at which they ran – plus their loads – as indicated by the disc on the front of the engine. The times of the passenger trains rarely varied by more than a few seconds, but the goods trains puffed their way along more slowly and unpredictably. We could tell whether they were carrying "meat, cattle and fish", or coal, or passengers, etc, by those discs. The passenger trains usually stopped at West Dulwich station – a couple of hundred yards down to the left. We listened to the "puffs" from the engine as they restarted to go uphill towards the Penge tunnel and had bets on whether they would make a series of rapid puffs as the wheels skidded – which they frequently did – or the more regular accelerating puffs.

As the train came into sight over the bridge, we could see the fireman and engine driver shovelling coal onto the fire to generate more steam – in the evenings the glow from their fire was quite spectacular. Although they made a noise, the trains seemed to me to be very friendly things and I loved watching them puffing up the hill. We learnt that the way the smoke and steam behaved on belching out of the funnel was an indication of the sort of weather we could expect – straight up and dispersing quickly meant good weather; falling to the ground indicated rain.

We also used to bet on which lamps would be lit first when the lamplighter came round at dusk carrying his pole to light the gas lamps lining our street and the road across under the bridge. Different lamplighters seemed to take different routes; some going up one side and then down the other, others zig-zagging across. We had little else to occupy our attention in those days. Everything moved at a slow pace and any little thing that happened was of interest.

In the evenings, when my mother and sister were knitting, sewing or making woolly rugs, I had nothing to occupy my attention – so I had to make my own amusement. Partly because my brother and sister were so much older, I became rather a lonely child. I made my main activity that of solving puzzles of all sorts – including those inside a box with a glass cover with tiny balls which needed manoeuvring into their correct holes and, later, mathematical and more complex ones. As a result, I became quite good at solving problems – often by just thinking logically about them.

In 1919, food was still short and we kept chickens in our garden – not only to provide eggs but also to help dispose of any food waste. The outer leaves of green vegetables were given to them raw, but most of the other waste food – like potato peelings or bits of meat gristle – was boiled up first. Whenever I smell boiling potatoes, it reminds me of carrying out a saucepan full of peelings and spreading them out for the cackling chickens to gobble up. Each chicken had a name and as far as possible we kept a record of how many eggs each laid. As soon as we heard a chicken cackling it was my job to run out to find and mark on the warm egg with a pencil the name of the cackling chicken. The chickens with the lowest marks went to the top of the list for eating. The breeds were mainly Leghorns, Wyandottes, and Rhode Island Reds, and the champion layer had the name Funny Bunny. Sometimes my brother would dig up worms for them to gobble up. I helped crush the used eggshells into small pieces which, together with a little grit, were fed back for them to eat. The eggs were delicious.

Amongst my main recollections of that period were the awful fogs we experienced. The only heating in most houses was a coal fire – such as the kitchen range. By early October every chimney in that area was belching out black smoke mixed with yellow sulphurous fumes. Even on windy days it often made me choke. Sometimes, when it was foggy, frosty or windless, it was impossible to see the ground, or any obstacle, more than a yard ahead. My mother used to wrap a woollen scarf round my head, covering my nose and mouth, in an effort to filter out the stinking soot from getting into my lungs as I crept cautiously up the road to school. The school had no heating and we sat at the desks wearing our overcoats and mittens. Between classes we had to go out into the playground and jump up and down, swinging our arms, to improve our blood circulation. My toes and fingers were covered with painful chilblains most of the winter.

Just before we had moved into 81 Alleyn Park the house had been redecorated and was damp. Our only heating was the kitchen range. In the spring of 1919 (that was the year after the awful flu epidemic had killed over 20 million people in Europe), I was incapacitated by a form of rheumatism which covered me with purple spots and which was attributed to the damp walls of our house. Our doctor said my only hope of recovery was masses of sunshine. Luckily, 1919 produced a marvellous summer. Every fine morning my sister or my mother carried me out and laid me naked on a mattress in the garden, where I remained for as long as it was sunny. By the autumn I was cured. As a result, I have always seized every opportunity to sunbathe – even in the tropics. I have never used sunscreen ointments and now believe – as the statistics tend to indicate – that the increase of skin cancer can be linked partly to the practice of putting chemicals on the skin and then frying it in with hot sunshine, instead of letting nature gradually provide protection.

In that connection I have never ceased to wonder at the amazing number of different chemicals that most ladies (influenced by the multitude of advertisements) have now been persuaded to use on their skins. Recently, when one of my daughter's friends visited us, I counted no less than 45 different bottles and tubes that she had laid out for use in the bathroom. She obviously had not read the brilliant book *Silent Spring*, by Rachael Carson. In my youth the only ointments I remember are Cold Cream, Zam-buk and Iodine. As a remedy for colds, we were given a lump of sugar doused with cinnamon.

My mother's eldest sister, "Auntie Flo", was a spinster who sponged off my father and caused friction everywhere; in retrospect, she was one of the most evil people I ever encountered. Together with my cousin Bowditch, she ran a girls' school, "Thurlow Grange", a quarter of a mile away. I was sent to the kindergarten there, but was soon expelled for being naughty – my aunt said that I was twice found kissing one of the girls. I have no recollection of that, but hope it was true.

Instead, I was enrolled at Dulwich College Preparatory School (DCPS), which was a couple of hundred yards up our road. The headmaster, W. R. M. Leake, had played rugby for England and was one of the finest characters I ever met. He ran a splendid school, with strict discipline, and had no hesitation in using his cane on the bare bottom of any pupil who misbehaved. That was an amazingly efficient deterrent; few boys ever risked getting a beating, and those that did never misbehaved a second time.

[Prohibiting that very effective (and less costly) form of punishment, which resulted from the UK joining the Common Market, accounts for much of the rapidly increasing problem of crime today – and the unnecessary payment by the public for the accommodation and living expenses of wrongdoers. Corporal punishment had been used effectively for millions of years – in the animal kingdom as well.]

At home, however, my parents considered me to be rather a naughty boy – not perhaps entirely without reason. One Sunday we were having midday lunch and the first course was hot soup. My brother and I were sitting together on one side of the table, him on my left. Facing us was my father on the other side. My mother was at the end of the table on my right, between my father and me. My brother whispered to me: "Bet you can't gargle with your soup."

I filled my mouth with a large spoonful, put my head back and started gargling. My brother then dug me in the ribs – causing me to burst out laughing. All the soup in my mouth shot across the table and splashed over my father. Roaring with anger, he leapt to his feet and took a swipe at me. I ducked and he missed. But his arm swung with such force that he hit my mother instead. That spilled her hot soup all over her. She leapt to her feet, berating my father. That gave me a couple of seconds' grace. I made one of those instant decisions that have so often saved my life. Like a flash I dived under the table, emerging the other side near the door, rushed out, slamming it behind me, and raced upstairs to the lavatory, where I locked myself in both with the key and extra catch. For the moment, at least, I was safe. Furthermore, I reckoned I was in a good strategic bargaining position – because the only other "convenience" on the property was a smelly bucket in a damp shed at the end of the garden, and it was raining.

Within less than a minute my father was hammering on the door, ordering me to come out. I was far too frightened to do so. I heard my father arguing with my mother about breaking the door down, so I quickly downed my pants and sat on the toilet – hoping that thereby it might at least delay my father spanking me. But my mother (thank God!) persuaded him against damaging the door.

Both my parents continued shouting to me to come out. But as time passed I noticed a slight change of tone outside. Instead of them periodically ordering me to come out, it became rather more like them pleading with me to do so. I realised the strength of my position and began formulating my terms. By 6 o'clock that evening the pressure (quite literally) on them was so great that they gave in to my demands – no thrashing, and supper in bed. My brother, I later learned, had not been so lucky!

In 1921, we moved to a much larger house up the road – 17 Alleyn Park. That had eight bedrooms, a ballroom, a billiard room and stables that had been converted into what became a garage. The large garden included a tennis court, fruit trees, vegetable area and greenhouses. Our staff included a butler, housekeeper, cook, maid and gardener. Soon after we moved in, workmen installed the latest magic – electricity. I was absolutely amazed that by moving a little switch on the wall at the top of the stairs, I could cause brilliant sunshine (even at night) suddenly to illuminate the hall below. I remember wondering what the savages in Africa would make of this apparent miracle. One evening in my bedroom, I wanted to unplug one of the electrical leads from the wall, but found it stuck in too tightly. So I used my penknife to help me lever it out. The blade of the penknife must have touched both terminals and the shock sent me reeling half way across the room, and my penknife had two blackened dents in its blade. That taught me a lesson never to be forgotten, but at the price of nearly being killed.

Later, as well, we had our first telephone installed in a cupboard in the hall. We had to turn a handle and wait for the operator to answer. She knew everyone in that area by name who had a phone and usually had a brief chat before connecting us to whomever we wanted to speak. She was often able to tell us that the person we were calling was, for example, out shopping. But, quite soon, with more houses having phones installed, we had to use only numbers.

To communicate with the staff downstairs, the main rooms all had a bell-pull handle by the fireplaces which caused the appropriate one of a row of bells to ring in the kitchen downstairs. Beside that bell-pull was a speaking tube with the mouthpiece sealed by a whistle to enable the person at the other end, by blowing into it gently, to "ring up". After lunch one Sunday I noticed that my father was sound asleep by the fire with his head near the whistle. So I stole down to the kitchen, put my mouth to the appropriate tube and blew with all my might. I could run quite fast, but he eventually cornered me between two greenhouses at the end of the garden. I still remember the thrashing that resulted.

Soon after we moved into that bigger house my father bought a De Dion Bouton open four-seater (at that time the "Rolls-Royce" of French cars) that we kept for many years. We toured around south-east England in it and, most summers, down to my father's old home near Evian-les-Bains on Lake Geneva. He also brought back from France a small two-seater that had an air-cooled engine at the front – a Sara – that eliminated the problem with the water freezing in cold weather. Both cars caused him to spend many hours (with help from my brother and me) fiddling with them in our garage.

Starting the engine on cold mornings, particularly the De Dion, was quite a lengthy process and sometimes took an hour or more. On cold evenings, all the water had to be drained from the engine and radiator, for fear of it freezing. Warm water (not too hot because that could cause differential expansion and crack the cold metal of the cylinder block) had to be carried out. Also, the spark plugs had to be unscrewed, taken out and heated up (usually by burning some methylated spirit in them) before being replaced.

Then it was a matter of cranking the engine round with the starting handle – an exhausting job which usually needed more than one person to complete, sometimes three. Backfires were frequent and – to reduce the risk of a broken arm – the handle had only to be pulled upwards, with the thumb and fingers always underneath. Even in warm weather it could be quite a lengthy, dangerous and tiring operation.

These cars had, of course, brakes on only the two rear wheels. They did not enable us to stop quickly, but they did have one great advantage – at least until the electronic anti-block system became available – over the later cars fitted with four-wheel brakes. We could ram the brakes on hard, even on a slippery road, and the car would not skid sideways, even if both wheels locked, and so could still be steered normally. With four-wheel brakes, because the front wheels have more weight forced on them, they grip better and allow the back to skid round sideways – often in a complete circle.

When we first got a car with four-wheel brakes we had to fit a warning red triangle on the back to warn following drivers that we could pull up more quickly. I was surprised that the introduction of the "brake-assist" when fitted to some new cars (which – in addition to the now standard anti-bloc – enabled them to stop in up to 40% less distance) did not require them to display a similar warning to following drivers.

I remember seeing the motorised buses (which succeeded the horse-drawn ones) in Dulwich with solid rubber tyres, but our De Dion had pneumatic tyres although they were very little bigger than the solid ones. They did not provide a very comfortable ride and my mother complained bitterly of being bumped about – particularly on the potholed roads of northern France and over the cobblestones in the French villages. So, on one trip in the early 1920s, my father decided to make a detour to Paris to have fitted a pair of the new Michelin "balloon" tyres. These made a big difference to the riding comfort of those in the rear seat, but could not be fitted to the front wheels because they were too floppy to withstand the sideways pressure of turning to steer the car. So, to get maximum benefit, my mother had to sit in the back of the car. I was not sorry to exchange seats and move to the front, where I had the benefit of the windshield protecting me from the wind and weather. There were, of course, very few cars on the roads. Sometimes, on our way down through France, if we met a car coming in the opposite direction, after perhaps an hour without that exciting event occurring, the drivers would stop to greet each other. If there was a café nearby my father and the other driver would have coffee together while discussing motoring matters. In our case the new balloon tyres created great interest.

Life was more leisurely in those days, but, with so little traffic and never any congestion, the trip down to Evian-les-Bains would have taken little longer then than it does today, but for the time sometimes spent repairing punctures. And the cost – of course – was far less.

The areas of France through which we motored down in the 1920s had suffered badly from the Germans in the First World War. On one trip with just my father and brother (1928) we stayed at a small hotel in Montdidier. Many of the other buildings in the village were still in ruins and I remember digging lead bullets out of the walls with my penknife. We had an excellent seven-course dinner with unlimited wine, two bedrooms (we brothers shared one) and breakfast – great bowls of café-au-lait, croissants, freshly baked bread, cheese and jam. The total cost (including service) for all three of us was four shillings and sixpence – in today's money that is less than 20p, yet the food and service were better than some luxury restaurants today. I cannot remember the price of petrol then, but I remember that in 1935 it was 9 pence per gallon in England, although rising to 10 pence in Scotland – less than 5p a gallon in today's money.

I noticed that at most houses in France there were hutches with larger rabbits in them than I ever saw in England. I learned that these were bred for eating – particularly in winter, when other food was

On Mer de Glace 1928

short. I also learnt why the French cooks were so renowned for their delicious sauces. In those days there was no way, except sometimes in winter, in which they could prevent meat from going bad. So when they cooked it they had to produce the strong sauces to make it palatable. The French are a very practical race and they waste little. Meat from horses, cats and dogs were also made tastier with those sauces. Washing up the dishes, since there was rarely any running water, was practically unknown. The plates, and implements, were cleaned with bread – the same plate being used for each part of the meal and then usually left in place for the next meal. Hence the custom of serving bread at the beginning of a meal – to facilitate cleaning the plate between courses.

At Grand Rive, near Evian, only a narrow road separated our house ("Les Bosquets") from the lake on which, from the age of seven, I used to row myself out to fish in water so clear that I could watch the fish nibble the bait 20 feet below. When swimming, we used to drink that water. In the 1960s, by comparison, if you happened to fall in you were advised to wash in disinfectant. It is, however, cleaner again now.

I often caught enough perch for our breakfasts: I gutted and cleaned them in the running water that was piped from a mountain stream into the trough beside the gate, before taking them in to my mother to cook. There was, of course, no running water in the house. The only toilet was located in a nearby outbuilding and consisted of a very deep hole in the ground, about three feet in diameter, and a movable wooden plank with a hole in it stretched across it. I was always frightened of falling in.

The water that was piped into the trough in our garden came from the same source – a larger stream coming down from the high mountains behind Evian – that also supplied the Evian Cachet establishment up the road. They bottled and distributed that drinking water throughout France. It was my father who first introduced Evian Water into England.

With no running water in the house, once a week my mother would walk with me to "Les Bains" – a large building about half a mile up the road in Evian – to have a bath. There, for a small payment, we had the use of a cubicle containing a bath with both hot and cold running water – although we had to take our own soap and towels.

My father's sister, Antoinette, and her husband Alexander Naz (who was Postmaster General of French Indo-China) usually came back from Saigon for a summer holiday at the same time as we did. They stayed at the Villa Vielle – a luxurious little house they had built in the grounds of my father's family home, Les Bosquets.

Les Bosquets (which has now been converted into the hotel/restaurant "Panorama" and the name Les Bosquets transferred to the original Villa Vielle) had a large covered veranda on the roof and I remember the absolute tranquillity of sitting up there in the evenings, sipping a glass of wine (yes, I was always allowed a little wine – but never any other alcohol) and eating Camembert cheese with a spoon, while watching the beautiful sunsets. Straight across the lake the lights of Lausanne would begin to appear, while to our right and behind us the last of the sun's rays would still illuminate the Dent d'Oche mountain on our right, and the Jura Mountains ahead. On the lake the barges with their enormous sails would slowly make their way to harbour – frequently with a member of the crew playing a mandolin. The only other sounds might be a distant hoot from the siren of a paddle-steamer crossing the lake, or a tinkle of bells from the cattle in the mountains behind.

Now, the noise of traffic roaring down the road, powerboats on the lake, aircraft in the sky, and the blaring of radios everywhere, have completely destroyed that tranquillity. And the sun is now frequently obscured by the spreading contrails of the many aircraft that converge into

My parents – Chamonix

the Geneva air lane. The Jura Mountains are often invisible due to the air pollution that tends to build up over the lake when the wind is not strong enough to blow it down the Rhone valley and away over the Alps. To me this is sad. But to the younger generation it is still a beautiful area, as confirmed by one of my grandchildren – Mark Heslop – who learnt to water-ski on the lake.

My grandfather once had the opportunity to purchase a large area of land across the lake at Ouchy – the large park in which the Beau Rivage Hotel now stands – at a price that I understood to be less than about one centime per square metre. He declined, claiming that it was far too expensive. Alas, land in that area is now some of the most highly priced in Europe.

In the early 1920s my father spent some time in Germany. He used to send me postcards every few days and I still have the stamps from them in my album. They give a vivid picture of the inflation that then ravaged that nation. The early stamps cost just a few phennig – a fraction of a mark. But that began increasing week by week until it became a mark, then several marks, with the later ones millions of marks – just to send the same type of postcard.

The collapse of the German currency enabled my father to buy some property near Hamburg very cheaply. We spent a holiday there and also at Travamundie on the Baltic Sea, with its large sandy beaches and bathing huts.

We only visited Evian in the summer. In winter that area can be very cold. My father told me that one year when he was young the Lake of Geneva was almost completely frozen over. He and his school friend Gros (whose daughter Annie came over to England in 1950 to help look after our three girls) were able to skate half way across the lake towards Lausanne. Also, that when he was doing his French National Service (in the famous Chasseurs Alpines regiment – which experience he was able to put to good use in the Second World War), his group were stranded in the mountains behind Evian at sub-zero temperatures in a blizzard which lasted so long and blocked them in with such deep snow that they were lucky to survive.

From about the age of ten onwards I sometimes also spent short holidays with my school friend Dudley Ashton in his parents' bungalow right by the beach at Shoreham-by-Sea. That area had no lavatories with running water – just a "thunder box" bucket located so the council workers could gain access to it from outside by raising a hinged wooden flap and so remove and empty the bucket periodically. Before lifting the flap, which had no catch to stop it being opened freely, they usually gave a warning shout to first check that there was no one perched on the wooden seat above the bucket.

To meet a popular demand from churchgoers, the council had recently erected three such lavatories, each in a wooden cabin labelled "Ladies", in the open ground about 40 yards from the local church, which itself was built on a large isolated patch of shingle. It was customary, after the Sunday service, for the churchgoers – all wearing their Sunday best, the ladies in their large hats and long flowing skirts, many with lorgnettes (spectacles held to the eyes with a long handle), and the men in top hats, some with monocles – to stay assembled, chatting together for quite some time just outside the church. Inevitably, the "Ladies" became used for the purpose for which they were intended.

We "little horrors" – Dudley and I, with another 12-year-old – saw a way in which we could enliven the morning for those assembled gentry. So, one Sunday, shortly before the service was due to finish, we furtively took up our positions, with one hiding behind each cubicle. Dudley and I were each armed with a birch broom, the other with a sooty chimney flue brush. We waited patiently, chuckling to ourselves – hoping that everything would go as planned and that we would not be caught.

The church service ended, the participants assembled for their usual natters outside the church and, in due course – as we had anticipated – three ladies detached themselves from the group and made their way into the establishments behind which we were hiding. We waited long enough for the ladies to become well seated, presumably with their voluminous undergarments either up round their waists or around their ankles. Then, at a signal from Dudley, we each lifted the flaps and pushed our brooms up between their knees. The result, as we had also anticipated, was absolutely hilarious.

Just like the pictures of old witches on their broomsticks, all three ladies burst out of the doors, screaming, clutching the broomsticks in their hands and trying to run with some undergarments around their ankles.

The effect on the assembled onlookers exceeded our expectations. With lorgnettes to their eyes, some of the ladies were gasping open-mouthed. Monocles fell in utter disbelief. The astonished look on the vicar's face alone repaid us for our efforts.

Before they recovered their composure, we little horrors had sprinted out of sight – each in a different direction.

Ten minutes later, when someone came looking for the culprits, I was sitting reading the Bible, clearly as innocent as driven snow.

My academic progress at school was not very satisfactory, but I won three medals on the sports field that helped compensate. I was quite good at maths, and solving problems by logical reasoning, but in most subjects I was hampered by my inability to memorise anything that I considered unimportant or uninteresting – like historical dates or the names someone had happened to give to the promontories round the coast of England.

For example, I failed one test because I could not remember the answers to two questions that were apparently considered to be vitally important. The first concerned how many wives Henry VIII had, and the second the date that William the Conqueror invaded our shores. To me, both were utterly irrelevant to our future and therefore of no importance whatsoever. But, for some reason that I still cannot understand, the teacher considered knowledge of the exact answers to be vital to the future of my world. All I could do was to try, by logical reasoning, to work out the answers.

Regarding Henry the Eighth, I had no information – no database – from which I could start making any calculations. But I thought that he must have been a pretty randy old sod for the number of women he actually married to be of any interest a century or two later. I had no idea how many others he had jumped into bed with. But I already knew enough about life to guess it was quite a few more than he had wives. So I chose a round figure for that – a total of one hundred girlfriends. (I now realise that this was probably a ridiculously low figure – but I was then only 14.) So one hundred tarts was the figure I used as a basis for my calculations. I vaguely remembered that he had a habit of chopping off his wife's head. For that reason it seemed likely that not more than about one in each dozen of his tarts would have been stupid enough to encourage their own demise by giving him the excuse "... till death do us part".

I therefore reckoned that only 12% of his one hundred girlfriends would have taken the marriage vows. So, on those calculations, I gave my answer – eight wives.

I protested when given no marks at all for that answer, pointing out that it really did not matter a hoot how ever many women Henry had actually married. Furthermore, my answer was only 25% out and therefore 75% correct.

Similarly with the William the Conqueror date. I knew it was a long time ago because the pictures of him indicated that the sort of hat and clothes he wore had been out of fashion for a considerable time. I vaguely remembered the figure 10 and had an idea that two of the digits were similar. So I guessed 1088. I was wrong by 22 years. But (in the year 1926) I pointed out that an error of 22 years in the 860 years that had since elapsed was only wrong by 2.56%. So, I argued, my answer was 97% correct and I should therefore get nearly full marks for it. The teacher of history could not follow that reasoning, but only memorise dates.

Those two incidents had quite an influence on my attitude to learning. I realised that teachers could only impart knowledge that they themselves had been taught. Most were considered clever solely because they had been able to memorise those things and so get good marks in exams. To them the precise dates, and the amorous escapades of past personalities, were the bread of life. To me they were of no importance whatsoever. So I decided to ignore, as far as possible, any subject that relied on remembering anything which was not likely to be directly relevant to my future life. Instead, I would study textbooks on, and teach myself, the subjects in which I was really interested. Amongst these were physics and astronomy.

Because I could not remember the exact date of William the Conqueror or the number of women who were stupid enough to marry Henry VIII, I nearly failed the entrance exam to Dulwich College. Luckily, my maths results and sporting record tipped the balance in my favour and I entered the College in 1926. But I am still amazed that not remembering the exact figures for such ridiculously unimportant events could have altered my whole life.

It made me realise that, in most cases, high academic qualifications resulted mainly from a good memory and, on its own, meant little except that their owners could impart that acquired knowledge to others – but that the really clever people in this world are those who had either inherited, or developed, the ability to use whatever knowledge they had to reason logically the further implications and so solve problems. And if the two were combined in one brain – that resulted in brilliance. Much later, after I had experienced working for several years with some of our most highly academically qualified scientists (which further confirmed my view), I had the opportunity to discuss this with Albert Einstein – and he wholeheartedly agreed with me.

In May 1926, England was almost brought to a complete standstill by the General Strike. Because the trains were not running, my father tried to reach his London office by car and needed someone to go with him. My brother, who had joined the London Rifle Brigade (part of the Territorial Army) on leaving school, had been called up as a Special Reservist to assist the police. So I went with my father. As we approached Brixton I saw that the few remaining buses had wire netting over all the windows to prevent the glass shattering when the baying mobs of strikers bombarded them with bricks and stones. It was my first experience of an unruly, threatening crowd of people, and it was very frightening. We were forced to turn back. Years later, when I was serving at Farnborough, I had to work with (and against!) some of the leading communists who had encouraged that uprising which had so nearly become a revolution on the Russian scale some nine years previously.

On another occasion, in November, I was with my father in the car returning to Dulwich when we ran into dense fog of a type never seen today – a mixture of sulphurous smoke from the chimneys and thick freezing mist. To enable us to reach home I had to walk the last half-mile in the gutter in front of the car, feeling for the curb with my foot and shining a torch behind me for my father to follow.

Also in 1926, I was taken up to London to witness a far happier event – the marriage of the Duke and Duchess of York. My father's office was in Pall Mall. We stood on a balcony of a neighbouring building overlooking the Mall and watched the procession go slowly past. The Duchess saw me waving frantically, as a child does, and she waved back.

That same year (for fees which amounted to £15 per term) I became a pupil at Dulwich College – "Alleyn's College of God's Gift". It was founded in 1619 by Edward Alleyn – a friend of Shakespeare – and was, I believe, second only to Eton in size; but otherwise very like most of the public schools against whom we competed in sports –

Dulwich College

Eton, Haileybury, Tonbridge, Bedford, St Paul's and many others. Fives, athletics, cricket and gymnastics (for which I won several cups) were my favourites. I was a day-boy (cycling to school, using an acetylene lamp if it was dark coming back). That enabled me to play tennis, billiards and snooker while at home where, in the evenings, we also played bridge or chess.

My father also taught me to play golf; I became a schoolboy member of the Dulwich and Sydenham Hill Golf Club. One day, playing the 4th hole (from memory I think it was about 420 yards) I had a good drive and a straight second shot from the fairway – but on reaching the green could not find my ball. Eventually, we looked in the hole. There was my ball. I was told that no one had ever had an "eagle" there before, so my father was particularly pleased. But I imagine that record has since been broken many times.

My father let me use an old telescope that had belonged to his father. The fascination of looking through the telescope at the

29

moon, Venus and stars generated my interest in astronomy. Later, my father gave me the old pocket sextant that his father had used. That increased my interest still further and by the time I started at Dulwich College I had a good idea how mariners had used the sextant, combined with a timepiece, to calculate their position from observing the sun, moon and stars. In consequence, I also became interested in magnetic compasses.

About that time, also, a family friend who was staying with us made me a radio receiver out of a cigar box, some copper wire and a crystal. Using that with headphones, moving a contact up the coil of copper wire, and juggling with a "cat's whisker" to get a good connection on the crystal, I was able to hear the announcer in North London say, "This is 2LO calling" (I think for the first time ever), and then listen to the news. It seemed almost like magic to me that a flimsy little device about six by ten inches, weighing less than a pound, could let me hear a man talking about ten miles away.

I mentioned earlier that, to augment our food supply, my father had shot blackbirds with a .177 smooth-bore gun that I later learned to use. I found that rather a heavy weapon and was given, instead, an air rifle of similar calibre with which I soon became quite a good shot. One afternoon I was down the end of our garden practising shooting at a cardboard target when my brother arrived with a friend.

"It's easy shooting at targets," said the friend, "but I bet you couldn't hit a bird – that one there, for example." He pointed to a chaffinch, in full song, on the branch of a tree about 20 yards away.

"Bet I can," was my reply. I took aim and fired. I hit the bird in the head and he fell to the ground. The song "little bit of bread and no cheese" was cut off in the middle and it was one I loved. After my brother and his friend had gone, I went over and picked up the dead bird, feeling very sad, and then buried it. As I was doing so I heard the song of another chaffinch – presumably calling her mate. But there was no reply – and this went on until I left to go back to the house. The guilty feeling of having destroyed the happiness of that bird has remained with me ever since.

I went down the garden the next morning, and several times during the day. That chaffinch was singing her little song repeatedly, often sitting on the branch where I had shot her mate. But she got no reply. The next day her song was weaker, and on the fourth day I heard no song, but found her dead on the ground beneath that same branch. I burst out crying. Why, oh why, had I caused such a tragedy? I was still crying as I buried her beside her mate. Whenever I hear a chaffinch I think back to that sad incident and the effect it had on me.

I had become quite fond of our cat. He was very friendly and often sat on my lap purring contentedly. But the stealthy, cunning way in which he would sometimes catch birds made me less enamoured of him. One day he was purring contentedly in my arms when he suddenly lashed out with his claws, leaving a bleeding scratch from my forehead to my chin. Luckily, he missed my eye. I never knew what caused him to do it – perhaps he had heard a noise that alarmed him and struggled to get to his feet – but whatever it was, I wanted never to have anything further to do with cats. I took an intense dislike to them. The consequence has been that they must sense my hatred of them and invariably make a beeline for me whenever I encounter one.

My Family

About 1927 we moved from Dulwich to 35 Cator Road in Beckenham, Kent. It was a quite large detached house, with tennis court and kitchen garden, in a private road facing the Ibis playing fields that belonged to the Prudential Assurance Company. The move meant that I now had to go to school by train from Penge station, through the tunnel to West Dulwich station. It took only about five minutes and the trains were usually exactly on time. The line by that time had been electrified using a third rail beside the other two to carry the current. That, and the new carriages, made it a very comfortable journey, although the goods trains were still drawn by steam engines that sometimes left the tunnel full of smoke. We were warned about the danger of touching the live rail, but one schoolboy was killed instantly when, while waiting for a train at West Dulwich station, he walked to the end of the platform to have a pee without realising that the water splashing onto the live rail would make a connection. Very sad, but death was instantaneous, and I can think of worse ways of departing.

On my 15th birthday I acquired my first driving licence and was given (at my request) a Matchless 250cc motorbike on which – not having ever received any driving instruction, apart from being a passenger in my father's car – I nearly killed myself several times. The first occasion was coming round a bend far too fast approaching a rarely used minor crossroad. The driver of a car coming from my right, after checking that the main road appeared to be clear and not expecting some maniac to come shooting fast round the bend, decided to proceed across just as I approached. I braked, swung left, trying to avoid hitting him, skidded, fell off and ended up with his front wheel pressed against my neck. Had he not stopped, but gone on even three inches further, I would not be writing this. Luckily, apart from a few bruises, and a gash on the ball of my left thumb where the gravel on the road had torn through my leather gauntlet to cut through the skin, I was unhurt. My motorbike was only scratched. The cut to the ball of my thumb, however, had a surprising result 40 years later.

My 15th Birthday

On another occasion, with my brother riding behind me on the pillion, we set off early one morning to visit friends in Worthing, about 50 miles away. On the way down something went wrong with the magneto. We had to push my motorbike two miles to the nearest garage, where it took nearly seven hours to repair. So we arrived in Worthing eight hours late and quite tired. Towards the end of our return journey, near Croydon, by which time I was very tired indeed, my brother suddenly realised that I had fallen asleep. He said afterwards that he dare not shout or wake me up with a jerk, so he himself steered us by leaning over from side to side while quietly telling me what to do, which I must subconsciously have reacted to, until I woke up. It was probably only for a few seconds – but he found it pretty frightening. Had I been solo, the ending might have been different.

Like most young riders with no instruction in those days, and with tyres that had little grip on wet roads, I also skidded through a few hedges, usually because I was going too fast. But I gradually learnt to ride it more safely.

Then, that same year – 1928, when I was 15 – I met a girl, seven years older than me, named Margery Barnard. (To differentiate her from my sister Marjorie, I nicknamed her "Bunny".) She had been invited, at the last moment, by my brother's girlfriend to make up a foursome for tennis in place of someone who was ill. I had never met her, nor many other girls, before. She and I played against my brother and his girlfriend. In spite of my brother being a far better player than me and Bunny being only five foot three in height, and weighing less than seven stone, we won.

I fell head over heels in love with her and that chance meeting on our tennis court began its control over the whole of my future life and led to a wonderfully happy marriage until her death 62 years later.

Bunny wanted me to let her come riding pillion with me on my motorbike. But I considered her far too valuable to put her life at risk like that. Instead, we played tennis together, she came to watch cricket matches in which I played, and the gymnastic competitions with displays in which I participated. We went to music recitals (recordings of Caruso, Gigli and Galli Curchi, etc) together and she played the piano, and me the drums, in a band that my brother had organised.

My father was fond of music and we had all been taught to play the piano, although his favourite instrument was the flute, which (folded into its three pieces) he had always carried in his knapsack during his military service in France. My brother played both the violin and saxophone – mainly the latter. I also played the flute and piccolo (which I still have). I tried playing the violin, but the mandolin became my favourite as it was not only less tiring but it enabled me also to sing while playing. Bunny often accompanied me on the piano. Although she had at first considered me too young, we gradually became almost inseparable and she gave me lots of encouragement to do well at school – and then afterwards.

Soon after I met her she had to have an operation on her nose. I was so upset at seeing her in hospital that I dashed round to the nearest shop to buy her a present. I hadn't a clue what to give a girl, but ended up buying her a small barometer. It was utterly inappropriate, but it gave us much pleasure. It was lost to us during the war, found and given back to us 4 years later, and is now one of my few relics of those happy days.

When Bunny went with her parents on holiday at Freshwater Bay on the Isle of Wight, I raced down on my motorbike via Lymington to stay nearby. I taught her to swim and we went boating together. Her father knew a great deal about Astronomy and helped me considerably with that subject. He was basically an artist and, via his company (the Grout Engraving Company), he was entrusted with the reproduction of the paintings at Buckingham Palace. He also made many pictures, oils, water or pen and ink, of scenes with which I had been associated.

Two years after I met Bunny I decided that I wanted her to marry me. She stressed the 7 years difference in our ages, but I pointed out that since women usually lived longer than men we would probably die about the same time, so that age difference was really an asset. She finally agreed – subject of course to her father's approval. So, as was then the custom, I prepared myself for that ordeal. I shaved and brushed my hair with particular care and, dressed in my best clothes and feeling very nervous, went round to face him. He asked the usual questions about my future prospects and how I proposed to maintain her, pointing out that I was still only 17 years old. I mentioned that I had an allowance of £50 per year, had passed my Matric, was already studying for a BSc with a place at university and a job in a big electrical engineering company already assured. That interview was, of course, just a formality. He knew perfectly well that his daughter and I were so much in love that whatever he said would not make any difference to the final outcome. He gave his approval.

My mother seemed rather miserable about it – but I gathered mothers often are at the thought of losing a son to another woman. My father, however, had always liked Bunny and seemed quite pleased. From then on Bunny became one of our family. But my mother, perhaps hoping that it would cause me to see less of Bunny, decided that we should move away from that area close to where Bunny lived – back to the Dulwich area.

So we moved to 47 Lancaster Road. It made little difference to me. Either by train, or using my motorbike, I saw Bunny every evening. Sadly, soon after we moved there my best school friend – Dudley Ashton – died of TB. He was the first in a whole series of my closest friends whose premature deaths have impinged on my life – and my career.

At school, encouraged by Bunny, I began working much harder. Having passed all the exams I needed before starting at university, I was more or less free to choose what work I did during my remaining time at school. So, together with Paget Bowyer (whose brother Vivian together with Dudley Ashton had been my main buddy at prep school), we started constructing a television set. Using the Baird principle, we finally achieved making two television contraptions that enabled us to transmit and receive pictures (like a large black blob on white paper) across the laboratory. We both left school later that year (1931) and I never saw or heard of him, or his brother, again until about 60 years later, when we all three found ourselves guests at the same wedding. Television, we then agreed, had advanced quite a bit since our pioneering efforts in the lab at Dulwich College.

My father always had a great interest in new inventions and finding simple solutions to complicated problems – a trait which I inherited. After learning to play golf – which he loved – he invented a golf club with a head that could be rotated, using a penny to unlock and lock it, to any desired angle, from putter to full niblick. Carrying only that club and a wooden baffy (like a brassy and about a No 2 wood in modern parlance), he did not need a golf bag or caddie to carry them – but just carried the two clubs, laying down on the ground the one not in use. He was soon playing to a handicap of plus four and won the championship at the Dulwich and Sydenham Hill Golf Club three years in succession. My brother inherited the big silver cup, but unfortunately sold it when the price of silver rocketed to high levels. The rotating head club was a brilliant idea and vastly improved the play of anyone using it – mainly because they got used to the swing of just one club. But the professionals got it banned for fear that their sales of clubs and golf-bags would fall – and caddies become redundant.

My father's love of music caused him to become excited about every new means of reproducing it. In the early 1920s we had, for example, one of the first Pathe 78 turntables equipped with a sapphire needle that could slide across the disc without scratching the grooves. Later, we graduated to wooden needles that I used to sharpen to produce a clearer sound from the more refined 78 discs.

By around 1930 my cigar box crystal set had been replaced by a very large six-valve radio receiver of considerable complexity and power. I think it was that year that my father brought home a framed oval picture that he hung on the wall near it. That was the first radio loudspeaker I ever heard. Previously, we always had to plug earphones into our receiver to hear anything. Instead, with two wires leading from a small gadget behind the centre of the picture plugged into the same socket used for our headphones, this reproduced speech and music of a quality that amazed everyone who listened to it. Behind the gauze on which the picture was painted was a thin, lightweight plate of corrugated metal, with a tiny exciter at the centre that caused the metal plate to vibrate and so reproduce the sound. It was, I believe, the first "flat speaker".

[Some sixty-odd years later, the company NXT (of Huntington) appeared to claim they had just invented and patented a flat loudspeaker. It seemed to me to be almost identical to the one we had used in 1930. So I wrote to Mr Azima, the head of NXT, mentioning this and asking to be allowed to visit him to listen to one of his design for comparison. I got no reply.]

Each autumn, as the trees started turning brown, the large horse-chestnut trees lining the gravel road beside the College, and those in the College grounds, began shedding their fruit and playing conkers became our main occupation. We would go early to school to be sure of filling our pockets with the shining chestnuts. Then, with a gimlet we would carefully drill the hole and string them on the cord. Some boys cheated by trying to make them harder by putting them in the oven for a few minutes, but they were usually found out and disqualified. The intensity of our interest in that competition seemed similar to that afforded to the World Cup today.

Each morning before lessons we always said prayers, sang a hymn, and listened to one of the senior boys reading the lesson. If ever we heard the National Anthem being played, we had to stand up to attention until it was finished. We had it drummed into us that we British had a great Empire, covering one fifth of the earth's surface. Having defeated the Germans (who considered themselves the master race) and rescued the French (good cooks with nice wines) from domination, we were clearly the finest race the world had ever seen. The Americans, of course, had helped a bit during the war – but they had originally been a British colony anyway and, but for some bureaucratic inefficiency long ago, would still be part of our Empire. (In fact, we Europeans owe a tremendous debt to the Americans for coming to our rescue twice. That is one reason why France – as a nation – which had capitulated completely during the Second World War, now has such an inferiority complex towards, and hatred of, the USA.)

Sadly, so many of our finest future leaders had been killed in the First World War that England was becoming governed by men of much lower calibre than formerly. Almost a generation of future leaders had been wiped out. So, at Dulwich College we were reminded that it was up to us to make up for this deficiency – in sport and in all other walks of life. "The future of Great Britain is in your hands," we were told when we were made prefects. It was Churchill who reminded us of that in 1940.

Dulwich College (like most other schools) had produced quite a few famous personalities – mainly in sports like rugby and cricket or in the Services. The current Commandant of the RAF College at Cranwell was an OA (Old Alleynian, as they were named). So was Shackleton, whose open boat was displayed near the science block; also P. G. Wodehouse, whose books sometimes used the school area as a background. Pupils there with me included the two cricketers S. C. Griffiths and H. T. Bartlett, and Gardner who won a VC, and several others who had distinguished careers.

Griffiths was such a brilliant wicketkeeper that I (also a wicketkeeper, like my brother) had no chance of beating him into the 1st XI, but I was captain of the 2nd XI for a couple of years. Mainly due to the encouragement I received from Bunny, I did rather better than my brother academically, but did not achieve quite the same sporting successes. Nevertheless, encouraged by my father, who had been a gymnast in his youth, I won several prizes for gymnastics; also for sprinting, high jumping and throwing the cricket ball. I also played fives, which helped me later get into the RAF squash championships.

I left Dulwich College in July 1931, sadly saying goodbye to my many friends – most of whom I never saw again. I was looking forward to going to university to gain a BSc and then starting my planned career as an electrical engineer with one of the giant companies that was expanding worldwide.

Little did I realise what actually awaited me.

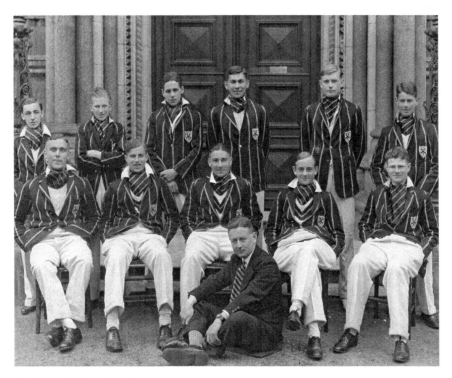

Cricket at Dulwich College

Chapter 3

The Great Depression

Although I had first listened at home to a radio news broadcast in the early 1920s – the famous "This is 2LO calling" – on the crystal set made out of a cigar box, at school we had no knowledge of what was happening in the outside world. Any news that was important to us, like the cricket scores or who had been selected to join Hobbs and Sutcliff for the England side (with Bradman on the other) reached us by word of mouth. None of us, I think, ever read the papers. When I left college in July 1931, none of my friends seemed to have any more idea about any "depression" than I had.

So I went away on holiday to Cornwall without a care in the world. I vaguely remember having heard that some financiers had jumped to their deaths from buildings in New York, but I really did not know what a financier was, and in any case, that locality – even in one of the fastest ships – was a good week away. The forecast, by the local fisherman, of the likely surfing conditions at Morgan Porth (near Newquay, Cornwall) for the next day was of infinitely greater interest to me.

When I returned to our home in Dulwich, just a week before I was due to start at university, my father and mother both looked so ill that I was quite shaken. My father then explained to me that the financial crisis affecting the Western world had finally hit him. Like many others in London, his company had been forced into liquidation. The banks were calling in their loans – some going bust. His business had collapsed. He had sold our car and several other things and so managed to repay all debts. He was not bankrupt and we were still just able to pay the rent for our house; but we had neither money nor other income beyond that.

So, instead of going to university, he said I would have to go to the Labour Exchange and try to get a job. Meanwhile, my mother would take in lodgers to try to make enough money to buy food for us.

I seem to remember my father saying it was some chap with a name like Lowenstein jumping to his death from a plane while flying across the English Channel that was the final straw. Also, a man named Hawtrey and a company called Swedish Match were involved. But I really did not understand what was causing such a change in our lives.

Next morning I took the bus to London to visit the Labour Exchange, hoping that my academic qualifications would quickly enable me to get a job. The scene there was unlike anything I had ever seen or visualised. A mob of dispirited, rather dirty, hungry-looking men and badly dressed boys stared at me, dressed in a suit, as I joined the long queue. Until then I had absolutely no idea of the magnitude of the crisis and the influence that it was having on so many people's lives.

The only remaining job available, as I learned when I eventually neared the head of the queue that day, was for a road sweeper – but someone ahead of me took that. I returned home feeling utterly depressed. My mother tried to cheer me up, but she too had been unsuccessful in finding anyone who wanted to become a lodger.

Every day that week was the same. No jobs available. No lodgers. The following week I was offered the job of becoming a salesman, on commission only, for the new "Goblin" vacuum cleaner. The firm gave me a couple of hours training with a bunch of other applicants, and then allocated me all the houses in a long street. I knocked at each door in turn. The only people that were prepared to listen to any proposal from me, and they were few, were clearly not in a position to afford anything at that time, and certainly not a luxury like a vacuum cleaner.

On the second day I realised that I was not suited to such a hopeless task and gave up that job.

Some of the people standing in the queue with me were clearly short of food. There were masses of unemployed, no social security and little to prevent them from starving. I remembered that I had been told that one of my cousins had died of starvation in Austria during the war. My pile of pennies for the fare to London was getting smaller. The outlook was so bleak that I started to become afraid – I feared starvation.

My mother found, or borrowed, enough money to pay for my fares to London for a few more days. Then, at last, a job was advertised for a clerk in a firm of chartered accountants – Wilson, de Zouche and Mackenzie. No one in the queue ahead of me had the necessary academic qualifications. I immediately applied.

One of the partners in the firm interviewed me. My maths qualifications appeared to help. He then mentioned that my name Vielle was rather unusual and asked whether I had had a relation who had served in the Navy during the war. He had also been an officer in the RNVR and remembered my father. That clinched it. I think I may have got the job anyway. But it made me realise that it might be whom you know, rather than what you know, that can really help in life.

My hours were to be 9 to 6 on weekdays, with one hour for lunch, and 9 to 1 on Saturdays. My salary would be one pound per week. My bus fares would take two-thirds of that – leaving me six shillings and eight pence (30p a week in today's money) on which to live – but with the prospect of a small increase after three months. I started the next day.

My office, which I shared with several inky-fingered clerks, some of whom were quite elderly, was in an attic in 2 Norfolk Street, Strand. My first task was to check the addition of the entries in the ledgers of the Chilean Nitrate of Soda – an enormous company that was in liquidation. At first I used to go home absolutely exhausted and with a splitting headache. But with practice I could soon add whole columns of six-figure numbers quite quickly with rarely an error.

I was made assistant to one of the qualified accountants and sometimes accompanied him when he visited firms – mainly pubs – whose accounts our firm was auditing. I became friendly with another clerk – Barry Aikman – who had joined the firm shortly after me. During each lunchtime I used every available minute trying to extend my knowledge by visiting different places of interest, including, for example, the art galleries and museums. The "Laughing Cavalier" by

Franz Hals in the Wallace Collection stands out particularly as one of the great masterpieces which inspired my love of art. Bunny later gave me a reproduction of it, which I still treasure.

The head of the accountancy firm wanted me to become articled, which would have led (in due course) to me becoming a qualified accountant. But the prospect of working (like he did) in a stuffy office for six days each week, mainly to help people and firms fiddle their tax returns, did not appeal to me as a main aim for the rest of my life. I wanted to put my knowledge of physics, maths and astronomy to better, and more exciting, use.

Opposite our office in the Strand was Adastral House – the administrative headquarters of the Royal Air Force – and in one of the windows I saw a placard which read: "Join the Air Force and see the World", with details of the Short Service Commission scheme. That offered successful applicants seven times the money I was earning with a bonus after five years.

I applied. I had all the right qualifications and also passed, at the RAF Central Medical Establishment, the extremely tough physical examination for future pilots with A1 category. At the final interview at Adastral House, the committee chairman said I would be accepted and granted a Short Service Commission for five years with a possible extension – but he then asked me:

"Why, instead, not try to get in to the RAF College, Cranwell, and so get a Permanent Commission? You will still be within the age limit to take the Civil Service Exam this summer."

I pointed out that we could not possibly afford the £250 fees for two years at Cranwell.

He asked more about my academic qualifications and sports. Then, whether my father had served in the war. Had he been killed in the war, I would have been offered a "King's Cadetship" at Cranwell, involving no cost at all. But the fact that he had been a Lieutenant in the Navy convinced them that I was the sort of potential officer they were seeking.

"Take that exam," he suggested. "The first six get a 'Prize Cadetship', which reduces the fees to £20 per year. If necessary, you could borrow that and repay it out of the seven shillings per day you receive as a cadet."

"And if I fail to win a Prize Cadetship?" I asked.

"Then we will award you a Short Service Commission. You are just the sort of chap we need in the RAF."

Everyone from whom I sought advice, except my mother (who was afraid I would be killed flying) encouraged me to have a go at it. The head of the accountant firm, although he wanted me to stay, said it would obviously be more the type of life for me, and Barry Aikman urged me to take the chance. My brother, who had wanted to go into the Army, said it was the obvious thing for me. Above all, Bunny was really enthusiastic, although it would mean us being parted for most of the next two years.

My mother now had a Japanese couple as lodgers. They paid enough for my mother to buy food for us all, and my father was working with an old friend in London to try to start up another business. So I left the firm (with a generous bonus from the senior partner) to study at home for the exam. I got up before six each morning to help my mother clean up and prepare breakfast for her guests, worked hard all day studying, saw Bunny every evening and went to bed exhausted but optimistic. I had no tuition, but taught myself from textbooks which I borrowed from the local library.

One of the optional subjects for which one could obtain extra marks in the Civil Service Entrance Exam for Cranwell was astronomical navigation. That was primarily intended for naval cadets; but, having made astronomy my hobby, I decided to tackle it. I believe that decision changed my life.

About 700 aspiring cadets took the exam, both for the Army and the Navy. After an agonising wait, I learned from *The Times* that I had won 4th place and a Prize Cadetship to Cranwell. That was followed by a letter from the Air Ministry with the joining instructions, other details regarding my future career and the pension to which I would become entitled, depending on my rank, in about 30 years' time. Under the conditions resulting from the depression, the latter was the most important of all – security and no future fear of starvation.

I was absolutely thrilled. So was Bunny – it meant that in the not-too-distant future I would be able to afford to marry her.

My name was added to the Roll of Honour in the Great Hall at Dulwich College and I received letters of congratulation from two of my former masters there.

It was the fear of starvation that had motivated me. My father losing all his money had been a blessing in disguise. My love for Bunny, the encouragement she had given me and the prospect (although delayed) of a life together, made me exceedingly optimistic for the future.

Chapter 4

Cranwell

The aim of the Royal Air Force College (like the much older RMA Sandhurst) was to turn the cadets, the majority of whom came direct from English public schools but with a few from other countries in the Commonwealth, into good officers and leaders with qualifications that would enable them to gain the highest ranks, and so form the nucleus of the future armed services. Cranwell, in addition, aimed to make them the best pilots in the world – for which medical fitness and sporting ability were even more important than academic qualifications. In consequence, the flying instructors were of the highest grade – but I was less impressed by some of the academic lecturers.

In September 1932, when I arrived, we cadets were accommodated in the old war-time hutted camp across the road facing the gates of the present building. We lived five to a hut. The only heating was a coal stove in the sitting room adjoining the dormitory – damn cold in the winter with the east wind from the North Sea blasting us, and stifling hot in summer without it.

September 1932 'C' Squadron

The Selection Board had eliminated most of those who were not of strong character, adventurous, good at sport and deemed likely to make good pilots. So I found myself joining a bunch of potential leaders, full of zest for life and adventure – but not (with a few exceptions) academically brilliant.

On arrival we had to fill in a form stating what sports we played – summer and winter. A typical cadet – the Earl of Bandon, who had been there a few years ahead of me – had, for example, filled his in:

Summer – *Fishing and Fu******.   *Winter – No fishing.*

He was a fine officer, with whom I later served. I have no reason to think his statement was inaccurate or misleading – but typical of a breed which helped win the Battle of Britain.

All cadets were expected to participate in every type of sport and game – from boxing and rugger to water polo, from fox hunting (for which some cadets had their own horses) and beagling (for which the College had its own pack of hounds) to billiards and snooker. As a result of the skill I had acquired with my air rifle and later with a pistol, I became Captain of shooting: I was also Vice-Captain of cricket and a member of our squash team. However, we were warned that neither as cadets, nor as officers later, were we ever to become involved in discussions about either politics or religion, and few of us had any idea of what was really going on in the world.

The cadets were divided into the three Squadrons, each subdivided into two academic levels relating to the performance in the entrance exams. I found myself in the top section of 'C' Squadron, in which there were just four of us: Jeudwine (Prize Cadetship), Henry Molyneux (King's Cadetship), "Dreamy" Williams (Scholarship from Johannesburg, South Africa) and myself. We four, for the whole of the next two years, attended every lecture, marched down to the hangars, sat beside each other at meals – did everything together. But, at the end of the two years, I felt I knew Jeudwine no better than the day I first met him. We other three formed a wonderful friendship.

Jeudwine was a most extraordinary chap. He was tall, had a face and neck like a giraffe, had few friends and never mixed much.

But he had an amazing career (DSO, OBE, DFC) and an even more astonishing death – which forms the basis of a novel I have yet to finish writing. (Details in a later chapter.)

Molyneux was quite different – small and plumpish, vivacious, full of fun, brilliant at sport, clever and a very loyal friend to me. He used to go out with the lads most Saturday

Molyneux, me & Dreamy Williams - Cranwell 1933

evenings. I always stayed in camp, studying or writing to Bunny.

Williams (rightly known as "Dreamy") was tall, handsome, a wonderful character, slow, deep thinking and rather reserved, but with a good sense of humour and large, unmistakable handwriting. He did not join the other lads on Saturday, but tended to go out alone. Towards the end we suspected that he had a girlfriend somewhere nearby, but he never gave any hint of it himself. We learnt later, however, that Dreamy's activities there later had a major effect on the life and family of my second daughter, Pat – of which I give details later in this chapter. After leaving Cranwell, Dreamy specialised in Engineering and I lost touch with him until after we had both retired, when his son, Andrew, used to come and stay with us.

In my first term the cadet in the next bed to mine was an Indian named Daljit Singh. That autumn, on 5th November, some time after we had gone to bed, we were woken up by a loud sizzling noise, followed by a thump of something falling on the floor. Realising the date, I, like the other three, just put our heads under the bedclothes waiting for the bang and then looked out to see what had happened. There was poor old Daljit standing dishevelled in his nightshirt, his turban blown off, his beard singed, and in his hand the remnants of a firework.

"Oh!" he exclaimed, "they do not do that in India. ... I tink I go home." That became a catchphrase if something went wrong.

We learnt to fly, to begin with, in an Avro 504N – a later version of the biplane designed in 1912 which was in action throughout the First World War. The propeller was made of laminated wood and designed to pull the aircraft to a top speed of no more than about 70 mph with the engine flat out. At speeds above that (eg in a dive) the engine could go no faster and so the propeller acted as a brake, pushing against the air and preventing the aircraft reaching much higher speeds.

While still at school in 1926 I had paid five shillings for a brief flight from Shoreham airfield as a passenger in a similar aircraft with Alan Cobham. That had been interesting. But the feeling of exhilaration of myself controlling an aircraft was far more exciting. In all my flying experience, nothing ever gave me more of a thrill than my first solo in that slow old aircraft. Being up in the sky alone and able to move myself about like a bird was completely different from being a passenger. I took to flying like a duck to water, and just loved it – particularly aerobatics and instrument flying.

One of the first things we were taught at Cranwell was how to pack a parachute. We never knew when we might have to jump. We used the seat type and never flew without one. It acted as a cushion attached to our bottom and fitted into the bucket seat. We each had our own, with the harness carefully adjusted to our size, and we kept them in our flying clothing lockers in the hangar. In the same way that my ghillie later always encouraged me to tie on my own flies when fishing for salmon or trout, so – for the same reason – we were encouraged to pack our own parachutes, or at least supervise it, so that if it did not work properly, then we could not blame anyone else.

In that, we were always carefully supervised by an expert and, once a month to test it, we had to stand on a chair and pull the ripcord, while the instructor watched that the parachute fell out correctly onto the floor behind us. On one such occasion a particularly unpopular cadet nicknamed "Queenie" had pulled his ripcord and then heard the instructor give a shout of alarm. Queenie looked round and saw that only three tightly packed bed blankets had come

out. He went as white as a
sheet and had to be helped
down from the chair. But he
got the message. The shock
transformed him into a much
more pleasant character.
He never discovered that
the blankets had only been
substituted that morning.

A different trick played
on another cadet as a

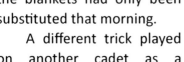

Avro 504 N

punishment was in the old huts where our heating was the coal
stove. Having been told that he was going to be branded on his
bottom, he had to watch a poker being made red hot in the stove,
then forced to lie over a chair with his trousers down. It was winter
and he did not know that another poker had been frozen in the
snow. The sensation derived from frozen iron on the skin is very
similar to hot iron. As they applied the cold iron to his bottom, they
simultaneously applied the hot iron to a piece of meat. He felt the
iron on his bottom, heard the sizzling and smelt the burning meat
that he assumed to be his own flesh. You can imagine his reaction.
But it did him no physical harm at all.

Our flying training was dominated by two things: learning how
to get out of a spin (which most aircraft went into automatically if the
pilot mishandled the controls at slow speeds), and how to make a safe
landing on whatever ground happened to be beneath in an emergency
– such as when the engine failed, we smelt fire or something went
seriously wrong with the aircraft – all not infrequent occurrences in
those days! That was also important, but less of an emergency, for
when we got lost or the weather got too bad to continue.

For the whole of my first year I flew only training aircraft – first
the old Avro 504N and then the Avro Tutor, which replaced it in early
1933. In these I learnt to do every type of aerobatics then known. I
remember the first time I did a bunt. We were flying level and my
instructor told me to loosen my collar and tighten my straps. Then he

pushed the stick forward and held it there until, having completed half a loop downwards, with us on the outside and my eyes nearly being forced out of their sockets, we were flying level again but upside down, with the engine spluttering; from there we did a half roll back. He then taught me to do a tail slide too. That consisted of pulling the stick back until the aircraft was pointing vertically upwards and holding it there until we started falling backwards through the air – a most extraordinary sensation. To recover, we applied full rudder, which tipped the tail to one side – thus allowing the aircraft to just tumble out of the sky, which usually resulted in it going into a spin.

Part of our training was also to recover from an inverted spin that we practised by rolling the aircraft onto its back, pushing the stick forward until the aircraft nearly stalled, then applying full rudder. That caused one wing to stall and flip the aircraft into a fast spin with the pilots on the outside. Spinning was so rapid that my eyes could not focus properly on the rotating ground below, and the blood was forced into my head, giving a feeling that my eyes were nearly popping out. It was not a pleasant experience – but valuable training.

My blind flying training was particularly comprehensive – mainly because one of my instructors, Sgt Monk, was exceptionally good at it – and I enjoyed it. He taught me how to recover from a spin flying blind in cloud, even though the instruments we had were very primitive. When flying blind, with my head in the cockpit and looking only at the instruments, the most difficult thing of all was to disregard completely all the sensations I was getting and to rely completely on what the instruments were telling me. Years later, when more powerful engines generated greater acceleration, one of my friends, O'Brian Nicholls, as well as several other pilots, were killed flying Canberras solely because they let these sensations overrule what the instruments were indicating. I happened to be given the job of finding out why these crashes had occurred and – thanks largely to my Cranwell training – was able to do so, as I explain later.

To practise blind flying in good weather we used a canvas hood fitted over the pupil's cockpit (to prevent him seeing outside), with the instructor looking out to ensure safety. My training to ignore my sensations began like that, with the instructor doing the take-off and warning me that I would get a sensation of climbing steeply as we accelerated. Then, flying level, he closed the throttle and warned me that I would get a sensation of diving. He demonstrated how other manoeuvres also created false impressions. He made me practise doing these manoeuvres on instruments until he was satisfied that I was proficient. It was the excellent flying training at Cranwell, and the splendid instructors I had there, to which I attribute my later survival.

My instructor also demonstrated to me that it is easy to let your eyes, focussed on the ground, override what your instruments are correctly indicating. A fellow cadet named Gard failed to remember that and so killed himself by stalling an Atlas aircraft while turning on the approach to land in clear weather. Four years later, from the deck of an aircraft carrier, I watched two similar crashes occurring (the second fatal) for exactly the same reason. Over 70 years later, in 2009, my godson (Colin Heslop) also crashed a light aircraft – apparently because pilots are still not being properly taught how to avoid that particular danger.

But my survival is also due to more than my fair share of luck – even at Cranwell! Although we used the hood over the cockpit on clear days, most of our instrument training was carried out flying in cloud. Sometimes several aircraft might be in the same clouds, although the instructors tried to avoid that. On one occasion I was blind flying like that with my instructor in dense cloud, and with both of us concentrating on the instruments, when we felt a sudden bump. After landing, we found the marks from the tyres of another aircraft on our upper wing. The occupants of another aircraft had felt the bump too. Had that other aircraft been a few inches lower, or us three inches higher, we would have all been killed. And Heaven only knows how often we had similar near-misses without us being aware of it!

Not everyone had my luck. Shortly before I left Cranwell, two of my fellow cadets, and their instructors, were killed in a collision – a New Zealander named Plugge, and a chap in my squadron named

Rutherford - although this had occurred in clear air while low flying. That tragedy, coupled with the earlier incident, had a lasting effect on me. It convinced me that the main danger in all flying is colliding with another aircraft – a view I still hold. In all my 25 years flying, that was my only real fear – and it was that which led me to invent an airborne anti-collision system, as I recount later.

As I mentioned earlier, there was much emphasis on spinning. That had always been the main cause of pilots crashing – right from the beginning of aviation. If either wing of an aircraft was not going fast enough through the air to hold it up, that wing would suddenly stall; the aircraft would flip over to that side and start spinning downwards, with the other wing going faster and so gradually making the spin more stable. That created a situation that was not easily remedied. The longer it was allowed to continue, the more difficult it was to get out of it. Some aircraft were much worse than others; but the training aircraft were specifically designed to make it easy to recover. We practised spinning on almost every training flight.

Because of the danger of getting into a spin, when flying in cloud we were taught always to keep the wings level – never to let the aircraft bank into a turn, because that was far too dangerous with the instruments then available. If we needed to change direction, we had to use only the rudder to make the aircraft skid round – side slipping – while concentrating on keeping the wings level. It was a most uncomfortable procedure.

On the 504 we only had four instruments to help us fly the aircraft. The first was an altimeter, which measured the atmospheric pressure at some place inside or outside the cockpit to give us a rough idea of our height (but only above where it had last been set – usually the last airfield from which we had taken off). The second was a gadget to measure the pressure of the air coming from a forward direction and so indicate our airspeed: that consisted of a coiled spring hinged at the top and attached to one of the wing struts with a flat piece of metal facing forwards, with a pointer at the bottom being forced over a scale graduated in mph. The third was a similar device placed at right angles to that on another strut, to measure the strength of the sideways wind (ie sideslip, which we also felt on our face). Both of these had to be located well away from the cockpit and the engine slipstream and so, in very dense cloud, sometimes became invisible or affected by ice. The fourth was a spirit level on the dashboard with a bubble, acting like an inverted pendulum, to confirm the feel we got from the seat of our pants. The Avro Tutor, which replaced the 504 N in early 1933, was better equipped with flying instruments.

The only other things we had to help us operate were a gauge on top of the fuel tank indicating the amount of fuel remaining, a watch to indicate time, a modified ship's compass, which was very difficult to use, a thermometer to warn of icing conditions, and a map, which was extremely difficult to use before it was (often) blown out of the open cockpit.

At the beginning of my second year at Cranwell, we cadets moved into the newly-built College, where we each had our own

New Cranwell College 1933

rooms. There were also several staff changes. The previous Chief Flying Instructor (C. N. Rowe, who played rugger for England and was, like me, an Old Alleynian) was replaced by Squadron Leader Martingell. Also, the Chief Engineer Officer was replaced by Squadron Leader Heslop, who had been a pilot in the King's Flight.

These two appointments made little difference to us, except that Heslop had a Rolls-Royce in which, on our weekends off, he used to give Molyneux a lift to his home in Yorkshire, which was close to Heslop's own destination: and – more importantly – Martingell had a very attractive and glamorous wife (Phyllis), who accompanied him to church each Sunday. She was the centre of attention for most of us cadets and excited our imagination during the otherwise tedious sermons. By an extraordinary coincidence, these three personalities later had a dramatic effect on my future family – as I explain at the end of this chapter.

In my second year I went on to fly operational types of aircraft in a flight commanded by Flight Lieutenant Beisiegel, who had recently been promoted to that rank. First, he taught me to fly Hawker Harts (a light single-engined bomber) and then I was selected to be a fighter pilot and went on to Bristol Bulldogs. Two events stand out in my memory concerning that part of our training.

One very cloudy day that winter, another instructor deemed the conditions ideal to give me my first experience of icing. We climbed up through solid cloud to a height of 12,000 feet, at which level the temperature had fallen well below freezing; with the wind whistling through the open cockpit. I was in agony from the cold. Also, I was becoming apprehensive that we might fall out of the sky because of the amount of hoar frost and ice that had built up on the front edges of the wings and struts. Furthermore, I knew the normal height limit for flying without oxygen was 10,000 feet and had little idea what happened above that.

The instructor (who was flying it) warned me that the aircraft had about as much ice on the wings as it could safely take without

Dining Hall - Cranwell

stalling and told me to take over control to get the feel of it. I did so – but shortly afterwards (flying in thick cloud only on instruments and possibly being a little light-headed without oxygen) I must have got the nose too high and stalled it. The next thing I knew, both from the sensations and the instruments, was that the aircraft had flipped into a spin. My instructor shouted, "I've got her", and took back control. I watched the altimeter unwinding as we spiralled down, with him struggling to correct the spin – a much more difficult task with all that ice.

10,000 feet ... 8,000 feet ... and we seemed to be spinning faster. And we were picking up even more ice on the leading edges of the wings and struts. At 6,000 feet we were still spinning and I began to wonder whether the spin had become too stable for us ever to get out of it, and at what height he would tell me to undo my straps and take to my parachute. Then I remembered we had been warned that getting out of the cockpit while the aircraft was spinning was extremely difficult, because one had to climb out from the top side – it was too dangerous to exit into the centre of the spin, as the aircraft spiralling down might then hit you or the parachute. We had also been warned that parachuting through cold clouds could cause the canopy to accumulate ice and so not function correctly.

At 5,000 feet the air felt warmer, but we were still spinning. I was following the movement of the controls with my feet lightly on the rudder and my fingers on the stick. We had full opposite rudder and the stick was being rocked hard forward with simultaneous bursts of engine. At 3,000 feet this suddenly took effect and put us into a vertical dive. We levelled out at 2,000 feet, still in cloud, and my instructor, in a perfectly calm voice, told me to take over control again. He told me to fly around at 1,000 feet until we lost all the ice and then land. My admiration for him – and my gratitude – knew no bounds. Ten years later that experience helped save my life.

Whenever I recall the confident way my instructor had called "I've got her", I am reminded of an amusing picture on one of the walls at the College. It was based (but exaggerated) on an incident that had occurred at Cranwell some years previously. The pupil, sitting in the rear cockpit, was depicted as just having made an appallingly heavy landing – so heavy that the aircraft fuselage had split into two just behind the instructor's front cockpit, leaving the rear half with the pupil in his cockpit on the ground. The instructor in the front half, unaware of this, is depicted with a bristling moustache opening up the engine to go round again and shouting, "I've got her" – just as my instructor had. The pupil, crouching in his cockpit now stationary on the ground, gleefully replies: "And you can bloody well have her!"

The other event concerns a "height test" which we carried out in clear weather. Our aircraft were not fitted with oxygen and we all had to experience the effects of lack of it at increasing altitudes. It only became significant above about 10,000 feet and the lack of oxygen had no lasting effect. Even if a pilot went far above that limit and became unconscious, then as soon as the aircraft fell below

10,000 feet he would normally recover and that would give him plenty of time to regain control before crashing. We each had to do one height test and were instructed to start descending immediately we felt light-headed and never to exceed 15,000 feet. Needless to say, competition between the cadets developed to see who could go highest.

I did my height test in a Hawker Hart. I began to feel a bit light-headed around 15,000 feet, but managed to climb to nearly 20,000. I was so elated that I decided to do a slow roll to celebrate. The next thing I remember was regaining consciousness and finding the aircraft out of control at about 8,000 feet, upside down, and diving very fast. I still do not know how we arrived at that situation. However, my training enabled me quickly to remedy matters and land safely.

One of the most difficult things was finding our way about – "cross-country flying", as it was called. We had no radio or other aids. The only navigation instrument we had was the ship's compass, whose direction pointer swung all over the place unless the aircraft was flying absolutely straight and level – a rare situation in a single-seater like the Bristol Bulldog, which I was now flying. Apart from the indications of our speed through the air (which itself could be moving in any direction), we had nothing but that compass, and a watch, to help us. Reading a map was almost impossible and I found memorising all the main features on it before taking off was too difficult. It was quite an adventure to get out of sight of the airfield or other prominent known landmarks.

One of our first cross-country training exercises was, on a fine day, to fly to Newark, Peterborough and back. These were such short distances that we had barely been out of sight of Cranwell and all of us arrived back on schedule, except a cadet named Yaxley. The hours passed and we feared he must have crashed. But that evening he turned up looking very sheepish.

He had managed the first two legs, but noticed from his map there was a village with the same name as himself – Yaxley – near Peterborough. He decided to fly over it to see what it looked like. But he had suddenly smelt something burning. We were taught, if we smelt fire, to switch off the engine immediately and make a forced landing. So that is what he did – concentrating on landing safely. Only then, on the ground, did he notice the large chimneys all around, with the smoke pouring up into the sky from them. The town of Yaxley was in the centre of the brickfields and it was the smoke from them he had scented. Yaxley himself, after a brilliant career which won him a DSO, MC, and DFC, had the bad luck to be a passenger in the aircraft carrying the Polish General which the Germans shot down over the Bay of Biscay later in the war.

At Cranwell we were taught to fly, to be leaders, to use our initiative, and manage our subordinates. But the academic side of our training was pretty awful.

The main thing I remember from our engineering training (apart from learning how to take an engine to bits and put it together again) was being given, on entry, a cube of metal precisely three inches square. We had the whole two years to file it down to a cube exactly two inches square. Now, I don't know whether you have ever tried filing a flat surface accurately –- but my cube quickly became the shape of a tennis ball. I had, however, learnt to use a lathe and with help from Dreamy Williams I managed to get some flat sides on it. This exercise again illustrated to me the irrational importance that teachers assign to things they themselves have learnt –- but which are utterly irrelevant to the future of their pupils.

Legal training, including how to preside over a court martial, was considered important. But the main thing I remember was the emphasis placed by the lecturer on the essential need to prove penetration if the charge was rape. We often wondered why he particularly laboured that point – we had varied opinions on his reasons.

To improve our social graces, we were encouraged to accept invitations to dinner that often came from residents in the surrounding county. Having come straight from school, some cadets were rather shy and socially inexperienced. I remember one such dinner when I was sitting on the right of the hostess – a most dignified elderly lady – at a mansion in the country. Her husband, wearing a monocle, was at the other end of the table. There were about eight of us altogether, including two other cadets, one of whom was on her left, opposite me. Like most big country houses in those days, they had no mains water – all came from a well or pond and was pretty cloudy.

Halfway through dinner there was a lull in the conversation. The cadet opposite me deemed it his duty to find a subject for conversation. So, noticing the glass jug of water standing on the table between us, he turned to the hostess and said:

"I notice that your water is very yellow."

I remember seeing the monocle drop from her husband's eye and her own expression of astonishment. There was utter silence for a moment; then, thinking she must have heard incorrectly, the hostess said:

"I beg your pardon?"

By that time it had dawned on the unfortunate cadet that he had made an awful faux pas. In an effort to remedy matters, he made it even worse by adding:

"Oh! I meant your drinking water, of course."

We were not invited to that house again.

One of our main tasks, during our two years at Cranwell, was to write a thesis on a subject of our own choice relating to the future of aviation – as Frank Whittle had done with his famous thesis on "Jet Propulsion" a few years earlier. To me, one of the main problems facing military aviation has always been navigation – how to find the target to bomb it, or to reach and land safely at the intended destination in any weather. My grandfather having been a Professor of Astronomy, plus the telescope and sextant I had inherited from him, had already resulted in me taking Navigation as an extra subject in the entrance exam to Cranwell. So I chose Navigation – astronomical navigation in particular.

However, while I was writing that thesis I felt pretty certain that the staff would never read through all the several hundred pages thoroughly. So I started off with quite a reasonable opening; then, to save work, I put in a lengthy middle (which was largely irrelevant) that I copied out of various books; but I wrote the end part myself very carefully. My hunch had been right – it was clear that the instructor judging it had not read it all, because I got full marks for it.

The whole of our strategic and war training was based on the assumption that the only conceivable foe that England would ever have to fight was France. Every lecture related to how we should plan to defeat the French and defend the South Coast from a French attack. No mention of Germany ever entered into any of the lectures at that stage – not even by the summer of 1934.

The cadet who passed out top had first choice of the available postings – and so on to the second and third down the line. First choice went to Don Stokes, who seemed never to do a stroke of work, slept through most lectures, but won most prizes and passed out top. He elected to go to a Squadron in India. Molyneux and I passed out second and third and so had next choice. There were vacancies for two pilots in 32 Fighter Squadron at Biggin Hill. That was the nearest airfield to where Bunny lived. So, at my suggestion, and because we had both trained as fighter pilots on Bulldogs, with which 32 Squadron was equipped, my friend Molyneux agreed that we should elect to go there together.

Bunny came up by train to attend our Passing Out Parade. Dreamy Williams had an open four-seater car in which he drove me to Grantham station to meet her. Driving back to Cranwell, Bunny and I were in the back seat and too preoccupied with each other to notice him nodding off. True to his nickname, Dreamy fell asleep at the wheel. We ended up in a cornfield and had great difficulty getting out again. But the next day after the passing out parade, at which we were awarded our commissions as Pilot Officers (signed by King George V), Dreamy drove us without mishap to Calthorpe station, from which Bunny and I had planned to go on holiday, together with her parents, at Mundesley on the Norfolk coast.

Sequel

When I graduated from Cranwell, in July 1934, the Chief Flying Instructor – Squadron Leader Martingell – signed my flying logbook with his assessment of my flying ability: "Above the Average". (Nothing very special about that, as many others had similar assessments. But the fact that I still have that logbook with his signature is of considerable interest to my second daughter – Pat.)

About a year and a half later, on 20 February 1936, I learned that Martingell, together with a pupil, Flight Cadet Tomlinson, had been killed in an aircraft crash 15 minutes after taking off in Tutor K3201 – the cause of which was never fully established. The aircraft appeared to have dived almost vertically into the garden of his married quarter in full view of his wife, Phyllis – the very attractive, vivacious lady whom I have already mentioned.

One theory was that the pupil's parachute had become jammed against the control column, another that he had "frozen" on the controls. Neither of these explanations appeared at all likely to me.

So, on my next visit to Cranwell (which was to play cricket for the Old Cranwellians against the cadets that summer), I decided to question the batman who had looked after Molyneux, Williams and me throughout our two years there. The batmen always knew everything (including all gossip) about what was going on in the camp.

"Was it really an accident?" I asked him.

He shook his head. "That's what the Court of Enquiry decided, but we have other theories."

"Such as?" I enquired.

But he refused to elaborate. "It's best left a mystery," he insisted.

I tried to extract information from some of the other batmen, but all my questioning was similarly unproductive. So I forgot about it.

Meanwhile, in April 1936, when I was temporarily based at Aboukir in Egypt during the Abyssinian War, I was ordered to fly a Blackburn Shark out to the aircraft carrier HMS *Glorious*, which was cruising about 20 miles north of Alexandria, to pick up two passengers, fly them to Cairo for a meeting and later return them to the carrier. One of those passengers was Squadron Leader Heslop, who had been the engineering officer at Cranwell. Luckily, the weather was fine and, with the Pyramids visible from 50 miles away, I completed the task without difficulty.

The following year, although I was unaware of it until much later, Martingell's widow – the gorgeous Phyllis – married Heslop (better known as "Slops").

Five years later, during the war, when Slops was a Group Captain and I was a Wing Commander, I found myself serving as one of his deputies at the British Air Commission in Washington, DC. As a result, my wife Bunny and Slops's wife Phyllis became great friends, with their first son Peter and our daughter Pam often playing together. Later, Phyllis asked me to be godfather to her second son Colin, and we stayed with them, first at their house near Washington – then in 1945, just after VE Day, at their house in Sonning in England. The following year Phyllis also became godmother to our second daughter Pat.

Some 20 years later, Pat had come down to Switzerland to spend Christmas with us at Gstaad, where we were then living. Peter Heslop, following in his father's footsteps as an engineer, was working for Rolls-Royce on aero engines in France and Switzerland. Bunny had a phone call from Phyllis to say that Peter was temporarily working at an airfield near Berne (quite near us) in Switzerland and suggested that we might like to have him with us for Christmas dinner – which we did.

That led to a romance and, a few years later, Pat married Peter Heslop.

Slops retired as an Air Vice-Marshal and died in 1976, and Peter's mother Phyllis died a few years later. When Pat was sorting out Phyllis's things, she came across many photographs of Dreamy Williams. Some were of him and (as she had then been) Mrs Martingell together. Also, there was a letter, in Dreamy's unmistakable handwriting – dated just four days after Martingell's crash – which made it quite clear that they were lovers. It read:

"Think of me as withdrawn
into the morning dimness –
Yours still – you mine –
Remember all the best
of our past moments –
forget the rest –
And so where I await
come gently on."

As I mentioned earlier, when we were together at Cranwell we had suspected that Dreamy's girlfriend might be one of the officers' wives.

Whatever caused that crash which made Phyllis a widow, it led to her marrying Slops which also resulted in our daughter Pat marrying their son Peter.

"It's a small world!" remarked Pat when we discussed it.

"Proof of the Chaos Theory." I replied.

To confirm what I now think may have happened (and so complete the story) I intend, next time I visit Cranwell, to study the photos of Tomlinson's term there to see whether he also had been a strikingly handsome cadet.

Chapter 5

Biggin Hill

During the Battle of Britain in 1940, Biggin Hill became one of the best-known airfields in the world and No. 32 (Fighter) Squadron one of the most famous flying units in history. When Molyneux and I were posted to that Squadron there in 1934, the airfield was just a relatively small grass field with a couple of new-type hangars – one for our squadron, equipped with Bristol Bulldogs, and the other occupied by 23 Squadron with Hawker Demons (similar to the Harts, but equipped as fighters with a machine gun in the back cockpit).

Because of the financial state of the country in the early 1930s, the Government had introduced strict economy measures that limited the amount of petrol the RAF was allowed to use. That restricted our flying and we rarely worked much in the afternoons. The politicians who were then in power had failed to realise that Germany was bent on rearming to become an aggressor again – and that increasingly obvious threat was ignored by our government. In consequence, there seemed no urgency about anything connected with the RAF.

Our aircraft, equipment and tactics had developed little since the last war; and with no imminent threat against which we were instructed to prepare, there was little incentive for us to do anything but enjoy the flying and the few other things our duties demanded. We lived in the officers' mess – just across the road from the airfield and with a lovely view over the valley – in accommodation of luxury hotel standard with a batman to look after cleaning our shoes and laying out our clothes, etc. So life went on at a very leisurely pace, with us having plenty of spare time to enjoy ourselves.

Getting third-party insurance for me to drive my 1928 Austin 7 two-seater "Beetleback" (which I bought for £15) was quite difficult because of my age and occupation, but one of the other young officers who had faced similar obstacles helped me arrange it. My experience of riding a motorbike – for which I never had any instruction nor, I believe, insurance – was the only help I had in learning to drive a car. There was, of course, no driving test in those days. Luckily, I rarely met another car when speeding along the narrow and quite twisty road to or from Beckenham to see Bunny – often in the dark, with headlamps so dim that they were quite inadequate.

The other pilots had an interesting selection of cars – as one would expect from such a varied bunch of adventurous characters. Two that I particularly remember were a splendid Bugatti owned by Freddie Shute – and a Daimler that Bill Hurley had specially modified. At the touch of a button in that Daimler, the back of the passenger seat suddenly collapsed to join with the rear seat to make a bed onto which the unsuspecting (or perhaps willing – I never discovered) passenger fell backwards into a rather helpless attitude. Bill had plenty of girlfriends. He also had quite a few officers wanting to borrow his Daimler.

The CO of 32 Squadron had, like me, been educated at Dulwich College and so wore the same "old school tie", which assured me of a good welcome. Molyneux and I were in "C" Flight, which was commanded by a splendid pilot named Kenneth Brake. He had been a cadet at Cranwell long before us and was now a Flight Lieutenant. Social duties necessitated all junior officers "calling" to leave visiting cards on their senior officers. Kenneth's wife Molly was kind enough to invite me to bring Bunny along to tea one day – which started a long friendship.

Since we were already experienced in piloting Bulldogs, Molyneux and I soon learnt to fly in formation with our flight leader (Kenneth), with our wings close in behind his and to stay in that relative position whatever attitude he manoeuvred into, whether in cloud or doing aerobatics – just like the Red Arrow pilots do today.

As I mentioned earlier, the primary role of the RAF was to defend England against an attack from France, and the main practice for that was to have, every day, a "Battle Flight" patrolling the skies over Kent and Sussex ready (in theory) to shoot down any hostile French aircraft that dared enter our airspace. In fact, we regarded the French Air Force as so incompetent that we never took that

'C' Flight 1934

'C' Flight 1934

danger seriously. Nevertheless, our masters in London insisted on us going through that routine – even though our guns were unloaded and we had little training on how to use them.

So, every morning a flight of three aircraft in close formation had to do a "Battle Climb" in almost any weather, unless the airfield was covered in fog or cloud, to 13,000 feet. We shared that duty with 23 Squadron, and (with three flights in each squadron) our turn for a battle climb came round about once a week. What use we would have been up there always puzzled us, because we had already used most of our fuel climbing up to that height and so could not remain on patrol for more than a few minutes before needing the remaining fuel to find our way back to Biggin Hill and land with an adequate margin of safely.

Our main armament comprised two fixed machine guns which were synchronised (we hoped!) to fire forward through the propeller; we could also carry a couple of tiny 20lb bombs attached to brackets which could be fitted under the wings. Although 16 years had elapsed since the end of the First World War, we had little better offensive equipment than our pilots had then – although the aircraft were slightly more manoeuvrable and reliable. I reckoned we were reasonably well equipped, in emergency, to frighten a herd of cows (at least with the noise from our engines) – but not much more.

Our main problem, except in fine weather with little cloud, was finding our way back to Biggin Hill to land before we ran out of petrol. With the wind blasting through the open cockpit, it was extremely difficult to use a map. Our only navigation aid was a primitive radio receiver that we could tune to listen to two ground beacons which transmitted a rotating directional beam through 360 degrees per minute with an extra omni-directional "pip" as it passed through north. Thus, by starting a stopwatch on hearing the "pip" and stopping it when we heard the rotating beam, the second hand on the stopwatch recorded the direction (but not how far) we were from the transmitting station. The main beacon was at Orfordness in Suffolk and measuring that bearing took well over a minute. Retuning and getting the bearing of a second beacon took at least a couple more minutes. Then, while memorising the first bearing and allowing for the distance travelled meanwhile, we could – in theory – calculate our location. But I found it impossible, while flying the aircraft in a bumpy cloud with one hand on the stick, my eyes practically glued to the flying instruments, to ensure we were still upright and not turning, also to handle the stopwatch and change the radio frequency and then complete the calculations of my position. I never got more than a vague indication that I was somewhere in the south-east of England. For larger aircraft carrying a navigator (to plot the results on a map), the system could be very helpful. For single-seater fighter pilots, the system was practically useless. But it was the only aid we had.

So, unless we could see the ground, our only way of estimating our position was by remembering in what direction, for how long, and at what speeds we had been flying. That was difficult enough and usually pretty inaccurate. But then we had to guess (and allow for) the wind speed and direction – which varied with height, and sometimes had a speed approaching that of the Bulldog – to estimate how far, and in what average direction, it had carried us, in order to guess where we were in relation to Biggin Hill.

Sometimes, particularly after climbing up through cloud and in close formation with the leading aircraft – which made it impossible to watch our instruments – we got it badly wrong. We always broke formation on reaching the battle climb height. On a signal from the leader, given by waving his hand (we had no other means of communication when I first joined 32 Squadron), the pilot on the right of the formation (in our case Molyneux) turned 45 degrees to starboard and the one on the left (me) 45 degrees to port, with the leader going straight on. That was to reduce the risk of us colliding with each other as we dived back down. Each of us then independently had to find our way back as best we could – and that involved getting sight of the ground without first crashing into a hill, and then recognising some feature from which we could decide the direction in which to fly to get back to Biggin Hill or – in emergency – find somewhere to land.

Since we had only enough fuel to keep us in the air for less than an hour, the weather conditions were unlikely to change much between taking off and landing – so we could usually (but not always) guess the likely weather for our return. Biggin Hill airfield is nearly 600 feet above sea level and was relatively free of fog. We needed the cloud layer to be at least 800 feet above sea level before taking off and then to remember that nearby Leith Hill (with a height just over 1,000 feet) was sticking up into the cloud and also, not far away, other hills were also giving the clouds a "hard core". For that reason, in poor visibility we always tried, when making our descent, to head for the English Channel, where we hoped to come out of the cloud over the sea before hitting any hills. We had some pretty narrow squeaks, but no one actually crashed while we were there.

To decide our location, having descended through the clouds, we relied almost entirely on recognising the village pubs, or reading the names on the railway stations – and we were allowed to fly low enough to do so. Furthermore, to assist us in recognising the pubs, the Air Ministry actively encouraged us to get to know every pub in our sector of south-east England by giving us a special petrol allowance to motor to them in the evenings. It was part of our training (and certainly the most popular part) to visit several different villages each week for this specific purpose. In those days there were (luckily) few other cars on the road – particularly at night – so driving back in the middle (or on the wrong side) of the road presented little hazard. We often restricted the speed of the driver (when returning back) by making him drive in a lower gear – one related (inversely) to the number of pints he had consumed.

That part of our training certainly proved its worth. On one occasion our flight had taken off in formation for the "battle climb" in rather murky weather and climbed up through cloud with me tucked in tightly on Kenneth's left and Molyneux similarly on his right. At times the cloud was so thick that I could not even see as far as Molyneux's aircraft and I dare not take my eyes off the wings and cockpit of Kenneth's aircraft even for a second to glance at my instruments. All I could do, in the turbulent air, was hang in beside him without any idea of which direction, whether turning or not, or the height at which we were flying. Then I saw him raise his hand and wave for us to break formation. I immediately turned left away from him, concentrating now on my instruments.

They indicated that I was at 9,000 feet. (Kenneth later told me that he had not climbed higher so as to give us extra time, in the murky weather, to find our way back to Biggin Hill.) I had no idea in what direction I was heading because during a turn the magnetic compass swings violently. All I knew was that I was probably over south-east England. I levelled up to let the compass settle and then started descending on a southerly course towards the English Channel, noting that my petrol gauge indicated that my tank was still half full – enough for nearly half an hour.

Concentrating on the instruments, as was essential in those bumpy clouds, I found it impossible even to try using the rotating beacons or for me even to get out a map in those conditions – let alone study it. I guessed I was probably somewhere around the Crowborough area. That meant it was probably safe to descend until the ground became visible; also that, by then flying North, I would eventually come to the long straight railway running from Reigate to Maidstone, which we often used to help us get back to base.

In fact, I must have been over 20 miles from there (nearer Hastings). When I came below the clouds I could see the ground ahead for about half a mile and when the railway did not appear I began to realise that I was completely lost. Unless I could recognise some landmark, I might have to land in a field and ask someone where I was – a very degrading procedure – but one which would soon be forced on me because of my dwindling fuel supply. I headed northwards, circling around each village that came in sight, hoping I would recognise one of the pubs. I suddenly did so – it was one near Goudhurst that we had visited just a few evenings previously. So I knew the railway line was still further ahead.

With great relief I flew further north and on reaching that railway line I turned left, flying along it low enough to check the station names – Paddock Wood, Tonbridge, and then turning right shortly after Penshurst, up the road to the White Hart at Brasted and so up the road back to Biggin Hill. That was how we used to have to navigate in anything other than clear weather!

Some of the pilots were pretty daredevil types who rarely thought much about potential hazards ahead – either flying or driving a car. One of these was the very dapper Hamish West – white silk scarf for flying and always dressed immaculately – who enjoyed making a "blue note" with his Bulldog to announce his arrival back at base. That involved putting the Bulldog into a vertical dive, with the engine at full power, directly over the airfield, before pulling out at about 1,000 feet and doing a loop before landing. The noise from the engine during the dive was termed "blue" and we always knew it was Hamish West who was arriving back. He was one of the officers that started making the White Hart at Brasted such a popular rendezvous for fighter pilots.

Just south of Biggin Hill lies Westerham Hill – a winding road with a very steep gradient. Most evenings, up to four others crammed into Hamish West's open Austin Seven to descend that hill en route to that pub at Brasted – although I only joined them once. The brakes on the car were barely adequate to cope with the hill – even without the extra load – and it was quite a frightening ride, particularly with Hamish driving, negotiating the bends at increasing speeds. At the bottom of Westerham Hill, where it straightens out just before the crossroads where an AA man was usually on duty, we reached our terminal velocity of around 45mph – for which reason Hamish had a mutually beneficial arrangement with that AA patrol man.

Hamish, engrossed in controlling the car, would get one of the passengers to start (about halfway down the hill) blowing the bulbous rubber horn, using the Morse code SOS to identify us. The AA chap, on hearing this, held up any other cars (if they happened to be around) in order to let us shoot safely through that crossroad. On our return journey Hamish would conceal a bottle of beer in a prearranged location in a hedge by the crossroads as a reward for the AA man to retrieve the following day.

The AA man always gave prior warning if he would be off duty, in which case two or three of the passengers would have to walk down the hill, holding the car back.

That arrangement worked splendidly for several weeks, with the AA chap always giving good warning of his days off. In retrospect, it was really a crazy situation with an accident just waiting to happen. But that is the type of chap that Hamish was – a brilliant pilot, confident and fearless: just the type who later helped win the Battle of Britain.

One evening, when I returned to the mess from having had dinner with Bunny in Beckenham, I found Hamish and several others in the bar looking very sorry for themselves, but luckily not badly hurt. The AA man had been called to attend to an accident a couple of hundred yards away. He had heard Hamish's horn and had run as fast as he could, but failed to get to the crossroads in time to prevent a car coming out. Hamish had skilfully managed to swerve round the other car, but had gone through the hedge at high speed into a field.

Flying at night had not been part of the Cranwell training, so that autumn, as the evenings began to draw in, Molyneux and I were scheduled to get our first experience of it. (We had no dual-control aircraft in which another pilot could have instructed or supervised us.) A landing strip on the grass airfield was marked by a flare path in the shape of a T by a line of paraffin burners, each about four feet high and spaced about fifty yards apart. They consisted of absorbent material that had been saturated with paraffin and held together in a wire cage to be set alight when needed. Each burnt for about an hour, before being replaced with a spare one which had always to be kept nearby and ready for use.

The method of training used was for the pilot to practise landing to the left of this flare path as it was getting dusk to get accustomed to it and then continue until the night had set in and it was dark. We were supposed to land as close to the first flare as possible and not to go beyond the last flare in the "T", as that marked the edge of the airfield where the land fell steeply away into the valley.

With no radio, our main communication from the ground to the pilot was by Aldis lamp — a powerful torch with a narrow beam — into which red or green coloured glass could be inserted or messages flashed in Morse code. The Bulldog had wingtip lights that could be seen from the ground, so the Aldis lamp could be aimed at a particular aircraft to give him a green or red signal. Alternatively, in emergency, coloured flares (red for danger, green for OK) known as "flaming onions" could be fired by the ground controller high into the air. The only way the pilot could communicate with the ground — in an emergency — was by firing a Verey pistol, which needed loading with a coloured flare cartridge, which might perhaps convey a message but was almost as likely to set the aircraft on fire.

The paraffin flares had not yet been lit when I took off for my first experience of this, although it was already dusk. For some reason, probably because someone had forgotten to bring a box of matches, there was then a long delay in lighting the flares. Each time I circled to land, I was given a red by the Aldis lamp and had to wait longer. By the time the flare path was finally ready, and I was at last given a green, it was pitch dark.

All that I could see was the flares and I had to judge my height by the angle between them and land as close to the first one as possible. So that is exactly what I did. As the aircraft touched down I felt a big thump, but attributed that to having made a heavy landing.

Feeling quite elated at the success of my first night landing — particularly as I had done so without the advantage of any dusk landing practice — I taxied back and started to take off for a second time. I had opened up the engine and was nearing take-off speed along the flare path when I saw a red "flaming onion" curling into the air ahead of me. For a moment I hesitated, wondering whether that was for me, but decided it probably was. So I cut the engine and aborted the take-off. My Bulldog rolled to a stop (we had no brakes) about ten yards beyond the last flare.

Looking back over my shoulder, I saw, outlined against the light of the flares, an airman running towards me. He climbed up beside me and shouted: "For God's sake, Sir. Don't take off. You've only got half a tail plane!"

He hung onto the wingtip to help me turn the aircraft round and I taxied back to the hangar, switched off and got out to look. The entire starboard side of my tail plane and elevator was missing. If I had completed that take-off, my Bulldog would have rolled over out of control and dived into the valley ahead.

My tail plane had hit the spare flare basket that had been left standing close to that first flare. That explained the bump I had felt.

The next morning I walked to the area where my Bulldog had rolled to a stop and saw the patch of burnt grass where the last flare had been located. I had finished up less than ten yards from where the ground fell steeply away into the valley. That generated a heartfelt feeling of gratitude to the chap who had fired that red flaming onion. Without that I would almost certainly have been killed.

After completing my night flying training later that month, my total night flying experience by the following July was still only one hour and twenty minutes. Night flying was rarely practised by fighter squadrons in those days.

We did a little firing with live ammunition against targets on the ground at Lydd by aiming the aircraft at them in a long straight dive from about 1,000 feet. That was good fun and we sometimes scored a few hits. But anyone on the ground defending the area with a machine gun would have found us an easy target. We also practised dive-bombing with tiny little bombs that only made a puff of smoke. But that was more difficult than shooting, because we had to allow for bomb trajectory after it was released; I don't ever recall hitting the target, although I often pulled out of the dive with only a few feet to spare, as that gave me a better chance. Otherwise, we practised aerobatics, sometimes in formation, cloud flying, spinning and landings.

Then, in March 1935, because of the threat that Italy was going to invade Abyssinia, what became known as the "Abyssinian Crisis" blew up. Most of us had not the slightest idea of where that country was located. We had only ever heard of it in relation to the definition of an "Abyssinian virgin" – the answer (apart from the one in the dictionary) being: "An Abyssinian goat that could run faster than an Abyssinian shepherd".

The incompetent idiots in our government decided that a show of force by the mighty British Empire would deter any such aggression. In fact, the Italians just cocked a snook and got on with the job. There was talk of war and most of the Royal Navy Home Fleet were ordered to combine with the Mediterranean Fleet in the waters off Malta. The RAF squadrons in Egypt were also to be reinforced. The Navy then found that they urgently needed more pilots in the Fleet Air Arm – to fly from their aircraft carriers.

In the ensuing panic, Molyneux and I were two of the pilots selected to help remedy that deficiency. With only a couple of days' notice, we were ordered to report first to RAF Calshot, near Southampton, to undergo a two-week training course on flying floatplanes. Following that, we were to go immediately to RAF Leuchars, near St Andrews, in Fife, Scotland, to fly Naval aircraft and practise landing them on a dummy deck marked out on the ground to resemble that of an aircraft carrier. We expected to be there for only three weeks before being posted to Malta to join one of the carriers then in the Mediterranean.

Calshot was the base from which we had won the Schneider Trophy in the seaplane designed by Mitchell who later, based on that aircraft, developed the Spitfire. [Interestingly, it was a sporting event, rather than any Government initiative, that resulted in that important aircraft development.]

In the RAF we used a balloon type of flotation waistcoat that was later developed to become the famous "Mae West". But, on reporting for duty at Calshot, we found that the Navy had just designed a new type of floating jacket for use by Fleet Air Arm aircrew. We RAF pilots were a bit doubtful about its buoyancy: it seemed more like a thick jacket to keep a sailor warm in a storm. So we decided to test it on a pilot wearing full flying gear. Molyneux, who was the sort of chap who went swimming on Christmas Day, was persuaded to volunteer.

Tutor - Calshot 1935   *Seal - Calshot 1935*

Having helped him put on the flotation jacket over his flying gear, we got him to stand on the end of the spit at Calshot and then jump into the water below – rather as if he had come down in his parachute. We had a rope ready to throw to him so that he could be pulled to a nearby ladder. At first the life-jacket and the air trapped in all the clobber he was wearing kept him well afloat; but as the seawater seeped into them, he began sinking. He tried to keep himself afloat by swimming, but was hampered by the heavy clothes.

We watched in horror as he sank out of sight. We were sure he had gone to the bottom, so it was useless throwing the rope. We began to panic – fearing he would be drowned. The air in his lungs could not last more than about a minute. One chap had rushed off to find a long boathook, and I had grabbed a couple of uninflated RAF life-jackets, intending to dive in with them on my arm, and pull the toggle to inflate them only after I had grabbed him. I was about to dive in when his head burst out of the water to a height of about a foot – giving him time to take another breath before he went down again. And this happened again each 30 seconds or so until we managed to haul him out.

It was largely the weight of his flying boots that had saved him. They had carried him down feet first and, because of the state of the tide, it was only about eight feet deep there at the time. With great presence of mind, he managed to keep jumping high enough out of the water to take deep breaths.

That was our first experience of the Fleet Air Arm. We reckoned it must have taken the naval scientists a long time to develop such an efficient type of life-jacket – but were glad that we were permitted to use the RAF type when flying Naval aircraft.

Another event concerned one of the instructors who trained pilots both on seaplanes and on deck landing on carriers. For this there were two types of Fairey Seal – one with floats, based at Calshot to alight on water, and the other with a wheeled undercarriage based at the nearby airfield at Gosport to land on a carrier or airfield. So far as the pilot was concerned, the two types were identical. Sometimes this instructor flew from Gosport in the land plane and sometimes from Calshot in the seaplane.

On one particular occasion he had taken off from Calshot in a floatplane. At the end of a two-hour flight, he forgot that he was in the floatplane version and made his approach to land on the airfield at Gosport. Luckily, the chap in the back cockpit shouted at him in time to stop what would have been at least a minor accident. So the instructor flew back to Calshot and alighted safely on the water there. Having switched off the engine, he started climbing out, pausing to thank his passenger for having alerted him. He explained his error by saying that he was sometimes a bit absent minded. He then stepped backwards, as he would on an airfield, straight into the water.

In the Fleet Air Arm we would be serving as part of the Royal Navy, so we were lectured on some of the traditions with which we would have to conform – like saluting the quarterdeck on boarding a ship and all that other nonsense left over from Nelson's days. I was a bit of a rebel. I had chosen to join the RAF, not the Navy. The flying, however, I enjoyed.

The only real difference between flying a land plane and seaplane was in the take-off and landing – the necessary control column movements being rather different. I soon got used to that, but the main problem was landing ("alighting" is the correct term) on the sea when the surface was glassy calm. There was nothing on which I could focus my eyes to judge my height. Also, it meant there was no wind to help reduce the relative speed of making contact – in other words, it meant hitting the water at higher speed. That was partly balanced by the ability to make the landing in any direction – also, unlike on an airfield, the landing area was not limited by any hedges. So, under those conditions, I learnt to make a long approach, descending very gently and just waiting apprehensively for the splash, which (when it finally happened) always gave me a fright.

Apart from that, the flying was a piece of cake and I felt that the two weeks allocated for that seaplane training was far longer than necessary. So, at the end of the first week, I reckoned that – with a little co-operation from my instructor, and from Molyneux letting me do my flying ahead of him – I could complete the course by midday Wednesday instead of the Friday evening. That would give me four clear days before I was due to report to Leuchars (in Scotland) on the following Monday morning.

Bunny and I had already been engaged for nearly four years and the thought of being parted from her if – as seemed likely – I was going to be sent to Malta for an indefinite period, did not please me one bit. I decided that it would make sense for us to get married first, so that she could then come out and join me there.

One problem facing me was that, before getting married, all officers had to get the permission of their commanding officer. That was only forthcoming if the commanding officer's wife, and the wives of at least two other senior officers on that station, had first met the girl socially and approved her as suitable to become an officer's wife. Pure snobbery. But who was my commanding officer? The one at Biggin Hill, Calshot, or Leuchars? And how long would the process take?

Such petty regulations or traditions have rarely held me back from doing what I wanted, so I decided to omit that formality. So, that Sunday, I phoned Bunny to suggest we should get married on that Thursday. She agreed and arranged a special licence to enable us to do so. My instructor and Molyneux co-operated. I left Calshot and motored up to Beckenham on Wednesday afternoon. On Thursday we were married in the church at the end of Cator Road with just our two families present. I left my car at her house and we took the train to London – to the newly-built Marble Arch Hotel, had dinner with our combined families at the Trocadero, spent the night at the hotel, took the train back to Beckenham next morning to pick up my car and then set off, in snow that was blowing into the car and all over Bunny and me, for Leuchars.

We spent a night at the Red Lion in Newark, another in Lockerbie, and installed Bunny in a boarding house in St Andrews on the Sunday. There we were astonished to discover the extraordinary atmosphere that then pertained in Scotland on the Sabbath – no games of any sort, not even card games; only religious music; no drinks at any pub or hotel except for genuine travellers, which resulted in mobs walking past each other to the next village at midday to qualify; and all sorts of other restrictions.

I reported to RAF Leuchars as instructed and began, with Molyneux and a few others (including Jeudwine), flying Naval-type aircraft and, for the first time, learning how to use a bombsight as well as practising dummy deck landings. During our first week there, on the Thursday, I nearly killed myself and Molyneux (which I deal with in the next chapter) and the following day had a message from Bunny that she had developed mumps.

A few days later, acting as bomb aimer in a Fairey 111F with Jeudwine as pilot, the air blasting up through the open hole containing the bombsight seemed to be hurting my cheeks more than usual. When we landed, my face was so swollen that I decided to get the doctor to examine it. He diagnosed mumps – which I had obviously caught from Bunny – and put me into an isolation ward (which I had to myself) in the camp hospital. I remember well the bloated round red face that peered back at me from the mirror. Luckily, it only affected the glands in my neck.

No one was allowed to visit me there and I found it very lonely. So, as I was getting better, I got a message to Bunny (who by then had recovered) and I bribed the medical orderly on night duty to leave the large window opposite my bed open. I well remember my excitement at seeing her leg appear as she climbed in through that window.

When I had fully recovered I was given ten days' sick leave to recuperate, so Bunny and I made that into our honeymoon – touring the Highlands in our Austin Seven in perfect weather. Motoring up some of the hills, we had to stop the car to collect water from a stream to add to the boiling radiator; we also quite frequently had to clean the plugs at the roadside. We found the beauty of Scotland – particularly Glen Affric – so entrancing, and we were so happy, that we forgot all about the Abyssinian Crisis and the separation it might entail. Our honeymoon was crowned, on a lovely evening, by the 1935 Royal Jubilee celebrations, when every mountaintop in Scotland had a bonfire on its peak – a scene of great emotion and beauty. When we later went to live in Switzerland, we were reminded each 1st August (the Swiss national day, which they similarly celebrate by lighting bonfires on each mountain peak) of that wonderful evening in the Highlands at the beginning of our marvellously happy marriage.

Apprehensive that we were going to be parted for an indefinite period, I reported back to Leuchars. There, to my delight, I learned that both Molyneux and I were returning to 32 Squadron for a further period at Biggin Hill before being posted to the Fleet Air Arm. The panic about Abyssinia appeared to have diminished.

When I arrived back at Biggin Hill, I was hauled up before the Squadron Commander to be reprimanded for having married without permission. Luckily, Kenneth Brake's wife Molly had already met Bunny and put in a good word for me. Happily, also, the fact that the CO (Squadron Leader Richardson) wore the same "old school tie" helped, and I got away with only a mild rocket.

At that time, officers were discouraged from getting married before the age of thirty, or had reached the rank of Squadron Leader, and got no marriage allowances at all. Their

Honeymoon in Scotland 1935

wives were not officially recognised and the couple were officially considered to be "living in sin". How things have changed!

In July 1935 our squadron took part in the Royal Review at Mildenhall, when the King and his three sons (two of whom became our future kings) drove in an open Rolls-Royce along the lines of parked aircraft, with us all proudly attired in our newly-issued white overalls. The fact that practically all the land-based squadrons of the entire Royal Air Force were lined up together on just one grass airfield and then flew past in formation gives an idea of the total size of the Royal Air Force at that time. It was more like being a member of an exclusive flying club, with everyone knowing everyone else and having a jolly good time, than being part of a serious fighting force.

That summer, the squadron moved to Practice Camp at Sutton Bridge on the Wash, where we lived in tents on the airfield, beside our aircraft, for a couple of weeks. We practised dive-bombing with live 20lb bombs (which hardly frightened the rabbits) and fired our guns with live ammunition at a drogue towed by another aircraft. That rarely resulted in any holes in the target drogue, but certainly terrified the pilot towing it.

Bunny was lodged in the pub at Sutton Bridge, just beside the bridge over the River Nene. We usually finished flying at midday and Bunny and I spent most afternoons motoring round the countryside. By then we had graduated from our Austin Seven to the long-nosed Standard Swallow Special ("Standard SS"), a sporty two-seater which did not go particularly fast but had a roar from the engine exhaust which made it quite impressive. That car was the forerunner of the famous "SS", which later became the Jaguar.

Most evenings, some of the other junior pilots would join us there at the pub beside the bridge for a drink. I would stay on there with Bunny after closing time and then motor back to creep into the tent just before dawn. One evening, shortly after opening time (6 pm), we were all outside the pub having a drink when Hamish West walked to the centre of the bridge and looked down at the water of the River Nene flowing slowly underneath on its way to the sea a few hundred yards distant.

"Anyone like to bet that I can't fly under this bridge?" he asked. Several of us challenged him with bets of a day's pay. So he climbed down and walked along the bank to assess the situation. It was a brick bridge with a curved arch and he reckoned that by flying with his wheels three feet above the water he would have about six feet to spare on either side of his wingtips and a good five feet in height.

"Right," he said confidently, "bets taken – providing there's not a cross wind. Be here at 12.30 midday tomorrow."

Next day was beautiful with no wind. We assembled on the bridge soon after midday with our mugs of beer (Bunny with a gin and tonic) to await his arrival. With hindsight we were pretty stupid to be standing right in the middle of that bridge – it would have been more prudent to have positioned ourselves a safe distance to the side.

Hamish West had taken off and climbed to about 7,000 feet. We watched him and heard the "blue" note of his engine as he dived the Bulldog vertically down with engine full on. At about 1,000 feet he pulled up into a loop, from which he continued his dive to level out about 200 yards away, with his wheels just above the water of the river. The Nene is quite straight there and he was heading towards the bridge. We could see the spray rising from the river behind him as his slipstream churned up the water.

As he approached he went even lower, with his wheels only about a foot above the water. But, even so, I got the impression that he was still too high. He seemed to be coming straight at us and not under the archway.

Molyneux was the first to realise the reason.

"Look out!" he shouted. "It's high tide! There isn't room!"

I grabbed Bunny and dived to the ground; the others did the same, beer mugs flying in all directions. At the very last moment Hamish too realised there was no longer enough room for him to fly under the bridge. He pulled back on the stick, and passed just over our heads with a deafening roar, missing the parapet, and us, by inches.

What we all had forgotten is that the Nene is a tidal river – with the water level changing by many feet. The previous evening at about six o'clock it had been low tide; at midday the high tide had left far too little space under the curved bridge for him to get through.

We had numerous similar escapades while we were stationed at Biggin Hill – cutting through the telephone wires to the lighthouse at Beachy Head when low flying round the cliffs; a pilot from 23 Squadron flying down Regent Street at night with wingtip flares burning while pretending to be at 10,000 feet; and many other crazy pranks. But that was the spirit that later made the pilots of Fighter Command Squadrons so famous.

Then, in September 1935, with the Abyssinian Crisis again flaring up, and the Navy again crying out for more pilots, Molyneux and I were posted to the Fleet Air Arm – him, unfortunately, to a different carrier from me and, sadly (as I explain later), I never saw him again.

But first (in the next chapter) I deal with a historical event – of which I believe I am probably the last person alive to have direct knowledge. I consider it to be far more relevant to events today than the number of women that Henry VIII married.

Chapter 6

A narrow escape

This chapter deals with the incident that happened, while George V was still King, on the Thursday after Molyneux and I had arrived at Leuchars – which led to me learning of an event which had occurred a few years previously.

As a preface I should mention that low flying was terrific fun and it was not uncommon for young pilots, full of the joys of spring, to indulge in low flying and sometimes to "buzz" people on the ground – particularly girls who they either knew or hoped to meet. That involved diving down and then flying straight at them with the wheels only perhaps a couple of feet off the ground and then pulling up over their heads at the last moment. Great fun for the pilot – but it could be absolutely terrifying for the person on the ground and sometimes cause an extremely severe shock. I know, from my experience of having often been buzzed, that when in a group of people the instinctive reaction – immediately the danger has passed – is for everyone automatically to laugh; but the effects of the shock, such as sleepless nights, come later.

The Air Ministry had made it a serious offence for any RAF pilot ever to low-fly over land without specific authority (with a court martial and dismissal from the RAF the standard penalty). But they were normally only charged if their low flying had caused some actual damage which provided solid proof of the regulations having been broken.

Amongst the Naval aircraft we flew at Leuchars was the Fairey 111F – a long-nosed, single-engined, very sturdy biplane which was easy to fly but heavy on the controls. Neither Molyneux nor I found the slightest difficulty in flying one; but, compared with the Bulldogs, the 111F was very cumbersome and slow to react. The pilot's cockpit was quite small, but behind that was a much larger cockpit designed to carry an observer and a gunner with room for them to stand up and move about. Both cockpits were wide open, with only the pilot having a tiny windshield.

On 14th March 1935, at 0830 hours, we reported as usual to the Flight Commander's office. As pilots of single-seat fighter aircraft, we had no experience of carrying any crew or of being passengers ourselves, so that morning Flight Lieutenant "Bobbie" Burns – a delightful character – detailed us to take it in turns, for forty minutes each, of being pilot and then passenger in a Fairey 111F.

We tossed a coin. Molyneux won and elected to pilot first. I climbed into the large open cockpit behind him to be his passenger. In those days, we used a motor vehicle (called a Hucks Starter) that was driven up to the front of the aircraft to start the engine. It had a long metal probe sticking out in front that hooked onto the hub of the propeller. When the pilot gave the signal, the driver let in a clutch that caused the probe to turn and so rotate the propeller to start the engine.

The Flight Sergeant, whose name I unfortunately cannot remember, was one of a fine breed of "old sweats" wearing medals from the First World War. He had by coincidence been stationed with us before and regarded us two pilots with fatherly affection as two of his "young boys". He had presented us with the Form 700 to sign, which certified that the aircraft had been properly serviced, and that we had carried out our own inspection – which in those days consisted of kicking the tyres to ensure they were properly pumped up, thumping the wings to listen for any undue rattles (really high-tech!) and checking that the rudder, elevators and ailerons moved freely.

He supervised the starting of the engine. Molyneux tested it to full power and by switching off each of the magnetos in turn while two airmen lay across the tail-plane to prevent the tail being lifted by the slipstream. Satisfied, Molyneux waved the chocks away; the Flight Sergeant saluted and gave us the all-clear signal.

A few moments later, as we were taxi-ing out across the grass, I did what must be the most stupid thing in my whole life. I leant over the front of my cockpit and shouted to Molyneux:

"Bet you can't frighten me!"

"We'll see!" he shouted back.

I decided to attach the tail anchor (the metal cable secured to the floor of the rear cockpit) to my parachute harness so that I would not fall out if he turned the aircraft onto its back, or subjected it to negative G by pushing the nose violently down, which could otherwise have thrown me out. I knew, of course, that he was a very skilful pilot and I was not unduly apprehensive. What I did not know was that he was quite familiar with that part of Scotland and Perthshire in particular. I, on the other hand, had never been in that area before.

In accordance with our instructions, he took off and climbed to 1,000 feet towards Perth. At first I stood up in the rear cockpit to get a forward view. But that gave me no protection from the slipstream and I found it more comfortable to sit facing backwards on a little seat which hinged down; that gave me a view only to the sides and to the rear. Near Perth, Molyneux put the aircraft into a steep dive, levelling out with our wheels only a few feet above the water of the River Tay. Then, banking into turns with his wingtip only a few feet off the water, he manoeuvred the cumbersome aircraft to follow the river contours northwards towards the Highlands.

From our experience of flying seaplanes at Calshot, we knew low flying over the sea was generally permitted; so it seemed unlikely that anyone would report us for low flying up a river.

Just north of Perth we came to a short straight section where Molyneux levelled out and went even lower. We were over the middle of the river, with our wheels practically touching the water. I saw a small boat setting out from the side with several people in it. I waved as we passed and they waved back. Only then did I see the pylon behind them and the high-tension cables stretching across the river and realised that we had just flown under them. Had I been looking ahead earlier and seen those wires (charged with 33,000 volts) I most certainly would have been frightened and Molyneux would have won his bet. Even just touching high-tension cables meant almost certain death – particularly for an aircraft with a tank full of petrol. But that danger had passed, so I put my mouth to the Gosport tube (the communication pipe leading to the earphone in his helmet) and shouted:

"Is that all you can do?"

He merely turned his head and grinned.

I tried to stand up to see what else lay ahead, but found the G force too strong because we were in a tight turn. Molyneux was struggling to manoeuvre us round the next bend; our wings were nearly vertical and yet the wheels were almost scraping the trees.

For the next ten minutes Molyneux followed the river, flying very low and skilfully. It was tremendous fun and a new experience being in the back cockpit with no measure of control. Once or twice my heart was in my mouth, but I pretended to be completely unconcerned. Eventually, as our time to land approached, he climbed up to 1,000 feet and headed back to Leuchars.

Then it was my turn. The entry in my flying logbook confirms that I took off that day at 0940 hours piloting Fairey 111F No S-1788, with Molyneux as passenger.

As we were taxi-ing out, Molyneux did an equally stupid thing. He leant over and shouted:

"Bet you can't frighten me either!"

The 111F was far too clumsy an aircraft for any aerobatics. The only thing I could think of was also to do some low flying. Not knowing that part of Scotland, I decided to use the River Tay as well – but starting from further north (hoping to find some bridge that I could fly under) and flying down towards Perth in the opposite direction to our earlier trip.

All went well to begin with. Then, when I was flying low down the middle of the river, a flock of ducks suddenly took off from the water right ahead of us. At higher levels birds are usually flying faster and can dive out of the way. But these had only just taken off and they had no room to dive. It was impossible for me to avoid them. We flew straight through the flock, killing several of them. Hitting birds has always been one of the hazards of flying, although this was my first experience of it, and these were large birds. Luckily, although it gave us both a fright, and I could see a couple of minor dents in the wing fabric and lots of blood and feathers sticking to the struts and wires which held the wings together, it did not appear to have done any serious damage to the controls or engine; so I was not unduly perturbed and carried on. Bird strikes were not usually serious at the speeds at which we flew in those days, although it was unusual to hit so many heavy birds together. I was glad that we were in such a sturdy aircraft.

I was trying to fly really low in the middle of the river, but that was not always possible. Some of the bends necessitated banking the aircraft quite steeply to avoid hitting the trees on the bank. Approaching Perth, I was in one such steep bank with the wings nearly vertical.

Too late, I saw the two pylons with the high-tension cables stretching across the river ahead. I had completely forgotten about them. I tried frantically to level out to climb over, or go under, them – but that was impossible. There was no time. I knew we were going to hit the wires; but there was not time even to worry about being killed.

Some people say that your whole life flashes through your mind on such occasions. Mine did not. My thoughts were probably similar to those of a chap who has fallen off Beachy Head and is nearing the bottom, but I have not yet met anyone in that category with whom to compare notes ...

We hit the cables fair and square in the middle. There was a blinding flash, a deafening bang, a tremendous judder and deceleration and then – suddenly – I realised we were still flying, although somewhat awkwardly, and that I could still just control the aircraft. My main reaction was complete astonishment and utter surprise to be still alive and – unbelievably – to have a faint chance of not crashing. I had instinctively levelled out and put the aircraft into a steady climb to gain enough height so that we could, if necessary, take to our parachutes.

Then a very white-faced Molyneux (who, I later learned, had thrown himself onto the floor, crouching against the bulkhead as soon as he saw the wires) tapped me on the shoulder and pointed to our starboard wing. Two strands of thick wire about 50 yards long were trailing from it and there were several gashes along the leading edge. I thought it was probably the weight and drag of those copper wires that was making the aircraft difficult to fly. I changed the throttle setting to test the engine; that seemed rather rough, but was still performing reasonably well.

After reaching a height at which we could have taken to our parachutes, I began testing the controls and varying the engine power as I would during a landing. In spite of the weight and drag from the wires on our wing, I found that I could manoeuvre it adequately. We conferred via the Gosport tube and agreed that we should make a forced landing without delay to take off the wires and assess the damage. I judged the wind direction by the smoke from a chimney and selected a large grass field. I made an approach to land, but was worried that the wires might catch in something on the ground and cause us to swing and crash. For this reason I was too high on my first approach and decided to go round again. My second attempt was spot on; we touched down just over the hedge and rolled to a stop with plenty of room to spare. (We had no brakes on that 111F – few aircraft had at that time – but the drag of the wires on the ground helped slow us down.)

Hoping that we might be able to fly back to Leuchars, I stayed in my cockpit and kept the engine running. Without a Hucks Starter it would have been impossible for us to restart it. Molyneux got out and prised the copper cables out of the gashes where they had torn into the wing. They comprised wire as thick as his finger and were heavy. He examined the wings and tail plane, then the rudder, elevators and ailerons, as I moved these controls to their limits.

He left the cables lying on the grass, climbed back and told me that he thought it would be safe to fly providing the engine and propeller were undamaged. I said I would test them by going to full power at the beginning of our take off. Then, if we did not accelerate normally, I would cut it while we still had enough room to pull up before hitting the far hedge. So Molyneux got out again to hang on to the wingtip to help me turn the aircraft round, taxi back and then turn into wind again. Our take-off went successfully, although the engine seemed to vibrate more than usual. A few minutes later we landed back at Leuchars.

As we were taxi-ing in, Molyneux gamely admitted that I had certainly won our bet and we had a rather forced laugh about it.

With the help of an airman on each wingtip, I manoeuvred the aircraft to a stationary position where the Flight Sergeant was waiting. I then switched off the engine.

Even before the propeller had finished rotating, the Flight Sergeant had already noticed the damage to the leading edges of the starboard wing and the blood and feathers on the struts and wires between the wings. He assumed it was all due to birds and not a very serious matter. But when the propeller stopped turning, he became really concerned. Molyneux had already climbed out and had joined the Flight Sergeant examining the propeller. It took me longer to undo my straps and parachute harness.

The Fairey 111F, with its Napier engine, was one of the first aircraft to be fitted with a metal propeller. Until then they had mainly been constructed of wood – and as we looked at it we realised that we owed our lives to it. The metal at its leading edge had five deep gashes where it had cut through and short-circuited the main high voltage cables before they touched the mainframe holding the petrol tank. It was that, and the luck of having hit the right wires, that had saved our lives. We had been doubly lucky. In a less sturdy aircraft, and without that metal propeller, I am sure we would have been killed – as were most other pilots who had the bad luck to hit high-tension cables.

I can still remember the look of concern on the face of the Flight Sergeant as he turned to me and suggested: "You've been low flying, Sir?"

I nodded confirmation and explained what had happened.

"You were bloody lucky, Sir, not to catch fire or crash," he exclaimed emotionally. "Thank God you were not killed. But now you've got another problem. And it's serious. You will be charged with low flying."

I nodded again. I realised that.

"The last pilot caught low flying in this area was dismissed from the service," he said gloomily. "It's bound to be reported, Sir, so you'd better have a good story. I only know of one pilot who ever got away with a charge of low flying. That was Mr Beisiegel – but that was a very special case."

"Beisiegel!" I exclaimed. "He was my flying instructor at Cranwell." Then eagerly: "What happened and how did he get away with it?"

"He was low flying and buzzed a girl who was in a garden. The low flying was reported and Mr Beisiegel was soon discovered to have been the pilot responsible. He was arrested and was going to be court-martialled. But then, suddenly, the case was dropped – all the witnesses refused to give evidence. That was because the girl was well known and had been pregnant."

He mentioned the lady's name (which seemed irrelevant to me at the time) and added, "She may have tried to run and fell – or it may have been just the shock – but we learned later that she had lost her baby – a baby boy – and she did not want any publicity. So her family insisted that the whole thing was hushed up and we were ordered never to mention it. So the charges against him were dropped. That's the reason Mr Beisiegel got away with it."

He then quickly added, "Oh! I forgot. I shouldn't have told you that, Sir, so please forget it. We were all sworn to secrecy about it."

To me, all that seemed immaterial to my case and my hopes of learning something that would help my own defence were dashed. The charges against me would not depend on witnesses. The damage to the aircraft and the broken cables were ample proof that I had been low flying – and there was no way I could deny it. So what he told me seemed of little relevance to my situation and I put it all into the back of my mind.

My immediate concern was to find some way of avoiding a court-martial. I was in a very desperate situation. I wondered what on earth I would do if, having just married Bunny, I was dismissed from the RAF. Then I remembered what my father had taught me – that every problem has a simple solution.

Deep in thought, and with the Flight Sergeant's words, "you'd better have a good story", ringing in my ears, I began walking slowly towards the flight commander's office to report the damage to the aircraft. I suddenly stopped and quickly returned for a brief discussion with Molyneux and then a word with the Flight Sergeant. By the time I reached the office, I had my story planned.

Flight Lieutenant Burns was at his desk. I told him I had a serious incident to report.

He looked concerned and asked: "Anyone hurt? Molyneux?"

"No, Sir. We're fine." The relief showed immediately on his face. "But," I went on, "we've got a bit of bird damage on the aircraft. And we've also cut the high-tension cables across the Tay just north of Perth – at Walkmill."

"You've been low flying!" he accused me, looking very severe.

"No, Sir," I said emphatically. "We had an emergency. I was flying at 1,000 feet when we hit a flock of geese or ducks. You can still see the blood and feathers all over the aircraft. It seemed to be flying a bit differently after that and I thought they had damaged the controls. I decided it would be prudent to make an immediate landing to examine them. I selected a good field for a forced landing near the River Tay and was in a steep turn on the final approach and didn't see the cables until too late and went straight through them."

"Christ!" he exclaimed. "You're bloody lucky to be alive. What happened then?"

"We didn't know it at the time, but it seems that the metal prop short-circuited and cut through the high-voltage cables, thus triggering the fuses, before any wires touched the wings or fuselage. So, effectively, we just flew through a batch of thick copper wires stretched across the river – and the aircraft was stronger than they were. We carried away about a hundred yards of cable trailing from our starboard wing. I was completely put off that landing and thought it best to climb quickly to a height at which we could, if necessary, take to our parachutes and where I could test everything and assess the damage. Although the aircraft was a bit difficult to control, I decided that it would now be doubly prudent to get the aircraft on the ground quickly to examine it. So I decided to make an immediate forced landing. I was worried about the trailing wires, but on my second attempt I landed safely. We took the wires off the wing and left them in the field. We checked all the controls carefully and I reckoned that it would be safe to take off again and fly it back here. So that is what I did."

"Bloody good show, Vielle!" was his generous comment. "I really congratulate you. Well done!"

He accompanied me out to examine the aircraft. There he saw the blood and feathers to confirm my story, also the squashed head of what to me looked more like a duck than a goose that the Flight Sergeant had found trapped in the undercarriage. The Flight Sergeant reckoned that it would only take a couple of hours to change the prop and repair the wings – no major damage.

Having examined the aircraft and seen the deep cuts in the prop, Bobbie Burns said:

"You did a good job, Vielle. I'm glad you flew it back here. Saved complications. Well done!"

I was elated. Not only did I appear to have escaped a court martial, but also his tone almost sounded as though he was going to recommend me for the award of an Air Force Cross.

Alas! My elation was short-lived. An hour later, I got a message to report immediately to the office of Wing Commander Maxwell. He had the reputation of being very fierce and short-tempered. He was the officer whose name hit the headlines in the press when his shotgun fired while he was cleaning it in their bedroom and killed his wife. So it was with considerable apprehension that I reported to his office that morning. I comforted myself with the knowledge that the shooting season was over and that he was unlikely to be cleaning a gun there. I knew that he played golf most afternoons and I noticed a bag of clubs leaning against the wall as I entered.

"Vielle," he roared, his face nearly puce with rage, "you are a bloody nuisance. The Chief Constable has been on the phone to me about you low flying and all hell has been let loose. The manager of the laundry at Walkmill complained to him about you cutting off his power supplies; it's stopped all work there and it will take several days before they can start again. He intends claiming damages from the Air Ministry. He said the ferryman and other people in a boat all saw you fly once under the wires before you came back and then hit them. I don't believe a word of the cock and bull story you told your flight commander. You were obviously low flying."

Seething with anger, he went on:

"You've cut power off for that whole region. And now the press have got hold of it too – so it will be in the afternoon Dundee paper. When it gets to the Air Ministry, it will reflect back on me – one of my officers breaking regulations. There's going to be one hell of a row and I shall have to spend the rest of the day dealing with it. Before I put you under arrest and charge you formally with low flying, is there anything you have got to say in your defence?"

I repeated what I had told Bobby Burns.

"I don't believe a word of it," he snarled.

"But the blood, feathers and remains of the geese on the aircraft are proof," I suggested. "And I have a witness – Molyneux – who was my passenger and will confirm it."

"But what about you first flying under the wires? There are witnesses to confirm that."

I had to be careful here not to incriminate Molyneux. "I will swear on oath, Sir, that I have never piloted any aircraft beneath those wires. I had never piloted an aircraft in that area before. It is obvious that if I had flown under those wires before then I would have known they were there and most certainly would not have hit them. That must have been an aircraft from somewhere else – we did see a couple of other aircraft in that area shortly before I hit the geese."

He glanced across to his golf clubs and then sat back silently for a while.

"It's a good story," he said finally. "I still don't believe it all. But I suppose it's just possible it could have happened that way."

I saw a faint ray of hope. His main concern, obviously, was to minimise his work and eliminate any detrimental effect on himself. If the incident were treated as a complete accident and not a case of deliberate low flying, it would be much better for him personally. Also, he could then probably go and play golf.

"Supposing, Sir," I suggested eagerly, "I rush out and see the manager of the laundry and tell him what actually happened. I think I could persuade him to withdraw all his accusations about low flying. It won't re-connect his electricity, of course, and he will have a claim for compensation. But if he is made to realise that it was a complete accident resulting from a genuine emergency, would not that simplify everything?"

He stared at me for a minute. Then he glanced towards his golf clubs again. My spirits rose.

I waited for what seemed an eternity.

"All right, Vielle," he said finally and rather more cordially. "Get going. If you persuade him, then I'll agree that you were not deliberately breaking regulations."

Within about twenty minutes, Molyneux and I had changed into civilian clothes and were racing in my Austin 7 (top speed 42 mph – downhill) towards Perth armed with a large-scale map on which we had pinpointed the field in which we had landed. The wires were still lying on the grass. We rolled them up into a coil and then, with great difficulty because of their weight, we managed to get them into my car. Then we made for the Walkmill ferry. The fare to cross the river was one penny. We could see the broken cables straggling down from the pylons and the ferryman who took us across could talk of nothing else. He said the laundry manager was mad with rage and had sworn to castrate the pilot responsible. When I told him I had been the pilot, he regarded me with awe.

"And you weren't hurt!" he said in amazement. "But you flew under them the first time all right – so why did you hit them the second time?"

"First time?" I asked. "What do you mean?" I went on to convince him that I had certainly never piloted any aircraft under the wires and that the accident resulted from an emergency. I said I was going to explain that to the manager.

He gave me a sympathetic look. "You'll be lucky! He's sworn to have your balls for a necklace!"

When we were shown into the manager's office, I said: "I am the pilot, Sir, who flew through your high-tension cables this morning, and I've come to explain and apologise."

He jumped up from his desk, spluttering with rage and pointing at me. "So you're the young bugger who cut off our electricity and frightened us all. Pity you weren't killed."

I stood bolt upright, staring at him unflinchingly.

"Just a minute," I said defiantly. "You don't understand. I was in a serious emergency – the aircraft was almost out of control. We had hit a flock of geese that damaged the aircraft. It was an accident that I happened to be in this area and hit the wires."

"Don't talk such bloody nonsense," he retorted angrily; "you had already flown under them once this morning. You were deliberately low flying and it is no good you denying it."

"You are completely mistaken. I did not pilot any aircraft under those wires," I retorted firmly. "If you saw an aircraft in this area earlier it must have been some other pilot. What time was that? I only took off from Leuchars at 0920 and then it was nearly half an hour later before I entered this area and had an emergency. I had to land urgently and descended to do so in a field the other side of the river. It was during my approach to the field that I accidentally hit those wires. We were extremely lucky to survive. It was your wires or our necks. I am extremely sorry and I've come to apologise."

He seemed slightly mollified, so I continued: "If you let me explain how the accident happened, it may help you get compensation from the Air Ministry."

That seemed to change his attitude. He sat down, motioned to us also to be seated, and then listened, without interruption, while I repeated my version of events.

"Furthermore," I went on, "the reason why we are temporarily up here at Leuchars is because of the Abyssinian crisis. Next week we are due to go to Malta to take part in the war against Italy if it breaks out. For that reason I got married last week. Now, having luckily escaped death today, we will probably be killed out there anyway."

He almost had tears in his eyes. "Oh, you poor young sods," he said, opening the cupboard in the side of his desk and taking out a bottle of whisky. "I thought you were just low flying."

He poured three glasses, saying: "Now I'm going to wish you good luck!"

Half an hour later, with slightly slurred speech, he was on the phone to the Chief Constable, and then to the Dundee newspaper telling them it had all been a mistake about him accusing us of low flying, and singing the praises of these intrepid young airmen who had so narrowly escaped death. At our request, he also telephoned RAF Leuchars to get a similar message to Wing Commander Maxwell (who was out playing golf).

We staggered back to the ferry and then drove back to Leuchars. There we deposited the two coils of wire in Bobby Burns' office as a sort of peace offering – copper at that time fetched a good price – and that was the last I heard of the incident.

It was not until three years later, in the summer of 1938 (shortly before the Munich Crisis, with war seeming imminent), when we were both at Cranwell to play cricket for the Old Cranwellians against the cadets, that I had any opportunity to discuss the subject with Beisiegel.

He had heard about me flying through those wires, but was extremely surprised that I knew about his low-flying incident and escape from being court marshalled. He said there had been strong pressure from the Royal Family on the Air Ministry to keep it all secret – but he confirmed what the flight sergeant had told me: that the lady who had been pregnant back in late October 1929 when he had buzzed her was the then Duchess of York.

"But can we be certain that it was a boy?" I asked.

"Oh, yes," he replied. "Had it been a girl they would have continued with my court martial. It was only after they realised the potential implications of it being a boy who was in line to become King that it was all cancelled."

"Had her pregnancy been publicly announced?" I asked. "If not, wouldn't it have been too early to tell whether it was a boy or girl?"

He shook his head. "Someone did suggest that possibility. They even tried to get the hospital records – but I think the actual miscarriage was either on the Royal Yacht or one of the Naval ships out in the Firth of Clyde. Later, the pregnancy of Princess Margaret only being announced at four months put an end to that. The sex of a boy can be determined from about twelve weeks."

Neither of us regarded the incident as particularly important – the Queen (as the Duchess had by then become) was still young enough to have more children – and we did not discuss it further. The threat that the war with Germany could break out any day was of vastly greater concern to us. Beisiegel asked me to keep all information about his low-flying incident to myself – which, apart from telling (in confidence) my family and a few close friends, I then did for the next fifty years.

However, when Prince Charles and Lady Diana started hitting the headlines in the press, Bunny suggested to me that the events concerning the Duchess of York (who had by then become the "Queen Mum") had become of such significance that I should write them up – at least as a record for historians. So I began doing so. Also, in the late 1980s, by sheer chance, I happened to go salmon fishing on that beat of the River Tay at Scone, just north of Perth, which included the area where those high-tension cables cross the river. That resulted in me getting further completely independent and unsolicited confirmation of the Queen Mum's miscarriage of a baby boy. It came from an elderly man who had had connections with Glamis Castle back in 1929. (I have written that coincidence up as a separate story.)

My first write-up of this Queen Mum story concentrated mainly on my own flying incident. I had done no research on where the Beisiegel buzz had taken place and had wrongly assumed that it was at her home at Glamis. I wrote a fictional beginning to the buzzing incident story, based on it having happened there, which turned out to be complete nonsense.

However, Her Majesty confirmed the buzzing incident, which she said had occurred while (as Duchess of York) she had been visiting her sister in Fife – close to the airfield from which Bieseigel was then flying. Also, I have recent evidence indicating that the actual miscarriage occurred in the location indicated to me by Beisiegal back in 1938. My further research has enabled me to fill in sufficient details to know that the whole story as now written is true.

Back in 1929, the Royal Family (probably King George V himself) – but only when they realised the implications of it being a boy who was in line to become King – would have wanted to keep the event secret. It would therefore be entirely logical for the Royal Family now to continue trying to deny that miscarriage. But neither the Flight Sergeant nor Beisiegel could possibly each (separately) have made up identical stories of which I later had the further independent confirmation (nearly 60 years later) of that resulting miscarriage.

If that buzzing incident had been so trivial that the group on the ground just found it amusing, it is unlikely to have resulted in a court martial. But laughing after being buzzed is the normal reaction of a group of people suddenly finding themselves safe after the terrifying shock of being buzzed.

I am publishing this story not only because I consider it to be of considerable historical interest – but also it is intriguing to contemplate what differences might have resulted if the boy had lived. Additionally, since I must now be the sole surviving person with direct knowledge of that incident, it could otherwise be lost for ever.

That prank by Beisiegel in 1929 may have completely changed the composition of the Royal Family as we know it today and is a good example of the "Chaos Theory" in operation. It was simply the slight movement, of about an inch or two, of the control column (for less than five seconds) of an aircraft in Scotland in 1929 that, had the boy lived, resulted in the death several decades later of a Princess in a road tunnel in Paris, as well as many other events like the Jubilee celebrations in faraway Australia the following century.

The main effect on me personally, however, resulted from that miscarriage being of a boy and not a girl. That was what caused the court martial of Beisiegel to be cancelled – instead of him being dismissed from the RAF. Otherwise he would not have become my flying instructor at Cranwell, where the skill with which he trained me largely accounts for my own survival during my subsequent 24 years' flying.

My survival from hitting those wires, however, was not due to any skill. It was due to that metal propeller and an amazingly large dose of sheer good luck – which latter unfortunately was not shared by several of my friends. In addition to the three cadets and two instructors killed flying while I was at Cranwell, another cadet of my term (Spurrier) had a fatal flying crash shortly after we graduated. Then, on 23rd May 1936, a year after I had flown through those cables, another one – Flying Officer P. W. Ashton, who won the Sword of Honour and was an excellent pilot – was flying in formation when his aircraft hit some similar high-tension cables. He was killed instantly. Three months after that, on 8th August 36, Molyneux accepted a lift in an aircraft flown by his squadron commander to go on leave and was a passenger in the rear cockpit of another Fleet Air Arm aircraft – exactly as he had been with me. But the Squadron Leader made a bad landing, the aircraft nosed over, and my great friend Molyneux was killed.

I was thankful that, in those days, I had Bunny to help console me.

Chapter 7

Fleet Air Arm

In September 1935, on being posted to the Fleet Air Arm, I completed my deck-landing training at Gosport in a flight commanded by Bruen Purvis – one of the RAF's finest pilots and with whom I later flew, early in the war, in the Wellington with the magnetic ring "halo" which we used to detonate the German magnetic mines in the Thames Estuary.

Under his supervision at Gosport, I made my first deck-landings in the slow old Avro 504N on HMS *Furious* – the training carrier with the flat deck with no superstructure protruding above it. With *Furious* steaming at 25 knots into a wind of 15 knots, the waiting seamen ("deck crew") could run alongside this slow aircraft, grab the wings and pull us down onto the deck! That was in the days before the aircraft were equipped with a hook to catch wires strung across the deck to help us land. In case we got it wrong, there was a small net along the side of the deck to hopefully prevent us falling "into the drink". After that, I graduated by doing four deck-landings in a Fairey Seal.

I was then posted to No 820 (Torpedo Spotter Reconnaissance) Squadron, whose home base was Gosport, and its carrier HMS *Courageous* – the flagship of the Home Fleet. Over a year was to elapse, however, before I landed on *Courageous*.

When I arrived, 820 Squadron was in the process of being re-equipped with the new Blackburn Shark aircraft, but one half of the squadron, still equipped with the obsolescent Baffins, had been rushed out with *Courageous* to the Mediterranean because of the Abyssinian crisis. I joined the half of the squadron that had been left behind at Gosport and began flying the Shark – a very easy aircraft to handle. Like the 111F, it had a large open cockpit behind the pilot. The design of the wires and struts that held the biplane together caused it to make a whistling noise and it became known as the "Whistling Shark". As soon as the full complement of 12 Sharks arrived, we expected to be sent by ship (with the aircraft in packing cases) to join *Courageous* either in Malta or Egypt.

Italy invaded Abyssinia on 3rd October 1935 and war with Italy seemed a distinct possibility. Everyone expected our squadron to be sent out to the Middle East urgently. But instead, Bunny and I spent a very pleasant winter living in digs at Lee-on-Solent, with activity at Gosport going on at its usual leisurely pace. We made perhaps one flight a day, working slowly through a training programme involving practice bombing, dropping dummy torpedoes, night flying and – on one trip to Farnborough – learning to be shot off a catapult ("accelerator") of the types used in carriers. These were originally intended for launching seaplanes from the port side at the front of the flight deck, but were used by us to leave more space for other aircraft to take off normally from the deck.

Then, in February 1936, by which time the Abyssinian crisis seemed to be nearly over, we were suddenly ordered to urgently go out to the Mediterranean to join HMS *Courageous*. We ferried the 12 Sharks up to Sealand, where they were to be dismantled and put in crates to be taken by ship to Egypt for re-assembly. The plan was that we would then fly them from there onto the carrier. We expected to be sent out in one of the many troopships on their regular runs to India and the Far East.

I hoped not to be parted from Bunny for more than a few weeks, because HMS *Courageous* was part of the Home Fleet. I had not yet had experience of the appalling inefficiency with which My Lords at the Admiralty ran the Royal Navy – and, particularly, the Fleet Air Arm.

Instead of going in a troopship as expected, we officers were put on a luxury liner (RMS *Orsova*) cruising out to the Far East. On our way out, off the coast of Spain, I was sunning myself in a deckchair, half asleep, when one of the others tapped me on the shoulder and said:

"Come and have a look. There is a most extraordinary ship approaching."

I went to the rails and saw this strange-looking ship in the distance. It was heading towards us and as it got closer one of the older hands said it looked like an aircraft carrier. Until then I had believed all carriers were flat, like *Furious*.

"It must be *Glorious*," remarked someone. But, as it passed us, an astonished shout came:

"Christ Almighty! It's the bloody *Courageous*!"

It was, indeed, the carrier that we were being sent out to join in the Med, and it was steaming in the opposite direction to us – back to England.

That was my first indication of the standard of efficiency that I could expect during my attachment to the Navy. It proved to be typical. The Fleet Air Arm – at that time – was justifiably the butt of a whole series of humorous cartoons depicting inefficiency and muddle.

On arriving in Egypt, we found a complete shambles. There seemed to have been no planning on where we should go. We started by being stationed at Aboukir – a glorious spot on the coast, where we lived in luxury in the officers' mess and had nothing to do except swim, play tennis and other games to while away the time until our Sharks arrived in their large wooden crates. These crates, when emptied, were all we had to use as offices, as all the accommodation was already in use by the squadrons normally stationed there.

I had been appointed Squadron Adjutant and was allocated a crate to myself in which, once a week, I counted out the money to be paid to the airmen who lined up on the sand outside to receive it. Another crate served as the CO's office, another as the engineering workshop – we had no other place to work, with flies and sand a constant menace.

The other half of the squadron had been left in Egypt to join us – making our total 12 officers, of whom half were Navy or Marine. My particular RAF friend became John Northey, who flew – as Molyneux had done – on the right of our flight formation. Each squadron had just 12 aircraft – each allocated to a particular pilot, who rarely flew any other.

Our chief engineer was a great big chap, well over six feet tall – Sergeant Pope – who supervised the mechanics who (when our aircraft finally arrived in their packing cases) put the aircraft together. My aircraft happened to be the first assembled and I was due to carry out the air test – the first time a Shark had been flown outside England. Pope insisted on coming with me on this test flight. He did this, I am sure, to demonstrate his confidence in the work carried out under his supervision, which had all been done under primitive and difficult conditions. I was very grateful to him. In fact, we had no problems.

Then, during the weeks ahead and in very leisurely fashion, we carried on with our so-called "training". That included doing dummy deck landings on a stretch of sand marked out as the deck of a carrier, or flying around aimlessly while our observer played about with his Morse key, trying to contact various radio stations. On one occasion I was sent out by lorry into the desert with a radio operator to set up a beacon there. One of the pilots spotted us and decided to "buzz" us. He flew directly towards me at low level. It was one of the most terrifying moments in my life. I threw myself flat on the ground, not knowing whether he would pull up in time to go over me. His wheels passed only a couple of feet over my head and the roar of his engine

Shark in Egypt 1936

108

Shark buzzing me in the Sahara May 1936

deafened me. I was badly shaken. That made me realise the extremely serious shock a pilot can inflict on anyone on the ground – as I have mentioned in a previous chapter involving the then Duchess of York.

HMS *Courageous* remained back in England having a lengthy refit. So, to keep our hand in, we made a few practice deck landings on HMS *Glorious* out at sea between Alexandria and Palestine. On 8th April, I was detailed to fly two senior officers from *Glorious* to Cairo and back – as I have already mentioned. Except for that flight, our flying seemed to have little purpose.

Near Cairo 1936

At the end of April our squadron moved up to Heliopolis, near Cairo. We started "work" (which mainly involved sitting around doing nothing) at 6 am and finished at midday. We then had the rest of the day to enjoy ourselves. The Abyssinian crisis had died down and no one seemed to know why we were there. However, it seemed likely that we would stay there for some time, so I decided to get Bunny out to join me. I arranged to rent a tiny apartment in Heliopolis and sent her a cable to come out on the next available ship. She and the wife of another officer (Dawkins) arrived a couple of weeks later. From then on we had a wonderful time, swimming at the club, playing tennis (and me cricket), visiting the Sphinx and other interesting places – generally having a splendid holiday.

At Saqqara, having followed the guide carrying his candle down the 39 steps into the tomb of this ancient pyramid, we were admiring the marvellous paintings on the walls when the candle went out. I do not recommend such an eerie experience to anyone. Finding ourselves suddenly in a pitch-dark tomb was not pleasant. Bunny was petrified. Luckily, John Northey had a box of matches and we went back up those steps rather faster than we had descended.

One afternoon I had an Arab guide, in his white nightshirt, accompany me to the top of Cheops Pyramid, where I took a photo of him. When we descended to rejoin Bunny, he drew some lines in the sand and forecast that Bunny would have two children and that I would return to that spot some time in the future. Bunny believed him and was convinced that he would be proved right. He was right about me returning (as I relate later), but it was partly because of his stupid prediction, which Bunny believed, that we ended up with three daughters – for which I am nevertheless grateful to him.

By July (1936), Bunny and I were running short of money. I was still not entitled to any allowances at all – still "living in sin". We put aside just enough money for her fare home, where she could stay with her parents; and, shortly before we reached that critical level of poverty, we booked a passage for her on a cruise ship which was due to visit several ports on the way home and which was due to leave

Bunny

Top of Great Pyramid

for England in ten days' time. Little did we guess that I would be in England in time to greet her when she arrived.

The day after we had booked her passage I had a problem with the Shark I was flying. I was cruising at about three thousand feet near the airfield, with an observer in the rear cockpit, when I suddenly felt an extremely strong vibration. The controls acted normally and the vibration did not feel aerodynamic in nature. But the moment I altered the engine setting, the vibration changed. I sensed danger – and reacted immediately. I not only closed the throttle – but also switched off the engine. That almost certainly saved our lives.

"Prepare for forced landing," I shouted down the Gosport tube to Lieut Wood, my observer. "Strap in tightly."

I surveyed the ground beneath us. Plenty of sand everywhere. No problem, and the airfield itself not too far away. I had practised forced landings often, but usually with the engine ticking over. This time my propeller was stationary, causing extra drag and a steeper descent – but I managed to land just within the airfield boundary.

My aircraft was towed to the parking area, where Sergeant Pope listened carefully to my reasons for my actions resulting in the forced landing. He climbed up a stepladder and removed the cowling to examine the strong metal struts that held the engine to the fuselage. Then one of the legs of his stepladder began sinking into the sand. He grabbed hold of one of the main struts securing the engine to the fuselage to steady himself, and it came clean off in his hand, causing him to fall and hurt his ankle. It was a scene I shall never forget – Sergeant Pope lying on the ground, holding the broken metal beam, staring up at the engine incredulously, and swearing about the pain in his leg. Two mechanics were also looking up at the engine in disbelief. Lieut Wood was congratulating me and I was thanking my sixth sense (which has saved me many times since) for causing me to switch off the engine when I did. Had I not done so, the engine would almost certainly have torn free and fallen off – making the aircraft so uncontrollable that we would not even have been able to get out and use our parachutes.

The remaining struts holding the engine were all found to be cracked and on the point of failure too. An urgent examination of our other Sharks revealed that most had serious cracks too. Our aircraft were obviously too dangerous to fly without major modifications to the engine mountings. They were dismantled and put back into their packing cases to be returned to Blackburns in England, and we pilots – just the day before Bunny was due to set sail – were put on a troopship (SS *Neuralia*) returning to the UK. Such was our opinion of Naval efficiency that we fully expected to pass *Courageous* coming out again!

The Shark was only one example of poor aircraft design by Blackburns – a company that even had the stupidity to name one of their aircraft a Skua after a species of seagull which suddenly folds its wings and dives vertically into the sea. That is precisely what at least one of the Naval Skuas did, killing the pilot.

On arrival in England, we were given six weeks' leave. I borrowed £15 with which to buy an open four-seater Lea-Francis, with which I met Bunny when her ship arrived at Tilbury. We then motored down to Cornwall, where we had a wonderful holiday at Gluvian Farm, Morgan Porth.

On our way back to rejoin 820 Squadron at Gosport, we were descending a steep winding hill on Dartmoor when I had to apply the brakes rather sharply. The car behaved very strangely. I only realised the reason when Bunny gave a shout and pointed to one of our rear wheels bouncing past us and disappearing over the hedge ahead. (It is quite annoying to be overtaken by your rear wheel!) The half-shaft, which was all that held the wheel on in that model, had broken. However, the local blacksmith soon repaired it and we arrived back only a few hours late.

At Gosport we had to revert to flying the old Fairey 111Fs and Seals, until modified Sharks became available in late autumn. That November, when flying the Shark 11 at dusk near Southampton, I noticed a tremendous glow in the sky towards London. I thought it must be a big fire. I learnt the next morning, with great sadness and sense of loss, that it was the Crystal Palace which – one way and another – had been part of my childhood and had given me a lot of pleasure. I would miss the weekly firework displays and seeing that impressive structure dominating the skyline.

That winter we continued – at a very leisurely pace – doing more training, which included, at long last, me actually making a deck landing on the carrier to which I had been posted over a year before.

HMS Courageous 1937

In January 1937, we embarked in HMS *Courageous* for the Spring Cruise for the combined operations of both the Home and Mediterranean Fleets in the Mediterranean. Each carrier always had its own attendant destroyer steaming along about a hundred yards astern to deal with any aircraft that crashed "into the drink" or had to "ditch". Just the carrier and its destroyer alone steaming along together was quite an impressive sight – particularly in a rough sea. But all the ships of the Home and Med Fleets cruising along in formation provided a truly magnificent and impressive sight – demonstrating the might of the British Empire at the height of its power. They included many famous ships - *Nelson, Rodney, Hood,* etc. and the three carriers *Courageous, Glorious* and *Furious* – as well as two flotillas of smaller vessels.

My cabin was in the bowels of the ship and, like those of most junior officers, it was only just large enough for me to get in through a narrow door and stretch out on the bunk. The only ventilation was a tiny pipe near the ceiling blowing in sooty air. We used socks tied over the pipe as a filter. I hated being cooped up like a sardine and strongly resented having to serve in the Navy. Our main exercise was playing hockey on the deck with walking sticks, if the weather and wind over the deck permitted it. We normally wore mess kit for dinner. The food and service were superb. But most of the officers drank far too much, as gin and rum cost practically nothing.

As one of the most junior officers, and as dictated by tradition, I had to take my turn sitting next to the C-in-C Home Fleet at dinner. I suggested to the Admiral that just one squadron of aircraft could sink the whole fleet and stressed that the deck of a carrier would be a particularly easy target for an aircraft carrying armour-piercing bombs; and, furthermore, that the designs of bombs would inevitably become more powerful in future years.

He was outraged at my suggestion that any ship could ever be sunk by bombing and made it clear that he regarded me as a complete idiot to propose such a stupid idea. That to me emphasised the low mentality, and complete lack of vision of My Lords at the Admiralty (of which group, incidentally, that twit later served as a member).

Spring Cruise 1937

Torpedo practice off Gibralta

He was typical of the senior Naval officers who later sent *Rodney*, *Hood*, and *Nelson* within range of enemy aircraft, which resulted in them being sunk so ignominiously. (HMS *Courageous*, with some of the friends I had made while serving in it, was one of the first to be sunk by the Germans.)

Several events during that Spring Cruise increased my disgust of the "Nelson mentality".

One afternoon, the whole combined fleets were steaming along in formation, with *Glorious* about a hundred yards away on our starboard side. My aircraft was unserviceable that day, so I had nothing to do but sun myself standing at the side of the flight deck and watch the others taking off. As I have already mentioned, the catapult is located on the port side at the front of the flight deck.

The aircraft carrier *Glorious* was cruising in line with *Courageous* to starboard and I watched an aircraft being hoisted onto the catapult to be shot off. The pilot was "Hoggers" Cornabe, who had been a cadet at Cranwell with me. (His nickname had been earned one evening after a guest night at Cranwell when, in a rather inebriated state – "hog drunk" – he had inadvertently walked through a glass door without first opening it – leaving him with a scar across his face for life. Hence "Hoggers".) I watched him climb into the cockpit, do up his straps and start the engine. He checked the controls, then opened up the throttle to run the engine at full speed and tested it. With everything apparently in good order, he raised his right hand to signal "standby" to the seaman on the deck beside him who held the signalling flag. That seaman then raised the flag over his head as a standby signal to the others concerned (who each in turn raised their flags above their heads too) and waited for Cornabe to signal "GO".

Nelson would have approved the method used by his successors to get the message to the mechanic (secluded in the deck below, directly underneath the catapult) whose job it was actually to pull the lever to shoot the aircraft off. To convey that message, a relay of four seamen, each with a signalling flag, was used. (Remember, the year was 1936 – not back 130 years earlier.)

Having given the GO signal – by dropping his hand – the pilot needed time to prepare for the extremely violent acceleration. Exactly ten seconds was the standard set interval between the pilot dropping his hand and the chap down below shooting him off. This was to give the pilot the time, after dropping his hand, to wedge his left hand behind the throttle to prevent it being forced back by the sudden acceleration, press his right elbow into his chest so that his hand on the stick would not be forced back either, and then ensure that his head was firmly against the pad behind it in the cockpit seat.

That ten seconds delay was arranged by three of those seamen pausing briefly before waving their flags at each other. The drill for all this was carefully organised.

I watched Cornabe drop his hand to signal GO. The seaman beside him immediately turned smartly away from the aircraft and, facing towards the rear of the flight deck, signalled to the next seaman. He, I knew, would turn towards the one on the deck below and count three before dropping his flag. He, in turn, would also count three before dropping his flag to signal to another who was standing inside the hangar and could only see the seaman on the lower deck in the stern, who would also count three before giving the order to fire.

But a moment after Cornabe had dropped his hand and the seaman beside him had turned to the rear, I noticed a large puff of smoke belch from the engine and the propeller coming to a standstill. The engine had clearly failed.

But the rigid procedure had started, and not even the sudden appearance of Nelson himself could have stopped it progressing to the end.

I watched Cornabe waving frantically to try to get the procedure halted. This must have attracted the attention of an officer on the Bridge, because I heard the siren of *Glorious* blasting out to alert her attendant destroyer for an emergency. Not being able to see what was happening on the deck of the *Glorious*, the captain of the destroyer could not possibly have visualised what sort of emergency had arisen, but must have given the order (probably in accordance with routine procedures) for full speed ahead to deal with it.

Meanwhile, and naturally enough, the seamen on the lower deck, who could not have had any idea of what was happening on the flight deck above them, lowered their flags in turn, in accordance with normal procedure, which resulted in the order to pull the lever to "fire" the accelerator and propel the aircraft into the sea ...

Hoggers Cornabe, when sober, was no fool. He guessed exactly what would happen. He knew it would be dangerous to try to get out of the aircraft and get clear of the catapult in time. Instead, he tightened the straps holding him in, released his parachute straps, inflated his Mae West and waited for the inevitable in a position to sustain minimum injury from the rapid acceleration as he was catapulted off – and then from the inevitable shock of hitting the water. He told me afterwards that he counted those seconds like he had never done before, waiting for the catastrophe that he knew nothing could prevent.

The siren blast from the *Glorious* had alerted everyone on the *Courageous's* deck and we all watched as Cornabe's aircraft, with the propeller stationary, was catapulted into the air, where, of course, it stalled and dived into the sea straight ahead.

Full marks for the helmsman of *Glorious*, who had immediately started a turn to starboard to avoid the area where the aircraft would splash into the sea; otherwise the carrier would have hit it. But, as with a bicycle on which the handlebar controls only the rear wheel, that turn to starboard also swung the stern to port, thus completely blocking the view from the destroyer which, now at full power, was rapidly gaining speed. In consequence, the helmsman of the destroyer – still ignorant of what had happened – gained his first view of the aircraft when it was only a few yards straight ahead in the water. Cornabe, who had quite a bit of experience of the Fleet Air Arm, had guessed what would happen and was swimming vigorously away from the aircraft buoyed up by his Mae West, with his arms going like windmills. Sure enough, the destroyer, now at full speed, smashed into the aircraft and sent it to the bottom.

In due course the destroyer managed to turn round and pick up Cornabe who, thankfully, was not badly hurt. Later, recovering from the trauma in the wardroom, he fully (and justifiably) re-earned his nickname of Hoggers.

On another occasion, the helmsman steering our own carrier, *Courageous*, had allowed the carrier to swing on to a heading where the wind was not coming straight down the deck. (He obviously knew nothing about flying and may not have realised the implications.) I was making my approach to land, but realised the deck was out of wind in time to allow for it – by making a crab-like approach and applying rudder just before touching down and catching the wires with my hook. I had climbed out of the cockpit and was standing on the deck watching the next aircraft coming in to land – flown by Flying Officer Solbe.

The carrier, I reckoned, was sailing at least about ten or fifteen degrees to starboard of the actual wind direction. Solbe had not realised this until too late. He fluffed his landing, missed the wires, and opened up his engine to go round again. But the wind coming from the port side drifted him to starboard and I watched with horror as his starboard wing hit the superstructure and caused him to crash onto the deck. Luckily, there was no fire and, miraculously, he was not hurt. The broken aircraft, without any of its costly instruments being first taken out, was simply pushed over the side into the sea. I doubt whether the Naval Officer responsible for steering the carrier out of wind ever got a rocket. Solbe got all the blame.

Solbe crashing on Courageous

Solbe Crashed

119

While out in the Med, my aircraft happened to be the one in our squadron which had the necessary fittings to have the heavy drogue-towing equipment attached to it. The drogue, which was to be the practice target for the guns in the various ships, was like a big windsock made of canvas which (at the end of a long wire) acted as a target aircraft about a mile behind the towing aircraft.

The equipment, in the observer's cockpit behind me, was a large horizontal drum onto which about a mile of metal cable was wound, with the necessary pulleys to let it trail out safely behind the aircraft with the drogue at the end. At the end of the drum, and sticking out from the side of my aircraft, was a small propeller which, when not in use, lay horizontal; but which, when turned vertically into the slipstream, derived ample power from it to rewind the wire back onto the drum quite quickly. There was also, for emergency, a handle that could be inserted directly into a gear driving the drum, for the observer to crank it in by hand – but that was a very slow and laborious task because of the drag of the aircraft speed through the air on the wire and drogue.

One fine breezy afternoon in February, it was decided that the whole combined fleets would do gunnery practice. Normally, that was carried out with practice ammunition, but this was to be live ammunition. I was ordered to take off at 4.30 pm and fly past all the battleships at 8,000 feet with the drogue streamed out one mile behind me so that they could fire at it with high explosives. My flight was scheduled to take no more than about half an hour, but I had the aircraft fuelled for an extra hour as a safety precaution.

As I was climbing up to that height I instructed my observer to start letting out the cable and drogue while I positioned the aircraft about twenty miles astern of the ships. Everything seemed in order and I instructed him to send a signal to the fleet (by Morse) saying so and confirming my height as 8,000 feet and speed about 130 knots. I then turned to fly past the ship formation about half a mile to the port of them.

As we came within range, I saw the flashes of the guns of *Hood*, *Rodney*, *Nelson*, *Royal Sovereign* and scores of other ships in the combined fleets opening fire. That was tremendously impressive. Then came the burst of their shells. That was even more impressive. Some, so my observer told me, were bursting nearer to us than to the target – some way above and some below. There was nothing I could do but continue on until we were out of range, but both my observer and I were relieved to have escaped unscathed.

It was not me but another pilot who later had a similar experience of one shell bursting ahead of the aircraft, which caused him to send the famous signal to the Admiral:

"Wish to confirm, Sir, that I am pulling the drogue, not pushing it."

The accuracy of the gunners was no better on my second run, and one shell did burst ahead of us, but way below and to the side. Looking down, I realised that the waves were now far bigger than when I had taken off. The problem, I supposed, was that the ships were pitching and rolling as the gunners tried to take aim. Nevertheless, they were missing, sometimes by more than a mile, a slow-flying target going in a straight line at a steady speed and height that they knew in advance. I wondered how a rolling and pitching ship would fare in a real aircraft attack.

At the end of our second run, to our relief, we were given the order (by Morse) to land back on the carrier as soon as possible as the wind was increasing rapidly. That was about half an hour before sunset. I could see the ships nosing into waves that were becoming larger by the minute, and the deck of *Courageous* rising and falling with the pitch of the ship. I was eager to land before the sea got any worse and before the light began to fade. I instructed my observer to wind in the drogue without delay. That normally took only a few minutes.

It was then that the real fun started. Being shot at with live ammunition was only a preliminary. The propeller for rewinding the cable jammed and would not wind in the drogue.

I told the observer to cut through the wire - but he could find no way of doing so. The emergency axe that was always stowed on the right-hand side in the observer cockpit (for use in a crash) had been taken out to make room for some of the drogue towing equipment. I dare not try to land on the carrier with all that wire and the drogue trailing behind us, because it would have dipped into the sea and caused a sudden drag which might damage the aircraft or cause me to stall and crash. So there was nothing else to do but wind it in by hand. And that, we knew, might take half an hour or so. I had enough fuel for that, but I took the precaution of adjusting the engine for maximum endurance at slow airspeed and descended to 3,000 feet to give the observer more oxygen for his exertions. He quickly tapped out a message in Morse to warn *Courageous* of the delay and then started winding in with the handle.

It was so exhausting that he frequently had to stop for a rest. At the end of half an hour, he had wound in little more than one half. Quite soon I was watching the sun descend below the horizon and the dusk turn into night. The "Green Flash" that evening, as the sun finally disappeared, was the brightest I had ever seen. I took it as a signal that all would be OK and felt slightly comforted by it.

Landing on a heavily pitching carrier in a rough sea was difficult enough by day, because the end of the deck would be rising and falling by many feet. Under the conditions now pertaining, all flying would have been cancelled. And, so far as I knew, no one had ever landed on *Courageous* by night, even in a calm sea. My own experience of night flying was very limited and had been near populated areas with plenty of lights on the ground by which I could orientate myself. It was, I decided, going to be quite a challenge to get down safely.

The officers in *Courageous* had no way of telling when I would be ready to land, but had turned the carrier into wind so that I could do so at any time. That resulted in *Courageous* streaming away from the rest of the ships in the formation. The lights from those ships had been helpful to me in keeping correctly orientated. As darkness had fallen, they had become brighter. But now they had receded into the distance as I circled around *Courageous*. On either side of the deck they had placed a row of lights to assist me.

The stars were bright above me, but below the sea appeared everywhere pitch black, broken only by the lights of the carrier

Try landing on that at night!   ***A Challenge***

and her attendant destroyer. I had no way of communicating with the people on deck and I felt very lonely. Also, my fuel gauge was warning me that my tank would soon be empty.

Eventually, my gallant but completely exhausted observer shouted to me down the Gosport tube that he had the drogue in and secured and our trailing radio aerial wound in. I descended to just above the level of *Courageous's* deck and flew past about fifty yards to the starboard side to judge her movements by looking at the lights on her deck. I adjusted my altimeter to read zero. That instrument, once I passed ahead of the ship and could no longer see her lights, would be my only indication of my height above the waves.

I judged *Courageous* to be now steaming at full speed to increase the wind speed over the deck and so reduce my landing speed relative to the deck. She seemed not to be rolling much, but she was pitching hard into the waves, and I judged the rear end of the deck to be rising and falling by at least fifteen feet. They had lit more flares. Beside them I could see deck crew crouching, ready to grab my wing tips immediately if I hooked one of the wires. I guessed the wind to be above 30 knots and the speed of *Courageous* around 25 knots through the waves. If I approached at about 80 knots (which would give me good control, even in the

123

turbulence, and ample speed to go round again if necessary), my speed over the deck should be no more than about 25 knots.

One of my main concerns (remembering the Solbe incident) was whether the carrier was steaming into wind accurately. I circled round, lowered my tail hook (to catch the wires) and made a long straight approach which would enable me to judge that wind direction. As the ship pitched, one second I was looking into the hangar on the lower deck with no sight of the lights on the landing deck, and a couple of seconds later all the lights along the deck became visible. But, so far as I could tell, I was not drifting sideways in relation to the ship. But the buffeting I got from the turbulence caused by the ship's superstructure added to my problems.

On my first approach I was not able to co-ordinate with the deck movements sufficiently well. As I was about to touch down, the deck fell away beneath me and I would have missed all the wires. So I opened up the engine to go round again. I think most of the ship's company were watching and, after that first failed attempt, were fully expecting me to crash. So, as he later admitted to me, was my observer.

Ahead was pitch-blackness with no visible horizon. Having been watching the bright lights on the deck, my eyes were not yet adapted to seeing the stars to differentiate between sea and sky. For a few seconds I even had difficulty making out the dimly-lit instrument dials on which I had suddenly become dependent. I could see nothing. Just blackness – but knowing there were big waves on the sea just a few feet below. It was an uncanny feeling to have absolutely no indication of the attitude of the aircraft, nor of our height or speed.

I just froze on the controls, hoping I was climbing. But it was only a few seconds before my eyes adapted and I began to see the stars above and the instruments again. I decided to make my next attempt at a higher speed so that if I missed landing I could immediately go into a turn, looking over my shoulder, to keep the carrier and destroyer in view as a point of reference.

My second attempt began well. I thought I had judged it correctly, but the carrier nosed down at the last moment, causing me to give a burst of engine to climb over the rising stern. That left me far too high above the deck as it again descended. But I was able to make a turn with the carrier in view as a reference point. Even in daylight, I decided, it would have been extremely difficult to land under those conditions.

After a third unsuccessful attempt, with my fuel gauge warning that I could not continue flying for much longer, I reassessed the problem. There seemed to be three choices. My observer could send a message in Morse (using the Aldis lamp) of our intention to ditch, asking them to slow down and illuminate a patch of water with searchlights, beside which the destroyer would be waiting to rescue us. We were both wearing flotation vests, the aircraft had a dinghy and the sea was not freezing cold.

Or we could climb up and parachute out, hoping they would find us and pull us out. Or I could crash the aircraft on the deck, as Solbe had done, and hope to be equally lucky. There would not be much petrol left in my tank to cause a big conflagration and the fire crews would be waiting anyway.

It was this latter course of action I decided on. Alighting on the sea in those waves would almost certainly mean the aircraft breaking up and sinking quickly. I never enjoyed swimming at night. Also, I hated wearing wet clothes. (I also remembered my mother's warning on sending me off to school: "Try not to get your feet wet!") But it was my lack of confidence in the destroyer being able to rescue us in those conditions that swayed me. Better, I decided, the devil you know.

Checking my fuel gauge, I reckoned I had just enough petrol for one further attempt to land before crashing. So I began my fourth approach, desperately trying to judge it correctly this time. I kept my speed high enough to ensure I could go round again if necessary and thought I had judged everything correctly. But at the last moment the movement of the deck again prevented me landing and I went quickly into my turn, keeping the carrier in sight.

As soon as my eyes re-adapted, I checked the fuel gauge. It was reading zero. I now had no alternative. I prayed that our fuel would last out for our final approach. The thought of the engine spluttering to a halt while we were over the sea was not pleasant.

I consoled myself with the thought that our speed, in relation to the deck, would probably be less than about 30 knots and that, although the aircraft might be badly damaged, we were unlikely to suffer any injury.

I warned my observer to prepare for a crash. (Quite unnecessary, as I learned later; he had been expecting one on every approach.) I undid my parachute harness and tightened my seat straps. This time I made a much higher and slower approach, intending to stall the aircraft as soon as I was over the deck.

We came over the rear end of the landing deck with about ten feet to spare and I immediately cut the engine and switched it off to lessen the chance of fire. The aircraft stalled and fell rapidly. I braced myself. But, by sheer chance, the deck was now also falling fast – thus reducing the force of impact. The undercarriage withstood the shock, the hook caught the wire, and the waiting deck crew quickly grabbed our wings. It was no worse than a normal, although rather heavy, landing. I could not, for a moment, believe our luck.

Although I disliked serving with the Navy, I always enjoyed flying – even the clumsy Fleet Air Arm torpedo aircraft. But, unlike piloting a single-seat fighter, most of it was really acting as a chauffeur for the observer in the back. Furthermore, I became more and more fed up with being cooped up in a vessel with my tiny stuffy cabin the only place where I could really relax. Above all, I was parted from Bunny, and she had no way of communicating with me. I sent her voluminous letters whenever we reached port, but she never knew where we would be next – and so could not reply.

That Spring Cruise lasted two and a half months. I had complained often about my tiny little cabin, claiming that, as Squadron Adjutant, I should be entitled to something better. As a result, during that cruise, I was moved to share an outside double cabin with Flying Officer John Northey. That led to a wonderful friendship and made life very much more bearable, but did little to relieve my dislike of naval routine.

One warm sunny afternoon we were relaxing on our bunks – John on the one under the open porthole, me by the wall opposite – when I was alerted by a scream from John. I became convulsed with laughter when I realised the cause and watched John frantically trying to catch the flying fish that had come in through the porthole and landed on his bare belly.

Whenever I happened to be duty officer at night, I had to visit the lower deck at regular intervals to see that the aircraft were all secure. I did not mind that unduly, but I also had many other tasks which I considered not to be the job of an RAF officer – such as descending at night into the bowels of the ship to the engine room, which stank of oil, climbing up and down the metal ladders, along the narrow gangways to see that all was well there. The heat and the stench of oil, particularly when the ship was heaving about in a rough sea, made me feel sick. Had I voluntarily joined the Navy I could not have complained, but I had joined the Air Force to see the world – not to inspect the bowels of a smelly sardine tin.

One other of my tasks, when I was night duty officer, was – together with a naval duty officer – to scrutinise all incoming and outgoing signals. I am reminded of the occasion when, on approaching Malta, the Admiral had given instructions for all his laundry, on arrival, to be quickly attended to. That resulted in the duty officer on that occasion writing out a signal to be sent by Morse code to Malta:

"Immediately on arrival, please send aboard the Admiral's washer woman."

Owing to an omission of one word by the radio operator, this was received in Malta:

"Immediately on arrival, please send aboard the Admiral's woman."

Back came the signal:

"Would the Admiral prefer a blonde or brunette?"

This caused considerable mirth. But when the omission of one word in the original was realised, a suitable reply was sent:

"Either will do. But between 'Admiral' and 'woman' please insert 'washer'."

We spent much time, particularly when bad weather curtailed flying, in the hangar deck, where the only place to sit was on the radiators beside the walls. They were invariably either stone cold or boiling hot. As a result, nearly all Fleet Air Arm pilots developed piles – an occupational hazard. One in our squadron – Flying Officer H. de C. A. Woodhouse – suffered particularly badly. We persuaded him to go and see "Bones" – the Naval doctor on board – who gave him a box of medication to help deal with it.

At the end of a fortnight, Woodhouse could detect no improvement whatsoever. So he went to "Bones" to complain that the prescribed treatment was doing no good and also that he found the taste of the pills so revolting that he always felt sick after taking them.

He returned looking quite green. He had been informed by an astonished "Bones" that the pills were suppositories and intended to be inserted – but not into his mouth. We all doubled up with laughter, but Woodhouse could never quite see the funny side.

In addition to our squadron of Sharks, the *Courageous* also carried a squadron of single-seat fighters – Nimrods. During that combined Spring Cruise, we carried out quite a lot of formation flying. Each aircraft had to take off singly and then join up with the leader to make a flight of three. The first aircraft to take off would make a fairly wide, complete circular turn to the left, followed by the second doing a tighter full circle turn to the right, so that both came up alongside simultaneously, to arrive in formation on either side of the flight commander as he took off in the third aircraft.

I was in my aircraft on the flight deck waiting for the turn of 820 Squadron and watching a flight of the Nimrods take off before us. The first aircraft had taken off and was doing its usual wide turn to the left. The next aircraft, flown by Lieutenant Jelf, RN, took off, doing a fairly tight turn to the right.

One of the first things I had learnt at Cranwell was that, if you are looking at the ground, you automatically tend to judge your speed by your movement over it – but this is dangerous if you are low down and have been flying into wind and then turn downwind.

This effect is magnified if your point of reference on the ground is itself moving (like a train) and enormously important if it is a ship on the sea moving into wind.

But that is exactly what Jelf must have done – judged his airspeed by looking at the carrier. I watched with increasing alarm as Jelf continued his tight turn. It was obvious that he had not allowed for this factor. He was clearly watching his flight commander on the deck beginning his take-off run and not paying attention to his own airspeed – or to the fact that the stalling speed increases considerably in a tight turn. As I feared would be the case, Jelf stalled the aircraft. I watched it flip over and crash into the sea.

Jelf was extremely lucky not to be killed on impact. It was also lucky that the crash had happened in full view of the attendant destroyer; that resulted in him being rescued.

Needless to say, Jelf was a very shaken pilot, and I assumed that his superiors would explain to him exactly why the accident had happened and the way to prevent a similar mishap in future. In my view, he should not have been allowed to fly solo again without further flying instruction and should certainly have been discouraged – indeed forbidden – from doing tight turns at low level. But, of course, there were no dual aircraft on which instruction could be given in an operational carrier; nor, I fear, any naval officers with sufficient knowledge of aerodynamics available to instruct Jelf correctly.

We were continuously at sea for about three weeks after that crash, before returning to English waters, where all the squadrons were due to disembark. During that time, Jelf did not fly at all. To our amazement, and for reasons none of us were ever able to understand, Jelf was ordered to fly an identical aircraft back to Gosport and to adopt exactly the same procedure as before to join the flight formation. We were sitting in our aircraft on the flight deck, awaiting our turn, and watching his take-off with apprehension. He made his turn to the right – exactly the same manoeuvre as before. We could see that he was again going to stall. And we watched him crash into the sea in exactly the same way as on his previous flight. But for the fact that we all had our engines running ready to take off,

I think there could have been a mutiny. We arrived back at our new base at Eastleigh, near Southampton, feeling very sad and pretty bloody-minded. There we learnt that, this time, Jelf had been killed on impact.

This further increased my resentment about serving in the Fleet Air Arm and being commanded by officers of another service who knew so little about flying.

After a spell of leave, we began, at the end of April 1937, rehearsing for the Royal Review, which was scheduled for 20th May in the Solent. That involved formation flying, together with all the other squadrons of Fleet Air Arm, over the combined fleets of ships being reviewed by the King on the Royal Yacht.

On one such rehearsal, I was flying on the left of my squadron which, in turn, was on the left of the massed formation of all the squadrons taking part. We were flying over the Solent on quite a bumpy day, which made it difficult to keep accurately in position in relation to the adjacent aircraft. I had, of course, to look to my right to keep station on my flight commander and so had a good view of the squadron on our right as well. I noticed that the aircraft flying on the extreme left of that squadron was having particular difficulty in keeping position. One second he was too low, and a few seconds later he was too high in relation to his flight leader. He was also rather too close to him. Both aircraft had observers standing in the open cockpits behind the pilots.

Suddenly, as that aircraft on the left was descending from being a few feet too high, I saw his wingtip hit the elevators on the tailplane of his flight leader's aircraft. That forced the elevators sharply down and put the flight leader's aircraft into a sudden dive. His observer had not anchored his harness to the floor and I saw him thrown out of the cockpit clear into the air – without a parachute. I still believe that I heard his screams as he began his fall to his death two thousand feet below.

[By a strange coincidence, I happened to meet the pilot of the aircraft responsible about 30 years later when – by sheer chance – I happened to be admiring the view from the top of the Empire State

Building in New York. He actually came up in the lift after me. Small world! I have had several experiences like that.]

The actual Royal Review was (even to my jaundiced eye) a grand spectacle – the massed squadrons of aircraft in close formation, flying over practically the total might of the Royal Navy, with the battleships, cruisers, carriers and destroyers dressed overall, steaming in formation past the Royal Yacht on which our King was returning the salute. Tremendously impressive. The fact that the aircraft were of little use for any war, for which we were still not beginning to prepare – in spite of the many warnings from the far-sighted Churchill – and the fact that each of the ships could have been (as many later were) easily sunk, did not seem to matter. We all had tears in our eyes. We were proud to be participating in such a splendid event and to be serving in the armed forces of a country that ruled one-fifth of the world.

Up to the spring of 1937, our squadron had been commanded by Lieutenant Commander Poole, whom I greatly respected. Also, we had as our senior observer a splendid chap named Pedder (who later became an Admiral), and his replacement was another outstanding navigator named Couchman (who also became an Admiral). They were all of a calibre which, when they became senior enough to take over from the deadbeats then running the Fleet Air Arm, would transform it. But in April of that year Poole was promoted and replaced by an officer with whom all the pilots, and observers, were so dissatisfied that there was nearly a mutiny.

One of his first mistakes was to try to lead the squadron, flying in formation, from Southampton to West Freugh, on the Mull of Galloway, in south-west Scotland, where we were due to have a month's practice camp bombing in Luce Bay. I had arranged for a pilot from another squadron to fly my aircraft on that trip. My excuse was that, as Adjutant, I had to go on ahead to ensure that everything was ready at West Freugh for the squadron's arrival. My real reason, of course, was so that I could motor up – taking Bunny with me.

The day after I arrived up there I had received – as expected – the signal notifying me that the squadron had taken off from

Southampton, with, also, their estimated time of arrival. I was on the airfield waiting for them to appear. Half an hour after their ETA, I became a little apprehensive at their non-appearance. Another half hour and I became more concerned. Then one of the aircraft landed and the pilot, livid with rage about the squadron commander, told me:

"The bloody idiot nearly killed us all. Hasn't a clue! We had to break formation and fend for ourselves. God only knows what's happened to the rest of them."

One by one, as I anxiously counted them over the next two hours, the remainder straggled in.

The squadron commander did not seem particularly concerned, but all the other pilots were fuming at the way he had led them up narrow valleys, completely lost in worsening weather, into situations where they would have crashed if they had remained in formation. Their main surprise, and even regret, was that he had not killed himself.

As Squadron Adjutant, I saw more of him than most. I judged him to be of extremely low calibre and quite unfit to command our squadron. My dissatisfaction with the Fleet Air Arm increased.

We spent a month in that lovely area. Bunny and I lived on a dairy farm, where they made "English Cheddar" cheese – the best I have ever tasted. Most days, the squadron practised bombing in Luce Bay and sometimes even scored a hit on the target. Most evenings, Bunny and I went motoring or shooting rabbits, accompanied by John Northey.

John had just become the proud owner of a brand new car; Bunny had just passed the recently introduced driving test in the nearby town of Stranraer. One evening, we had motored to a remote field on the farm; John and I got out to go shooting rabbits. He suggested that Bunny should drive his new car back to the farmhouse, where we would all meet up later. About twenty minutes after she had departed, we saw a pathetic little figure running across the fields towards us. Bunny, with tears streaming down her cheeks, stammered out that she had driven his car into the stone wall at the farm entrance. From her description, we visualised his shiny new car to now be just a heap of crumpled metal.

132

John, after the initial shock, was quite marvellous. He pretended not to be the least bit concerned. He comforted her, dried her eyes, and assured her that any damage could easily be repaired. I knew what a tremendous blow it was to him and admired him enormously for pretending so well. Sobbing again, Bunny led us to the gateway where she had misjudged her turn and hit the wall. In fact, the damage was largely superficial – a broken lamp and buckled wing.

Subsequently, in all her years of driving in many different countries, Bunny was responsible for only one other accident. That was when, driving in the New Forest, she lost her way; she spotted a Walls Ice Cream "Stop me and buy one" vendor sitting on his tricycle by the roadside ahead and decided to ask him for directions.

"Excuse me," she called, as she approached, "can you tell me …?" Thump! She had failed to stop and hit the front of the tricycle. The startled chap was thrown off, making a complete somersault before landing in a bush. Luckily, no serious damage resulted, but she always approached Walls Ice Cream vendors with diligence thereafter.

That year Empire Air Day occurred while we were at West Freugh and we put on a flying display for the public. I was given the job of doing the commentary over the tannoy system. It was my first experience of broadcasting and was all impromptu. After initial nervousness, I quite enjoyed it and the experience helped me later when I made radio and television broadcasts.

Our pleasant month there, flying from an RAF Station but living on a farm, made me realise the enormous difference between the enjoyment of life ashore and the boredom of being imprisoned in a carrier. I had never wanted to be in the Fleet Air Arm, which I regarded as highly inefficient, right from the beginning. But that month in Scotland decided me that, at all costs, I must find a way of escaping from being cooped up in a carrier and get back to the type of life I had chosen.

When we returned to Southampton, I learned that HMS *Courageous*, with our squadron aboard, was scheduled to participate in the Navy's summer operation of "showing the flag" along the south coast of England. This involved the ships moving slowly along the coast, anchoring off various holiday resorts, and being open to visitors who came out in their hundreds, in all sorts of little boats, to wander round the ship and have things explained to them. Brighton was to be our first holiday resort to visit.

I was scheduled to be off duty that weekend and had been given three days' leave. I arranged for Bunny to come down to Brighton, where I could meet her. But, at the last minute, my leave was cancelled and I was detailed to be one of the officers (dressed in No 1 uniform – breeches and tight puttees) on the flight deck where our aircraft would be lined up for the visitors to see and examine. My job would be to answer any questions and also make sure that no damage was done to the aircraft. I was absolutely livid that my arrangements to meet Bunny had to be cancelled.

That weekend, the weather was brilliantly hot, the deck burning my feet, and my head sweating under my stiff uniform cap. Then the mobs started arriving – fat women in shorts, some dragging screaming kids around sucking gooey sweets and being sick; giggling girls stinking of cheap perfume; parties of school kids; men lighting up their pipes near aircraft full of petrol. And Flying Officer Vielle was expected to answer all questions civilly, help people climb up to look inside the cockpits, explain how everything worked, and make sure no damage was done. And all this instead of being ashore with Bunny!

That was the last straw. By the end of that day I decided that I would no longer tolerate serving in the Fleet Air Arm. Even if it wrecked my career, I would find some way of escaping from the sardine tin and all the antiquated associated traditions that ruled life within it. I sought the advice of John Northey, who sympathetically agreed with my suggested plan of action.

That evening, in the cabin I was sharing with him, we discussed my proposed scheme and he offered his full co-operation. He recommended that I should tell our flight commander, John Cullum, of my intentions and then enlist the help of the two other RAF junior officers in the squadron – Woodhouse and Solbe. No one else was to know. All three agreed to co-operate, but would officially know nothing whatsoever about the plan.

For the next two nights I did not go to sleep at all. John, Woodhouse and Solbe took it in turns to be with me both by day and night to keep me awake and make sure that I did not fall asleep. Then, on the third day, while flying in formation, I pretended to fall asleep in the air, letting my head fall forward and putting the aircraft into a gradual dive, which became steeper as I descended. I ignored the screams from my observer in the back, who thought we were about to crash into the sea. Then, as though waking up, I pulled out of the dive just before hitting the water and climbed back up to rejoin the formation.

All the pilots in our squadron had seen this happen and the Squadron Commander demanded an explanation. I put in a written request to be taken off flying. I reported that I was finding it impossible to get adequate sleep in the carrier and had nearly crashed that morning (as many had witnessed) by falling asleep in the air. Our Squadron Commander had no option but to forward my request, accompanied by his own report on the incident he and my observer had witnessed. His report went to "Wings" – the naval commander in charge of flying. He in turn forwarded them, doubtless in triplicate, through the official channels that led eventually right up to the Admiral.

Meanwhile, John Northey and the two others continued taking it in turns to ensure that I got little sleep either that day or during the following night. They had a difficult job keeping me awake. The next morning I reported sick. By this time the effect was beginning to show on my face, and particularly in my eyes, that I was in very poor shape. "Bones" (not surprisingly) categorised me as unfit to fly until I had a full medical examination at the Royal Air Force Central Medical Establishment (CME) in London.

Then there occurred something that made me look with a little less antagonism towards the senior naval officers. The Admiral, on receiving the report (probably in quadruplicate by that time), offered me the use of one of his cabins that was reserved for visiting VIPs if that would help me sleep. I had difficulty in talking my way out of that one, but managed to persuade him that his kind offer would make no difference. In fact, I knew I would fall fast asleep the moment I was left alone.

Meanwhile, the ship had been cruising along the south coast, showing the flag at other ports. I was excused flying, but the others still kept up their vigils to prevent me sleeping more than an hour or so at a time. As we approached Weymouth, a signal arrived from Air Ministry recommending that I had two weeks' leave before reporting to CME to be examined. So, at Weymouth, I went ashore and phoned Bunny.

We had two glorious weeks' holiday at Gluvian Farm in Cornwall, swimming and surfing at Morgan Porth, sunbathing, sleeping and walking long distances over the cliffs. I became suntanned and was soon in excellent physical condition again.

Needless to say, at CME the doctors could find nothing wrong with me and categorised me A1 for flying. I shall always remember the kindly and understanding look on the face of the senior medical officer at my final interview there. He studied the various results on his desk and said to me:

"Nothing wrong with you. You're as fit as a fiddle." Then he looked at another file and smiled at me. "You're married, aren't you?" he asked.

I nodded. He continued, "And you don't like serving in the Fleet Air Arm and being in a carrier? That's all that's wrong with you, isn't it?"

"Oh, no!" I began defensively. "I can't sleep ..."

"Nonsense!" he interrupted, putting on a broad smile. "Try pulling my other leg! Would you like me to arrange a posting for you out of Fleet Air Arm?"

I nodded eagerly. He referred to the file again. "I see you have a good flying record. You enjoy flying?"

"Tremendously," I assured him. "I just love it."

He smiled again. "Good," he said, "I'll have a word with postings. I'll recommend that you're given a good flying job back in the RAF."

Two days later, my posting to Cardington to take over command of the Ferry Flight came through. To be given command of an independent flying unit while still such a junior officer was wonderful news. And the Ferry Flight was one of the most interesting and challenging flying jobs in the RAF. That posting altered my whole career.

Bunny

Cornwall 1936

Cornwall 1937

Chapter 8

The Ferry Flight

Cardington

On 24th August 1937, Bunny and I motored up to RAF Cardington, where I took over as Officer Commanding the Ferry Flight. While I reported for duty, Bunny motored into the nearby market town of Bedford to find accommodation for us. At 4 pm, as arranged, she was waiting for me in our little open Morris two-seater, to take me to the Red Lion at Elstow, where she had arranged for us to have a large bedroom upstairs and a private sitting/dining room downstairs plus all meals for 30 shillings per week. We could just afford that.

The dear old lady who ran that pub looked after us magnificently and we were very happy there. But the Red Lion is located at a small road junction and was quite noisy – even in those days, with much of the traffic still horse-drawn. Our experience of living on that farm near West Freugh made us long for the open countryside again. So, after a brief spell in an apartment in De Pary's Avenue, and a ghastly few days in a damp cottage near the river, we put an advertisement in the local paper for farmhouse accommodation. We received several replies – amongst them one from Phyllis Measures at Blackburn Hall, Thurleigh. That simple little letter turned out to have such an influence on our lives – and the lives of our children – that I am writing separately about Blackburn Hall. We lived there throughout the 18 months I served at Cardington.

Blackburn Hall

Charlie Measures off hunting

Aerial view of Blackburn Hall

Blackburn Hall

Royal Air Force Station, Cardington, had been Britain's main airship base until, after the crash of the R101, which resulted in the Government decision to abandon airships, it had become one of the main recruiting and equipment centres. The two large airship hangars were in use – one for storing old aircraft and the other housed the rapidly expanding Balloon Wing that was hoping to provide London and other cities with some protection against low-flying enemy aircraft with a Balloon Barrage. The balloons were tethered to mobile winches by steel cables designed to cause any aircraft hitting them to crash.

The station comprised well over 3,000 personnel in various wings, commanded by senior officers from the Equipment, Engineering and other branches. The station commander was a General Duties (ie flying) Branch Group Captain. The Ferry Flight was a completely separate unit, with me reporting direct only to the Group Captain. I was only a Flying Officer, and far junior in rank to the Wing Commanders, Squadron Leaders and Flight Lieutenants in the other branches, but I was the

The Ferry Flight

Me with my Hurricane

Vickers Virginia

Autogyro

next most senior General Duties Officer to the Group Captain. So I had automatically (in theory) to take over command of the whole station in his absence. I was afraid this might cause friction, but they were all such a splendid bunch that there were never any problems. It was, however, a little embarrassing for me, aged 24, sitting in the Group Captain's chair while dealing with an airman on a charge, to have to call in wing commanders to give evidence as witnesses and then interrogate them (like I would someone junior to me) before I could pronounce the accused not guilty or guilty. The accused could always opt for a court martial; but, knowing the maximum I could impose was 28 days' imprisonment, usually elected to accept my judgment.

Apart from that, however, I had no administrative duties. My task, together with six experienced sergeant pilots under my command, was simply to fly any aircraft – of whatever type – from wherever it happened to be – to wherever the Air Ministry wanted it. Each afternoon I would receive a signal updating the list of different types of aircraft, their numbers, and the locations between which they were to be flown. This meant that I had to be capable of flying every type of aircraft with which the RAF was equipped – including the new ones coming into service – and then also train my other pilots to fly them (safely) to any airfield in the UK as well – a challenge which we never failed to meet (and without ever damaging any) for the whole time I commanded that unit.

We usually flew them direct to their destination, but sometimes to Cardington to keep them for a day or two if that simplified our work, or if I decided to use them to train my pilots, or (with the larger ones) to carry us around. How I organised it was entirely up to me. We had neither radio nor any other navigational aids and no route weather forecasts. All we could do was phone our destination to find out what the weather was like there – but we often found it had changed before we arrived.

My office was a wooden shed near the airship hangars. The six sergeant pilots were much older than me. They clearly regarded this young "fighter pilot" becoming their CO with some apprehension. However, it was not long before my Cranwell training (plus my experience in 32 and 820 Squadrons) showed them that – while less experienced on large bomber aircraft – I knew as much about flying and aviation generally as they did and certainly exceeded their skills doing aerobatics. Within a month they fully accepted me and together we formed an excellent team.

Although I had no administrative duties – no records to keep, no reports to write – I was confronted with one problem which caused me some concern. A young GD Pilot Officer who was attached to the Balloon Wing, but for whom I was his immediate superior officer, came to me asking for advice on whether he should marry a girl that he had reason to believe had been made pregnant by the local chaplain.

We were the only pilots allowed to use Cardington airfield; the whole area was prohibited to other aircraft because of the danger of flying into the balloons and their wires. Our aircraft were maintained by civilian staff and in the whole time I was at

Cardington we never had a single technical problem with any of the hundreds of aircraft they serviced for us. That was largely due to the chief engineer of the storage unit, Mr Whittaker, and his deputy, Cooke. The latter had been one of the only survivors from the crash of the R101 airship in Beauvais a few years earlier. His first-hand account of that event was riveting. Strangely, he preferred not to fly in aircraft and rarely did so, but said he would willingly go up in an airship again.

To ferry my pilots around, we used whatever aircraft happened to be available – including some unusual ones that had been stored for years in the airship hangars. Amongst these, for example, was the Prince of Wales' aircraft – the Blackburn Special. We had no instruction manuals or any other pilots to advise us – we just got in and flew them. Because I had never previously flown an aircraft with more than a single engine, one of my more experienced sergeants came with me as second pilot to advise me how to handle a Vickers Virginia – a bomber with two engines produced in 1922 – and a Valencia, in which we often ferried pilots around. After that I always made a point of flying any new type myself first and then instructing the others.

New types of aircraft began appearing on our lists with greater frequency – and the numbers to be moved were increasing as the factories began gearing up for the war, which even some of our dim-witted politicians were at last beginning to realise might materialise.

Amongst these aircraft was, for example, the first Wellington ever built. I flew down to the Vickers factory at Brooklands to collect it. There I met, for the first time, the chap who designed it – Barnes Wallis, with whom I had many contacts later. That Wellington was due to go to Martlesham Heath for the RAF test pilots to put it through its paces.

Before handing over the aircraft to me, the Vickers chief test pilot (Mutt Summers) asked me whether I had ever flown with a constant-speed propeller.

"I've never even heard of one," I replied.

143

"In that case," he said, "I think I had better do a circuit and bump with you before you fly it alone – it will probably seem a bit strange until you get the hang of it."

I was glad to have the chance of flying with one of our most famous test pilots and particularly glad to have him demonstrate the difference in handling an engine fitted with this new type of prop. It proved to be a very strange experience – particularly on approaching to land – to find that moving the throttles made little difference to the noise of the engines. I flew the Wellington back to Cardington, where I experimented with it and then demonstrated it to the other pilots.

The most extraordinary of the 48 different types I flew there was the Cervia Autogyro "Rota". I enlisted the help of our engineer, Cooke, to help me fathom out how everything worked. It had a normal engine and propeller in the nose to drag it through the air. It had no wings to provide lift; but rotating blades above the pilot's head – like a modern helicopter. It had a normal rudder on the tail controlled, as usual, by the pilot's feet. But the Rota had no ailerons or elevators and, instead of the normal control column, it had a sturdy metal bar, slightly curved and with a knob at the end, hanging down from the central rotor pivot a few feet above the pilot's head. That control stick (which inevitably became known as the "donkey's prick", which it closely resembled) needed considerable force to make it tilt the rotors in relation to the fuselage and so cause the aircraft to bank into a turn, climb or dive.

Unlike the helicopters (which appeared later), the rotor blades were not driven by the engine when in flight; nor did it have a propeller on the tail to control direction. Instead, there was a drive, with a clutch, between the main engine, with its propeller in the nose of the aircraft and the rotors – but that was only to get them rotating prior to take-off. Thereafter, the engine only provided the forward speed through the air: the airflow itself kept the blades rotating. An engine failure had no direct effect on them. But the Rota could not hover and so needed a few yards of level ground on which to land.

The first time I flew it at Cardington the other pilots and several mechanics had gathered to watch the take-off. Cooke started the engine for me and then stood well clear. I ran up the engine and tested it. Then, with the engine running slowly again, I let in the clutch to drive the rotors. There was a grinding noise and shaking of the aircraft as the rotors began turning – as with some of the early helicopters. I gradually opened up the engine until the rev counter reached a red mark on the dial. The rotors seemed to be going quite quickly. I had been holding the aircraft against the brakes but the aircraft began creeping forward. So I disengaged the engine from the rotors and released the brakes simultaneously. The engine, now freed from having to drive the rotors, increased the power to the propeller quite dramatically. That accelerated us forward. After just a short run I gave a gradual heave on the control and we became airborne. I made sure the airspeed was adequate and climbed up to a height from which, if necessary, I could safely bail out by parachute. I then practised all sorts of manoeuvres to gain experience. On landing, I found that about ten yards was adequate.

I then taught the Station Commander, and others, to fly it.

One day, while flying the Autogiro, I ran into a thunderstorm. My airspeed was only about 50 mph, but I was in that storm for longer than I had expected. Also, there was hail in it – quite big hailstones. To my horror, I saw that the rotor blades were being damaged as though being sandpapered down to a smaller size. I had often before flown through hailstorms in ordinary aircraft with wings; but they were designed to withstand hail and sandstorms. This was a different matter. My sole means of support was rapidly being diminished before my eyes.

Because I had no desire (nor the ability) to fly this strange contraption blind on instruments, I had already been forced down by the cloud to a low level to keep visual contact with the ground. So I quickly landed on the nearest patch of grass I could find. It was far, far smaller than would have been necessary in any other type of aircraft. There I let the rotors stop, but kept the engine running sufficiently fast for the propeller to blast most of the hailstones from settling in the cockpit. Then, when the storm had passed, I switched in the clutch to start up the rotors again and flew back to Cardington.

An examination of the rotors revealed that I had indeed been wise to land. They were not constructed to rotate in large hailstones.

Years later, flying helicopters, I realised that I could not have coped flying these more complicated contraptions without far more information, such as a Pilot's Handbook or at least more comprehensive prior advice. It was much easier and more fun when aircraft were less sophisticated.

Also stored in the airship hangar I found the three Avro Tutors that had been fitted with special carburettors to enable them to fly upside down and also strengthened to do aerobatics inverted. They had been used at the annual RAF Displays at Hendon and had coloured markings on their upper wings to make it easier for the spectators on the ground to see which way up they were flying. I arranged for one of them to be serviced and, after practising bunts and outside loops (for which I always had to take off my tie and loosen my collar), I gave upside-down aerobatics displays on Empire Air Day, first at Cardington and then – arriving there flying upside-down with my head about 50 feet from the ground – at nearby Henlow. Great fun. I also used that aircraft to demonstrate inverted spins to a couple of my pilots – the others did not volunteer.

I found it interesting that while I do not like heights and get a mild panic attack near the edge of a cliff or looking down at the ground from a high building, flying upside-down at any height never had the slightest effect on me. I enjoyed it. However, as I shall explain later, flying low (the right way up) towards the edge of the Grand Canyon in the USA forced me to turn away – my instinctive sensations caused a reaction that was too strong for me to overcome. It would have been interesting to see whether I would get the same sensations if flying inverted over a cliff edge – but I never had the opportunity to try that. The countryside around Bedford was too flat.

That absence of hills near Cardington was a bonus when we were returning there in bad weather. We were not usually flying great distances and our mental calculations, based on our compass and airspeed indicator, usually got us within about 20 miles of home. So we could descend fairly safely through the cloud until we could recognise some landmark and find our way by following a road or railway. In fact, by chance, we found a way of getting back and landing at Cardington when most airlines and other aircraft were grounded by bad weather.

One misty day with a layer of low cloud, I took off from Sealand, near Liverpool, to fly back to Cardington in a Swordfish. I had climbed up through the murk to well above the layer of cloud, in the hope of getting occasional glimpses of the ground. Looking ahead, I suddenly noticed a cluster of barrage balloons shining brightly in the clear sunshine and realised that they must be at Cardington, about a hundred and forty miles away. So they provided a homing device that would not only lead me there, but also indicate the wind direction for landing. I subsequently arranged with the Wing Commander commanding the balloon unit that whenever we had clear weather above a cloud layer and needed help to get back, we would telephone him before taking off. He would then arrange for one or two balloons to be flown at sufficient height to guide us home.

We then carried these ideas further. We arranged to have ribbons of different shapes and colour attached at specific heights (controlled by the length of wire released), with the winches placed in line about fifty yards to the left of where we should land on the airfield. By using these, I found I could descend and land safely in far worse visibility than I had ever dared previously. Having three balloons lined up made it even easier.

The ribbons on the balloon cables served another purpose. They enabled me to check on the accuracy of our altimeters in measuring our height above the ground as we flew past. That proved what I had always suspected – aircraft altimeters could give a pretty inaccurate indication of height above the ground. The errors varied considerably between different types of aircraft. There was, I believe, no better way of checking the setting and the accuracy of altimeters in flight.

Ever since the earliest days of cross-country flying in bad weather, errors in altimeters, and the settings that pilots put on them, have probably been the biggest single cause of air crashes – flying into mountains, hitting high ground, or crashing on the approach to land. I mention later how this was almost certainly the cause of the Duke of Kent being killed, early in the war, while being navigated by a fellow Cranwell cadet named Moseley.

After I had been in command of the Ferry Flight for a few months, the station commander, Group Captain A. A. B. Thompson, who had often flown with me and who was himself an outstanding pilot, upgraded my rating as a pilot from the "Above Average" I had first gained at Cranwell to the highly coveted "Exceptional" – a rating I then retained throughout my career.

During my 17 months at Cardington, we ferried hundreds of aircraft, of 47 different types, without a single accident. I think it was that, and my pilot rating, plus passing the preliminary French interpreter's examination, which resulted in me having received accelerated promotion to Flight Lieutenant and then, the following year, to Squadron Leader.

The nearest I came to an accident in the Ferry Flight was when I was flying a Swordfish in poor visibility. It was raining, and to keep below the cloud I was flying at about 400 feet to follow the stretch of straight railway line near Basingstoke. I was keeping that railway line just in sight below me to my left. A pilot in another aircraft must have been doing the same thing – but he was flying in the opposite direction and keeping the railway line in sight to his right. We missed colliding head on by inches. The sudden roar of his engine made me look up. I caught a glimpse of his wheel passing just over my head before I hit his slipstream, which temporarily jerked my Swordfish out of control.

This near miss further convinced me that collisions were the main and constant danger we were facing when flying. (The only exception in my 25 years' experience was later, when I was flying a Canberra above 50,000 feet – at which height I knew there could be no other aircraft in that vicinity.) Again, I had been incredibly lucky.

Nevertheless, I viewed it more positively – that I would have been incredibly unlucky to collide with what was probably the only other idiot stupid enough to be flying in that area under those conditions. It taught me that, with the increasing numbers of aircraft flying, and until we got better navigational aids, following railway lines in bad weather was similar to driving the wrong direction along a motorway! Potentially very bad for your health!

We had to collect numerous Swordfish from the manufacturers (Fairey). To do so, we had to land at their small grass airfield named Heathrow near Slough. We used the nearby big reservoirs to help us find it. Heathrow is slightly different now!

One day (I think in early 1938), a friend of mine named Anderson landed (with special permission) at Cardington in an Anson to have lunch with me, during which he told me about something very strange. The previous day he had made a lengthy flight out over the North Sea, during which he had been ordered to zig-zag about and change height and direction in any way he liked, but to have his navigator keep a very careful record of exactly what he had done. His radio transmitter and receiver were to be switched off completely throughout the flight. On landing, he had been met by a couple of scientists who presented him with a record of all his movements and these compared exactly with the record that his navigator had maintained. He was absolutely astounded and asked me whether I had any idea how they had done it. All I could think of was that they had been able to detect the noise from his engines, but we agreed that was unlikely at those distances and, carried sideways by the wind, would not have been accurate enough. We agreed it was a mystery – almost magic. It was, in fact, one of the early trials of RDF (Radio Direction Finding) by Watson-Watt and his team at Bawdsey, near Felixstowe. I later learned that the principle of what became Radar had been proven in a test on a Heyford in February 1935 and that Anderson's flight over the North Sea in the Anson was part of the continuing trials. [But for that timely invention of Radar, we could not have won the Battle of Britain and Germany would certainly have invaded Britain.]

In the spring of 1938, the station commander was promoted to Air Commodore and posted to command one of the groups in Bomber Command. He was a highly regarded officer, but he was also, unfortunately, very tall. Soon after he left, I learned that, while near a bomber aircraft at one of the stations in his new command, he had inadvertently walked into one of its rotating propellers and been killed. This incident had a profound effect on the design of the next generation of bombers. His shocked contemporaries at the Air Ministry decided to make it safer for the aircrew and mechanics to move about under their aircraft. That was the sole reason – nothing to do with aerodynamics or engineering – why the Stirling and other bombers had such high and awkward undercarriages.

The nearest any of my pilots came to disaster was when the youngest of them (Sgt Sutton) was flying an Anson back to Cardington in deteriorating weather conditions. The clouds, in which there was severe icing, were getting lower and lower as he approached the airfield from the north-west, and it was beginning to snow. Luckily, he had already completed the exhausting task of winding down his undercarriage in anticipation of landing at Cardington. Just five miles short of the airfield, flying only about 50 feet up, he found the clouds were right down to the ground on the slight hill between him and the airfield. He had run out of sky in which he could fly and there was insufficient room to turn; so he cut the throttle and simply landed straight ahead. That field happened to be part of Blackburn Hall Farm, where Bunny and I were living. One of my other pilots flew it back safely the next morning.

We had to ferry quite a few Miles Magisters from an airfield near Reading. The Magister was a new small, fully aerobatic, single-engine training aircraft with dual open cockpits. I had incidents with two of the many that we collected from the manufacturers there. The first was when flying at about 2,000 feet and one side of the metal engine cowling suddenly tore off and was flung violently backwards by the force of the slipstream. It gashed my shoulder, tore off my epaulette, missing my head by less than an inch, and cut a hole in the fuselage behind me. Luckily, it did not hit the tailplane or rudder and I was able to land safely. (Hence, incidentally, the lack of one epaulette in the photo of me beside the Hurricane fighter which many years later appeared in the *Daily Telegraph*.)

The other Magister incident was on a similar flight on a lovely day when, full of the joys of spring, I decided to do a slow roll. That, unexpectedly, resulted in the engine failing – it just fluttered to a stop, even though I had completed the roll and was right way up again. In spite of all my training, it came as quite a shock to find myself with no engine over the Chilton Hills. But I managed to land safely in a rather bumpy field and needed to get to a telephone to report the incident and request help. The nearest likely place where I would find one was a large house several hundred yards away. So, leaving the aircraft to look after itself, I made my way towards it, clambering through hedges and across ditches until I arrived at the front door.

A gorgeous girl opened it, but, on seeing this rather grimy stranger clothed in flying kit, nearly slammed the door in my face. However, she finally let me in. Then, as I explained my predicament, her attitude changed completely. She appeared overwhelmed to meet an intrepid birdman that had so recently been dicing with death. Her parents were apparently out. She insisted on helping me clean myself up and made me a cup of tea before she would even let me use the telephone.

I got through to the nearest RAF Station (Halton) and arranged that a guard for the aircraft would be sent out, plus a couple of mechanics to see if they could fix what I felt sure was trouble with the carburettor. She did not want to let me leave, but I had to get back to the aircraft.

The mechanics soon fixed the trouble and I took off to continue my flight. Arriving over the airfield at Cardington, I decided to check the functioning of the engine by doing another slow roll. The engine again failed, but making a forced landing there on the large airfield was considerably easier than into a small field in the Chilterns. My experiences resulted in slight modifications to the Magister, which went on to have an excellent record.

With war now threatening, most of the new fighter aircraft were being delivered urgently direct by the manufacturer to the squadrons.

I managed to borrow a Hurricane for a few days and then flew across to 19 Squadron at Duxford to get experience flying Spitfires. Its shape reminded me of watching the Schneider Trophy races on the Solent while I was still a schoolboy. It was a lovely aircraft to fly, but when I came in to land the first time I got quite a shock. No one had warned me that the engine obscured all view ahead when in the tail-down landing attitude. I could not see the runway and had to judge my height and direction by looking out to the side. But I soon got used to that. Overall, however, I preferred flying the Hurricane.

The most enjoyable to fly of the pre-war fighters were the Gloster Gauntlet and Gladiator. But I may have been prejudiced, because they were the first types in which I did aerobatics inside a closed cockpit – the first with a canopy to protect my head from the blasts of air that hitherto had made all flying, and particularly slow rolls, so uncomfortable. The difference between flying in an open cockpit and a closed one is similar to the difference between driving an open car at 100 mph in a blizzard to being in a luxury air-conditioned saloon car today.

The Lysander was one of the most interesting aircraft I flew. It had extraordinary landing characteristics which made it ideal for the type of clandestine operation for which it later became famous. I never discovered whether it had been designed with that in mind – dropping and picking up spies behind enemy lines at night – a pastime in which several of my friends were later employed.

We became very accustomed to changing from flying one type of aircraft to another. During one day, for example, I piloted five different types – two of which I had never flown before. With the threat of war with Germany increasing, so the expansion of the RAF was accelerating and the numbers of aircraft being produced by the aircraft factories increased dramatically. By the summer of 1938, I needed more pilots to cope with these numbers. Unfortunately, the experience and skill of the new ones posted in did not match that of my original team and caused me to limit most of them to flying just one or two types on which I had personally checked them.

In August, I motored Bunny down to stay with her parents in Beckenham, Kent, to have our first baby. I went on to Cornwall for a holiday while awaiting its arrival, then rejoined Bunny at Beckenham in September when Pam was born. The international situation was worsening and it was at last becoming clear (even to our blind politicians) that Germany intended taking control of the whole of Europe. The Munich crisis blew up, war seemed inevitable and I was recalled to Cardington urgently. It was at too short notice to take Bunny and our baby with me.

The RAF was on War Alert and I could not leave my post at Cardington, although I was desperate to get my wife and baby away from London before the bombing started. But the station commander, who knew about our new baby, helped me to do so. He detailed me to take some urgent secret papers to Squadron Leader Macfadyn in the Plans Department at Air Ministry. To ensure the safety of those documents, I was to go by car and he said that he would not expect me to report for duty until the next morning – thus giving me time that evening to pick up Bunny and our baby.

We expected war to start any moment – probably with an air attack on London. Bunny and I put little Pam (all four pounds of her) into her carrycot behind us in my open two-seat Morris, with her gas mask ready beside her. Then, having said goodbye to Bunny's parents, fearing that we might never see them again, and with our own gas masks ready too, we set out through London, expecting any minute to hear the shriek of air raid warning sirens. We arrived back at Blackburn Hall with great relief.

The next day the threat of war seemed to be temporarily delayed – Chamberlain returned from Munich with his famous "bit of paper" and "peace in our time" – and life returned, on the surface, to normal. But there was increased urgency to prepare for the war that now seemed inevitable and we were inundated with work. Great fun – and with a wonderful spirit of co-operation everywhere.

All ex-Cranwell cadets were encouraged to learn foreign languages and also to specialise in a chosen subject such as signals, armaments, navigation or engineering. If they did so successfully, then accelerated promotion usually resulted. I had chosen Navigation as my specialist subject, and in consequence was posted, in November 1938, to undergo the Specialist Navigation Course at the School of Air Navigation at Manston, in Kent.

The Ferry Flight, from the little unit I had commanded, later expanded into an enormous organisation – Ferry Command. The two large airship hangars at Cardington still dominate the skyline near Bedford and remind me of the happy days I spent flying in that area – and of the wonderful months we spent living with the Measures at Blackburn Hall.

Chapter 9

Navigation

The art of navigating accurately to the intended destination has been one of the main problems facing all living creatures since the beginning of the world; and most birds, animals and fish have developed that skill – often by means beyond human comprehension. Some living organisms use the sense of touch. Taste may help salmon find their way back to their pet river. Scent or sound, carried in the air, can indicate direction for slightly longer ranges to most mammals, but are affected by the wind. The eyes can detect, with amazing accuracy, both direction and distance, but only in clear visibility. Some birds are believed to use the earth's magnetism and celestial bodies to navigate enormous distances. A recent theory is that turtles travel thousands of miles to their breeding grounds guided only by the earth's magnetism. Even cats and dogs have been reported finding their way home from hundreds of miles away. Exactly how is still a mystery.

By 1938, some radio aids for flying along particular routes had been developed for use in civil aviation – but in wartime all these could be jammed; also, they would have to be switched off in case they helped the enemy. So we RAF aircrew, except the pilots in Fighter Command being controlled by radar and radio, unless we could see the ground clearly enough to recognise distinguishing features which corresponded with those shown on the map, had about as much chance of reaching our intended destination as would a salmon with wings flying over the Sahara Desert. The human body had not developed the necessary skills, nor had the scientists yet developed enough gadgets, to enable us to do so.

We could take off and fly about in almost any weather, but finding our way accurately to a target to bomb it, or an airfield on which to land, in any area without sufficient visibility for the aircrew to recognise features on the ground (or sea) was virtually impossible. We had, in fact, no reliable way of navigating anywhere accurately.

The difficulties increased with the distances we could fly, the length of time we were airborne and, usually, at night.

Watson-Watt had discovered in 1935 that radio waves could be reflected back from an aircraft and so, up to about 100 miles from a ground radar station, could detect where and at what height an aircraft in the sky was located. This was already coming into use to detect enemy aircraft and direct a fighter by radio to intercept it.

But no one had yet devised a reliable way of enabling a bomber pilot to find his target or bomb it accurately unless he could see the ground. However, if he could see the ground, then enemy gunners on the ground, and other aircraft, could see him too. Also, because of inadequate instruments, he had to approach the target in a long straight run to aim the bomb, thus making the plane an easier target.

The methods of navigation taught at the RAF School of Air Navigation at Manston in 1938 were exactly the same as those that had been used by the merchant ships and the Royal Navy in previous centuries in navigating the oceans. Those methods were referred to as "Dead Reckoning" or "DR Navigation", which depended primarily on measuring the speed and direction of travel from a known starting point, with allowance for the tide or current (or, for aircraft, the wind) to calculate the resulting position. Additionally, when weather permitted, the altitude of various stars, sun or moon above the horizon could be measured (but only inaccurately in a bumpy aircraft) and used to calculate, by quite complex mathematics which took many minutes, the approximate position in which the ship or aircraft had been when those observations of the heavens had been made.

Those two methods were all that we could be taught at that time and neither would enable us to navigate an aircraft accurately. The Air Marshals running the RAF since its formation may have remembered the dogfights over the Western Front in 1918 in planning how Fighter Command aircraft would operate, but they had failed to realise the imperative need for accurate navigation in our bomber and reconnaissance aircraft and the necessary instruments to permit that. As I explain later, however, it was the activities of some communist scientists at our research establishments that were responsible for our navigational deficiencies.

So all we could be taught at Manston was DR and astronomical navigation – both of which we practised in Ansons flying over the English Channel or North Sea. We rarely found the target, often got lost and had to follow the coastline to get home. We only flew occasionally at night when (if we were lucky) our astronomical observations sometimes confirmed that our position was probably somewhere in Northern Europe.

Our military aircraft were simply not equipped with the necessary instruments and aids to enable us to function efficiently. Our compasses were based on a ship's binnacle and swung wildly around in the accelerations experienced when flying. Our air speed indicators were less accurate than a ship's log; the winds more variable than the tides; everything happening much more quickly; and (unlike navigators in a ship floating on water) we only had a limited time before shortage of fuel would force us to land – or crash.

After undergoing the eight-month Specialist Navigation Course, I would have been able to navigate a ship round the world, but could still not guide an aircraft anywhere accurately in anything but good weather – and that only with prominent features on the ground within sight.

I became very critical of this situation. I realised that our instructors could only teach what they had been taught – and that went back to the methods, with only small improvements, used by Nelson and Drake. Our two instructors, Flight Lieutenants Richardson and Moseley, taught us all they knew – but the quality of that knowledge could be judged by Moseley later navigating the aircraft carrying the Duke of Kent into a mountainside in Scotland and so killing all the occupants.

To judge our position by observation of the stars necessitated first measuring the angle of selected celestial bodies above a horizon that (when flying) does not normally exist. So, an artificial horizon had to be generated – and the only known practical way in 1939 of producing that was by use of a spirit level or pendulum which, in an aircraft, was so inaccurate as to be virtually useless.

Mariners could (in clear weather) use the sea horizon as a very accurate reference. But flying, we had to rely on a bubble of air in a curved tube of liquid. Any airline passenger who has tried to drink a cup of tea under turbulent conditions will appreciate our problem. Even in smooth air, the hand-held "bubble sextant" rarely gave reliable accuracy, and under most flying conditions was almost useless.

Even on the ground it was not easy, using the only bubble sextants then available, to work out exactly where one was on the earth's surface. I spent many evenings lying back in a deckchair in our garden taking sights on the stars with a bubble sextant to work out my position. After twenty minutes' calculations, my observations were just as likely to indicate that I had been in Paris or Edinburgh as in our garden in Kent. Doing the same thing in an aircraft in bumpy conditions extended that to Bordeaux or even Berlin. But that was the only independent way we had of fixing our position.

Meanwhile, as the early months of 1939 passed by, it was quite clear that war was becoming more and more likely. Also, that the RAF was so badly equipped – particularly navigationally – that, while Fighter Command might just be able to defend England against a German air attack, the RAF were very badly equipped to retaliate. Our future prospects, if Germany went to war against us, were not good, and we navigation specialists (who realised this better than most) and our wives, particularly those with young children, feared for their future in England.

Amongst the other officers with me on that course was one from the Royal Canadian Air Force, Flight Lieutenant Frank Miller, who later became an Air Marshal and head of that Force. He was due to return to Canada at the end of the course. His wife Dorothy and my wife Bunny became good friends. Dorothy used to visit our bungalow at Minnis Bay and one day, when playing with little Pam in her pram, she said to Bunny:

Our Bungalow   *Minnis Bay*

"If ever you feel it is getting too dangerous in England, just get Tubby to send us a cable warning us, and you bring Pam over on the next boat to Canada. You can come and live with us there until the war is over – we'll look after you."

Amongst the officers on the staff of the School were several who became lifelong friends of mine – amongst them Don Stokes (and his wife Bunch), Wilf Oulton (and his wife Terry) and many others. I did not know it at the time, but Dorothy Miller had made the same offer to Terry Oulton, who also had a baby – Peter.

In spite of the gloomy international outlook, and our utter disgust with the politicians in Westminster, we were a very happy group, making the best of the threat of war and determined to enjoy ourselves before it began. Some evenings, however, I used to go alone for a walk along the cliffs at Minnis Bay, wondering what the future held for Bunny and Pam. I certainly did not expect to survive for long myself if war broke out.

During the Navigation Specialist Course, we spent a week with the Army, learning how to survey with a theodolite to prepare maps. I also had a brief spell navigating a submarine. But for me the most important subject (which has helped me ever since) was meteorology – learning to forecast the weather. We used to plot the pressure from weather ships in the Atlantic and other stations in Northern Europe, joining up the isobars to form a weather map.

Then, using winds and temperatures, we would decide the likely movements of weather fronts and so forecast the weather for the flight we were intending. At the end of the course, I was elected a Fellow of the Royal Meteorological Society (FRMetS).

We also spent a week at the Admiralty Compass Observatory at Greenwich – the ancient establishment set up to develop compasses for naval ships, but now also responsible for designing our aircraft compasses. Even Nelson might not have found much new to excite him. To us pilots it was as stimulating as studying anthropology at the British Museum. The Naval staff there appeared to have no conception of the needs of a pilot flying an aircraft. There are, of course, many problems facing anyone designing any compass to be accurate – particularly one for use in aircraft.

The approximate position of the North Pole is well known and practically all maps mark its direction. A magnetic needle, however, does not point to the North Pole. If freely suspended, it points downwards to a location (which slowly drifts about) much nearer the centre of the earth, but which, from Greenwich (if measured horizontally), is roughly in the direction of the North Pole.

On the other side of Iceland, however, a freely suspended magnetic needle points almost vertically downward. That makes it difficult to measure the horizontal direction of the North Pole – the basic information the navigator needs from his compass.

So, even in England, a weight has to be added to the south side of the needle to keep it horizontal. That, to a Boy Scout in England, makes little difference. But if he uses it in a car and the driver slows down, the heavier (southern) end will shoot forward, giving a completely wrong indication.

In an aircraft, particularly in bumpy weather, that effect is magnified. When the aircraft banks, the compass needle, now out of the horizontal, swings violently, seeking to point to the magnetic pole deep down towards the earth's centre. The angles, and consequent errors, differ all over the world.

To complicate the problem still further, the location of the compass was usually about the last item of equipment to be considered in the design of an aircraft. The engineers sometimes located bits of iron near where the compass was finally placed or the electricians ran wires with varying electric fields quite close to it. Trying to compensate for their effect on the compass was an impossible job. The magnetic compass was, nevertheless, the primary instrument on which all our navigation was based.

By 1938, however, most RAF aircraft were also fitted with a standard "instrument panel", which included a directional gyroscope that could be set from the compass and retain its indications of direction during most aircraft manoeuvres. Its accuracy, however, was still dependent on the setting taken from the magnetic compass.

I will not go into the inaccuracies of the airspeed indicators or of the altimeters and their QFE-QFF settings. The fact is that, in 1939, as had been obvious for many years, the Air Force was so badly equipped – particularly as regards being able to navigate – that Bomber Command was pretty incapable of fighting a war.

While I was on that course at Manston, shortly before the war, this dismal state of affairs had at last penetrated the skulls of our masters at the Air Ministry, whose flying experience was, in many cases, still limited to dogfights during the First World War. They decided that some officer, a navigation specialist about the rank of Squadron Leader, who seemed likely to be able to work with the scientists (usually referred to as "Boffins") should be sent to the Instrument Department of the Royal Aircraft Establishment at Farnborough. The intention was that he should speed up, guide, and assist the work of the boffins there to help solve urgently this glaring deficiency.

My prior knowledge of astronomy (resulting from having used my grandfather's sextant at school) and my physics background had helped my progress. I think it was that, coupled with my experience of flying so many different types of aircraft and my "Exceptional" rating as pilot, that I happened to be the officer chosen for that post in preference to other candidates. David Waghorn (whose brother had been in the Schneider Trophy team) was obviously a more experienced navigation specialist than I was at that time. David,

June 1939

however, was shortly afterwards posted to Boscombe Down, where he worked closely with me.

On 1st June 1939, I was promoted to Squadron Leader and on 12th August was transferred to the "Special Duty List" to take up that new post at RAE Farnborough.

We were sad to leave our bungalow at Minnis Bay. Although cold in winter, that area had some of the best weather in the British Isles. We decided that Bunny and Pam should go and stay with my mother and sister, who were now living at Burgess Hill in Sussex, until we found somewhere to rent near Farnborough. Since, at last, I was now entitled to marriage allowance, we would be able to afford something a bit more appropriate. I sold my Morris and bought a 1½-litre MG Drop-head Coupe.

The prospect of working with the scientists at the RAE was exciting. But I had no inkling of the tremendous influence that it would later have on my career and whole future life.

Chapter 10

The Royal Aircraft Establishment

RAE Farnborough was the main base in England for research and development for practically everything connected with flying. Much of the work – particularly for the RAF – was highly secret. It was a civilian organisation controlled by Civil Servants, over which neither the Air Ministry nor the Royal Air Force had any direct control. The test pilots there included some civilians, although most were ex-RAF officers who had been on Short Service Commissions. A few other regular RAF officers with specialist qualifications had, like me, been attached to RAE to help guide the scientists ("boffins") on the practical aspects of their work – for example, Cedric Bell to the Radio Department. Also, across the airfield at the Institute of Aviation Medicine, there were mainly RAF doctors such as Bill Stewart, with whom I worked closely and who later became head of that organisation.

To begin with (and also later), I lived in the civilian Senior Staff mess with the other scientists – not in the RAF Officers' mess – and (until war broke out) rarely wore uniform. I had become, in effect, almost a "boffin" myself.

I found myself Joint Head, together with Harold Pritchard (with whom I shared an office) of the newly-formed Navigation Section. That was one part of the much bigger Instrument Department headed by Jack Richards. The staff comprised as strange an assortment of boffins of all ages as one can imagine. Some of these scientists were so specialised in their particular field that they knew little about the outside world; others had wider knowledge – some had brilliant brains, others were just drearily plodding along, waiting for their pensions. All, almost without exception, were interesting and quite friendly towards this newcomer in their midst.

Harry Pritchard was a highly regarded Senior Scientific Officer. He had earlier been working on radar with Watson-Watt at Orfordness,

163

Harry Pritchard   **Jack Richards**

and after the war he was the scientist in charge of the Atomic Bomb tests. He and I got on splendidly together and became great friends.

One of the most famous pilots at Farnborough was A. E. Clouston – always known as "The Colonel". He had recently broken yet another record – his flight to Cape Town and back in the Comet – and was making plans to have a go at breaking the transatlantic record. He proposed using a modified Hampden, and invited me to be his navigator. Our plans were well advanced to have a crack at it in mid-September – before the autumn gales. But the obvious threat of war with Germany was already casting its shadow on our hopes of together breaking that record.

At the beginning of September, I was spending the weekend with Bunny and Pam, who were still staying with my mother and sister at their house in Burgess Hill. We listened almost continuously to the radio, with the news getting worse and worse. At 11 o'clock we heard Chamberlain's announcement that we were at war with Germany. We listened in complete silence. My mother was in tears, remembering the First World War. So was my sister. I looked across at Bunny, with little Pam in her arms. We said nothing, each engrossed with our own thoughts. Bunny and I knew that I would have little chance of surviving a war. I again wondered what the future would hold for her and our darling little Pam.

We half-expected to hear the wailing of air raid sirens, or the sound of aircraft overhead – even the bangs that I remembered from when I was a baby. But there was no sound, apart from the sobs from my mother, and the radio droning on.

Then, with a heavy heart, I went into the bedroom to change into uniform. I kissed them all goodbye – not knowing whether I would ever see them again – got into our MG, and drove back to Farnborough to report for duty.

There, everything appeared quite normal – a complete anti-climax. People were talking more excitedly perhaps and the guards at the gate now had revolvers, tin hats and gas masks in their belts, but there was nothing else to indicate we were now at conflict with the most aggressive power the world had yet experienced.

At RAE the next morning, work continued absolutely normally. It was quite uncanny. So I too just got on with my job. But the Colonel and I agreed that our planned attempt to break the transatlantic record would have to be cancelled.

The war did not, at first, develop into the sort of conflict (with bombs dropping on England) that everyone had expected. So Bunny and I rented quite a large house in Farnham, about 10 minutes' drive from RAE, where we lived very comfortably, with a maid to do the main chores. Apart from some shortages, and petrol rationing, it was little different from peacetime.

My father, at that time living on his yacht at Evian-les-Bains, came over to England to offer his services. Having been an officer in the RNVR during the First World War, speaking several languages, obviously very fit and knowing Germany well, he was welcomed with open arms – just the sort of chap they wanted, particularly to work in Intelligence. They immediately offered him a commission. When, however, he filled in the forms showing that his age was 62, he was unceremoniously rejected as being over the age limit of 60.

He returned to live in France, feeling very bitter, and I did not see him again until the war ended.

However, he still retained his British nationality and when France surrendered in mid-1940, he escaped across the lake of Geneva in his yacht to Morges and served with the British Consulate in Lausanne. His knowledge of the mountain passes across the Alps, gained from his French National Service with the Chasseurs Alpines, proved invaluable in helping many (who might otherwise have become inmates – or worse – of German prison camps) evade capture and rejoin the Allied forces.

My brother had been a member of the Territorial Army ever since leaving school, first in the London Rifle Brigade and then in a cavalry regiment (Inns of Court), and was commissioned immediately war broke out as a Major, to serve mainly in the RASC in Burma. He was twice captured by the Japanese, but escaped. I did not see him either until after the war.

My primary task at RAE was to do everything possible to speed up developments which would enable our aircrew to fly, and navigate, more accurately. That involved first surveying each project concerning navigation that was in progress in the Instrument Department. I would then discuss it with Wing Commander Mackworth, in the Operational Requirement (OR) section of the Air Ministry, and with the navigation specialist officers at the Command for which the equipment was intended – usually either Bomber or Coastal Commands. If possible, I would test any new development myself in the air, and then discuss critically each project with Harry Pritchard. Together, we would then try to decide priorities and put most pressure on those most likely to be of use in the near term.

In fact, the whole programme had been in an appalling state of unco-ordinated muddle. Many different instruments were being developed – each of which would present on a separate dial to the navigator different information which collectively might have enabled him, given enough time (say a couple of hours) working quietly at a desk on the ground, to work out very roughly where he had previously been located.

Harbour-Evian le Bains where father kept his yatch

So the first thing I had to do was explain to the boffins that aircrew, wearing an oxygen mask, with frozen fingers or gloves, travelling at, say, a couple of hundred mph and being bumped about, would be quite incapable of using most of the currently planned instruments.

To illustrate the crazy situation that I found, I will mention one of the first projects that I scrutinised – the Periscopic Drift Sight – an instrument to enable the navigator to measure drift (and so calculate in what direction and how much the wind was additionally causing the aircraft to move). It had been designed by RAE to meet the requirements laid down by the Operational Requirements branch of Air Ministry some years previously for Bomber and Coastal Command aircraft. A dear old boffin, who was brilliant in his field of optics, proudly showed me the result of his several years work. It was a magnificent instrument and I would dearly have liked to test it in the air. Unfortunately, it was so enormous – nearly as big and heavy as a submarine periscope (on which its design was based) – that the RAF had no aircraft into which it could be fitted. Also, it needed such precision of manufacture that it would have been extremely costly and, under wartime conditions, impossible to produce. The dear old boffin was absolutely devastated when I pointed out these simple facts to him. He showed me the specification on which he had worked so hard to meet, and he pointed out, with tears in his eyes, that it completely fulfilled every detail. It did – but was quite impractical for use in RAF aircraft. I felt terribly sorry for the old boy. But that was only one of the many examples of effort being misdirected, either through lack of knowledge of the practical application or – as I later realised – quite deliberately by Meridith (the former head of the Instrument Department) and Richards (who had succeeded him in that post).

At the other extreme was a small, complicated piece of machinery, like a watch with several tiny dials that would have been impossible to read, or adjust, in a bumpy aircraft. It was theoretically capable of enabling sidereal time to be calculated from a setting of Greenwich Mean Time, to assist the plotting of astronomical observations. I explain later that we were soon able to eliminate completely the need for any such device.

There was no co-ordinated plan to develop instruments that would enable our aircraft to navigate or bomb a target accurately.

At the outbreak of war, the newspapers had invited anyone who had ideas that might contribute to the war effort to submit them to the authorities – who then referred them to the departments concerned. Anything concerning navigation ended up on my desk. Many were useless, some relevant to work we were already starting to do – but one which seemed to me to be brilliant, and a possible solution to all our problems. It proposed an arrangement of fast-spinning gyroscopes which would measure any movement from the originally set position with an accuracy which only decreased slightly with the intervening time – in other words, an inertial navigation system. The principle had been known for years. If only the RAE boffins had previously put their effort into developing that, then the RAF would by then have had few navigational problems and we would have won the war far earlier.

Why, I asked Pritchard, had RAE not developed an inertial navigation system for the RAF?

"That," he replied, "is a question you should put to the former heads of the Instrument Department here."

Unfortunately, as Pritchard pointed out to me, now the war had started we could not develop, and then produce, gyros of sufficient accuracy to make it worthwhile. Later, of course, the inertial navigation system became the main (and I believe only) basic system of navigation which was independent of radio and is used worldwide. It would have made such an enormous difference to our ability to bomb targets accurately that the war, had Germany dared to start it, could have been quickly ended.

Within a few days of war breaking out, some of the most brilliant brains from the universities and industry began joining the boffins at Farnborough to help with the war effort. Several of them lived in the civilian mess (which I was also still using) and I got to know them well and I had the privilege of helping them by advising them on the practical flying aspects. There were several others, who did not live in the senior mess and worked in various other departments, with whom I had little contact. One of these was Professor A. A. Hall, who, not only because of his close association with Jack Richards, was believed to have strong communist sympathies. The Professor of Astronomy from Oxford University (Plaskett) joined our Navigation Section and the inventor of Vitaglass (Lamplough) worked in an adjoining office, using optics for measuring airflow over aeroplane wings, but also became interested in our navigation problems.

I put the problem of designing something simpler to replace the Periscopic Drift Sight to Lamplough. Within a week, with help from me, he came up with the design of a small gadget that we thought would do the trick. Pritchard arranged for a trial model to be made up in the workshops. Lamplough flew with me to try it out. A second model, weighing about a pound, cheap to manufacture and easily fitted to any aircraft that needed it, was produced two days later. I rushed with it down to Pembroke Dock to try it out on an anti-U boat patrol over the Atlantic in a flying boat, then tried it in a bomber, demonstrated it to other navigation specialists, and recommended its adoption. Quite soon it was in production and being fitted to all appropriate aircraft – the Drift Recorder Mark 2. It did everything that the big Periscopic Drift Sight could do – and more. Within just a few weeks we had a better instrument than that dear old boffin had produced in several years – not only through incorrect practical guidance, but under the directions of Meridith and Richards. Lamplough (quite rightly) got an award for it at the end of the war.

If, so quickly, a problem like that could be solved, why then was the RAF so badly equipped with other instruments and equipment – oxygen, autopilots and all the rest? I discovered the answer – and the reason why that deficiency persisted, but with a temporary break when Germany invaded Russia, right through to the Cold War. It is a sad, but true, tale.

Shortly after Bunny and I had moved into a house in nearby Farnham, I learnt that the wife of Jack Richards (the Head of the Instrument Department) had fallen ill and had to return to her home in Wales, so leaving him to fend for himself. So I invited Jack to come and stay with us for a week.

The first evening (after a couple of gins) Jack talked of nothing but communism and the superiority of the Russian form of government. All that week he tried to convert me into becoming a communist. At that time I had so little knowledge of politics that I hardly understood what he was talking about.

I subsequently mentioned this to Harry Pritchard. He expressed little surprise:

"Didn't you know, Tubby," he asked, "that Richards, together with Lockspeiser and Meridith, was one of the ringleaders in the Communist uprising here back in 1926? He is one of the most ardent communists anywhere."

Meridith, he explained, had been head of the Instrument Department before Richards and was now with Smiths Instruments Ltd (one of the main companies which produced the instruments for aircraft). Lockspeiser was in a senior position at the headquarters that controlled RAE. All three he mentioned (as I was later able to confirm from my personal contacts with them) had brilliant – even if distorted – brains.

Richards had originated from a very poor mining family in South Wales and one of his family (I think it was his father) had died of

Lockspeiser

Meredith

starvation. He had had a very deprived childhood, but managed to win a scholarship that resulted in him getting a first class degree and rising to his present position. He had, not unnaturally, an enormous chip on his shoulder and genuinely believed in communism.

At the beginning of the war, it should be remembered, Russia was not allied to us – quite the opposite. These three ardent communists, and all their associates, had been doing their best to prevent all RAF aircraft (although our defensive fighters had been less affected) from being properly equipped. When Germany invaded Russia, however – as I shall explain later – then Richards and his pals were transformed (temporarily at least) overnight and developments that they had previously opposed as being impossible were achieved in a flash.

I was far too ignorant, during my first tour of duty at Farnborough, to imagine that many there could be working for Russia against British interests. My suspicions concerning Richards increased, but it was not until the Cold War (after his pal Fuchs was convicted, and Richards was head of the important Telecommunications Research Establishment at Malvern) that I gained sufficient solid proof of his subversive activities. (These, incidentally, I reported to the head of RAF intelligence, but was, at that time, advised not to disclose them to anyone else.)

Two of the main resulting deficiencies (in addition to our lack of Navigation facilities) in our aircraft in the early years of the war were proper oxygen equipment for the bomber aircrew, and a decent autopilot. Both of these deficiencies were directly due to Richards (and his predecessor Meridith) and resulted in the unnecessary deaths of many of our aircrew. I was at the meeting where, in spite of the unanimous recommendation in favour of the Sperry autopilot, which was readily available and far superior to the one being developed at RAE, Richards manipulated matters (both then and later) to ensure the much less efficient RAE type was fitted to our aircraft.

But, in spite of the evil influence of Richards and his pals, a tremendous amount was achieved at RAE. Amongst the many developments with which I was involved in those early days of the war, I will mention only a few.

The Germans had developed a new magnetic mine with which to sink our ships. The older type had required the ship to touch the mine to make it detonate, and minesweepers could thus clear a safe channel through those. But this new type of mine was detonated by the magnetic properties of the iron in the hull of any ship that passed over, or near, them. In consequence, the mines could lie on the seabed, where it was difficult to detect, or sweep, them. Such mines were most effective if placed in a narrow channel used by many ships.

The Germans chose the Thames estuary as one of the best locations to lay these new mines and increasing numbers of our ships using that channel were being sunk. RAE was asked to find a way of countering this serious menace. One of the prominent scientists who had recently joined us – George Thompson – had a brilliant idea. Together with other scientists, he came up with an answer.

A Wellington was fitted with an enormous circular magnetic ring stretching almost from nose to tail, and wingtip to wingtip, with the idea that by flying over the water at low level it would generate a similar magnetic effect to that of a ship and so detonate the mine. Bruen Purvis tested the aircraft so fitted and found, rather to our surprise, that it handled quite well. Flying that contraption over measuring instruments laid on the ground indicated that it produced enough power to detonate the mine – providing the aircraft flew low enough over the water. But that raised the problem of whether the explosion of the mine would also cause the aircraft to crash. The speed at which the aircraft should fly, and its height, became vital factors. If too fast, the fleeting effect on the mine (designed to be detonated by a relatively slow-moving ship) might not work. The boffins, hard at work on their slide rules, came up with what they thought were the answers.

Two problems remained to be solved. How was the pilot to be sure he was flying at exactly the correct height – particularly if the water was calm, which made it impossible for the pilot to judge it accurately? And how was he to ensure that he had correctly covered every part of the area, particularly in bad visibility? These problems were clearly ones that belonged in our department – and solutions were required urgently.

Radio altimeters had not yet been developed. I had, however, recently carried out flying tests on an experimental sonic device to help a pilot land in fog. It comprised a powerful loudspeaker that transmitted noise downwards, and a sensitive receiver that measured the time for the echo from the ground to return – thus indicating the height. A "sonic altimeter". It worked well and I had carried out blind landings with it. I proposed that that should be tried on the Wellington. But Richards opposed the idea and made sure it was not available ("returned to makers for major modifications") and it was never tried.

Instead, to measure height, we arranged for a couple of fly fishing rods – one a long salmon fishing rod, the other a shorter trout rod, each with two wires running down it to an electrode at the end – to be pointed vertically down from the aircraft when over the water. The pilot had to descend until the tip of the salmon rod was touching the water; thus completing the electric circuit which produced a green light on the dashboard. But a red light from the trout rod indicated that the aircraft was too low. That enabled the pilot to control his height over the water to within about three feet.

The navigation problem remained the last hurdle. Harry managed to get hold of a fairly bulky instrument called a Brown Static Gyro. Taking that with us, and several other instruments, we drove in my MG down to Manston, where Bruen and the aircraft were waiting for us. We did not know how long we would be in that area, so Harry had decided to bring his wife with us.

I dropped Harry off at the airfield for him to supervise the installation of the Brown Static Gyro in the Wellington, while I motored his wife to a hotel at nearby Minnis Bay. There I helped his wife book a double room for them and – as there was no porter – I carried their suitcase up to their room for her and then rushed back to the airfield.

With me as navigator, Harry adjusting the gyro, and Bruen piloting the Wellington, we flew back and forth over the Thames estuary, with me trying to ensure that no area was missed. All the time, we expected an explosion beneath us and prayed that the boffins had done their sums correctly. We were all pretty apprehensive and tensed up.

We did not, however, detonate any mines on that flight. After we finished flying, that evening I motored Harry back to the hotel, dropped him off at the entrance to join his wife and motored back to Manston, where I had a room in the Mess. On arriving back at the Mess, I was given an urgent message from Harry asking me to return to the hotel immediately – which I did, wondering what on earth could be the matter.

I found Harry in a furious rage, stamping up and down outside the entrance, where he informed me that he had been ejected by the manageress and her husband. It took me quite a while to help him get it sorted out.

The strait-laced manageress, with whom Harry's wife and I had booked the double room, had seen me go up to her room with her, and assumed I was her husband. She had not noticed my subsequent immediate departure and was convinced that I had spent some time in the bedroom with her.

Then, in the evening, another man (Harry) had turned up, demanding to share her room for the night. The manageress automatically assumed that the attractive lady upstairs was a prostitute and that she (the manageress) could be accused of running a brothel if she permitted that. So Harry had not been allowed to go up to his wife's bedroom – nor even to have dinner with her.

It took me quite a few minutes (with Harry's help) to convince the proprietors otherwise. (What a difference from attitudes today!)

On subsequent flights, many magnetic mines were detonated. The first one proved the accuracy of the calculations – but only just! The upward blast of water hit the tailplane – but that forced the elevators up and so jerked the aircraft into a sharp climb. Startling, but not dangerous. Later, however, there were some pretty narrow squeaks, with bottom hatches being blown in; and other methods of measuring height were developed. From memory, I believe these were the forerunners of the intersecting light beams later used by the Dambusters.

I mentioned earlier the Sonic Altimeter. That was an entirely new type of instrument and it gave me the idea that perhaps we could use it for a completely new type of navigation – using the measurement of contours on the ground to follow a predetermined path to a destination. It would, of course, only be accurate enough at fairly low levels – otherwise the echoes from other parts of the ground would confuse it. With the help of George Gardner, a splendid boffin who was in charge of the "Queen Bee" Section (developing pilotless aircraft, at that time used mainly for gunnery practice and therefore expendable), we worked out that we could send a Queen Bee (basically a Tiger Moth – a small biplane) all the way to Berlin without a pilot. It could only carry a very small bomb, but would, throughout its flight, make a noise like a loud siren to frighten all within hearing distance. Above all, it would prove to the Berliners that Hitler's claim that no enemy aircraft could ever bomb Berlin was false.

In the spring of 1940 I was told that my proposal went as far as the Cabinet, but was turned down for the reason that it might encourage Hitler to retaliate by bombing London (which, at that time, the Germans had not yet seriously attempted)!

One of the main navigation projects at RAE had been, for several years, to try to develop a better type of magnetic compass – one which gave the pilot a steady reading on a dial in the dashboard, instead of him having to peer down and guess the average from a swinging needle by his side. The design, however, of the Distant Reading ("DR") Compass was based on a "Heath Robinson" idea which, in practice, would obviously be unsuitable. The entries in my flying log book record that I spent many hours flight testing it in various aircraft, which confirmed its inferiority compared with other designs; but Richards insisted on continuing with it. Other designs – mainly American ones – were far superior and immediately available. But through sheer momentum, and the evil influence of Richards, the RAE version had been adopted for most of our aircraft, thus making Bomber and Coastal Commands far less efficient than they should have been.

As soon as the war started, I had been appointed as one of the team of specialists whose duty it was to rush to any German aircraft that was shot down, in order to extract all the instruments before the souvenir hunters could do so, and take them for examination back to the RAE. When the first German bomber was shot down near Edinburgh, I rushed up there in my MG to do so. The Heinkel had crashed near Gifford. When I arrived at the site, the whole area was swarming with sightseers. Luckily, I managed to persuade anyone who had already extracted any instruments to give them to me and I collected the whole set. The hotel at Gifford was thoroughly overcrowded and I had to sleep that night in the only available space – on the floor in the bar – with the instruments safely hidden in my greatcoat beside me. Back at Farnborough, the boffins were, like me, surprised at their sophistication. The Germans appeared not to have the handicap of some scientists working against their national interests.

A development had been started long before I arrived at RAE to try to simplify the procedure for determining position from observation of the stars – astronomical navigation. The calculations alone, after a sextant observation on a couple of stars, could take up to a quarter of an hour to complete. One of the inputs was sidereal time – which differs both from local time and GMT. So the complicated instrument I mentioned was under development to simplify that task. That, to me, was just nibbling at a tiny part of a much bigger problem. So I took a few steps back to get a full view of the whole issue, asking myself: what is the real aim?

As in a ship – from which practically all our navigation practices have evolved – the navigator worked on a chart on the table. Therefore, he wanted the result of any astronomical observation to appear on his chart as a single point showing his position. It was nonsense to expect a navigator to fiddle with slide rules for a quarter of an hour (possibly with shells bursting round him over Germany) to work that out, convert it into latitude and longitude and then plot it on his chart. All data had, I decided, to be projected down onto the chart on which he was already working – preferably automatically.

[That principle, on which I insisted, also influenced several other future developments – including the Air Position Indicator (API) and Ground Position Indicator (GPI). These, based on an Air Log, merely calculated the DR position in the same way as the old mariners did – but mechanically and continuously.]

I knew that Commander "Daddy" Weems in the USA (with whom I later formed an excellent friendship) had produced a series of Star Charts giving lines of the altitude of the main stars. With help from our astronomer, Professor Plaskett, and from Pritchard, I had the Weems Star Charts transferred on to film. Because a projector to cover the area of the chart would be far too costly, and difficult in wartime to produce, Harry designed a simple little 35mm projector that we could slide over the chart to cover just the small area on which the navigator was interested. I felt we were beginning to solve the problem, but when I tested it in the air I found it quite useless – bumps and acceleration made it slide about too much. So, I decided, it would have to be a fixed projector above the chart – but with the optical industry already overstretched on other projects, that presented a difficult problem.

I mentioned this to Lamplough. He came up with the suggestion that we could use just a simple torch bulb (attached to the roof above the navigator's table) shining through the film, with the lines on it producing a shadow on the chart. I tested that and found it worked almost better than a wide-angle lens projector and produced less distortion. We called it the Shadowgraph. But that left us still with one problem – the automatic calculation of sidereal time to roll the film to the correct position for that location and time.

I consulted the Admiralty Nautical Almanac Office, Harry, Richards, Plaskett, and others. No one came up with any ideas. Sadler, head of the Almanac Office, said it was impossible – so did Plaskett. Then, one morning, Lamplough (to whom I had also mentioned the problem) arrived very excited. He had come up with a brilliant idea of incorporating, into the film, a way of completely eliminating the need to calculate sidereal time.

We proposed this to our Professor of Astronomy – Plaskett. He worked intensively on it for two days. He then presented me with a lengthy treatise proving mathematically, and conclusively, that it could not possibly work. Lamplough (who knew nothing about astronomy, but had a very logical brain) argued with him and suggested we should try it out. I knew that some specialists can get so involved in their particular subject that they cannot see the wood for the trees, and persuaded Harry to go ahead and construct what we then called the Astrograph, which incorporated Lamplough's new idea, which we named "Astrograph Mean Time". I tested it. It worked perfectly. It was fitted in all suitable aircraft, greatly helped our navigators and saved many lives.

The navigation specialists at Bomber Command were Wing Commander Toni Ragg (who, I believe, had been the first pilot to land an aircraft on a platform under an airship) and Squadron Leader Chilton, with whom I worked more closely when he became deputy to Mackworth at the Air Ministry.

One day I had a call from Chilton to say that Kelly Barnes (one of our small group of Navigation Specialists), while piloting one of our flying boats near Iceland, had become lost and made an emergency landing there. Iceland was a neutral country at that time and so he faced being interned there for the duration of the war. The cause of him getting lost had been the apparent failure of his compass in that area.

"Top priority, Tubby," Chilton told me. "You've got to find some way of preventing this happening again."

I immediately realised that it was the same old problem of the magnetic compass needle trying to point down to nearer the centre of the earth at the magnetic pole, instead of horizontally towards the North, as I have already explained. The solution, therefore, was to determine direction from some other source. At night the Pole Star gave an approximate direction of North. But that was rarely visible, even at night, during most of the summer in northern latitudes. So we needed something easy to use (day or night) that would enable us to establish the direction of North.

I quickly researched (at the Science Museum and British Museum in London, Greenwich Observatory, etc) all the types of gadgets that the Chinese, Romans and other early navigators had used, seeking ideas. Within two days I had completed a diagram of the sort of instrument I wanted to try. The workshop then constructed a rough working model.

I tested it in the air. It worked. With just one figure taken from the Nautical Almanac and my watch giving me GMT, that gadget could determine North pretty accurately, day or night, providing I could see the sun, moon or stars. It could also be used to help a bomber returning from Germany to fly at the correct latitude to reach his home airfield.

Rather than run the risk of Richards finding excuses to delay it, I rushed with it in my car to the instrument makers Hughes, where my navigator friend Francis Chichester (then only of "Seaplane Solo" fame) was helping them with aircraft instrument design. He was quite excited about it. We went in together to see Everett, the chief engineer, to get his opinion. He too was excited by it.

There was no point in me patenting my invention – serving officers were never entitled to any proceeds from patents they took out. So I offered to let Everett take out a patent for my invention in his own name if, in exchange, he would quickly have a couple of properly engineered models constructed for me to test and demonstrate to Coastal and Bomber Commands. He did. Also, he was so convinced of the urgent need for such an instrument that he started planning immediately for his company to produce it.

I tested and then demonstrated the models he produced in both flying boats and bombers. The tests were successful and the Astro Compass was fitted to all appropriate aircraft. In addition to its use for determining direction in Arctic waters, it helped several aircraft return safely from raids over Germany that might otherwise have been lost. My original model was designed for use in the northern hemisphere, but the Mark 2 model was for use worldwide. At the end of the war (like Lamplough for the Drift Recorder) I was given a government award for my invention of the Astro Compass.

Meanwhile, the pilot who had been interned in Iceland – Kelly Barnes, who was one of our most brilliant and enterprising ex-Cranwell cadets and under whom I was later privileged to serve – had not relished the prospect of being interned in Iceland, away from his girlfriend, for the rest of the war. So he organised a brilliant escape to England (which hit the headlines), grabbed his girlfriend, married her, and got her back with him to be re-interned in Iceland, where they enjoyed a prolonged honeymoon until Iceland joined in the war against Germany and released them.

Professor Blackett (the discoverer of Cosmic Rays, who later became President of the Royal Society) was one of the many scientists who had joined RAE on the outbreak of war. I had mentioned to him the awful problem of the pilot having to fly in a long straight line approaching the target in order to aim his bomb. He came up with the idea of developing a relatively simple gyro-stabilised bombsight that would alleviate that problem, and which could also be used at lower levels. The Americans already had very complicated ones (like the Norden), but Richards had successfully prevented progress along those lines in England. Blackett sought my advice as an aircrew (although my experience as a bomb aimer was limited to a few flights in that capacity at Leuchars and Manston) and I was able to help him with the design and testing of it. It went into production and helped improve our bombing accuracy – providing, of course, the aircrew had found and could see the target. (That latter restriction remained the main difficulty for most of the war.)

For the first few months that I was at Farnborough the "Phoney War" with Germany mainly involved Bomber Command only dropping leaflets over enemy territory. Then the real battle started – the invasion of France, Dunkirk, the rejection by France of Churchill's offer that we joined together as one country, the French surrender, and the successes of the German U-boats sinking our ships in the Atlantic.

The fact that the French even blocked their runways to prevent our aircraft taking off showed how far they were prepared to go over to the German side to save their own skins. I felt no sorrow when I heard that – to prevent it falling into German hands – we had sunk the French Mediterranean fleet. Morale throughout England fell to its lowest level. Several of the civil servants at Farnborough were advocating that we should surrender immediately. I knew, only too well, the small size of Fighter Command compared with the German Air Force – also the limitations of Bomber Command.

Many other people, including some politicians, also began advocating surrendering to the Germans. It was a terribly depressing time. Looking back, I have often wondered what the result of surrender would have been. Hitler's hatred of the Jews – largely because he had caught syphilis from a Jewish girl – would certainly have resulted in the massacre of all the Jews in England, and the Jewish state of Israel would not have been formed and so reduced the Palestinian problem. Also, he might have conquered Russia and put an end to communism. But, at the time, we were only concerned with the immediate future – and that looked so terrible that morale fell to a level which few people now realise. Surrender looked to many the only option.

Then came Churchill's magnificent speeches. In a few minutes the whole situation changed. From deep gloom, everyone became excited and utterly determined never to surrender. Even if we did not win the war, we would rather die than let the Germans rule us. But, led by Churchill, we now even had a faint chance – and hope – of winning. The sudden change in everyone seemed like a miracle. It has since become fashionable to denigrate Churchill. Anyone not in England at that time cannot possibly have any idea of the enormous debt we owe to that great man or pass judgement on him.

We knew that the coming battle for air supremacy would decide our future. I felt that any developments on which we were then working at RAE would be too late to have much effect on that. So I put in a request that I should be posted back to a flying job and given command of a fighter squadron.

Expecting to be parted from her anyway, I persuaded Bunny that we should take advantage of the offer from Dorothy Miller for her to take Pam to Canada. If things went badly in England, I argued, they would be safer there. If we won the war, then they could come back – or make a new life in Canada. I sent a cable to the Millers at Trenton, Ontario; their reply came back immediately, inviting Bunny to take Pam there.

We had moved from the house in Farnham to a delightful cottage in the nearby village of The Sands, next to the golf course. I remember walking up and down our lawn there, debating with Bunny what would be best. Finally, I persuaded her that she should go to Canada. I rang Harry to say I would not be in the office the next day – urgent business in London.

I drove up to London early next morning and was in the shipping office near Pall Mall immediately it opened. I told the chap behind the counter that I wanted a berth for my wife and baby on the next ship going to Canada and produced the cable from the Millers to prove she had accommodation to go to there. (Without that she would not have been allowed to go.) He said they were all fully booked for weeks ahead. I was, of course, in Squadron Leader's uniform with my tin hat and gas mask slung from my shoulder, and my loaded pistol in its holster.

I took out my pistol and laid it on the counter.

"Look," I said, "I am in deadly earnest. It is imperative that I have a berth on the next ship going to Canada. I insist that you find me a berth on it."

He turned a shade paler and disappeared into the back office.

He returned: "I have managed to find a berth, Sir. The train to Glasgow leaves London at 6 pm tonight, but you will need to be there much earlier to fight your way through the crowd."

I wanted to know the name of the ship, but he explained that none of the staff there knew the names of any of the ships – just the numbers of berths available. All shipping movements were closely guarded secrets.

I rushed back to Bunny, armed with the boat tickets and train reservations, pausing only at the bank to cash a cheque for all I could afford. Bunny cut open Pam's teddy bear and stuffed it with those banknotes to give her money on arrival in Canada. We packed just Bunny's essentials into a suitcase light enough for her to carry herself. Then, with heavy hearts, we motored to the station in London and fought our way through the milling crowds of people seeking to evacuate the capital. When I kissed them goodbye, Bunny and I were in tears and Pam was crying. We knew it was unlikely that we would ever see each other again.

But, as I drove back, I consoled myself with the thought that I had done the best thing for them. I knew I could not expect any communication from Bunny until she arrived in Canada – which, if they were sailing in a convoy, would be at least ten days.

I returned home feeling extremely sad. Without my two darlings, the lovely cottage seemed more like a mortuary. I wept copiously and, although I am not religious, I went down on my knees and prayed fervently that they would reach Canada safely and that I would see them again.

The next morning I bought myself a small pocket atlas in which to mark the location in Canada to which they were heading, and my estimation of where, each day, they would be on their voyage across the Atlantic. At RAE, I threw myself into my work with increased fervour, trying to forget.

Then, on the third day after they left, came the announcement that the Arandora Star, en route to Canada from Glasgow with hundreds of women and children on board, had been sunk. The area given was exactly where I calculated Bunny's ship would be. It came as a tremendous shock. I tried desperately to find out whether she had been on that ship, or the name of the ship she was on – but with no success. Wartime secrecy about shipping was too tight. But I assumed they must have been on it. Life seemed hardly worth living. I hoped my posting to a fighter squadron would come through soon.

But a visit to RAE by the Inspector General of the RAF put an end to those aspirations. The Air Marshal had come to discuss the work and value of the RAF officers attached to that organisation. He was apparently advised by the senior boffins that my varied flying experience and navigational knowledge had proved of such great help to them that the value to the war effort of me staying at RAE would far exceed me being employed just as a pilot. In spite of my protests at my interview with him, Air Chief Marshal Sir Edgar Ludlow-Hewitt ruled that I was to remain at RAE on the Special Duties List. Air Marshal Sir Roderick Hill (who was my boss on the Special Duty List in London) confirmed that to me in a handwritten letter, adding that the knowledge I had acquired about several highly secret projects would in any case now prohibit me from any operational flying that would risk me being captured by the Germans.

Meanwhile, believing that Bunny and Pam were both dead, I began facing up to life without them. It was too depressing to remain alone in our cottage. I decided to move back into a room at the Senior Staff Mess at RAE – just outside the main gate and up the hill on the left, with a good view of the airfield. I suggested to Dr Temple (the brilliant mathematician from London University and one of the most delightful characters I have ever had as a friend) that he should move into our cottage and get his family down from London to join him – which he later did.

It was nearly two weeks since Bunny had left and I had still heard nothing. Hope had faded. I was packing up my things at The Sands to make that move when a telegram arrived. I was loathe to open it. I feared that it was confirmation that Bunny and Pam were dead. Eventually, with trembling hands, I tore open the envelope. I could scarcely believe my eyes. It was, in fact, a cable from Bunny in Halifax saying they had reached there and expected to be staying with Dorothy Miller in a few days' time. I sat down, crying my eyes out with relief. It was one of the most emotional moments in my life. It is impossible to describe my feelings.

From a letter she had written the same day that she had sent the cable, but which took nearly two additional weeks to reach me, I later learned that two ships in their convoy had been sunk, that Pam had been ill and nearly died, but was now in hospital, but that she and Pam were being looked after marvellously by the Canadian Red Cross, with Pam recovering fast and that they hoped to go to the Millers the following week.

Unknown to me at the time, Wilf Oulton had also accepted the invitation from Dorothy Miller to send his wife Terry and her baby to Canada. In consequence, Dorothy had arranged for Bunny and Pam to move (almost next door) to stay with her sister Nancy, who was married to another RCAF officer, Bob Cameron.

Wilf Oulton, who had been commanding a Coastal Command Squadron at St Eval in Cornwall, had been posted to the Operational Requirements branch at the Air Ministry in London and so was in daily touch with me. He and I had decided that if a German invasion was successful and we surrendered, we would each make our way to a rendezvous on the Welsh coast. There, in a cove that he knew from his childhood in that area, he arranged for a small boat to be adequately provisioned to enable us to sail across the Atlantic with a view to joining the RCAF – and our wives. We planned it all in some detail. We would first sail south and go via the Azores to avoid the headwinds. I prepared the charts and navigational instruments we would need to get us to our destination.

I was the only RAF officer in the Senior Mess and my companions there were about a dozen of our top scientists who had come to RAE to help the war effort and had decided to make the Senior Mess their temporary home. Those "Super Boffins" were wonderful characters, each brilliant in his own field and all extremely friendly towards me. We all fed together at the same large table. I learnt more during those meals and discussions than I would have done at any university – in a whole variety of subjects. It was there, for example, that I first learned about the possible development of an atomic bomb and of the technical problems of constructing one.

The main building, in which we also had our bedrooms, had a cellar that we could use as an emergency air raid shelter. I used to park my MG on the other side of a tree near the corner of the building. Although Farnborough had never been bombed, the air raid warnings were so frequent that we tended not to pay much attention to them, unless we heard the noise of approaching aircraft.

One afternoon, although the sirens had given warning, a few of us were having tea there in the dining room when I thought I heard aircraft and rushed to the door. I saw, coming straight towards us (memories of 1917!) from the far end of the airfield, a large formation of aircraft at about 8,000 feet. (I seem to remember that they were the first – and last – Italian raid on England and that they were all shot down before they left our shores.)

I saw the first bombs start falling from the aircraft. I shouted to the others to get down to the cellar, and rushed there myself, strapping on my tin hat and getting my gas mask out of its case. We put on our gas masks and waited. We heard the bangs getting closer, followed by a tremendous bang that shook the building, loosening the bricks in the roof of the cellar – one of which fell out and dented my tin hat, temporarily stunning me.

When there were no more bangs, Willie Wilson (one of the test pilots who had been having tea with us) crept out to have a look. He called for us to come out. At the corner of our building there was a crater about 15 yards across and about 12 feet deep, made by the bomb that had just missed our building. The tree that had stood there was about 60 yards away; but my MG, a few feet from the edge of the hole, was still parked there completely unharmed. The bomb must have been fairly deep in the ground when it exploded, with the blast going high above my car. I was far more concerned with my car than I was with the narrow escape we had experienced.

The airfield, however, was now of completely different appearance. To our amazement, the whole area nearest to us seemed completely white. Very puzzling. The only building that had suffered any damage was one adjacent to the sick quarters – that appeared to have taken a direct hit. The mystery of the white airfield was only solved when "Septic Sam" (our resident doctor) explained that the bombed building had contained all the medical records of everyone there since the First World War. They now resembled a layer of snow on the airfield.

Septic Sam deserves a mention for his well-earned reputation for rapid reaction in emergency. A year or so previously, an aircraft had crashed on the airfield. The pilot had been hurt and was trapped in the cockpit, with the aircraft nearly on its back. Another pilot, who had just landed, rushed to try to help the injured pilot and had managed to make a hole in the fabric at the side, through which he was trying to reach the pilot. He had squeezed his way through the hole and was kicking with his legs trying to get further in when Septic Sam arrived in his "blood wagon". Septic Sam saw the kicking legs and assumed the owner was badly injured and in agony. So he promptly gave the gallant rescuer an injection in his leg to render him unconscious. Both, however, survived.

Most of us preferred to use a doctor in the nearby town.

I was based at RAE throughout the Battle of Britain. We kept any Spitfires and other fighters (which we were using for research) fully armed and ready in case we could assist. We were not directly involved – except on one occasion while I was flying a Magister (a trainer with no armament) at near-stalling speed to test one of the instruments. I spotted a Messerschmitt diving towards me. I managed to escape by flipping the Magister into a spin and only pulling out at a very low level.

Apart from working even harder to help provide the aircrew in the front line with better equipment, there was nothing we could do but listen to the news, and hope.

We all knew the outcome of the battle for air superiority would decide the future of Europe. The rumour went round that the Germans planned to castrate all Englishmen. Abolish our favourite sport? Not bloody likely! We listened to the evening broadcasts anxiously to learn the latest scores of our Hurricanes and Spitfires. Our future was on a knife-edge. I then learned of the official estimate that if the Germans continued attacking our fighter airfields for even just four more days, then Germany would probably win that battle. Without those airfields, Fighter Command could not have continued to put up enough resistance. Hope was beginning to fade – at least amongst those of us who knew how desperate the true situation really was.

It was the brilliant decision by Churchill – to send a couple of aircraft to bomb Berlin – that saved Europe. That caused Hitler, furious at the breach of his promise that Berlin would never be bombed, to order their bomber attacks to be switched from our fighter airfields to bomb London. We all regretted the casualties and damage in London, but that was THE turning point in the war. Few people realise that – but it gave Fighter Command the breathing space to recover – resulting in us winning the Battle of Britain.

They were tremendously emotional days – for everyone. When, for example, I was getting on a bus in Piccadilly, the conductress refused to take my proffered fare and instead, looking at the wings on my uniform, she put her arms round my neck and kissed me, saying, "Thank you, thank you all!" I felt the same about the Air Raid Wardens, and the wonderful people in London who withstood those awful raids (some of which I personally experienced) – we were all in it together.

The danger of an invasion across the Channel remained. The powerful speeches by Churchill, to which everyone listened on the wireless, rallied the nation to a degree that is difficult to understand in England today. The strong emotions they generated cemented a bond between everyone. I still get tears in my eyes when I listen to recordings of those wonderful speeches.

At Farnborough, in our spare time and to get some exercise, we helped the workers build tank traps (blocks of concrete) on vulnerable approaches to the airfield. I also lectured members of Dad's Army on how to differentiate between enemy planes and our own. And in case the Germans did invade, we made plans (while resisting every step) to continue the fight elsewhere.

By that autumn, I had instigated every development for new types of instrument that I thought could help the navigator. We had considered inertial navigation instruments, but the development and production of gyros with the necessary precision were still considered impossible in England during wartime. The best hope for navigational and bombing accuracy lay in the radio developments going on at other establishments.

We knew the Germans were using intersecting radio beams for their night bombing of cities like Coventry. Don Stokes, I later learned, was flying most nights trying to trace and track these beams. That was the type of development that would most help our bombers. Counter-measures to bend the beams and also develop our own were where the radio developments were leading. Oboe and GEE were already being discussed and a Doppler navigation aid was also on the horizon. The key development that I advocated was for the radio boys to find some way of presenting the navigator with a picture of the prominent points on the ground below.

With the danger of an invasion decreasing, the Air Ministry had started planning for a much longer war than previously, and it was decided to move much of the training to Canada.

One afternoon in late August, I received a phone call from Group Captain P. D. Robertson – the CO of the School of Air Navigation, that had by then moved from Manston to St Athan in South Wales. He said that the school was to be moved to Canada and he wanted someone right up to date with new developments to ensure the graduates were trained to operate them. He said he had asked Air Ministry to appoint me Chief Instructor and to be his deputy and was ringing up to warn me that I could expect that posting to come through any day. This carried with it the implication that I would be promoted to Wing Commander. With most of the developments with which I was concerned at RAE nearing fruition, and future gadgets to aid the navigator more likely to come from the radio boffins at TRE – as indeed they did – I felt it was a logical time to take on another challenge.

I also received a phone call from Chilton saying that another reason for me being sent to Canada was so that I could brief the relevant staff of both the US Army Air Force and the US Navy about all the recent navigational developments in England.

My posting came through a few days later and I motored down to St Athan in South Wales in a state of euphoria that I might soon be reunited with Bunny. To my surprise, I found that my deputy at the Navigation School would be Don Stokes, who had passed out of Cranwell just senior to me, but who (because of my accelerated promotion) was now junior to me. I feared that might cause resentment, but there was none – just loyal co-operation. Don was a splendid officer and remained one of my best friends until his death a few years ago.

We understood that our new location would be Port Albert, near Goderich – a small town on the banks of Lake Huron, in Ontario. For security reasons, however, only the CO, Don and I were supposed to know that. We also understood that the new airfield and accommodation would all be ready for us on arrival.

We managed to organise that Don's wife and baby should accompany him. The only other officer for whom I was able to arrange that he should take his family was a newly-commissioned young doctor – Basil Kent – who expressed his everlasting gratitude.

Group Captain P. D. Robertson ("One Eye Robbie", as he was affectionately known) was a wonderful character. Before the First World War he had served before the mast in the Merchant Navy. That had left him with a vocabulary that was the envy of all to whom he recounted his wealth of stories about life at that time. During the First World War he had become a pilot, but subsequently lost an eye and had his face and lungs badly burnt pulling another pilot out of a burning aircraft that had crashed. For this he had been awarded the Albert Medal.

While Don looked after the continuing instructional side of the school, my main task was to organise the transportation of several hundred personnel, 30 aircraft with spares and other equipment, across an ocean in wartime to over a thousand miles inside another continent, with winter approaching. That was a completely new sort of challenge and proved an interesting experience.

Meanwhile, at St Athan – just to show the pathetic state of our defences – all our slow old Ansons, with relays of any pilots with wings (whether staff or pupils) to fly them – were on standby, day and night, to take off at 20 minutes' notice, armed with just two 20lb bombs and the pistols in their belts, to help repel a German invasion! Meanwhile, all our ground personnel helped Dad's Army patrol the airfield to deal with German parachutists.

I was not allowed to mention anything about the move to Bunny in my letters, but tried to hint that – just possibly – we might soon be reunited.

Chapter 11

Chief Instructor

In November 1940, the German attacks on our shipping were causing so many casualties that we decided to move the Navigation School to Canada in two parts in the hope that at least one half should survive the journey. Robbie and I went with the advance party with half the instructors and men. Don would follow with the remainder a couple of weeks later.

For the first part of our voyage across the Atlantic our ship was in a convoy of about twenty others, with a couple of destroyers to help protect us all. We experienced one alert, when we seemed to be under attack from a German submarine, but the destroyers dealt with that satisfactorily. But later, as we entered waters further away from Europe, which were therefore deemed less dangerous, the two destroyers departed to take up other duties and all the ships in the convoy separated out, each heading independently for its own destination. It gave us an uneasy feeling to see the destroyers depart, and the other ships gradually disappear over the horizon, while knowing that there might still have been a German U-boat following us, waiting for the chance to sink us.

Throughout the voyage we had, of course, to wear flotation jackets (day and night) and carry out frequent boat drills because of the threat. I thought of the worrying time it must have been for Bunny, particularly after two ships in her convoy had already been sunk. I had been appointed OC Troops and thus had the additional responsibility concerning the conduct of all the personnel. That was not too difficult in the rough seas we encountered, because most of them were too seasick to cause any trouble.

The day after the departure of the destroyers we ran into a Force 11 gale that made the ship slow right down – a worse gale than any I had experienced while serving in the Fleet Air Arm. I remember standing with Robbie, in a sheltered nook on deck, with him telling me of his experiences in ships before the First World War. Both of us were apprehensive that a German U-boat might still find us, but – unlike me – he was not the slightest bit scared of the enormous waves thudding against our bow or the howling wind sending the spray flying as high as our mast – he had experienced far worse earlier in his life.

At Halifax, the Canadians gave us a tremendous welcome. At the first opportunity I phoned Bunny. I did not know her number but only the area, so the Halifax exchange put me through to Trenton, where the operator said:

"Oh, you want the little English lady staying with Nancy Cameron. I think she's in. I'll put you through." That was the measure of the personal service – from 1,000 miles away – that one received in those days.

As I have already mentioned, wartime security had prevented me from telling Bunny about my movements or destination. All I had been able to convey to her was that there was a slight chance that we might be reunited. So when I told her I was in Halifax, she was too emotional at first to speak coherently, but finally understood we would soon be meeting in a place called Goderich – only just over a hundred miles from where she was.

Robbie and I, with our three hundred officers and men of the advance party, spent two days on the train, passing through scenery enhanced by the marvellous colours of the trees in that Indian summer. Arriving at Port Albert, we found that construction of the airfield and accommodation was far from finished – the contractors' dates had slipped badly. With winter approaching, it was not easy to cope – but it was amazing how, in wartime, everyone mucked in and co-operated. By the time Don arrived with the other half, we were ready, in a makeshift way, to start instructing the pupils.

One very touching gesture was to find, awaiting us, small bundles of warm clothes – like hand-knitted woollen socks, each pair labelled with the name of the person who had donated them – with a note wishing these valiant airmen from England a hearty welcome. They were, I believe, organised by the Canadian Red Cross and were symbolic of the warmth with which we were everywhere received.

Goderich - Canada

Bunny and I had a wonderful reunion at the hotel in Goderich. I remember Pam running towards me as soon as she saw me, excitedly shouting, "Daddy! Daddy!" We could not believe our luck in all being together again. The local papers reported our reunion, and helpful residents quickly found us a lovely bungalow to rent on the cliff overlooking Lake Huron. Our lawn and garden went right to the cliff edge. It was idyllic. Frosty mornings, wonderful colouring on the trees, and beautiful sunsets over Lake Huron. We were very, very happy.

Then it started snowing. And it continued snowing. The area for about ten miles inland from Lake Huron had massive falls compared with further inland – which often had bright sunshine, while we had continuous snow. This is because the west wind picks up moisture crossing Lake Huron and deposits it as snow on the adjacent land; but, having then travelled only over land, where it picked up no more moisture, the air becomes brilliantly clear. Whoever decided to locate the airfield at Port Albert, instead of in an area further inland, either needed his head examined – or, more likely, had a financial interest in that particular piece of land being taken over by the Government.

Sometimes I could not get along the coast roads to the airfield ten miles away, in spite of the highly efficient snowploughs. And the airfield itself was completely unusable for several days on end. Furthermore, because the snow came from a relatively thin layer of cloud, with the sun shining above, the diffused brightness badly affected our eyes. That winter we sometimes had howling winds with temperatures below minus 30 C, and soon learnt never to touch cold metal with bare fingers, or go out when it was snowing without strong sunglasses.

The local community in Goderich were just wonderful. On learning that two other officers were bringing their wives and children with them, they made sure there was somewhere suitable for them to rent, and then gave them a splendid welcome.

We ran two types of navigation courses. The main one was the Specialist Navigation Course for selected officers – like the one I had undergone at Manston – and the other for groups of pupils on a shorter course to turn them into operational navigators for Bomber and Coastal Commands. Amongst the officers attending the Specialist course were many who became good friends of mine or served with me later. Amongst the former was a young ex-Cranwell cadet named Jimmy Stack, who later (as Air Chief Marshal Sir Neville Stack) became Gentleman Usher to the Queen and – much more importantly – was my guest, with his charming wife, fishing the River Lochy in Scotland a few years ago. Many of the others remained friends during their lifetime; but most, unfortunately, are no longer around.

One of our handicaps at Port Albert was the narrow roads on the camp – all were single track, with few passing places. We had a civilian liaison officer – a French Canadian from Quebec – who had been given complete authority to deal with the contractors on behalf of the Headquarters in Ottawa. I later found that all roads should have been double width, and that various other things had been skimped by the contractors – but also that the French Canadian had acquired a splendid new house in Quebec! (I was later told that a branch of the same firm of contractors had built it for him.)

Similarly, there seemed a strange shortage of things in the Officers' Mess, where I had appointed a Flight Lieutenant as the

Mess Secretary to deal with the contractors who supplied us. He, I then found, had suddenly acquired a lovely new car that I knew he could not have afforded himself. These were my first experiences of business practices that I later learned were pretty commonplace. Nothing in my Cranwell training – or previous experience – had prepared me for that sort of thing; but I was moving up the learning curve quite quickly.

Robbie was a wonderful CO and the school ran very smoothly. Don looked after most of the academic training: I concentrated more on the practical flying side and helping the CO run the station. The flying, apart from the delays caused by bad weather, was very similar to what had been routine at Manston and presented few problems. The only serious incident was when two of our aircraft collided in mid-air, about 40 miles from the airfield, while flying at night – a chance of one in a million – and we never discovered why it had happened. But that reinforced my feeling that collisions were the main danger in flying.

We had, of course, the usual crop of incidents. Two of the airmen, while clambering over the jagged rocks of ice that built up near the shore on the frozen lake, fell in and were drowned. Two others, unfamiliar with the Canadian flora, were out on a long walk and happened to use the leaves of poison ivy as toilet paper. That resulted in them spending a couple of very uncomfortable weeks in hospital.

Meanwhile, the local residents welcomed our wives into their community (Bunny, Don's wife Bunch, and the wife of our young doctor, Basil Kent – all with young children) and we led a pleasant social life. (The Kent baby – Roderick – later became chairman of Close Brothers.)

I remember Bunny and I being entertained at dinner in the old, rather gloomily-furnished house the Kent's had rented. All round the dismal dining room walls were even more dreary oil paintings of the owner's ancestors. Basil had commented on how dark and depressing they found that room – particularly the pictures. I looked round the walls and could not but agree with him. One picture in particular, of a really fierce and ugly woman, caught my eye.

"That one," I said, pointing to it, "is really horrible. If I were you I'd get rid of it. Having that hawk-eyed old witch looking down at meal-times is too awful for words."

His wife burst into tears.

"That," Basil explained, "is the only possession we were able to bring with us. It is a painting of her mother."

I am often quite good at putting my foot in it. On that occasion, I could think of no way of extracting it.

The aircraft we were flying were the same type as we had at Manston – the Anson – and much of the training was similar. But I had introduced into the lectures details of the new types of equipment that was now beginning to be fitted in newer aircraft – for example, the Astrograph, Drift Recorder and Astro Compass.

In addition to flying the Ansons, I was also able to fly a Beechcraft of the RCAF. I then learnt, for the first time, of the navigation facilities – the Radio Range system – used throughout North America, in conjunction with the Bendix Radio Compass. I had never heard of it before and it was a real eye-opener to me. The RAF had good pilots, but as regards aviation, in its broader sense, the Americans and Canadians were way ahead of us and their aircraft far better equipped.

England could not produce enough aircraft and it had been decided to purchase several different types of aircraft from the USA. To help ensure those aircraft (eg the Mustang) met our requirements, an office known as the British Air Commission ("BAC") had been opened, first in New York and then moved to Washington DC, to be nearer the US Navy and Army Headquarters. Wing Commander Tony Ragg (with whom I had worked closely when he was at Bomber Command) was Chief of the Navigation and Instrument Branch of the BAC. (At that time, early 1941, America was still at peace – although quietly helping us.)

When Tony Ragg learnt that I was now in Canada, he arranged for the head of the Instrument Department of the Bureau of Aeronautics, US Navy (Admiral Clyde Smith) and the senior navigator of the US Army Air Corps, as it was then (General Skippy Harbold) to visit Port Albert so that I could brief them on the developments going on at Farnborough that might help their own work. That also resulted later in a visit by Ed Link – the inventor of the Link Trainer – and then the decision to locate his new Link Astronomical Navigational Trainer at Port Albert, so that I could arrange and supervise the testing of it both for the RAF and American forces. Thus began my long friendship with Ed Link that had quite an influence on my life.

Don helped me with the tests of the new Astronomical trainer – a large rotating dome representing the sky with the stars projected onto it, with a section of an aircraft underneath equipped with the instruments that a navigator was being trained to use to determine his position. Many of our staff were involved and one of them – a brilliant Canadian named Ken Maclure – developed a new system of navigation in response to the problem I gave him of navigating across the North Pole. We named his system "Grid Navigation", which became widely used in northern latitudes.

The Canadian winter was very tough for dear old Robbie. The burns he had sustained during the First World War had not only cost him his eye and a badly disfigured face, but had also damaged his lungs. He developed pneumonia and Basil Kent (our doctor) warned me that he was unlikely to survive. By that time, my promotion to Wing Commander had come through and I automatically took over command as soon as he became ill.

Miraculously, Robbie managed to pull through. To help his convalescence, we invited him to stay with us in our comfortable bungalow. But it was still touch and go whether he would survive. We received, from time to time, a batch of newspapers from England. I was careful not to let him see any, as they often had announcements that some of his friends had died or been killed. I thought it would depress him and hinder his recovery.

One newspaper announced the death of his great friend Group Captain Ap Ellis, who had served with him in the First World War. I hid that paper carefully away – fearful that the news of his friend's death would have on him. Our maid found the paper and was carrying it through the sitting room to throw it away, but Robbie saw her with it.

"That an English paper?" he demanded. "Give it to me – haven't seen one for ages."

Bunny and I watched anxiously for what effect the news of the death of his old friend would have on his frail health. His reaction was completely different from what we expected.

"I've beaten him!" he shouted excitedly, and from that moment his recovery became rapid. Each time he read of another of his friends succumbing, he would exclaim, "And I've beaten that bugger too!"

He took an extremely positive attitude to life. But the doctors decided that he was too frail to stand another cold winter and he was posted to the warmer climate of Patricia Bay, on Vancouver Island. After the war, he went out to Australia to join his daughter. We corresponded regularly until he died there, aged 92.

That spring, Terry Oulton and her son Peter (who had stayed in Trenton with Nancy's sister, Dorothy Miller) came to live with us in Goderich. Wilf Oulton, meanwhile, was winning himself a DSO and DFC fighting German submarines in the Battle of the Atlantic. Following that, Wilf was posted to Washington as part of the British Delegation advising the US Navy on anti-submarine warfare. Terry then went down to join him there.

The Canadian people were marvellous to us and did everything they could to help. The North family, who owned a department store in Toronto, invited me to send up any of my officers who were in need of a rest to their luxurious log cabin on Smoke Lake in Algonquin Park, up in the wilds north of Toronto. That was typical of the generosity and friendliness that we found everywhere in Canada. Bunny and I took advantage of that offer ourselves for a couple of weeks in the summer. I learnt there to handle a birch-bark canoe (in which Bunny and I won the race one week) and to fish for black bass. We were enthralled by the wonderful peace and beauty of that area and returned to Goderich very refreshed.

That June, we had the exciting news that the Germans had invaded Russia, in spite of their peace pact with Hitler, and were advancing on Moscow at the rate of 20 miles per day. The Russians, apparently, were completely unprepared and were now pleading with us for assistance. If Germany conquered Russia, it would have eventually made it worse for us. But, remembering Napoleon's mistake, we greeted the news with enthusiasm and welcomed the fact that we now had a new ally in the struggle against Hitler.

I was beginning to find my job as Chief Instructor less challenging, now that we had brought the training up to date for the new equipment. It was becoming too routine – scores of pupils arriving, similar lectures and flying exercises, and the usual farewell speeches. I looked forward to visits from senior US Navy and Army Air Corps officers, who several times visited our navigation school to discuss future navigation developments with me.

Following one of these visits, Tony Ragg rang me up to say that the British Air Commission had received a request (which he had passed on to the Air Ministry) from both the US Army Air Corps and the US Navy Bureau of Aeronautics that I should be made available to act as liaison between their scientists and the Farnborough boffins. The Air Ministry, he said, had approved that request. Also, since he had just been promoted to Group Captain and would be leaving that post, it had been decided that I should take over his job at the British Air Commission.

I was thrilled at the prospect of again becoming involved in stimulating new projects. I knew also that Don was far better qualified to be Chief Instructor than me and would also, presumably, be promoted to Wing Commander, which he richly deserved.

We were sorry to leave Goderich and the many Canadian friends who had made us so welcome there. The other lasting memory of that area was of the wonderful sunsets reflected from the calm water in summer, or shining onto and through the great waves of ice that built up over Lake Huron in the winter. Sitting in the bay window, near the cliff edge, looking due west at the setting sun shining through those rocky pieces of ice sparkling in all the colours of the rainbow, was just magical.

Nevertheless, it was with great excitement that Bunny and I set out with Pam in our Ford Coupe to motor down to Washington to take up this new challenge. As a neutral country, America would not, of course, allow the wearing of foreign uniforms. So I again found myself posted to serve on the "Special Duty List" – this time as a civilian "Government Official".

Motoring via Montreal down through Vermont in the beautiful Indian summer weather in October 1941, with the colouring of the trees at their brilliant best, was an experience that I shall never forget. The challenge of this new job was also exhilarating.

Chapter 12

The British Air Commission

My posting to the RAF "Special Duty List" to take up my appointment as Chief of the Navigation and Instrument Branch at the civilian establishment known as the British Air Commission, Washington DC, was dated 11th October 1941. We motored down via Montreal, through some of the loveliest scenery we had yet seen. The trees in the Adirondack Mountains – indeed, all the way down – were in their full autumn colours and we found Washington to be one of the most beautiful cities we had yet visited.

Terry and Wilf had invited us to stay with them when we first arrived. We then spent a couple of weeks at a pleasant hotel in the country a few miles outside the capital at Chevvy Chase, until Bunny found a lovely furnished house to rent in nearby Silver Springs, on the edge of a wooded park, which became our home for the next three years. One of the first things I did was to buy a 35mm Kodak camera (at a drug store for $40 – about £8), with which I started taking the thousands of colour slides which record most events in my subsequent life. One of the first of those was of Pam using a stick to guide little paper boats down the stream in the woods just a few yards away from our house. [It was just like one of the pictures in Winnie the Pooh and brought tears to Pam's eyes when I gave her a copy shortly after Bunny's death.]

Tony Ragg arranged for me to be issued with an additional passport as a "Government Official" and also a special security pass, which gave me access to American Army and Naval bases and to information in the highest security classification (at that time "Most Secret"). He also confirmed that I would not be permitted to go on operations over Germany or run any risk of capture, because of the highly secret information that I would be acquiring.

He then took me on a brief tour round the USA to meet the main people with whom I would be working at the various aircraft manufacturers, instrument firms and research establishments.

At the latter I met, in particular, Major Tommy Thurlow at Wright Field, Ohio (the US Army Air Force equivalent of RAE Farnborough), where he was head of the navigation department, and Lieutenant Commander Chick Hayward, who was head of the corresponding US Navy organisation in Philadelphia. We three worked closely together for most of the war.

[The US Army Air Corps later became the US Air Force. To save confusion, I will refer to it throughout as the USAF.]

Tommy was already famous as the navigator and co-pilot for Howard Hughes when they made their record-breaking flight round the world. Chick was one of the most highly-regarded officers in the US Navy. Both, also, were test pilots. We three became great friends and worked as a team together splendidly. Chick was very popular with the ladies; he had a lovely wife and family, but he always claimed that his life's ambition was to live to the age of 99 and then be shot by a jealous husband.

BAC comprised a happy and dedicated bunch of fairly senior boffins, administrative staff, solicitors and a few RAF Specialist officers like myself. It was headed by Sir Richard Fairey, with Air Marshal Sir Roderick Hill, aided by Air Vice-Marshal R. O. Jones (two of our finest officers) as the senior RAF representatives. I already knew them and many of the boffins from my Farnborough days.

My immediate boss was Group Captain Heslop ("Slops"), who had been the engineering officer at Cranwell when I was a cadet and whom I had flown to Cairo while we were both in the Fleet Air Arm. He was happy to let me handle everything in my Navigation and Instrument Branch without interference, which meant that I could travel anywhere necessary (either flying myself in aircraft put at our disposal by the USAF, by train or by airline) and do anything that would help either the US forces or the RAF to fly or navigate better.

My Branch was concerned with navigation in the widest sense. That included all the aircraft instruments a pilot and his navigator needed to take off, do their job, and land back safely. The flying instruments needed by the pilot were similar in most types of aircraft, but the navigational and other requirements depended on the type of mission the aircraft was undertaking. But getting an aircraft to the correct position to do its job, or accurately cover an area of sea searching for submarines, still presented great difficulties, even without any enemy opposition. Enabling a transport aircraft to arrive at its destination was slightly less difficult, because the destination would normally be in friendly hands. But the final phase of any flight, which involved arriving accurately enough to land safely, was common to all missions. There was, at that time, no way of enabling the pilot reliably to do this in bad weather – that problem still lacked a solution. My Branch also covered autopilots, cameras for aerial reconnaissance and oxygen equipment.

Radio developments – on which accurate air navigation would clearly become largely dependent – were such a vast field that these were handled by a separate branch, headed by a splendid boffin (Dr Barton), with Cedric Bell (who had been at RAE when I was there and now was a Group Captain) as his deputy. We worked closely together.

We at BAC were very busy, but the Americans (not yet being at war) were far more relaxed and packed up work early on Friday afternoons – which meant our offices were closed as well. In consequence, Bunny and I took advantage of weekends to explore the area around Washington – the parks in their autumn colours, the buildings and monuments in the bright sunshine, and the surrounding countryside and mountains.

One Sunday afternoon, eight weeks after we arrived, we returned from a picnic in the Blue Ridge Mountains to find my secretary (Miss Umbsen) sitting on the doorstep of our house, waiting for us. She ran to our car as we turned into the drive to give us the news that the Japanese had attacked Pearl Harbour. She was so incoherent that I did not at first fully grasp the magnitude, or implications, of what she was trying to tell me. She was panic-stricken that Washington would be bombed that night. We took her inside and Bunny made tea to try to calm her down.

We tried listening to the radio. The news about the bombing of Pearl Harbour seemed true – but it was difficult to make sense of all the excited comments. One thing was clear, however – America was now at war with Japan. I was pretty certain that would soon mean with Germany too. We felt elated that England, at last, would not be left alone any longer in our struggle against Hitler. Exactly as the sinking of the *Lusitania* by a submarine (alleged at the time to be German – but was it?) had brought the USA to our rescue in the First World War, so the Japanese attack on Pearl Harbour caused the same result in the Second World War, although it was not until four days later that Germany (this time) declared war on America.

In spite of the awful casualties at Pearl Harbour (and perhaps because we had become accustomed to even more terrible news in Europe – Norway, Holland, Belgium and the London Blitz), the belief that America would now come into the war on our side was such a profound relief that I could barely conceal my excitement. I knew their armed forces were not well prepared, but I had already learnt enough about America to know the speed and determination with which that would be remedied. For the first time since that idiot Chamberlain had waved his bit of paper, saying, "Peace in our time", I began to feel confident about the future for England. I felt as though a great weight had been lifted off my back. I was able, quite convincingly, to reassure my secretary that she need have no fear whatsoever of any bombs falling on Washington and that she could go back to her home quite safely.

That evening, I received several phone calls. The first was from a panic-stricken director of an instrument company in New York with whom I had become friendly.

"Tubby," he pleaded, "I need your advice. You've been through this bombing business in England and know all about it. My wife and I are all packed up ready to leave. How far do you think we should go to be safe when bombs start falling on New York?"

"Bombs on New York?" I exclaimed. "How on earth do you think the Japs could reach you there?"

But he was in too much of a panic to listen to reason. "Who thought they would bomb Pearl Harbour?" he replied. "Better safe than sorry. We've arranged to go and stay with some friends about 50 miles away. Do you think that will be far enough?"

I gave up. "You'll be quite safe there," I assured him.

"Thanks, Tubby. It's a great comfort to have your advice. We're leaving right away."

The other phone calls were in similar vein. Most Americans, I realised (and it remains to a lesser extent still true today), were so involved with their own communities and so self-sufficient inside the USA that they knew little of the outside world. That highly intelligent chap in New York had never been outside the USA. Few Americans had travelled outside their own country (except sometimes to Canada or Mexico) – there were not many ships, and practically no aircraft, in which they could do so. He had no idea that the distance from Japan or from Germany far exceeded the range of any bomber then available.

That day, America changed dramatically. Until they themselves became directly involved in the war, most Americans had taken little notice of us British. Many of them had regarded our war with Germany to be a local European problem. But after Pearl Harbour we British suddenly became very popular and our advice on every subject was in great demand. Overnight, I had become a VIP so far as all my America friends and acquaintances were concerned. Bunny and I were inundated with invitations and the volume of calls for advice and co-operation overwhelmed my Branch at the BAC.

As I have mentioned, most air navigation throughout the American continent relied on the use of the Radio Range system – ground beacons that guided airliners along predetermined tracks. Additionally, a radio compass could be tuned into any of these beacons to show automatically on a compass dial its direction. In consequence, the accuracy of their magnetic compasses (and any other navigation equipment) was of little importance. Also, with the exception of a few pioneers, their aircrew were not skilled in, and knew little about, any other methods of navigation.

In any area accessible to enemy bombers, all radio beacons would have to be switched off, as they would otherwise assist the bombers to find their targets. So, like our own Bomber Command aircraft, the American bombers would have no reliable means of finding their way to a target in Japan or Europe, or of hitting it – even if they found it – unless they could see the ground. (This was one of the factors later influencing the USAF to concentrate on daylight raids against Germany.)

The demands on me in connection with the navigation problems came not only from the USAF and US Navy Bureau of Aeronautics, but also from airline pilots, the instrument firms, and the aircraft manufacturers. These latter had never worried unduly about the accuracy of the magnetic compasses in the aircraft they produced, but they now requested my help in showing them how, in England, we "swung" a compass to eliminate (or compensate for) the errors in it. In consequence, I was rushing from one manufacturer to another, from New York to California to Seattle, trying to help.

I became thoroughly overworked and caught a bug from Pam. This developed into a splitting headache with a line of extremely painful blisters on my forehead going towards my eye. Ed Link, whom I happened to be visiting in Binghampton, saw that I was unwell and recognised the symptoms of shingles. He strongly advised me to get back to Washington immediately to see a doctor – warning me that otherwise I might lose the sight of my eye. I took his advice.

I was treated by a German doctor who Bunny found living nearby. He traced the origin of my shingles to the bout of chickenpox that Pam had suffered a week or so before – and the stress of overwork. Pam only had a mild attack, from which she had quickly recovered. But my shingles were more serious and extremely painful. He gave me a smallpox vaccination to cure the shingles, and morphine to ease the pain. That treatment, and Ed Link's good advice, saved my eye.

Ten days later, I had recovered sufficiently to motor down to Florida to recuperate. The people I met there were marvellous to me. As a guest on a luxurious motor yacht, I caught the biggest sailfish so far that season – an event that resulted in publicity in the local press. That led to me being approached by a retired scientist who had recently developed a method of making a gyro-compass more accurate – and then by others with inventions that might help the war effort – all of which I passed on to the appropriate boffins.

Now that America was officially allied to us in the war against Germany and Japan, both the USAF and Navy became more relaxed in handing over secret information about their own developments that might help us. I thus became the centre for the exchange of this information, not only with the Air Ministry and RAE Farnborough, but even between the USAF and US Navy, who were each largely ignorant of what the other service had been doing. One of the important things we achieved, through "Standardisation Committees",

1941

was to ensure (whenever practicable) that all future American aircraft instruments and equipment would be interchangeable with British designs – and also between the Naval and other air forces.

To cope with the amount of work, I had additional staff – three RAF navigation specialists, an additional photographic specialist and a couple more boffins from the UK; also five Canadian girl secretaries, who worked splendidly with me for the next three years.

Soon after I returned from recuperating in Florida, I (a Wing Commander) had to escort two Group Captains (Tony Ragg and Kelly Barnes – the latter being the pilot who had been interned in Iceland) on an overnight visit to an American firm. I told Alice, my head secretary, to make the necessary hotel reservations, and make sure they (as senior Group Captains) had good accommodation, as I wanted to impress them.

I spent the night in a luxurious suite of rooms and felt sure they would be at least as comfortably accommodated and – I hoped – suitably impressed with the arrangements I had made.

But disaster loomed. At breakfast the next morning, before I could ask them if they had spent a comfortable night, as I intended, they swore at me for them being crammed together sharing a small room and voiced their dissatisfaction with my arrangements in no uncertain terms. Needless to say, I did not dare mention the luxury I had enjoyed.

On my return to Washington, I told Alice to demand an explanation from the hotel. The answer was quite simple. In the USAF a Captain, as in the British Army, is a junior officer. Furthermore, in the USAF it takes three Groups to comprise a Wing – exactly the opposite of the RAF. So, in America, a captain in a Group ("Group Captain") is pretty low in the scale. On the other hand, the Commander of a Wing ("Wing Commander") is the equivalent of a General. So the hotel receptionist had arranged our accommodation accordingly.

It made me realise how ridiculous were the names given to the various RAF ranks. This was accentuated for me when, several years later, we were staying at Reids Hotel in Madeira. Two groups, each comprising about 30 tourists, one lot being Japanese and the other German, had recently booked in. When we arrived, Bunny enquired if there was any mail addressed to Group Captain Vielle. The receptionist replied:

"We usually keep the mail for each group separately. Which group is he captain of – the Japanese or German?"

However, everywhere I went in America as a Wing Commander I was treated as a VIP. I did not complain.

One of my early trips to New York was with Chick Hayward to the Bendix Corporation to meet Vlad Reichel, the chief engineer, who became one of my best friends and exerted quite an influence on my life. He spoke English (and German, French and several other languages) with a Russian accent. In the 1917 communist uprising in Moscow, he, a member of the Russian aristocracy, was against a wall facing the firing squad and waiting to be shot. His wife Zika, an amazing woman, had organised a group of friends to create a loud disturbance behind the firing squad. That enabled two other friends to help Vlad climb over the wall behind him and, together

Vlad Reichal visiting us in Gstaad many years later

with Zika, escape from Russia. In 1919, Vlad had worked for British intelligence, but later moved to the USA, where his excellent brain and strong personality enabled him to rise to the top of a big and important corporation, Bendix.

When I met Vlad, I was immediately impressed with his charm and old-world dignity. On being introduced, he bowed, then led us to a part of his office where, with great ceremony, we were served tea from an exquisite Chinese teapot. He told us of his respect for ancient Chinese customs and philosophy. He was quite unlike most Americans I met. Only when we had leisurely finished our tea did he start discussing the object of our visit – namely, the new type of compass he had developed: the Gyro Fluxgate.

Together with Tommy Thurlow, I had already tested the Gyro Fluxgate in a Beechcraft flying from Wright Field. We were comparing it with another new type of compass, the Magnesyn developed by Kollsman. The object of our visit to Bendix was to arrange further tests, this time with Chick Hayward in a Hudson. Following that test, in January 1942, I reported to the Air Ministry and to RAE Farnborough that the Gyro Fluxgate was far superior to anything we had in England. I received instructions to arrange for one to be sent urgently to Farnborough for test.

In January 1942, Chick and I flew a Hudson up to Montreal, taking Vlad and the only other Fluxgate with us to fit in another Hudson due to be flown to England. I had asked Don Stokes to select a navigator to go with it. He recommended one of the instructors at the Navigation School – Flight Lieutenant Chandler, whom I knew well. The pilot, who was a Polish Officer serving with the RAF, was able to converse more freely with Vlad in a language that I assumed to be either Polish or Russian. We fitted the new compass in the Hudson, briefed the pilot and Chandler fully, then tested it in the air with them so that they would be able to demonstrate it in England. I had signalled Jack Richards at Farnborough to warn him that it would soon be on its way and gave details (in code) of the aircraft in which it was fitted. Farnborough would also have been notified of (or could easily find out) the planned aircraft movements.

The aircraft with Chandler and the Fluxgate took off to fly to England. It was known to be OK after crossing the Canadian Atlantic coast. Then nothing was ever heard of it again.

That was a shattering blow to us all. Vlad, in particular, was devastated; he felt sure that the aircraft had been intercepted, diverted to a German-held airfield in France, or shot down. I wondered at the time what part Jack Richards, to whom all the information would have been passed, had played in that incident. Later, when I had more evidence of his subversive activities, my suspicions about Richards increased. Whatever the cause, however, the loss of that aircraft set back all RAF aircraft being equipped with a far superior type of compass.

As soon as America declared war, all personnel in the US armed forces were required always to wear uniform when in public. We, of course, did likewise. No one had ever seen an RAF uniform before in America. That sometimes led to me being mistaken for an airline pilot, or even a porter, but also – when they realised that I was a member of British services that had faced Hitler alone for so long – resulted in me being lavishly entertained.

That regulation about wearing uniform had one amusing consequence. At one of the hotels (I think it was in San Antonio) that was used by the airline pilots and hostesses, as well as USAF officers, many residents were woken up around midnight by loud screams. Thinking it might be a fire, some opened their bedroom doors to peer out. They saw a half-naked girl running screaming down the corridor, closely followed by a naked, clearly excited, man. The hotel manager received several complaints about the disturbance. The man was identified as a USAF lieutenant and the manager put in a serious complaint to his commanding officer, who felt compelled to have the offender charged.

But there was some difficulty in deciding the exact charge. It would have been bad publicity for the USAF to have an officer accused of attempted rape, or of creating a public disturbance. So it was decided to charge the lieutenant under the regulation compelling him, when in public, always to appear properly dressed in uniform.

At the court martial, the defendant did not deny any of the evidence against him and admitted that he had appeared naked in public, and therefore not wearing uniform, and that he was chasing the scantily-clad airline hostess down the corridor. It seemed obvious that he was guilty.

But his defending officer, while admitting all the evidence about the incident, nevertheless claimed that the lieutenant was clearly not guilty of the particular offence with which he had been charged. He pointed out that the paragraph in the regulations compelling the wearing of uniform in public had a sub-clause that read:

"Exemption. When an officer is engaged in sport, he may appear in public appropriately dressed for the sport in which he is engaged."

The president of the court, trying to stifle his laughter, had no option but to acquit the defendant.

During the next few months, I spent most of my time flying from one location to another in the USA, testing new equipment, assessing new inventions, advising companies about instrument requirements or helping sort out compass problems – usually with Chick or Tommy, but sometimes flying myself in whatever aircraft happened to be available or using the airlines. Because, right early on, I had helped the Chief Pilot of American Airlines and become friendly with him, the American Airline pilots often let me act as co-pilot: that experience of civilian airline flying proved valuable later.

My primary task was passing information regarding developments in England and their urgent requirements to any organisation or scientist in the USA that could help; also, passing information back to the Air Ministry and the Farnborough boffins from the scientists working on similar projects in America. My five secretaries were kept extremely busy. My work led me to meet, and work with, some of the top scientists in the USA. At one scientific gathering, for example, I found myself sitting beside and conversing with Albert Einstein – as I have already mentioned. I greatly treasure that memory.

At Philadelphia, Chick let me fly several US Navy aircraft, including the original experimental Catalina flying boat (XPBY). There too I practised flying a glider – easy enough, and the absence of any noise a sheer delight.

Wherever we went, Tommy, Chick and I – either individually or together – were entertained royally. After working hard all day, we usually continued our discussions, or negotiations, in more pleasant surroundings at the expense of the firms we were visiting. When in New York, we were usually entertained for dinner by Vlad at the 21 Club, where I first became friendly with Xavier Cougat and others. When in California, it was mainly senior officials from the aircraft companies or instrument firms who took us to various well-known restaurants and nightclubs. In Hollywood, the president of a big film corporation showed me round the film studios. I watched how they made the films and met many of the famous actors and actresses. That, incidentally, reduced my enjoyment of films for evermore. Having seen some of the gorgeous creatures looking ravishing during each brief shot, but watching their bitchy behaviour and sometimes foul language show their true character when the camera was not on them, and the way each bit was shot and then artificially joined up, caused me to analyse the way the films were made rather than enjoy the story they depicted.

Washington in Winter

In Washington, Bunny and I had a busy social life too. But that was mainly to introduce visiting senior RAF officers and high-ranking boffins from England to the US senior brass and scientists with whom I was working, or attending functions connected with the US Services or the British Embassy.

Lady Halifax with our eldest daighter Pam & Peter Heslop!

In June 1942, I made my first trans-Atlantic flight, taking off in a Liberator from Montreal, refuelling at Gander and landing at Prestwick after a total flight time of 18 hours. I lived at the RAF Club in Piccadilly and spent a month bringing myself up to date with developments at Farnborough, visiting various operational stations, and flying a Bomber Command Wellington to get experience of the new navigational radio device "Gee" (one of the first radio systems to help a navigator determine his position) and the completed version of the API (Air Position Indicator), with which I had been concerned at RAE and which later became the Ground Position Indicator.

Having brought myself right up to date on developments, and operational needs, in England, I was a passenger in a BOAC Clipper (flying boat) from Poole Harbour to Shannon, where I transferred to a Sikorski "Excaliber" (also a flying boat) for the 24-hour flight to La Guardia (New York). Being tucked up in a luxurious bed by an attractive hostess, and fed freshly cooked eggs and bacon for breakfast, was very different to travelling by air today. Furthermore, I felt much safer flying over large expanses of sea in a flying boat aircraft designed to alight safely, in emergency, on the water – and in the absence of other aircraft with which we might collide.

In August, back in the USA, I had my first experience of flying with airborne radar designed to detect ships, or enable a navigator to detect prominent objects on the ground – like buildings concentrated in a town. These new airborne radars were fitted in two Liberators nicknamed "Dumbo One" and "Dumbo Two" (because of the enormous bulbous noses in which the rotating radar dishes were fitted) based at Langley Field. They worked on a wavelength of 10 cms and gave me – for the first time – the facility to view prominent objects on the ground ahead through cloud and fog. I found this tremendously exciting – it opened up a completely new world for the navigator. In England, a similar development became known as "H2S".

A couple of weeks later, I flew with a further development (by MIT at Boston) of this ground-scanning radar, working on a wavelength of 3 cms. This gave much better definition and enabled a reconnaissance aircraft to detect even a submarine periscope under good conditions.

These new developments, combined with Gee, revolutionised bomber navigation. Another radio development, Oboe, helped the bombing accuracy of single aircraft. They still did not, however, define the target accurately enough for the bomb to hit it. Only a bigger bomb, as I repeatedly stressed to the boffins, or a guided bomb, could be sure of demolishing the intended target. I was already aware (right from my evenings at Farnborough chatting with the scientists) of the potential of an atomic bomb, and knew vaguely about it being developed.

Practically every week I was flying different aircraft, often with either Tommy or Chick, testing new equipment developed by various firms. Several new types of compass, and autopilots, were amongst the interesting new instruments submitted by industry that we tried out. Some went into production, while others fell by the wayside.

On one such trip with Tommy, we were in Texas, near enough to his in-laws' home for him to arrange for us both to stay the night there. His in-laws had a large ranch in a sparsely inhabited area about 40 miles from Dallas. We arrived in the afternoon and received a warm welcome. I was the first English person they had ever met and my English accent amazed them. (There was no television in those days and radio only from nearby stations). I heard his mother-in-law on the phone inviting all her friends – which was effectively everyone within 30 miles of their home – to come and listen to this Englishman speaking.

By early evening, I was surrounded by a couple of dozen Texans sitting in a ring round me, listening with astonishment to the way I spoke. They were also fascinated by my accounts of life in England. I, in turn, was very interested in the lives they led on their ranches. Breakfast the next morning was an enormous steak and a pint of beer. I saw the men with their ten-gallon hats mounting their horses to go and round up the cattle, as we left with his mother-in-law to drive back to the airport. I learnt the origin of the term "ten-gallon hat": it had nothing to do with its size or capacity – it was the pressure of water that the material could withstand without letting any seep through. In other words, a measure that guaranteed that it was waterproof.

Meanwhile, Chick had been promoted to Commander and Tommy to Colonel. Both had acquired assistants, whom I got to know well. Norm Hays, who had been attached as a student to the Navigation School when I was Chief Instructor, became an assistant to Tommy. Pliny Holt (whose father headed the Holt Caterpillar organisation) became deputy to Chick. After the war, each of these became godparents to my younger daughters.

To gain experience of US Navy operations, I flew as co-pilot on Atlantic patrols in a PBY flying boat, during which we carried out tests of the newly-developed Long-Range Navigation System (LRN), which was similar to Loran – a sort of long-range Gee.

When I first arrived in Washington, I had to do most of my long-distance travelling on the civilian airlines – mainly in the Douglas DC2 or 3, that later became better known as the Dakota. They never flew above ten thousand feet, so that, even in clear weather, the passengers frequently had an extremely bumpy ride. Carrying a total of about 22 passengers, they normally had to land several times to refuel on a journey from Washington to the West Coast.

I had also sometimes used the trains until, on an overnight journey, I was sound asleep in my bunk when the train collided with another and my carriage was derailed. I woke up on the sloping floor, concussed and somewhat bruised. After that, I got Tommy to arrange with the USAF commander at Bolling Field (just outside Washington) for me to borrow a suitable aircraft in which to fly myself around whenever I needed it – also, if I wanted to take passengers in a larger aircraft, a master sergeant engineer to accompany us to look after the aircraft. This excellent arrangement continued throughout my service in Washington and was extended to a couple of other RAF officers serving with me. Chick made similar arrangements for me to fly US Naval aircraft.

On one of my trips to MIT Boston to discuss developments with Dr Draper and his staff, Tommy, Pliny and I were being entertained in the evening at the Coconut Grove – a famous restaurant and nightclub. It was very crowded, particularly in the large downstairs area that seemed to have only one exit. I became acutely uneasy about what would happen if there were a fire, or anything else that caused a panic. I never like crowded areas, but this one generated real fear in me. Suddenly, the vision of the Zeppelin in flames flashed across my eyes. I decided to get out right away and persuaded the others to leave with me and go somewhere less claustrophobic.

Two evenings later, I was in the bar of a hotel in Mexico with one of my staff, Rod Harman, waiting for Tommy to join us. When he arrived, Tommy looked very distressed.

"Have you heard the news?" he asked. "That goddam Coconut Grove went up in flames last night. It was one of the worst disasters ever – only four people managed to get out of that downstairs area. Over 200 were burnt to death. How right you were, Tubby, to get us out of there!"

The glasses in our hands were not as steady as normal as we drank to our lucky escape. My fears about a fire had been justified and – on a similar occasion a few years later – another vision of that burning Zeppelin saved my life. I think it was that tragedy at the Coconut Grove that caused some states in the USA to introduce a regulation that all doors in such establishments must open outwards to prevent the exit becoming jammed.

We were in Mexico that evening because I had been due to fly down to Trinidad, where the Royal Navy had a navigation training school at which I had been invited to lecture the staff on the latest developments in navigation equipment. I had suggested to Tommy that he should come down there with me, together with Rod. We naturally wanted to take photographs during our trip, but colour film was in short supply. As a result of my activities in connection with aerial photography, I had become friendly with several of the scientists at Kodak, including the inventor of Kodachrome. So I had phoned him, mentioning the shortage of the film for my camera and my coming trip through Central

America and the Caribbean. Within six hours, a present of fifty rolls of Kodachrome film had arrived on my desk. That enabled me to record the whole of our trip.

We had chosen to fly ourselves in a Hudson, starting from Wright Field, where Tommy was based, and so stayed the first night in Mexico. Our next stop was Guatemala City, where we stayed at the main hotel in the centre of the town. Before dinner, we were in the bar beside the window overlooking the main street. Outside, ragged and barefooted beggars ambled past, but all the streets were amazingly clean – no rubbish anywhere.

Tommy (who had stayed in that area before) reminded us that alcohol had a far more potent effect at that altitude (about 6,000 feet up) and suggested we drank only half pints. These were served in special mugs, made at the local pottery and engraved with the hotel name. I suggested that we should keep these unusual mugs as souvenirs, but Tommy immediately warned me to be very careful. Pointing out of the window, he explained:

"Look at the streets. See how clean they are! That is because Guatemala has proper laws and enforces them. If you went outside and dropped a cigarette packet – even a fag end – and left it lying there, you would probably get six months' hard labour in one of their prisons. If you are caught stealing – death is the punishment. For God's sake, Tubby, if you want one of these mugs, then go to the desk, buy one and get a receipt."

I expressed surprise at such draconian laws.

"Try it out," suggested Tommy. "Put a dollar bill on the window ledge outside and see whether anyone dare touch it."

I did so. We watched as several beggars passed by. They saw the money, looked at it, but not one of them touched it. It was a lesson I shall not forget. I often now think that if the penalty, in England, for illegal parking or breaking the speed limit was the automatic confiscation of the car and contents, then few would ever break those laws. Then, perhaps, our police could concentrate on preventing crime. Until the punishment is sufficient to deter a wrongdoer, the police cannot win, and crime will increase.

I still have that mug amongst my travel souvenirs. But, as Tommy advised, I went to the desk to purchase it. In fact, the manager gave it to me as a gift, together with a signed document saying so.

The next day, we flew over San Salvador, Honduras, Nicaragua, Costa Rica, and spent the night in Panama. Tommy did most of the flying – very easy with the Sperry autopilot – Rod helped with the navigation, while I concentrated on photographing the rainforests and other interesting features over which we passed. The following morning we crossed Columbia and the tip of Venezuela, before landing at Curacao to refuel. Then on to Port of Spain in Trinidad – all in beautiful weather.

Toni Snowball (another Navigation Specialist), who was on attachment there, looked after us for the couple of days that I spent lecturing the staff; before we set off again to fly up the circle of Caribbean islands to Puerto Rico. There we stayed at an unforgettable castle hotel at the end of a large sandy bay near St Juan. Looking out at the Atlantic rollers sweeping into the bay reminded Tommy and me of similar conditions for excellent surf riding that we had experienced together in California. There was not a soul in sight, and the beach was completely empty, as the three of us waded in and swam out to begin some of the most exciting surf riding I ever experienced. No surfboard – we did it in the old-fashioned way, just riding the waves on our tummies. After about half an hour, we were exhausted and waded back onto the beach. To our amazement, it was now crowded. A whole mass of people had assembled to watch us. As we reached the sand, they started clapping and cheering us. I imagined that it was because we had not been using surfboards and they were impressed with our prowess without them. But even so, their excitement seemed excessive.

None of us could speak their language, but they followed us, clapping and cheering, until we reached our hotel. There too the staff seemed excited. The manager then gave us the explanation. That bay was full of sharks and all swimming was forbidden. Few who had ever swum there had survived. Somewhat shaken by this news, we at last understood why the crowd had gathered. We quickly made our way to the bar to celebrate our lucky survival. Again, the hands holding our glasses were a little unsteady.

In St Juan itself I witnessed scenes of poverty and squalor that I had never imagined existed. I was pleased to get back to the luxury of our hotel.

The next day we continued circling the Caribbean, flying over Dominica and Haiti, before landing at the US Naval base at Guantanamo Bay in Cuba, where we spent the night, before continuing to Miami. There I left Tommy and Rod to fly back to Wright Field, while I returned to Washington by Eastern Airlines to attend a meeting in the US Naval Department.

In mid-December, as a result of my suggestion to increase the co-operation between Farnborough and the US scientists, Harry Pritchard arrived to spend a month with me going round the various firms and research establishments. In particular, we concentrated on several new types of autopilot. Lack of a good autopilot still remained one of the main deficiencies in British aircraft, thanks to the obstructive activities of Jack Richards. I gathered from Harry, however, that, when Germany had invaded Russia, Jack Richards became a changed man – doing all he could now to help the RAF get better equipment to fight the Germans and so help his comrades in Russia.

In January (1943), I was able to arrange demonstrations for Harry of various new autopilots (Jack and Heinz, Sperry, etc). Amongst the other new developments, I took him to Boston to fly with the 3cm ASV (like the H2X) that gave so much better definition – for navigation as well as for detecting submarines. I missed him when he left to return to England – not only for his friendship, but also for the stimulating discussions we enjoyed together about the future.

In March, Pliny Holt, Rod and I were engaged in a series of trials of new sextants. In April, together with Chick Hayward, I flew a PBY5 to Bermuda and a PBM3 (both were flying boats) back to Norfolk testing Loran (the long-range equivalent of Gee) and two new types of sextant. I could not see, however, any hope of ever being able to determine position accurately by using – in an aircraft – a sextant and astronomical observations. In an emergency, perhaps, one could get a fix within about 50 miles, but that took time and skill. Inertial navigation, if gyroscopes could be made more accurate, or radio devices based on distant beacons, held out the best hope for determining position. The principle of using differential timing of radio signals – the forerunner of the global satellite system in use today – seemed, even then, the obvious answer in the future.

In May, Tommy and I began testing (and then demonstrating to AVM Mansell and "Slops", now an Air Commodore) another new autopilot – the A 10. They were surprised at the number of different and highly efficient autopilots there were in the USA, compared with the primitive one that RAE had produced.

Later that month, accompanied by Tommy and RO Jones (now an Air Marshal and senior RAF officer at the BAC), I made another transatlantic trip to England, also in a B24 (Liberator), via Dorval, Gander, and Prestwick. Admiral Clyde Smith, head of the Instrument Section of the US Navy Bureau of Aeronautics, who had become a close friend of mine, came over separately. We all stayed in London – me, as usual, at the RAF Club in Piccadilly. At night, London was very quiet (except during air raids), with virtually no traffic at all. I remember one night, to win a bet, reaching 80 miles an hour driving a motorbike down Piccadilly with Tommy on the pillion.

We had demonstrations of all the latest navigation instruments and bombing devices at Oakington, where Wing Commander Cribb ran the Bomber Development Unit. We attended briefings for our aircrews for their bombing raids on Germany, and debriefings on the return of those that had survived. That was a very sombre experience and emphasised the importance of getting them better equipment with which to do the job. It brought home to us, very vividly by the empty chairs at the debriefings, the utter stupidity of making aircrew fly their aircraft in a long straight line to aim their bombs, thus simplifying the task of the German gunners. In 1950, my invention of a new bombing system ("Red Cheeks", which became "Blue Steel" and was the origin of the Cruise Missile) to avoid that, had part of its origin in my experience at those debriefings.

I then flew Tommy and Pliny (who had come over in a Naval plane) down to St Eval in North Cornwall, just near Morgan Porth, where Bunny and I had spent many holidays. Wilf Oulton was commanding one of the squadrons there and we accompanied him on an Atlantic patrol, during which he demonstrated, in a Halifax, the Coastal Command equipment and tactics – including the low-level bombsight that, nearly four years earlier, I had helped the scientists (led by Blackett) to develop.

That evening, as a result of Wilf detailing a group of airmen to search along under the cliffs, we enjoyed what I think must have been one of the finest meals (mainly crabs and lobsters) served in England during the war. Pliny, in particular, was tremendously impressed.

"I thought you were short of food in England!" he remarked to Wilf. Little did he realise the effort, and sacrifice of food coupons, that had gone into providing it.

Tommy and Pliny, who had not had any experience of being bombed, were amazed at the calm way in which people in London (where we stayed most nights) went about their normal business, except when an air raid was actually in progress. On two occasions we had to take shelter in Underground stations and they were tremendously impressed with the high morale of the Londoners.

Tommy and I spent a couple of days with the C-in-C of the USAF in England, discussing their operations against Germany and their navigational problems. I also stayed with Don Bennett, discussing instrument developments in the USA that might help his Pathfinder Force. He was one of the best informed, and most efficient, aviators that we ever had in the RAF. That, and his record-breaking flight in the upper half of the Mayo Composite, made him a source of envy (and jealousy) amongst many of our senior officers. I had first met him when he was still with BOAC and based in Bermuda. We kept in touch after the war until his death in Switzerland many years later.

In July (1943), I flew back to La Guardia in a PAA Clipper. Our flight time in the air was 25 hours, but the comfort of our surroundings and excellent meals served by unhurried hostesses made that a much more pleasant experience than the shorter time of flights over similar distances today.

Shortly after returning to Washington in July, I flew AVM Mansell (who had taken over from RO Jones) and Dr Barton (the head of our Radio Branch) up to Boston to show them the performance of the latest navigational and bombing radar – the American H2X. I considered it superior to the latest British version I had just seen in England.

At MIT Boston, I had become friendly with one of their most brilliant scientists, Luis Alvarez, who showed me his latest idea to improve radar definition. The clarity of a picture depended partly on the size of the dish (like a modern television dish) that rotated in the nose of the aircraft. Since it had to rotate (like all radar dishes) to scan the area of ground ahead, its size was limited by the amount of room in the nose of the aircraft.

So Alvarez had come up with the idea of a much longer but non-rotating antenna that would have only a limited field of view ahead. This consisted of a hollow perforated rod with a sliding wave-guide inside, which could be housed in an artificial wing across the nose of the aircraft – rather like a cat's whisker. That lengthened the base of the antenna by around three times – with a corresponding increase in picture clarity, although it could only cover a sector of the ground ahead of about 40 degrees. This was fitted onto a B24 on which I carried out many tests. We called it the Eagle Antenna. It gave by far the best picture I had yet seen and I expected it to be widely used. Alvarez, unfortunately, then left MIT to go and work on the Atomic bomb. After the war, when he was at CalTech, he was the recipient of a Nobel Prize. A few years later (as I shall explain), I revived his Eagle Antenna to be used in a quite different way, with great success.

By August, I had convinced the Air Ministry of the superiority of several types of American autopilot – particularly for aircraft like the Mosquito. At last they gave authority for several to be fitted. So, taking Rod Harman with me, I flew up to the nearest unit equipped with Mosquitos (RCAF Greenwood, Nova Scotia) to fly one, and gain experience on these splendid aircraft. On the way back, I landed at Newark, where Tommy had made arrangements for me to fly a Mustang 111 – a lovely aircraft to fly – in which I then gave an aerobatic display.

Although there was no rationing of food in America, there was a shortage of some items they had previously imported – particularly the delicious Canadian hams. So, whenever any of us had to visit Canada, we usually brought back one or two hams, in spite of a recent US law banning the import of such items. My immediate boss now was Air Commodore Buckle – about 17 stone, a sense of humour to match, and a delightful character who had little respect for any regulations of which he disapproved.

We both had reason to visit Toronto, so we decided to fly up there together from Bolling Field, with me piloting a C45. We, and a couple of staff we were taking with us for the ride, collected our parachutes, plus a couple of spare parachute bags, from the store there, before boarding the aircraft. The weather was perfect, with just a layer of cloud at about 4,000 feet. To practise instrument flying, I decided to fly all the way in that layer of cloud. It was just at the right temperature to make ice form on our wings and by the time I landed at Toronto I had a good inch of clear ice on the leading edges. I broke off a piece about two feet long and, concealing it behind my back, went with Buckle into the Meteorological Office to check the weather for our return. The duty forecaster said that would be OK – no change expected. I then asked him if there was any chance of icing in that layer of cloud.

He shook his head. "None at all, Sir. No danger of any ice in that cloud."

Producing the stick of ice from behind my back, I said:

"I flew up in that cloud and this is the result." I then banged him on the shoulder with it. Buckle roared with laughter, but the poor forecaster did not see the joke. Even today, using massive computers, the Met chaps often get it badly wrong. In those days their forecasts were rarely correct.

Buckle had arranged for four hams to be available for our return journey and put two into each of the spare parachute bags we had brought with us. On arrival back at Bolling Field, I went to sign in at the Control Tower as having completed the flight, while the others started unloading the parachute bags. Because we had come direct from a foreign country, the resident US Customs official (who we had met before) had strolled casually across to the aircraft and asked Buckle the usual question of whether we had anything to declare.

Buckle explained that we had only been up to Toronto for a brief meeting and said "No". The Customs chap noticed the others struggling with the parachutes, which he knew had to be returned to the store about fifty yards away.

"Here," he offered, picking one up, "let me give you a hand with these."

By chance, the one he had picked up contained two of the hams and as he was walking across the tarmac with the others, by which time I had rejoined them, he remarked:

"This parachute is damned heavy."

Quick as a flash, Buckle replied: "Yes. It's one of the new experimental types."

The Customs chap made no further comment, but helped us deposit the parachutes in the store; but I think he probably guessed what he had been carrying. Buckle and one of the others returned to retrieve the hams as soon as the Customs man was out of sight.

That autumn (1943), the main emphasis of my work was changed. I was appointed to handle all exchanges of information between the USA and England on Guided Missiles (which included Rockets) – the types of weapon that the authorities deemed likely to dominate future warfare. It was all, of course, classified Top Secret. One of our most talented boffins (Dr Bill Stephens, who was assistant scientific attaché to the British Scientific Mission in Washington) was appointed to work with me on producing a comprehensive review of all developments in the USA concerning these new weapons. It became one of the happiest associations of my life. We worked closely together until I left Washington 18 months later and we became great friends. [His obituary was in the *Daily Telegraph* of 23rd August 2001.]

Our first practical tests of any Guided Weapon took place at Eglin Field in November, when, with me flying a C45 and with Bill Stevens beside me, we were trying to follow and watch the manoeuvres of one of the first guided bombs ever tested. It had been released, and guided, from an aircraft flying above us. The entries in my logbook read:

"Diving beside Guided Bomb No 1 (Torpedo)."

"Low flying, looking for GB1."

Those confirm my memory that it was far from successful. Trying to follow the bomb, by spiralling down in a small twin-engined aircraft, was not easy. I might, perhaps, have been successful in a Spitfire, but I do not think we ever found where that first guided bomb had ended up.

One of the early attempts to control a bomb onto the target was codenamed "Operation Dove". Several pigeons were trained, over a period of a few weeks, to peck at a particular point in a picture on the screen in front of them. When they hit the point accurately, they were rewarded (immediately to begin with, but only after a series of pecks, as they became more proficient) with a grain of corn. The picture on the screen in front of them was what they would see in front of them in a falling bomb. The picture would be produced either visually through a lens, television, or radar in the nose of the bomb. The pecks from the pigeons would make electrical contact behind the screen to manoeuvre the bomb (via aerodynamic fins, like tiny wings, on the outside) accurately to hit the point at which the pigeons were pecking.

The scientists got Dove working quite well in the laboratory. But they failed to appreciate the effect of accelerations on the senses of the pigeons. The scientists had themselves never experienced the effect of unexpected weightlessness – as pilots often do – nor realised the inability of anyone in free-fall to point accurately at some object: otherwise they would have realised the difficulties facing the pigeon.

As soon as I heard the proposal, I gave my opinion (based on my experience of weightlessness and sudden accelerations in an aircraft) that it was unlikely to work. The boffins did not have the practical experience of flying to visualise what would happen. I warned them that the sudden lack of any gravitational force as the bomb dropped from the aircraft would cause the bird instinctively to struggle to open its wings and would make it too confused to peck correctly. Then, the tilting down to a different angle would disorientate the bird. Furthermore, if it did peck accurately to correct the bomb's flight, the sudden resulting accelerations would make it impossible for the pigeon to continue. I was proved right. So, after a lot of money and effort had been spent on it, "Dove" (or "Pecker", as some called it) was abandoned.

In addition to covering Guided Missiles, however, I still had continuing responsibility for other developments as well. Bendix had fitted their new A4 autopilot in a Mosquito that I tested and then demonstrated. Also, to please the workers at Bendix, I gave them an aerobatic display in the Mosquito in which they had fitted it.

That December, a team of instrument specialists – mainly boffins from Farnborough, but including the communist Meridith of Smiths Instruments – arrived for discussions with their American opposite numbers. I had arranged to fly them round in a Hudson transport from Bolling Field to the various meetings via a route that I thought would give them the most pleasure and enable them to see some of the more interesting parts of the USA. For some reason, possibly to see his communist comrades, Meridith had arranged his own itinerary, leaving me with eight passengers – plus, of course, the USAF engineer sergeant who usually accompanied me to look after the servicing of the aircraft.

We set off on 28th December via Palm Beach, Florida; then via Galveston, El Paso, Colorado Springs, to spend New Year's Eve at a hotel in Albuquerque. Knowing there would be a big New Year's Eve celebration, perhaps I should have warned them about drinking at that height (6,000 feet) above sea level. I, as always when flying, went to bed early without any alcohol. But they were still in a pretty bad state when, after a late breakfast, they staggered up the ladder into the aircraft – one senior boffin expressed anxiety that he might have fathered a child during the night, but could not even remember the girl's name.

I had chosen that route particularly to show them the meteorite crater, and the nearby Grand Canyon, over both of which I intended to fly at low level to give them a better view. But when I sent the sergeant back to warn them we would soon be over the crater, they were all sound asleep. As I approached the Grand Canyon, low flying about a hundred feet above the ground, I experienced a most extraordinary sensation – similar to that I get when walking towards the edge of a cliff. I simply could not go any nearer – an overpowering force took control of me. It was the first time that I, while flying, had ever experienced such a sensation.

I was forced to make a steep turn to avoid going over the edge of the cliff (which, at that point, drops vertically down for several thousand feet). I was later told that the overpowering sensation I had experienced was a panic attack caused by fear of heights. Immediately I turned, I was perfectly normal again. So I climbed up a little and made another approach – this time with the autopilot switched on and with my hands over my eyes for the few seconds before we passed over that cliff edge. Then everything was normal again and I flew on over the Sierra Nevada to Burbank, where we had a week of meetings arranged in the Los Angeles area. We stayed at a hotel in Pasadena and I took, during the weekend, the opportunity to motor up to the Mount Wilson Observatory. I had visited there several times before and always found it a fascinating place. The giant telescopes were very different from those my grandfather must have used and were better positioned (for clear air) than most in Europe.

My next flight was one of the most memorable I ever made. It was on 24th January 1944. I had the group of 8 senior scientists as passengers and we were due for an important meeting at Boeing the next morning. So I took off in the Hudson before lunch from Los Angeles for what should have been an eight-hour flight to Seattle. The weather over the whole of that side of America was pretty awful, and even worse weather was approaching from the Pacific. This was expected to close all the airports in the Los Angeles area soon after we left. But good weather was forecast for the Seattle area. Also, both San Francisco and Salt Lake City were forecast to have good weather as diversions for me to land en route if I needed to do so.

We took off and climbed up into very bumpy cloud – rather worse conditions than had been forecast. Approaching San Francisco, I asked for another weather report. They advised me that the whole Seattle area was clear and was expected to remain so. My main diversions were both OK, although Salt Lake City had deteriorated a bit. As expected, all airfields in the Los Angeles area had closed in behind us; so I continued North, still in cloud, flying at 10,000 feet. Among the countryside ahead were Mount Shasta (14,162 feet) and several others nearly as high. But with my Bendix automatic radio compass and the Radio Range beacons to help me, I had no fear of getting off a safe track through all the mountains.

Half an hour after passing San Francisco, I received a radio call to advise me that weather conditions had deteriorated far more quickly than anticipated. San Francisco and all airfields south were now closed, as was my other main diversion – Salt Lake City – as well as all other airfields in that direction. The conditions at Seattle, however, remained good and they advised me to continue. It was obvious to me, however, from their repeated calls updating me with the latest weather reports, that they were becoming concerned for us.

An hour later, still in turbulent cloud, so was I. Already, ice was beginning to form on our wings and the aircraft was becoming more difficult to control. With mountains all round and beneath us, I dare not go lower. Then I received the alarming message that the bad weather had reached the Seattle area too and all airfields that side of the Rockies were now closed. That was extremely worrying. I asked for an emergency diversion. They said an emergency airstrip at The Dalles (of which I had never previously heard) was our only hope.

I was asking for more details about the weather there, when the aircraft gave a sudden jerk and the radio went dead. The sergeant sitting beside me said:

"That's our aerial gone! Too much ice!"

I looked across at him. His face had gone deathly white. He had probably never been in a situation like this before. Nor had I.

With the ice now nearly half an inch thick on the leading edges of our wings, it was not surprising that the extra weight and drag of ice on the wires stretching to the tail fin had caused it to break. It meant that we had lost our only means of communicating with the ground; also, that our Bendix radio compass would no longer function correctly.

We could still pick up the sound from the Radio Range beacons through our radio compass – our sole remaining navigation aid – but it would no longer point to the beacons automatically. Instead, we would have to wind the loop round manually using the little handle in the cockpit roof, with us listening to the signal strength to judge the direction. I knew, too, that we could not stay airborne much longer – the weight of ice would become too great.

[We learnt later that the ground controller, not hearing any answer to their urgent calls, assumed that we had already crashed into a mountain. Nevertheless, just in case we managed to reach The Dalles, he had given instructions for the lights to be switched on at that emergency landing strip.]

"Get the radio charts," I instructed the sergeant. "Turn up The Dalles page and hand it to me."

To ease the bumps, and because I was worried that the autopilot might not cope with all that ice on our wings, I had been flying the aircraft manually. But I now switched it in again so that I could study the chart. It showed the emergency airstrip to be in a remote area beside the Portland River. Apart from the emergency landing ground and a radio beacon, it had no facilities. The landing pattern for The Dalles called for accurate flying between two mountain ranges, with Mount Hood (11,245 feet high) on our left, but with the landing strip only a few hundred feet above sea level. I had no way of knowing the wind direction and speed; nor could I rely on the accuracy of our altimeter setting, due to the probable variation in atmospheric pressure since I had set it in Los Angeles. But I had no other means of measuring our height. I also feared that the airspeed indicator might become iced-up.

Some half-hour later, struggling in the turbulent clouds to control the aircraft with still more ice on the wings, and turning the handle in the roof to judge the direction of The Dalles beacon, we finally passed over its cone of silence. That indicated we were directly above it. I immediately began my descent, following the pattern and procedure laid down in the radio chart. The sergeant did the timing for me with his watch for each turn. We knew, as we went lower, that the slightest error could run us into one of the mountains.

The air was extremely turbulent and I had great difficulty in steering an accurate course on each leg of our procedure turns. Also, as we went lower, the freezing rain became worse and we were collecting ice at a faster rate. I knew the amount of ice on our wings would cause the aircraft to stall at a much higher speed than normal. To allow for this, I kept our speed well up. From the change in headings each time we approached the beacon, I could tell that the wind was from our left, and from the difference in timing (passing backwards and forwards over the beacon), probably about fifteen knots.

I lowered the wheels, adjusted the flaps and allowed an extra 30 knots on our final approach speed. I descended lower earlier, praying that we would see the ground before we hit it. I knew I could not rely on the altimeter correctly telling us our height. That last minute had us pretty tensed up.

"Ten seconds to go," announced the sergeant. The altimeter was indicating that I was already BELOW ground level.

I continued descending. We both knew we would hit the ground during the next few seconds – either as a crash or, just possibly, a landing.

I eased down still lower. According to the altimeter, we were now flying well below ground level, but still in cloud – an experience I never want to repeat. I was concentrating on the instruments, while the sergeant was peering ahead through the ice-covered windshield, hoping to get a glimpse of the ground in time to warn me.

Suddenly he shouted: "Lights ahead!"

I glanced through my side window. We had come out of cloud with the ground about 50 feet below us. Ahead, through the ice on our windshield, I could see the blurred light of the beacon and just pick out the airfield. I kept up our speed until, just about three feet from the ground and drifting to the right, as I had anticipated, we reached the landing area. I throttled back, kicked on the rudder to align our wheels with the direction in which we were moving over the ground and the aircraft fell out of the sky – a heavy but not too bad a landing.

I applied the brakes. They had no effect. I never discovered whether this was partly the result of the brakes on the wheels being too iced-up to function, or entirely due to the ice on the ground from the freezing rain; but it was obvious that we were in danger of overshooting the end of the airfield. I used the rudder, and a slight burst of our port engine, to make the aircraft skid sideways in a wide circle, hoping the wheels would break through the layer of ice and dig into the grass. That certainly helped.

We came to a standstill just a few yards from the edge of the airfield where, below us, we could just see, in the gathering darkness, the raging river below.

For a few seconds I just sat there, stunned at our amazingly good luck. The sergeant too was silently staring at the river. Then he turned to me and said something very complimentary. I thanked him for his help in getting the timing right.

I taxied back, parked facing into wind on the grass near the beacon and switched off the engines. I felt completely exhausted, but very elated. We had been flying in turbulent cloud for six hours, and the last part had demanded intense concentration – but also it had been exhilarating.

I sat there watching my passengers getting out. The first one went flat on his back on the ice. Then they wanted to know where we were and why we had come there. I had not wished to alarm them while we were in the air. But the excited sergeant explained what had happened, stressing how lucky they were to be still alive. They then seemed quite appreciative of my efforts.

Looking round the outside of the aircraft, I was amazed that we had been able to continue handling it with that amount of ice, plus the passengers and baggage. The freezing rain was now adding more ice.

There was no one about – nor a telephone – so we had no method of letting anyone know we were there. The airstrip was far from any human habitation. The sergeant set off, walking along the icy road towards what he reckoned was the nearest village, while we took shelter in the aircraft. Luckily, because it was midwinter and we were heading for Canada, we all had warm clothing in our baggage.

Meanwhile, the air control authorities assumed we had crashed in the mountains; but, rather by chance, had sent the maintenance engineer to check that the beacon at the airstrip was in working order. The sergeant, who had already been walking for ten minutes along the road towards The Dalles, saw the lights of the approaching vehicle and waved it down. An hour later we were all being exceedingly well looked after – indeed, feted like heroes – by the local residents in a hotel in The Dalles. The sergeant excitedly recounted every detail of our recent experience to our audience. I went to bed early, but my passengers celebrated their lucky escape.

The next morning, we were driven back to the airstrip. The weather was fine, with a layer of cloud at about 1,000 feet, but the temperature was still below freezing. The aircraft not only had the ice on the leading edge of the wings, but now also had a layer of clear ice, caused by the freezing rain, all over the wings and fuselage. We had no way of defrosting it.

I decided that our only hope of continuing our journey that day would be for me to get the aircraft up into the sunshine above the cloud and into the drier air, where the ice would gradually evaporate. To do so, I wanted the aircraft to be as lightly laden as possible. That meant leaving the passengers and baggage there and then returning to pick them all up. With its fuel tanks now less than one quarter full and the weight of ice being balanced by lack of passengers and baggage, I reckoned that I could get the Hudson to over its stalling speed before I reached the end of the airfield and then further increase speed if necessary by diving down towards the river – like we used to when taking off from the deck of HMS *Courageous* when the aircraft was heavily laden.

The sergeant declined to accompany me. He and the others clearly thought I was mad. But having first removed the ice from the propellers (which we did with rags heated by the exhaust from one of the vehicles), checked the engines and then the full movement of all the controls, I decided it would be safe. They helped remove all the baggage, and waved me goodbye as I opened up for take-off. I reached 100 knots well before the airfield boundary and climbed up happily away. I headed for a break in the clouds over the river and climbed into the bright sunlight and clear air above. The scenery was startling. Snow-covered mountains, dominated by Mount Hood, were thrusting though a white blanket of cloud – so brilliant that I had to put on dark glasses. It was unbelievably different from the previous day. But the turbulence I experienced flying up and down the valley above the river between the mountains was the worst I ever experienced. I did not realise at the time that just along the Portland River was one of the most secret establishments connected with the atomic bomb development. It was a prohibited area for all aircraft and I flew up and down it several times. (That had repercussions later.) It took nearly an hour for the sun and dry air to evaporate all the ice.

I landed back, took the passengers and baggage on board, and flew the remaining two hours to Seattle without incident. There the sergeant had a new aerial fitted.

The meetings at Seattle started later than planned and lasted until the following evening. I decided to fly back to Washington overnight, dropping off one passenger at Salt Lake City. The weather forecast, apart from some thick mist in the valleys, was excellent. Shortly after dusk, I took off, climbed up to 10,000 feet, switched in the autopilot, and sat back to enjoy what I expected to be a very easy and straightforward trip. As I have already mentioned, my only real fear in flying was colliding with another aircraft. In consequence, I tended always to keep a good lookout. About an hour into the flight I suddenly saw, ahead and to my right, a red light that appeared to be at a similar height to us and not changing in angle. I instantly realised that it must be the port wingtip light of another aircraft on a collision course with us. Quick as a flash, I cut out the autopilot and rammed the stick forward to dive beneath it. Thankfully, I could then see no aircraft. But, to make sure, I made a turn to the right before resuming course. Only then did I start climbing up to cruising level again.

That near miss had quite shaken me and I thanked my lucky stars that I had seen the wingtip light in time to avoid a collision and was now keeping a sharper lookout. Suddenly, as we were approaching our previous height, I saw his red wingtip light again in the same relative position as before. I rammed the stick forward again, dived a thousand feet, then made a 360-degree turn to the right, so that I would be at least a few miles behind him. My passengers, by the way, were complaining bitterly about being lifted out of their seats by my violent dives, but I was putting safety before their comfort.

Knowing that the other aircraft must now be miles away, I began climbing up to our cruising level again. Suddenly, I saw the red glow again – still in the same relative position. I stared in disbelief and was preparing to dive again.

"It's the moon!" said the sergeant. "It's just rising."

It was. As we climbed higher, more of the moon appeared over the horizon, and as we dived it disappeared. It was brilliant red – just like a wingtip light. I felt a bit of a fool when I explained the reason for my manoeuvres to the others.

When we were approaching Salt Lake City, the controller advised me that the airfield was closed due to fog, with visibility on the ground less than 100 yards. But from above I could see the runway lights quite clearly through what was really a thin layer of mist. So I overruled him, landed, dropped my passenger and took off for Washington without too much difficulty. Our flight time was 12 hours and we arrived in time to enjoy a hearty breakfast, before I went to my office.

An account of our flight from Los Angeles, and my solo one getting rid of the ice, was spread around the local USAF by the sergeant. At Bolling Field, in particular, RAF pilots became regarded with increased respect. But the CO at Bolling Field warned me to be very careful, in future, of entering prohibited areas. The fact that I had dropped off the sergeant before flying up and down that area of the Portland River had caused me to be suspected of being a spy trying to obtain information about a highly secret establishment there.

That January (1944), I tested (in an AT6) a completely new form of altitude gyro. Until then, all "artificial horizon" instruments were liable to topple if the aircraft banked, dived or climbed beyond fairly small limits, and so give incorrect readings. This new one had no such limitations and was the forerunner of an improved blind flying panel. I also tested yet another new type of autopilot – the A5 autopilot in a B24.

In February, my old friend David Waghorn and one of the head boffins at the Ministry of Supply, Ivor Bowen, came over on a visit. Some months previously I had been given, by Admiral Clyde Smith, a new type of fountain pen, which the inventor in South America had offered to the US Navy as being capable of writing underwater, or in the air, where, in the reduced pressure, normal fountain pens leaked badly. David spotted that pen on my desk and was intrigued by it. He thought it could be developed and exploited commercially. We agreed that, if it ever proved a success, he would give me half of any proceeds he received. He took it back to England with him and showed it to his friend Miles (of Miles Aircraft). He, together with help from the Shipman family, put it into production. I was not commercially minded, otherwise I could have made a fortune out of that invention.

In March, I made (in a Hudson) some of the first flights ever with the automatic blind landing system developed by Sperrys. To my amazement, having switched it on at a safe height several miles from the airfield, the equipment – through the autopilot – controlled the aircraft to approach the runway with complete accuracy to within a couple of feet from the ground without me touching the controls. This, I considered, was one of the greatest advances in flying I had yet experienced. I demonstrated it to Ivor Bowen, whose branch at the Ministry of Suppy was responsible for that type of development in the UK. When the Sperry system was further developed (some three or four years later), it enabled an aircraft to take off from New

York, cross the Atlantic and land at the Blind Flying Experimental Unit (BLEU) in England without the pilot ever touching the controls.

The following week, I flew Ivor Bowen and David Waghorn down to Boca Rotan in Florida to test, and then demonstrate to them, a different type of Blind Approach system. The Sperry one had depended on a narrow radio beam, transmitted from the ground, which was automatically interpreted by a receiver in the aircraft that controlled the autopilot. The "Baby GCA" (Ground Controlled Approach) system was a tiny, short-range version of the Radar Stations that detected approaching enemy aircraft that was used to direct our fighters to intercept them. This "baby" one fitted in a small truck and could be moved to the runway in use. If located near the end of the runway, it gave a picture of the exact position of the aircraft approaching to land, thus enabling the controller to tell the pilot what to do during a blind approach. It was very successful and became, in one form or another, the mainstay at most airfields for helping an aircraft to approach the runway safely, and even land, in fog.

Meanwhile, Steve was conferring with the US boffins about their plans for developing several different types of Guided Bombs. In April, I flew him to the main USAF test station at Tonapah in the Nevada desert. Apart from the remains of a few huts left there many

Las Vegas from the Air

239

years ago by explorers seeking gold, and a runway built in the sand, it seemed to have no connection with the rest of the world. There was no accommodation, so I made Reno and the small village of Las Vegas our main bases. Their main attraction for visitors was the Nevada laws that enabled anyone staying there for a few days to obtain a divorce. In consequence, it attracted many people for that reason. To keep them occupied while in that isolated desert area, the Nevada laws had been relaxed to permit gambling and that, in turn, attracted more visitors. When I was there, it was just a tiny village with a few gambling dens and a couple of nightclubs.

The guided bombs I tested were of various varieties. The first was AZON, which was so named because it could be controlled in AZimuth ONly. Lying in the nose of a B24 and using a normal bombsight to line up on the target, I released one from a height of about 10,000 feet. It looked like a normal bomb, but had larger fins on the tail and the pilot had to continue flying the aircraft on a dead straight line, while I, using a small control stick, could move the fins on the tail of the bomb to make it go left or right. It worked, and it landed nearer the target than it would otherwise have done.

That, I believe, was one of the first successful tests ever made of a guided bomb – the forerunner of the laser-guided bombs used today. But it had three grave disadvantages. The aircraft had not only to make the usual long straight run-up to the bomb release point, but then had to continue flying straight until the bomb landed – giving the crew even less chance of surviving enemy gunfire; it gave no greater accuracy as regard distance; and it needed clear weather conditions. The addition of further fins to enable the bomb aimer to control distance was impractical because, once the bomb has been dropped, it appears to fall way behind the aircraft, thus preventing the bomb aimer from judging that distance. Its main use, therefore, was for attacking a long straight target, like a bridge, road or railway line – preferably not in range of enemy anti-aircraft guns.

During the next few months I tested several further developments of Guided Missiles – GB4, GB6, GB8, etc – and, together with Steve, wrote a voluminous report covering all of them. The Ministry of

Supply and Air Ministry seemed pleased with it, but 5 years later had forgotten the comprehensive report existed and wasted millions on duplicating projects that had already been shown to be impractical – as I shall mention later. But both the USAF and US Navy were full of praise for our report, because they were able to learn, for the first time, what the other service was doing in that highly secret field.

The next development after AZON was to put a camera in the nose of the bomb to relay back to the bomb aimer a television picture of the ground towards which the bomb was heading. This had the advantage of allowing the aircraft to manoeuvre away immediately the bomb had been released. Using a little control stick and watching the picture it relayed back onto my screen, I had little difficulty, from 10,000 feet, in guiding it to hit the target. But it could only work in perfect weather conditions and also suffered from misting up if dropped from a layer of colder air, or passing through a layer of cloud.

To overcome that difficulty, the boffins tried putting a small radar transmitter in the nose of the bomb to replace the camera, but the definition was not adequate, except when the target was as prominent as a large ship in a calm sea. There were a host of other developments that we tested and covered in our report.

In May, I happened to be at a dinner in New York at which Pliny Holt was also present. We often used to tease each other, comparing the RAF pilots with US Navy ones. He asserted that no RAF pilot could land on a small carrier. (He was unaware that I had served in the Fleet Air Arm.) So we took a bet on it and I claimed it was so easy that I would do it and even a British Naval Observer, who was not a qualified pilot, could do it with a couple of hours' training. I had in mind Commander Hopkins (who later became an admiral), who was on our staff in Washington as an Observer and was secretly taking lessons in the hope of getting his pilot wings.

A few weeks later, I took off from Norfolk, Virginia, flying a US Navy Avenger to take up the bet. Hopkins, having done some more training, was himself flying in another aircraft beside me. We found the carrier (USS *Charger*) about 50 miles offshore. He made the first landing. I made a longer approach to give me more time to judge conditions. As had been my experience in the Fleet Air Arm, a "Batman" was stationed to the side of the deck, armed with a couple of tennis-sized bats with which to signal to the approaching aircraft whether it was too high or too low during the approach. When in *Courageous* I had rarely taken any notice of them, preferring to use my own judgement. But when this one gave me an urgent signal that I was too low, I climbed higher. He repeated the signal. But I knew I was already too high. He signalled again to go higher. That completely mucked up my approach and I decided to go round again.

On my subsequent approaches, I ignored the batman completely and made four good landings. When we landed back at Norfolk, I mentioned to Hopkins the incorrect signals from the batman and explained exactly what had happened. He was at first a bit puzzled. Then he laughed.

"Did no one tell you that the US Navy batmen give exactly opposite signals from the British? One indicates your position – too low or too high – and the other what you need to do, go higher or lower."

"Two allies divided by a common language!" I replied. But I had won my bet.

From my flying logbook, I see that I then carried out tests of other guided bombs – different versions of GB8 and GB4. But I cannot now remember details.

In June, I took advantage of an invitation to visit the USAF blind flying school at Brian Field. There, flying in a Harvard with one of their top instructors, I did 17 hours intensive instrument flying. The standard was far higher than any I had previously experienced. I learnt how, in an emergency, to carry out a completely blind landing (although it might be a pretty heavy one) on any airfield that had the standard radio beacon, even if the only receiver was just the loop of the radio compass – rather as I had at The Dalles.

Flying an Expeditor back to Washington from Brian Field at night, I ran into a tornado for the first time. It was an interesting experience. I had often flown through thunderstorms before and experienced the aircraft being struck by lightning (which normally does no harm, as the aircraft is bonded), but had never before known such violent updrafts and downdrafts. Another pilot happened to be flying back to Washington in a similar aircraft and also hit that tornado. He reported that he had been cruising at 10,000 feet, but found himself in a downdraft which, in spite of him using full throttle to climb, forced him down to 1,000 feet, before the next updraft lifted him back to his cruising height. When he landed at Bolling Field, the wings of his aircraft were found to be bent upwards.

My experience was less frightening, but the violent turbulence and lightning were pretty impressive. The glow from the lightning conductors on the wingtips was the brightest I had yet seen. Another RAF pilot (Sidney Hughes) was later attached to the USAF Bad Weather Research Unit, whose job it was, flying sturdy aircraft, to seek out hurricanes and tornados to fly through. These days, of course, storms can be forecast and avoided – particularly at the much higher altitudes used by aircraft with pressurised cabins.

In June, on a visit to Lakehirst, I had the opportunity to gain experience in a US Naval "Blimp" – the type of airship they used for coastal patrols. It was considerably bigger than the barrage balloons at Cardington, but much smaller than the Zeppelin, and – being filled with helium – less likely to go up in flames. The controls were extraordinary. The rudder bar was similar to that in an aircraft. But, instead of a control column, it had a large steering wheel (exactly like the ones in the old sailing ships) to control the ailerons, and another similar large wheel at the side of the pilot (at right angles to the other wheel) to control the elevators. This was perfectly logical for a sailor, and exactly what Nelson would have expected; but a bit confusing, at first, for me.

The most amazing thing to me about the Blimp was the ability to become stationary in mid-air, switch off the engines, and push out a plank of wood to enable an engineer to walk out and make adjustments to, or repair, either engine. Meanwhile, we could hear the cackling of chickens, and people talking, on the ground below. Taking off and flying the Blimp was easy enough, once I got the hang of it. But getting the Blimp down in a gusty wind and safely secured to its mooring mast was a manoeuvre, I decided, best left to the experts.

The main advantage of the Blimps was that they could stay airborne for very long periods – providing they were not in range of enemy gunfire, from ground or aircraft. Their main disadvantage, like all airships, was their inability to cope with the extra weight caused, in really bad weather, by freezing rain or snow. Nor would I have enjoyed flying one in very turbulent air.

At the end of June, I was appointed to accompany two VIP scientists from England to a series of high-level meetings. For the next three weeks I flew Professor Sir Melville Jones (a wonderful character, with whom I became very friendly and later visited at his London flat) and Ben Lockspeiser (who later, as Sir Ben Lockspeiser, became deputy head of the Ministry controlling RAE and TRE) all over the USA and the west coast of Canada. I used a Lodestar for the longer journeys and an Expeditor for the shorter ones. For some of the meetings, we also had Steve and Dr Barton (our head of radio). I arranged the routes, and the hotels, to make the tour really enjoyable for them. All our flights and meetings went without a hitch. The whole tour proved to be a great success.

At Eglin Field (while they were attending meetings at which my presence was not required), I took the opportunity to fly the P38 Lightning, fitted with engine booster controls – one of the first aircraft to have this extra power to accelerate it. I also flew the Kingcobra (P63).

When visiting Vancouver, I arranged for us to stay at a small hotel along the coast at Coral Beach. We all had a swim and then a drink on the terrace overlooking the sea and distant mountains as the sun went down. I was having an interesting chat with Melville Jones. Then Lockspeiser began playing the piano – the 'Moonlight Sonata', one of my favourites – and he played it brilliantly. We listened in silence, watching the shadows deepen across the water. It was one of those magical moments in my life that stands out clearly in my memory. Could the player really be a communist who had been working against British interests, I wondered?

Melville Jones & Lockspeiser

Melville Jones, Lockspeiser with Steve & me above

245

At the beginning of September, I flew Steve out to the West Coast again to test more guided missiles at Tonapah. We expected to be away for a week and, since there were several spare seats, I offered to take a couple of the junior staff with me. One of these was a Flight Lieutenant Taggart – a chap about the same shape as me and also with a similar clipped-black moustache.

We spent the first night at Salt Lake City – mainly because I wanted to have a look at the Mormon Temple there – and I set the take-off time for 11 o'clock the next morning to give the others time to see the city too. Everyone knew that I was very strict about being punctual to the second when flying, and that anyone late would be left behind.

I set off walking through the city to the Mormon Temple shortly after breakfast. I was, of course, in uniform. On my way back to our hotel, about 10 o'clock, a US Army police car screeched to a halt beside me and two USAF policemen – one with sergeant's stripes on his arm – accosted me. The sergeant demanded to see my identity pass. I felt pretty annoyed by his attitude and ordered him first to salute me as a senior officer and then produce his own pass and authority to accost me in this manner.

He was completely taken aback by this. He reluctantly saluted and produced his identity pass.

"And you," I said to his companion, "salute and produce your pass." He too reluctantly saluted, but on searching his pockets could not find his pass.

"I don't know what the hell you are up to," I said, "but here are my passes." I produced my RAF identity card, indicating to them that (in their eyes) I was the equivalent of a general, and my USAF pass for entering their airfields.

The sergeant looked nonplussed. "We were instructed to arrest you," he explained.

"Right!" I said firmly. "I am placing your companion under arrest for failing to carry his identity card and I order you to take him back to your commanding officer and have him charged."

He turned to the other.

"We'd better go," he said, and began moving towards their car.

"You salute before you go," I ordered.

Looking defiantly at me, they gave me a half-hearted salute and departed. I continued my walk back to the hotel, paid my bill and took a taxi to the airfield.

At two minutes to eleven, I started the engines, although one of my passengers, Flight Lieutenant Taggart, had not yet arrived. None of the others had any explanation for his absence. At 11 o'clock, I began taxi-ing towards the take-off runway, but a radio call from the tower instructed me to wait. I saw a car approaching fast from which, as it stopped beside us, Taggart hurriedly emerged. I waited for him to get in and then proceeded with our flight to Las Vegas.

After landing, I reprimanded Taggart for being late. He then explained what had happened. Just like me, but ten minutes later, he had been walking back to the hotel when a car had drawn up beside him and three armed police had bundled him into the car and taken him to the USAF base, where he was brought in front of the Colonel and charged with being a Canadian (for whom an arrest warrant had been issued) who was suspected of being in that area masquerading in RCAF uniform. The Colonel assumed that Taggart was the same person that his sergeant had tried to arrest earlier, and had told them to return and get me by force.

It did not take Taggart long to prove his identity to the Colonel. He mentioned the serious consequences that might arise if, because of their actions, he missed being with his Wing Commander for the flight. That created some concern and he was rushed to the airport. But that was not the end of the matter. Taggart's baggage was still at the hotel.

I instructed Taggart what to do. He rang up the Colonel, saying that, unless his missing baggage was delivered to him within three hours, then his Wing Commander, who was a personal friend of the USAF Chief of Staff (Hap Arnold), would report the incorrect arrest of a British officer, with a request that the Colonel responsible should be reprimanded.

Taggart's baggage arrived two and a half hours later in a B25 flown by a Major, who also handed me a note of abject apology from the Colonel.

The next day, together with Steve, I tested, in a B25, yet another form of guided bomb – GB9. There were so many different developments that I cannot now remember which one that was. Following the failure of "Dove" (or "Pecker"), we had fitted television cameras, and then short-wave radars, into the nose of bombs to transmit the pictures to a controller in the aircraft that had dropped them. But these ran into a whole series of insuperable problems, even in clear air conditions, which rendered them impractical for use from high-flying aircraft. So far as I recall, only the AZON was ever used successfully.

Jointly, Steve and I wrote a comprehensive review of all the ideas, developments and tests that had been carried out by either of the US services or industry in the field of guided missiles – including rockets. Copies went, I knew, to the Air Ministry in London and to RAE.

Steve, of course, had many academic qualifications. I had none – apart from the FRMetS – but around that time I was elected an Associate Fellow of the Royal Aeronautical Society, also an Associate Fellow of (what later became) the American Institute of Aerospace Sciences.

For several weeks, intelligence reports arriving from England had suggested that the Germans were preparing to launch a new type of missile against England – probably London. It was believed to be rocket propelled, but it was not known whether it would be just an unguided projectile, or a guided missile. It was named "V2". Our main fear – amongst those of us who knew about the atomic bomb development – was that it might have a nuclear warhead. I was selected, and put on standby, to go to England to bring back to America any details of the guidance system that could be extracted from the first one to arrive.

In consequence, on 13th September, I made the 20-hour flight across the Atlantic in a Clipper. The luxury inside the aircraft, the excellent food and comfortable bed made it a very pleasant flight – also good experience when the captain let me take the controls for a couple of hours during the night.

I immediately went to Farnborough to discuss all available details of that first "V2". In fact, the V2 had no guidance system – it was effectively aimed just like the shell from a gun. And, to our relief, there was no indication that it was designed to carry a nuclear warhead. So I took the opportunity of my visit to gain experience of flying some of the latest aircraft at Boscombe Down – over a dozen of them that week, all solo. I also visited operational stations in each command to bring myself up to date.

In October, I returned to Washington in a Skymaster, via Iceland and Newfoundland, to find that my main deputy, Rod Harman, was becoming a bit broody. He had decided, to the dismay of all my five secretaries, to get married to an American girl – Kaki Leopold – and wanted me to be best man. Kaki's family came from one of the southern states and she was a Lieutenant in the US Navy, serving in the Bureau of Aeronautics Instrument Department. Rod's family were, of course, in England and could not possibly make the trip across in wartime to be present. So Bunny and I felt a special responsibility for Rod. I quizzed him closely to make sure he was not making a mistake, if he expected mainly to be serving in the RAF in England in future, in choosing an American officer to join him so far away from her own family and friends. But he reassured me that was what he wanted. Her parents, who were quite wealthy, made all of the arrangements for the wedding.

That ceremony was arranged to be held at midday in Arlington Church, and, since a marriage between an RAF Officer and a US Naval Officer was unique in Washington, several Air Marshals, senior diplomats, US Admirals and Generals were included in the invitations. A few days before the wedding, Kaki's family moved into the Mayflower Hotel, and for the evening before the wedding they arranged one of the most elaborate and enjoyable receptions that I ever attended. My speeches, and Rod's, were well received and everything looked good for the ceremony the next day.

As planned, I met Rod in his apartment the following morning at 9 o'clock to check that all was in order – ring in my pocket, a spare curtain ring too; he properly shaved and uniform buttons polished; overnight rail tickets and reservations for their honeymoon in Canada, etc. I noticed that he seemed very agitated – but put that down to nerves.

We then took a taxi to the Mayflower Hotel, where Bunny was waiting for us in the bar. It was at that stage that Rod dropped his bombshell.

"I'm doubtful about going ahead," he announced. "I am not sure about marrying Kaki."

I looked at my watch. It was 9.45. Just over two hours to go.

"It's for you to decide, Rod," I said. "I'll get everything cancelled if that's what you want. There's still time. I'll get you a drink while you make up your mind. Dry Martini?"

He nodded. The drinks arrived. Bunny and I did not want to influence him either way. He could not make up his mind. Should he or shouldn't he? More discussions. Still no firm decision. He asked for another Martini. I had one as well.

At 11 o'clock, Bunny left us to go to the church, believing Rod had decided to go ahead. But 20 minutes later (and another Martini), he decided against it. It was now too late for me to stop everyone assembling at the church and I decided the only way to handle it would be for me to go there and make the announcement to the assembled gathering at midday – a pretty daunting task, to which I certainly was not looking forward.

I ordered another Martini and told Rod that was how I would deal with that part of the problem. I said I would then return to rejoin him in the bar to decide how we would handle Kaki and her parents.

"Oh! My God!" he said, "You can't do that. It would be terrible ..."

A porter, arriving to say that the car to take us to Arlington Church was waiting at the front door, interrupted him.

"Rod," I said, "you have one minute to make your final decision."

He swallowed the remainder of the Martini in one gulp.

"All right," he said, "It's on. Let's go!"

His attitude was similar to that, in more modern times, of a bungee jumper with an obvious fault in the rubber walking out on a plank over the Niagara Falls to start his dive.

I had purposely ordered the car a bit early to make sure we would not be late, and we arrived at the church with ten minutes to spare. An usher escorted us round to a side entrance near the altar, opened the door and pointed to where we should take up our positions when we entered. He suggested we should do that at exactly one minute before midday. The bride, he told us, was already on her way and the whole programme should be exactly on time. He left us standing beside the open door.

By this time, as can be imagined, both Rod and I were not too steady on our feet. In fact, we had considerable difficulty, out in the open, in not falling over. Rod again began expressing doubts about going through with the ceremony. So, to take his mind off that train of thought, I began telling him jokes, at which, in our inebriated state, we both began roaring with laughter. We had completely forgotten that, through the open door, this would be heard by many of the assembled gathering of VIPs inside. We had also omitted to remember about the time.

Suddenly, our raucous laughter was interrupted by the arrival of an usher, who gave Rod a note, handwritten on the back of the wedding programme, from Kaki:

"Are you going to marry me or not?"

I looked at my watch. It was 12 10 (I learnt later that Kaki had arrived exactly at midday and had been waiting for ten minutes at the church entrance for us to take up our positions.)

Together, trying to look sober, we walked in. Rod tripped on an uneven flagstone but I managed to catch his arm to stop him falling flat on his face, and we took up our positions. As Kaki approached, in uniform, I looked round at her. Had Rod seen the look on her face, I would certainly have had difficulty in restraining him from dashing for the open door again. I felt like making a run for it myself.

But the ceremony, and the subsequent reception, all went off splendidly. Later, I accompanied them (both still in uniform) to the station and saw them safely installed in their state-room on the overnight train to Montreal to start their honeymoon.

During the night, I was woken up by a phone call from the police. Apparently, Rod had been arrested for breaking one of the laws then in force by taking a girl, to whom he was not married, across a state border. A Customs official, when checking their tickets and passports, had noticed the RAF uniform and the US Navy uniform on the coat hangers, and then that their passports were of different nationalities. Also, when Rod was standing by the door answering questions, Kaki had not helped by shouting from her bed to Rod:

"Tell him I'm your wife, you fool."

That, according to the official, was what the girls usually claimed. But in this case I was able to provide confirmation that it was true and managed to arrange that they could proceed on their honeymoon.

About that time, my main secretary, Alice Clayton, also became broody. She fell in love with a Dutch officer, whom she later married. (We kept in touch until she died a few years ago.) He had escaped from the Germans in Holland, and spent three months making his way across France and into Spain. He then managed to get to the USA, from where he helped organise the Dutch resistance.

Amongst the staff at the BAC, there were surprisingly few other romances or scandals, although one of my boffins had a very vivacious wife who ran the typist pool during the day, but preferred more exciting activities outside working hours. Also, amongst her staff there was a gorgeous redhead who felt it her duty to console some of those officers whose wives were not in Washington.

In the autumn of 1944, the owner of our house wanted to return to Silver Springs, so we moved to a bungalow in Bethesda. Then Steve and I decided to send our families down to Florida for the winter. We rented a large apartment at Daytona Beach, because I knew I would be doing quite a lot of flying from the nearby airfield and could fly Steve down there with me fairly often.

In January 1945, Jack Richards arrived for a four-week visit to the USA, during which I was with him all the time flying him round, staying in the same hotels and attending meetings together. I got to know him very well and could not but admire his brilliant brain – as I had that of his comrades Meridith and Lockspeiser. His communist sympathies were so apparent that I felt embarrassed introducing him to some of my friends. But he was now clearly doing everything in his power to help Britain, the USA and Russia become more efficient at fighting Germany – a completely (at least temporarily) changed ambition from his earlier attitude.

However, on one occasion he wanted me to take him to a particular hotel in Florida, although we had no meetings arranged in that area. I happened there to overhear him in conversation, jabbering away in a language I could not understand (it turned out to be Welsh), with a chap to whom he did not introduce me, but with whom he disappeared for a couple of hours.

In February, I flew down to Daytona Beach to carry out some test flying on a Mosquito fitted with the new Bendix autopilot. Having checked everything thoroughly on the ground, including the performance of both engines, I taxied to the end of the runway for take-off. The airfield itself was built on land elevated just a few feet above the swamp towards which I would be heading. The engines on the Mosquito were pretty powerful and both propellers rotated in the same direction, giving the aircraft a strong tendency to veer to the right, particularly on take-off.

I opened up for take-off and was about half-way down the runway when the right engine lost power. That aggravated the tendency for the aircraft to swing right. I did not have enough flying speed to continue on one engine, so I throttled back and applied the brakes. But we had already swung off the runway onto the grass; that reduced the grip of the brakes and we were rapidly approaching the end of the airfield. Ahead lay the swamp – part of the Everglades. My only hope was to make the aircraft swing further to the right, hoping that the undercarriage would give way and so help me stop. It did – and we came to rest with my left wingtip actually touching the water. Looking down, I could see three alligators with their eyes staring up at me.

That was quite a fascinating sight – but also quite frightening. I had never before worried that flying might result in me being eaten alive, but I was too petrified to move in case the wing dipped further down and the aircraft slipped into the water. If that happened, I did not expect the cockpit canopy to provide much protection against the rows of teeth of which one of them, possibly in boredom, but to me more like licking his lips in anticipation, had given me a terrifying view. I dared not try to climb out of the cockpit, nor open the canopy to do so. I had no alternative but to sit there, staring back at them and hoping that help would arrive in time. The wind was now coming from our left and so helping hold down our raised starboard wing. Twice I felt the wing and fuselage slip further to the left and was near a state of panic when, probably less than two minutes after the duty officer in the control tower had seen the failed take-off, help arrived. The crash vehicle secured the Mosquito, dragged it back and helped me out. The undercarriage was quickly repaired, the engine changed, and that Mosquito was flying again the next day.

In early spring, Bunny and Pam came back to Washington before I could find suitable accommodation to rent. "Slops" was due to return to England, and his wife Phyllis invited us to go and live with them at their secluded wooden chalet just outside Washington – with the suggestion that we should continue there when they departed, which we did. By that time I had been promoted to Acting Group Captain.

My friend Chick had returned from a tour of duty in the Pacific and I met him for lunch in Washington. He was now a much-decorated Captain, and amongst his medals I noticed he had a Purple Heart – the American award for having been "Wounded in Action".

"How did you get that?" I asked. "Were you badly hurt?"

He laughed heartily. "We were having dinner in the mess one evening," he began, explaining it was on one of the Pacific islands within range of the Japanese bombers, and then continued:

"Then the sirens blasted off to warn of an air raid. So we all rushed outside and dived into the slit trenches. They were about two or three feet deep – quite adequate to protect us from shrapnel from bursting bombs, unless we got a direct hit. Next to me was a quite attractive Officer from the nursing service and I started chatting to her. The bombs started dropping and the air raid seemed to be going on and she was getting frightened, so I offered to help protect her by lying on top of her. She welcomed the suggestion with open arms. The bombs were getting nearer and I suggested that we might as well enjoy life to the full while we still had the chance – and she agreed. While we were making love, my bare bottom happened from time to time to be protruding above the slit trench. A bomb fell nearby and a piece of shrapnel cut right across both cheeks. I screamed with pain at just the moment she screamed for other reasons. Never," he concluded, "has the 'Wounded in Action' citation been better deserved."

Both Chick and I knew about the Atomic Bomb developments and discussed when it was likely to bring the war to an end – and the likely future for the world thereafter. We were both saddened by the news that our great friend Tommy Thurlow had been killed. He had been visiting his family for a lunchtime celebration in Texas and, taking off soon afterwards in a Hudson, appeared to have stalled it and crashed.

Around the same time, I received news that David Waghorn, then an Air Commodore commanding the Photographic Reconnaissance Unit at Benson, had also been killed. He had been visiting his old station, Boscombe Down, flying one of the high-flying reconnaissance Spitfires. Similarly, after lunch with his friends there, he had stalled after taking off – just like Tommy Thurlow. It increased my resolve never to drink if either flying or driving – a rule to which I strictly adhered.

From my schooldays onwards, my life has been punctured by the deaths of so many close friends, some of which have had quite an impact on my life, that it is quite uncanny. In the case of Waghorn, it may also have deprived me of a small fortune. Some years after his death, I received a message from his widow to contact her about the Biro (that came via her brother Barry Aikman), but for some reason I was not able to do so.

In April, Group Captain Leonard Cheshire VC arrived in Washington on a brief lecture tour. I flew him and Air Marshal Iles up to Flint (Michigan) for a lecture and dinner, at which Cheshire was guest of honour. He gave a good speech, but he was clearly a strange and unbalanced character – even before he was the RAF observer on the atomic bomb raid on Japan. I was not surprised at his even more erratic behaviour thereafter.

Also that month, we received instructions that we were to brief a visiting group of Russian scientists, giving them information about any development in which we had been engaged – including, in my case, guided weapons. I suspected that this originated from Lockspeiser or Richards and their highly placed communist comrades in the Ministry in London. I consulted Buckle and the Air Marshal, telling them of my suspicions. They agreed. The Russian delegation learnt little of value from me.

By the early spring of 1945, it was obvious that the war with Germany would soon end. I felt that my main task in Washington was nearing completion. If I was going to continue my career in the RAF, it was obvious that I should get back to more normal duties. I had several offers of jobs in the USA – two from instrument firms to become their test pilots, if I could get out of the RAF. But, much as I had enjoyed life in the USA and their progressive attitude, after many long discussions with my wise old friend Vlad Reichel (who had been through it all himself), I decided against becoming an employee in any industrial organisation. Rejoining our many friends (and relations) in England appealed more to Bunny too. My love of flying, the challenge it offered and the exciting life we led, made me decide to continue in my chosen career with my many friends in the RAF.

So I applied to be taken off the Special Duty List and be given a command. An old friend from Cranwell days – Rex Boxer – was appointed to replace me, but would remain in England until I returned there. My application that Bunny and Pam should travel back to England with me was turned down. Because I had sent her to Canada at my own expense five years earlier, I would have to arrange and pay myself for her to return – just as I had when she had joined me in Egypt when I was a Pilot Officer. Some other officers were treated better and I resented that.

In recognition of my services, Admiral Clyde Smith, at a ceremony at the Bureau of Aeronautics in the US Navy Department, presented me with one of the only remaining chronometers that had been specially designed to help navigate the first flight to the North Pole. It stands beside me as I write. I was also informed that I had been recommended for the US Legion of Honor. In return, I had recommended Clyde Smith, Chick and Pliny Holt for British awards that they later received.

Then a strange thing occurred. Bunny had a visit from an American who knew that I was due shortly to leave Washington. He suggested we should move into a house owned by a friend of his as paying guests. The wife wanted company and the cost would be almost negligible. It would, he pointed out, be so much better for Bunny to have someone to look after her when I left and also so much easier for her to pack up and leave when she wanted to. I was away at the time, but agreed with Bunny on the phone that it made a lot of sense. So we did that.

The people whose house we moved into were very strange. Bunny suspected that while we were out they searched through all our belongings and particularly any papers I had there. I never took home any secret papers, so, although annoyed, I was not alarmed. Then, one evening, the man had a friend visit them and invited me (but not Bunny) to join them for a drink. They tried to get me drunk (without success) and the visitor started quizzing me about Uranium 232 and other aspects of the Atomic Bomb. I guessed that I was probably being interrogated by the FBI and that this was the reason for getting us to that house. My flying up and down that prohibited area near The Dalles, having previously dumped the sergeant who normally accompanied me, was probably the origin of their suspicions. I did my best not to disclose that I had any more knowledge of any atomic bomb than any schoolboy who had studied physics.

The following day, our hosts departed on a holiday, leaving us alone in that house until we had both left Washington. We never saw, nor heard from, them again. It was all very strange.

The evening before I left Washington, I had a long session with my immediate boss, Air Commodore Buckle, to brief him on all outstanding things that might need further attention. At the end, as an afterthought, I said:

"I expect you know all about the Atomic Bomb? Its design and when and where it will probably be dropped?"

He stared at me as though I was mad.

"Atomic Bomb!" he exclaimed. "What the hell is that?"

He had never heard of it and knew absolutely nothing about any such development. So I explained both of their designs to him and the plans for their probable use against Japan.

The next morning, I said a sad goodbye to Bunny and Pam (who was now the spitting image of Shirley Temple) and made my way to New York to catch the boat home. This time, however, I expected to be parted from them only for a few weeks. Nevertheless, I felt pretty bitter that the RAF would not allow us to travel together.

I had, at that time, not the slightest idea of the repercussions my informing Buckle about the atomic bomb would have. Nor did I have any inkling that Donald Maclean – whom I heartily disliked – was passing much more detailed information about it to the communist comrades of Jack Richards.

Chapter 13

Oakington

In early May 1945, I sailed from the USA to Scotland in the former French luxury liner *Isle de* France, which had been converted into a troopship. I was the senior officer aboard and became "OC Troops" of the 3,000 assorted service personnel that included 400 US Army nurses.

My accommodation was a suite next to that of the ship's Captain, to whom I was responsible for their discipline. I appointed three other officers and the senior US Army nurse to assist me in this task. With no alcohol permitted on board, and everyone in good spirits at the prospect of the war in Europe soon ending, we had few problems.

However, on the third day out, the Captain said that one of my officers – an RAF Squadron Leader who seemed particularly attractive to the nurses – was causing him some concern. On the two previous evenings, this officer had been demonstrating his powers of hypnotism and the Captain was worried that if anyone fell overboard then this chap could receive the blame.

My enquiries revealed that the Squadron Leader appeared to have the most extraordinary powers. Very quickly he could persuade the volunteer to do the most ridiculous things – like going up to a piano when someone was playing and interrupting them by striking a particular note, or moving something to a different place. Although several of the nurses had volunteered and become mesmerised, nothing nasty had been suggested as resulting therefrom.

I interviewed the Squadron Leader. He had the appearance of being half Indian and possessed the blackest and most piercing eyes of anyone I had ever met. I found him dignified and charming. I had never met a hypnotist before and had a most interesting discussion with him. When confronted with the problem of someone disappearing overboard, he immediately undertook not to exercise his hypnotic powers again while we were at sea. He kept his word – in spite of several of the nurses challenging him to

259

try exercising his powers over them. I hardly think any hypnotism was needed.

The day before we were due to reach dock near Glasgow, the news finally came through that Germany had surrendered. I was with a group on deck discussing some of the implications when someone, who had been looking out to sea on the port side, gave a shout and called our attention to a disturbance in the water about a couple of hundred yards away. The lookout on the bridge must already have seen it too, because our ship was already beginning a sharp turn to starboard.

Sensing danger, I dashed up to the bridge, where the captain and several others had their field glasses trained on that area.

"It's OK," he announced. "They've raised the white flag. They want us to accept their surrender."

It was quite a shock to realise that the U-boat had been in a position from which it could have fired a torpedo into us. The Captain decided against stopping – his job was to get us quickly and safely to our destination. Instead, since the German submarine could already have reported our position, he broke radio silence to inform Naval HQ of the location of an enemy vessel wishing to surrender.

That evening, although the ship was "dry", a surprising number of the service personnel appeared drunk and the party went on all night – luckily without causing me any problems.

Although the capitulation of Germany had been expected, the actual announcement that war in Europe was finally at an end, after five and a half years of hardship and suffering, caused tremendous emotion and exuberance. Some of the aircrew, however, expressed disappointment that they were to be deprived of the opportunity to smash more of Germany and so take revenge on the nation that had killed some of their loved ones. Few today can have any realisation of the strong feelings that the German attempts to conquer Europe – and particularly England – for the second time in less than 30 years, had generated.

We remembered the pictures of the troops in the Flanders mud trenches being ruthlessly massacred by the hated Germans during the First World War and the deliberate bombings of civilians and babies during the Blitz on London more recently. Why had they done this? We cheered when Bomber Harris gave the Germans some of their own back. It was he, and the valiant crews of Bomber Command, who had kept up the British morale when we were otherwise helpless to attack. So it was not surprising to me that some of the 3,000 serving personnel in that ship regretted that all their training to retaliate against the hated enemy would now be wasted.

Overall, however, there was tremendous joy and high spirits. I was very grateful that there had been so little alcohol aboard.

Approaching our destination near Glasgow, we were intercepted by an RAF launch, out of which a Wing Commander and two Squadron Leaders of the RAF Police climbed on board, demanding to see me privately. I interviewed them in my suite, wondering whether we had some criminal on board. The Wing Commander handed me a sealed envelope, saying that it was from the Chief of the Air Staff (Air Marshal Portal).

I had not the slightest idea what it might contain. The letter was in his own handwriting, very cordial in tone, starting *Dear Vielle* and going on to say that I was in possession of certain information of such extreme importance and secrecy that I was to speak to _no one, under any circumstances_, other than the three officers he had sent to assist me, until I had spoken to him personally in his office, which he instructed me do as soon as possible.

The Wing Commander watched me read the letter and then explained that they had orders to arrange everything I needed to get down to London without me having to do anything and, in particular, not speak a single word to anyone else. They would deal with everything, and a first class compartment on the train had already been reserved. I was completely mystified. But, quite clearly, these were orders that had to be obeyed.

The next morning, on arriving at the Air Ministry, I was shown into the great man's office. He greeted me cordially, waved me to a chair and apologised for any inconvenience his instructions might have caused me, adding that I had done nothing wrong and indeed was to be congratulated on my work in the USA. I wondered what it could be that he wanted to interview me about.

"Tell me everything you know about the Atomic Bomb," he said.

Remembering that Buckle had been completely ignorant of any such weapon, I thought, 'Oh! My God! Doesn't he know anything about it either?'

So I launched myself into a description of the two designs, their likely effect and the plans for them to be dropped on Japan.

When I finished, he told me that my knowledge of the Atomic Bomb had caused absolute panic in Washington. The whole project was shrouded in such extreme secrecy that only a very few people were supposed to know anything about it. The fact that the American authorities had discovered that an RAF Group Captain was familiar with the project had resulted in diplomatic exchanges with the Prime Minister.

[I later learned that Buckle had passed on the information I had given him to the Air Marshal, who was also completely ignorant about any such development. The Air Marshal had gone to the civilian head of BAC, who also knew nothing about it, but considered it of such importance that he told the British Ambassador. I never discovered whether it was him, or the spy Donald Maclean on his staff, who had notified the US authorities that I knew all about it. But the fact that a Group Captain with a French name, not directly involved in the project, had gained so much information set the alarm bells ringing that security had been breached. One possible explanation (suggested perhaps by the CIA) was that I might have been a spy. That caused the removal of my name from the list of officers to be awarded the American Legion of Honor. The most urgent thing was, however, to discover how I had obtained my information – whether there was some leak in the security that would permit others to obtain similar data.]

The CAS asked me how I had acquired my information. I explained that physics had been my best subject at school; of my discussions with the scientists at Farnborough; my association with several of the scientists who went to work on the bomb, and with

Dr Stephens, who had carried the total world supply of Uranium/ Plutonium from England to the USA to start the project; and, finally, my conversations with an unnamed Captain in the US Navy.

He seemed satisfied with my explanation and told me to write a brief summary of it so that he could pass it to the US authorities to allay their fears that there had been a serious breach of security. He instructed me never to discuss my knowledge of the project with anyone, wished me good luck and dismissed me.

[Several years later, at a social gathering, I happened to meet Lord Portal again and reminded him of our conversation. He told me that at the Yalta conference (at which he was present with Churchill and Roosevelt) when they had informed Stalin of the plan to drop an Atomic Bomb on Japan, Stalin had sat quietly for a while before replying and then said, quite simply:

"That will surprise them!"

I have often wondered why Stalin's own lack of surprise should not have alerted Churchill and Portal to the fact that Stalin already knew just as much about the Atomic Bomb as Churchill did – via, as later emerged – Donald Maclean in our Embassy in Washington and others, like Jack Richards and his pal Fuchs in England.]

That period around VE Day, which reminded me very much of the rejoicings in 1918, is unforgettable. These days one can see pictures on television of the excitement of the spectators and players when one of them happens to kick an inflated bit of leather into a net. Compare that with a deadly game that lasts for over five years and then scale up the reaction, and that might give some idea of our feelings in 1945. We were all, in spite of the rationing and food shortages, partying and singing in the streets until after midnight. Being allowed to have lights showing after dark was alone a transformation! Everyone seemed extremely happy – deliriously joyful – that, against all the odds, the hated Germans would no longer be able to disrupt our lives or kill our friends.

A couple of weeks after VE Day, I went up to Liverpool to meet the boat carrying Bunny and Pam. I had tried to buy a secondhand car (no new ones were yet in production and the war against Japan still took priority), but any serviceable ones were rare and the roads, of course, almost empty of any traffic. I had to bring them back by train to Sonning, where Phyllis and Slops had invited us to stay with them.

While Bunny and Pam stayed with them there, I attended the Senior Commanders' course at Cranwell (designed to bring senior officers returning from service abroad up to date with administrative regulations), followed by a short course in Transport Command. I found it rather fun being back on normal duties with many of my old friends.

On 28th July, I took over command of RAF Oakington – one of Bomber Command's biggest stations, which had just been transferred to Transport Command to become one of the main bases from which additional troops from Europe would be transported to the Far East to intensify the war against Japan. In addition to Oakington camp itself, several other units also came under my command, including the Cambridge University Air Squadron and various satellite stations, like the airfield at Bourne.

The station had no officers' married quarters, so I arranged that Bunny and I would move into the cottage that had been requisitioned for the previous commanding officer in the adjoining village of Longstanton. It had no heating and was sparsely furnished, but became the centre of much social activity, where many new friendships took root.

Amongst my key officers were the station doctor, Flight Lieutenant Ian Donald, who had previously served with Wilf Oulton in the Azores; Mike Fleetwood, the CO of 86 Squadron, who had won the DSO for saving the lives of hundreds of prisoners by finding the *Altmark* off Norway; and Terry McComb, CO of 206 Squadron, with his OBE for his exploits against submarines. The local civilian doctor, William Hertzog (who was an Olympic athlete and the nephew of the South African Prime Minister), and his wife Alfreda, also became good friends.

The day I took over command of Oakington, these two squadrons, each equipped with 30 Liberators that had formerly been employed on long-range operations against German shipping and submarines, arrived together with all their personnel – bringing the station to around some 3,000 in all, of which about 300 were officers. The bomb bays of the Liberators were being modified to carry about 22 passengers each and our main task would be to ferry troops and aircrew out to India for Operation Tiger – the invasion of Japan.

I dared not give any hint of my conviction that an atomic bomb would make preparations for an invasion of Japan a waste of time.

The week after I took over command at Oakington, the news of the atomic bomb hitting Hiroshima blared out from every radio. That morning I was having breakfast in the Mess, sitting next to one of my officers who, in civilian life, was a stockbroker, and I mentioned that I had been expecting it.

"Oh! My God!" he exclaimed. "Why didn't you tip me off – I could have made you a millionaire."

The thought had never occurred to me, but of course that news generated massive changes to the value of various stocks within seconds – many of which he could have predicted. Another missed fortune!

But my mind had been more concerned with running the station – such things as organising around 9,000 meals each day with strict food rationing in force, keeping the men happy while waiting to be demobbed, and everything on this large station working smoothly and efficiently. Also, of course, I was running what in effect was a long-distance airline with a fleet of 60 passenger aircraft.

After the second atomic bomb was dropped on Japan two days later, I became even more convinced that preparing for Operation Tiger was quite unnecessary. But the Japanese did not finally surrender for a further three weeks and we had to continue with our preparations.

On VJ Day (2nd September 1945), Bunny and I motored across to Blackburn Hall to celebrate final victory on both fronts with our old friends the Measures. We had a wonderful party and Pat, our second daughter, was born 9 months later. That day was also marked by their son Julian gashing his leg badly on the bumper of my staff car, which caused me to rush him to the nearest hospital – at the

USAF base at Thurleigh, on the land adjoining their farm – where everyone, including all the doctors, was already so drunk that Julian received nearly a pint of penicillin slopped onto his leg.

The euphoria that erupted on VJ Day was wonderful to behold – both on my station and throughout England. The joyous reaction was infectious. It is difficult to convey the feelings of those of my officers who had been selected to go out to the Far East to fight Japan, on learning instead that peace, after exactly six years of war, had finally arrived. It was not until later, when the way the Japanese had treated their prisoners became better known, that our hatred of that nation – although they had never bombed England – began to match our hatred of the Germans.

After VJ Day, our main task went into reverse and became primarily that of bringing back troops from the Far East, including – in particular – those who had been Japanese prisoners of war. That task of repatriating the PoWs from Japan was one of the most emotionally satisfying tasks ever entrusted to me. It also engendered such enthusiasm in all my aircrew, and amongst everyone on my station, that morale was sky high.

The splendid bunch of aircrew manning our two Liberator squadrons had carried out their wartime tasks magnificently. But their hurried wartime training had been, of necessity, limited to enabling them to do a specialised job and – quite naturally – they knew little about aviation outside what they had been trained to do. This became apparent when we started having numerous engine failures. Nearly all their previous flying had been below 2,000 feet over the sea, and they had learnt the correct engine settings for maximum endurance at those levels. Now they were cruising at 10,000 feet to avoid mountain ranges, but no one had told them that the engines needed completely different settings for flying at these higher altitudes. It was only when my engineer officer and I went up with them to watch their handling of the engines that we realised the cause of the failures. We quickly produced new engine handling instructions that cured that problem.

Similarly, they had only flown those aircraft always with the same equipment and weight spread around the fuselage. They had never learned about the need to consider the centre of gravity. But now that we had replaced the bombs, depth charges and all the other equipment with passenger seats which might, or might not, be occupied, that weight distribution became a vital factor in the stability of the aircraft. I only realised this after Mike Fleetwood reported trouble with a wobbling nose-wheel when taxi-ing fast. When I learnt that he had no passengers in the back, the reason became obvious and was quickly remedied by the use of a Centre of Gravity calculator to which I had become accustomed in the USA as a matter of routine.

Although the Liberators were fitted with the Bendix Radio Compass, because there had been few ground beacons switched on during wartime, the aircrew had little knowledge of its use for navigation or of attempting to land in bad weather. So I got my radio officer to rig up a simple little transmitter and locate it in a wheelbarrow at the end of the runway. Using that, I then demonstrated to Mike Fleetwood – to his astonishment – that without a navigator and just me flying the Liberator with my head right down in the cockpit looking only at the instruments (but with him keeping a lookout for other aircraft), it was relatively easy to carry out a practically blind landing using the Radio Compass and just that little beacon – as I had to do on that flight to The Dalles.

By moving the wheelbarrow to the end of whichever runway was in use, our aircrew were able to navigate back to Oakington and land in far worse weather, with greater safety, than other stations in our group. That generated great interest at Group HQ and necessitated me demonstrating the method to several of the senior staff.

Because morale is influenced partly by the quality of the food, I made a habit of going into the airmen's mess at lunchtime at least once a week, sitting down with them to taste what they had been served. I would also inspect the fingernails of the cooks and the plates for cleanliness. The airmen just loved that. Most of the RAF cooks, although they tried hard, would never have qualified for a Michelin

Rosette. Some were below a standard that I considered acceptable. So, breaking the regulations, I advertised in the local press for ladies with cooking experience to volunteer to come and help prepare better meals. "Mum's Kitchens" resulted in a vast improvement and the airmen were delighted. I also staggered the times for meals for different sections to eliminate queuing. Then, again breaking with normal practice, instead of the airmen being allowed only weekend leave which, after the time they spent travelling, gave them very little time at their destinations, I introduced a roster of 10 days on duty followed by three days' leave. That amounted to the same total time off, but gave them a much larger proportion of it with their families or girlfriends. They really appreciated that. Oakington became so popular that airmen from other stations applied to be posted to us. It was, in fact, a very happy station.

Oakington, like most other stations, had quite a large contingent of WRAFs amongst the administration staff, with their own women officers. The head one, a Flight Lieutenant known as the "Queen Bee", was on my immediate staff in the HQ building. She happened to be an extremely attractive and vivacious girl, whose duty included keeping an eye on the behaviour of all the girls. I relied on her completely. Her duties necessitated her making official visits to, for example, the sergeants' mess and reporting direct to me on anything involving the personnel under her command. I had never before had any dealings with WRAF personnel.

My first experience of the complications they could cause was when Ian Donald reported to me, shortly after I had arrived, that one of the WRAF cooks – an exceedingly fat one – had gone to him complaining of stomach pains and before he even had time to examine her had started giving birth to a baby in his surgery. She apparently was so ignorant that she had not even known that she was pregnant.

But my next problem was more difficult. The morning after VJ Day, the senior NCO on the station – a Warrant Officer with two rows of medal ribbons from the First World War – asked for a private interview with me. He informed me that the Queen Bee (as was her duty) had visited the Sergeants' Mess during the celebrations the previous evening, when everyone was in pretty high spirits. Then, in keeping with the general atmosphere, she had taken her stance on a table and, to roars of applause, had done a very sexy striptease. He – the Warrant Officer – emphasised that he was not complaining. Indeed, he said it was the best performance he had ever seen, but he thought I ought to know about it for the sake of future discipline. I thanked him and he departed.

I sat at my desk for a while, wondering what the hell I ought to do about it. Nothing in my training or experience had prepared me for that sort of problem.

Before I had time to clear my mind, my Adjutant informed me that the Queen Bee wished to see me urgently and then ushered her in. She looked more glamorous than ever and gave me a sweet smile. How the hell was I going to give her a rocket? I thought she was going to mention her previous night's performance, but she immediately launched into a series of minor problems resulting from the previous day's celebrations, including a couple of alleged rapes and a complaint against one of her WRAFs from an airman's wife on which she needed my directions about the action to be taken. And all I wanted to do was get down to the airfield to go flying!

I decided not to discuss her indiscretions with her. Her sweet smile and twinkling eyes – as she probably hoped – made me realise that would be far too difficult a task. Instead, after she had left, I rang up the Queen Bee at Group HQ (a WRAF Wing Commander) and asked her to come and see me about a matter I preferred not to mention on the phone. The result was that my Queen Bee was discreetly posted to another station without me having to discuss the matter with her. I was, however, very sorry to see her go. So, I imagine, were the members of the Sergeants' Mess.

To get the station ready for its new task, we needed all sorts of things that were in short supply. It was thanks to another vivacious and attractive WRAF equipment officer (Betty), that we got them. There were still some USAF stations left in England, but they were winding down and had masses of equipment they were going to leave behind. So, whenever we needed something, I mentioned it to Betty. She would then rush off and charm the US officers into letting her take it. She was the most efficient equipment officer I ever had.

The repatriation of the PoWs from the Japanese prison camps was planned for them to be first transported, by our Far East Command, to hospitals in India, where they would recuperate for a few days, or several weeks, depending on their condition. Our job was then to fly them back to Oakington, from where they would go by road on the final stage of their journey in England to be rehabilitated near their families or friends. At the same time, our aircraft would be taking out replacements from Europe for some of our Army personnel serving in the Far East.

The route we flew out to India and back was usually broken down into several sections and as many as forty of my aircraft could be in the air at the same time. In the eight months I commanded Oakington, our aircraft did more passenger miles than BOAC had done in the whole of its history. The routes we used depended on the forecast, and the actual weather conditions – which often differed quite considerably. I remember one typical occasion when, at my 8 o'clock morning meeting in the operations room, the Met Officer had forecast a fine day. At ten o'clock, sitting in my office, I noticed that the weather had deteriorated badly and decided to check for myself by studying the charts in the Met Office. I motored down in my staff car, but the rain was so heavy that I got soaked just getting into and out of it.

"Any change in your forecast?" I asked the duty met officer as I entered.

"No, Sir," he replied. "I expect the fine weather to continue throughout the day."

He then noticed the water dripping off my cap.

"Oh! My God!" he exclaimed. "Is it raining, Sir?"

I examined his chart and was able to point out to him where he had incorrectly joined up the isobars and so omitting to depict the approaching front. He was, of course, working in the base of the control tower with windows that were still blacked out. But with each forecaster (unlike today) having to draw their own weather charts, errors like that often occurred. It was usually better – for the local weather forecast – to consult the 80-year-old gardener who had lived in that area all his life.

On the route to India, our first stop was usually either in Southern France or North Africa – and from there to Egypt, perhaps with a stop in Malta. Then Iraq or Aden, and finally India. A single crew would fly the same aircraft all the way out and back, with overnight stops as required at the various staging posts. One advantage of this was that the aircrew got to know their aircraft well and could detect the slightest change that might indicate the need for servicing. But it also had a surprising disadvantage.

Bunny, who ran the "wives club", told me that several of the officers' wives were beginning to believe that their aircrew husbands must have girlfriends at the staging posts, because they arrived home so exhausted that they were unable to make love. These complaints became more frequent. So, at one of my regular meetings with our brilliant young doctor (Ian Donald), who helped me and the squadron commanders keep a close eye on all the aircrew for any sign of strain, we discussed this at considerable length. He too had noticed that the aircrew were becoming more fatigued than would normally have been expected from the amount of hours they spent flying.

I interrogated several of the more senior aircrew about conditions at the staging posts. This indicated that most of the aircrew were far too tired after flying to chase girls; also that there were no brothels readily available at the staging posts.

We concluded that there must be some other cause of aircrew fatigue. Ian Donald finally came up with the answer. This was the first time in history that such long flights from East to West and return had been regularly made by the same pilot. He decided it was the constant changing of the time zones, sleeping in a different one each night without their bodies having time to adapt, that was causing the problem.

So, as an experiment, I changed the routine. Each crew would be allocated a section of the route, flying one way in the morning and returning later that same day so that they slept in the same time zone each night for a three- or four-week tour of duty. That solved the problem and the aircrew became far less fatigued and their wives content.

Ian Donald thus became the first person to recognise what later became known as "jet lag". To confirm this, I organised for one aircrew to fly down to Cape Town and back. They experienced far less fatigue than they had flying similar distances East and West. I recommended Ian for the award of the MBE – which he was awarded.

Ian Donald, who later became Professor of Gynaecology at Glasgow, was one of the most remarkable men I have ever met – and not only in the medical field. He started trying to play the piano while at Oakington, simply because he found one that had been left there by his predecessor in sick quarters. He appeared not to have a musical ear and complaints reached me about the awful noises he was creating – often late into the night. But he was determined and he persevered. Ten years later, he was playing at concerts. Similarly, he took up oil painting and often invited me down to see his latest efforts. They were awful. But by the time he left Oakington, it was just becoming possible to distinguish what he was trying to depict. He persevered. Twenty years later, he had one hung in the Royal Academy. These were not his only achievements.

Shortly after he was demobbed, he rang me up from St Thomas's Hospital in London, asking me to visit him there as he wanted my help. He took me into a surgery where he was experimenting on a cat that had been drugged to lie still – so that the amount of air it breathed in and out was similar to that of a newborn baby. His aim was to find a way of keeping newborn babies alive if they were not breathing properly – I think he called them "blue babies". To do his experiments with the cat, he needed something to detect airflow in or out of its mouth. If there was none (or too little), he wanted something automatically to switch on an artificial respirator that he had already constructed.

I suggested attaching, in front of the cat's nostrils, a very thin lightweight hinged metal flap which, if it was stationary for more than, say, five seconds, would cause the respirator to switch on. With a bit of help from me, he constructed a tiny mask incorporating the flap to put over the face of the cat. We found that it was sensitive to its breath. The respirator remained switched off so long as the hinged flap showed the air was moving in and out. If there was no movement of the flap (which we held stationary to pretend the cat was not breathing) then, after an adjustable time setting of, say, five seconds, a small electric device switched the respirator on for a few cycles and then paused for just enough time to see whether the cat was breathing on its own (simulated by us releasing the flap). The sequence was automatically repeated whenever the flap became stationary. It could thus apply artificial respiration only when needed, so assisting a baby to learn to breathe. That, in 1945, was quite an advance. Ian developed this further and I believe his invention helped save the lives of many babies.

A couple of years later, Ian came to see me to get my help in obtaining and modifying the sonar device that our reconnaissance aircraft had used for detecting submarines. I managed to get hold of one and get it modified to meet his requirements. He then used its sonic wave transmissions first to get a reflected picture of the baby kitten inside a pregnant cat and then developed it into the prototype of the ultrasound scan that is in general use today.

Ian was brilliant, but his wife was a bit absent-minded. A few years later, Bunny and I were invited to dinner at their house in Glasgow, where he had become Professor of Gynaecology. We were having drinks with them both in the sitting room where, after quite a long time, Ian looked at his watch and suggested to his wife that it was time for dinner. She led the way into the dining room, with a table beautifully laid out, and we all four took our seats. After we had been chatting for about a quarter of an hour, Ian again looked at his watch and said to his wife:

"Is dinner ready, darling?"

She looked startled.

"Dinner?" she replied, "Oh my God! I'd forgotten completely about it. There isn't any!"

Luckily, there was a fish and chip shop not far away.

Back now to when Ian was still thumping on his piano at Oakington. Our "trooping" task was well under way. The returning aircrew, after a short debriefing, would be served bacon and eggs – special aircrew meals allowed in spite of food rationing – in a room in the control tower. They felt they were doing a really worthwhile job – far better than chasing submarines out in the Atlantic and trying to kill the occupants.

I made it a point – at whatever time of day or night – of personally meeting each aircraft carrying any ex-PoWs to welcome them home. Many of the ground crews would gather on the tarmac to see the passengers unload and then to cheer them – each in turn as they stepped onto the ground. It was always a tremendously emotional scene. Some of those officers and men, on getting out of the aircraft, would kneel down and kiss the ground – their reaction at being back in England after years of ill treatment by the Japanese.

I had arranged a small reception centre in the corner of one of our hangars where they could sit and be served tea or coffee by some of our WAAFs, before they boarded coaches to take them to their next destination.

One of the ex-PoWs, an army Major who I had greeted, immediately asked me whether I ever knew an RAF officer named Jeudwine.

"Yes," I answered, "he was a cadet with me at Cranwell."

"Is he still alive?" he asked in a very agitated manner.

I nodded, adding, "But I haven't seen him since before the war ..."

I hesitated. I was going to add that Jeudwine had been captured by the Japanese but had escaped in a most astonishing series of events that had hit the headlines in the papers and won him a DSO, but something about the Major's demeanour alerted me to be wary about mentioning that. He seemed very agitated.

"I know he served in Bomber Command," I said. "The last I heard was that he was commanding a station somewhere north of here."

He became even more agitated and asked: "Is he married?"

I explained that I had not seen Jeudwine since 1935 and had no idea.

The conversation ended soon afterwards. But thinking about it later that day, I decided that it had seemed exceedingly strange. It became even stranger when, a couple of days later, I read that Jeudwine, with whom I had flown at Leuchars and knew to be a good pilot, had been killed flying an aircraft into the side of a hangar at the airfield he commanded. I became interested and unearthed a remarkable story that, some years later, I used as the plot for another novel I intended writing named "The Jeudwine Story" or "The Ghost of Salembou" – about which more later.

One evening I received a phone call from John Northey (my old friend with whom I had shared a cabin in HMS *Courageous*). He was now a Colonel in the Indian Army – at home on leave, but due to return to India in a month's time. He said he was planning to get married in about ten days' time and wanted me to be best man. I asked him how long he had known the girl and he said three weeks. I suggested that was rather a brief period in which to make such an important decision.

"Don't worry, Tubby, I know what I'm doing."

I sincerely hoped he did, because we were all very fond of John.

The wedding was to be at Chichester cathedral and he and his parents would be staying at The Ship Hotel, just up the street from there. Bunny and I booked in there to join them. Knowing that there would be a shortage of alcohol (which was still rationed), I raided the mess bar and obtained several bottles of gin to take with me. In the old Daimler (with the pre-selector gears and fluid flywheel) that I had recently managed to acquire, we motored down on the afternoon before the wedding and spent most of the evening with him and his parents. John's mother seemed dead set against the wedding, mainly because John had only known the girl for such a short time, but my supply of gin helped smooth the evening along.

The wedding was scheduled for mid-day. After we had breakfasted together, I checked that all preparations were in order.

Both he and I were wearing uniform. Then – just as had been the case with Rod Harman – he suddenly got cold feet and said he could not go ahead with the wedding. His mother seemed pleased, but his father was not.

I was becoming quite experienced at handling this sort of situation and I had two bottles of gin left. I felt that – either way – they should now be put to good use. John was at first adamant that he would not go along with the wedding. Then it became an almost exact repeat of the Rod Harman event and, shortly before mid-day, John and I staggered down the road to the execution. The wedding photograph taken of us holding each other up, and the look on the face of the bride, tell the full story.

When, a couple of weeks later, John took his wife, Joey, back to India with him, I arranged for all their baggage to be flown out on one of my Liberators. It was a wonderfully happy marriage and we enjoyed their friendship immensely. They attended our golden wedding anniversary in the South of France and were in good health until a few years ago when, sadly, both passed away.

Shortly after John Northey's wedding, I heard that my brother John had recently returned from Burma after surviving his 5 years in the Far East and was at Catterick Camp (in Yorkshire), waiting to be demobbed. I sent an aircraft up to fetch him and he joined me at a guest night in the officers' mess at Oakington. It was a very happy reunion. Around that time also, I received notification of my OBE for the work I had done in the USA.

In early September, with the station running smoothly, I decided (with permission from my AOC, David Atcherley) to fly one of the Liberators myself out to India, leaving my deputy Terry McComb to run the station during my absence. I asked Terry to select one of the pilots in his squadron to come with me as second pilot. He recommended Squadron Leader David Beaty, who had won a DFC and bar flying fighters in the defence of Malta, before transferring to Liberators. (That chance recommendation, by Terry, had a very considerable effect – some 14 years later – on the lives of both David Beaty and me.)

John & Joey's Wedding

I interviewed David and accepted him to be my co-pilot, together with his normal crew. During the next 11 days, I flew the Liberator for about 60 hours, with him as my co-pilot. We went out via various staging posts to Celyon, where we stayed a couple of days relaxing at Mount Lavinia, overlooking the sandy bay, before returning via Lydda, Athens, and Naples. The flying was simple, and the staging posts adequate.

During that time together, I became quite friendly with David, although he was a very strange character. He dreamed of becoming an author and had, he told me, actually started writing a novel. But he had little sense of humour and not, I thought, much imagination. Nevertheless, I encouraged him to persevere. He intended to leave the RAF to go into civil aviation and later I helped him get a job as a pilot in BOAC, where he became involved with flight refuelling. Bunny and I also encouraged his friendship with Betty – my highly efficient and attractive WAAF equipment officer, who later became his wife.

In December, I flew another Liberator (this time with a co-pilot from Mike Fleetwood's Squadron) with a full load of passengers to Delhi, returning via Malta. Meanwhile, I demonstrated, in various aircraft, the blind landing techniques I had learned in America.

The C-in-C of Transport Command, Air Marshal the Hon. Sir Ralph Cochran, who had headed 5 Group in Bomber Command during the latter part of the war, was reputed to be one of our most efficient officers. He announced that he was going to inspect all stations under his command. To get prepared, I decided to put a spy at the station he was due to inspect before Oakington, so that I would know what, in particular, he would be looking for. The spy reported that stones on the runway and wasted food in dustbins were his main anathemas.

I was always particular about anything being on the runways that could damage aircraft, but took the extra precaution before he arrived of getting the airmen to sweep every inch of them. I then appointed Terry McComb to make sure that there was not a scrap of food in any of the dustbins in the airmen's mess and to brief all the kitchen staff that there must be no food lying around when the C-in-C arrived to inspect that area.

Cochrane arrived and, having inspected the Guard of Honour, the first thing he wanted was to drive down the runway with me in my staff car. He seemed pleased with that part of his inspection. Next, he decided to go to the airmen's mess, where Terry was waiting. Terry, having saluted him, gave me the thumbs-up indication that he had personally checked all the dustbins. I was preening myself for further praise. As expected, the C-in-C raised several dustbin lids to look inside. At one near the door from the kitchen, he gave a roar of disapproval.

"Look at this, Vielle," he said furiously. "This is the sort of thing I will not tolerate."

I looked inside. There was a pile of newly-buttered bread lying on the bottom. I looked at Terry. He looked inside, unable to believe his eyes.

"I'm sorry, Sir," I explained to the C-in-C, "but that is directly against orders."

I turned to Terry: "Find the culprit. Punish him and report to me in five minutes."

Luckily, that was the only thing Cochran found to criticise and we passed on to the Operations Room, where, while he was talking to the aircrews, Terry explained to me how that bread had got into the dustbin in the brief period between him inspecting it and the C-in-C finding it. One of the cooks had just placed that newly-buttered bread on the table for lunch when the C-in-C had entered. Having been instructed that there was to be no food left lying around when the C-in-C appeared, he had, in panic, quickly thrown it into the dustbin.

In the Operations Room I told the C-in-C that I deplored the lack of navigation facilities at his airfields compared with the USAF in the USA. He obviously resented my criticism and demanded an explanation. I explained that just putting a tiny radio transmitter in a wheelbarrow at the end of the runway had greatly increased our operational efficiency. Also, using just the Bendix Radio Compass, I had no need of a navigator to fly myself to almost anywhere, whatever the weather. He had never heard of either the Radio Compass or the Radio Range. Instead of inspecting the rest of the station, he spent the time learning about them from me. I knew that Cochrane preferred his station commanders to have a chest full of DSOs and DFCs, but he was clearly impressed by me opening his eyes to aspects of aviation and navigation of which he had been ignorant.

A week later, I received an invitation from Cochrane to have dinner with him and Lord Trenchard (the founder of the RAF). I felt this to be a great honour. Both he and Trenchard invited my views on several subjects and I welcomed the opportunity to express some of my thoughts about future developments. It was an evening I shall never forget.

By the spring of 1946, our trooping task was coming to an end. All the ex-PoWs fit enough to be flown home had been repatriated and there were now fewer troop movements. In April, perhaps as a result of his earlier visit to Oakington and our discussions, the C-in-C appointed me to become special advisor on transport matters to the new Vice-Chief of Air Staff – Air Marshal Sir William Dickson – who was about to make a tour of RAF stations out in the Far East. I regarded that also as quite an honour.

I was sorry to leave Oakington and the many friends we had acquired there. But most of these (together with their wives) remained friends for life: Ian Donald; Terry McComb; Mike Fleetwood, who lived in our house there with us for a while with his unruly son, who later formed his famous band (Fleetwood Mac), and their daughter Susan, who became an actress; and many others.

I reported to Northolt to find that Dickson would also have a Group Captain of the Equipment Branch and a couple of Wing Commanders from other branches accompanying him and that the tour was to be made in a VIP Lancastrian – a converted Lancaster with kitchen, berths for sleeping, sitting/dining room, cooks and stewards.

Sir William Dickson arrived for take-off that evening. I had never met the little man before, but he had the reputation of being a very good staff officer and was diplomatic at handling civil servants. I soon discovered that he knew virtually nothing about flying or modern aircraft. For example, he did not even know what an autopilot was. He (like so many of our senior officers) had drifted up, since the First World War, in staff jobs without having any real interest in, or knowledge of, modern aviation. He was not qualified, in my opinion, to be in command of any flying unit – yet later he became Chief of the Air Staff and then Chairman of the Joint Chiefs of Staff!

Our first stop was to be Shaibah in the Persian Gulf, which involved 15 hours' flying from Northolt. After taking off, we all enjoyed a good night's sleep, and breakfast was served at 8 o'clock GMT, when we were at about 10,000 feet over Iraq. Dickson ordered two boiled eggs – which he specified were to be cooked for 4½ minutes. The eggs arrived and were, of course, almost raw. Dickson turned to the steward, absolutely furious:

"Corporal, I said four and a half minutes. These are raw. Take them away and give me two more – and this time make sure they are boiled for exactly four and a half minutes."

The corporal looked quite frightened. He dare not explain to the Vice-Chief of Air Staff what every schoolboy knew – that the temperature at which water boils depends on the air pressure, so that making tea up a mountain is more difficult, and cooking an egg by boiling it at 10,000 feet takes far, far longer than it does at sea level. When the steward had departed to the kitchen, Dickson said:

"Damned idiot! Doesn't know his job!"

I and the others thought it prudent to remain silent. Five minutes later, the steward returned and placed two more eggs in front of Dickson. He then stood back, looking rather plaintively at me, while waiting for the inevitable explosion. These two eggs were, of course, equally raw.

Dickson exploded. He expected his orders to be obeyed. He swore at the corporal and told him again to get back to the kitchen, cook two more and make damn sure they were four and a half minutes exactly. The corporal was looking at me pleadingly. I nodded to him to go back to the kitchen, then said to Dickson:

"This time, Sir, I'll go out to make sure they do it exactly as you want."

I followed the corporal to the kitchen and told the cook to give them about double the time specified. The steward looked at me gratefully. He returned in due course and placed the new eggs in front of Dickson. This time they were to his liking.

"There you are," he said, "but why could they not time the four and a half minutes correctly without a Group Captain supervising them?"

I tried discussing autopilots with him. As I have mentioned, he did not know that any aircraft had them. I turned the subject to guided missiles – he knew nothing about them. The same with blind approach systems. Rockets – yes, he knew about the German V2 – but dismissed that type of weapon as being too inaccurate ever to be of value. Even with an Atomic Bomb in the nose?

"That's impossible," he retorted, as though I was a child. "It could never be made small enough to go into a rocket."

I already knew, of course, that the Americans were developing one that could easily do so. I tried other subjects. Supersonic aircraft?

Ridiculous – they could never get through the sound barrier without breaking up. I gave up trying – I was obviously embarrassing him by trying to discuss anything connected with modern aircraft, warfare or future developments.

Our next stop after Shaibah was Ceylon, where we stayed the night in a luxury hotel. As every officer who has served in the Middle East and beyond knows, it is customary (indeed mandatory) always to wear long sleeves and trousers after dusk – partly for protection against mosquitoes. The Vice-Chief, when he joined us to go in to dinner, was wearing shorts. The head waiter, as I expected, refused to let him into the dining room. I tried to persuade the head waiter to make an exception by pointing out that Dickson was an Air Marshal – a VIP – but the reply I got was that he didn't mind who he was, he was not prepared to let that "scruffy little man" enter his domain. It was very embarrassing having to feel ashamed of a senior officer. Eventually, I managed to arrange that we were served dinner, with the little man still in his scruffy shorts, in a private room.

The AOC Ceylon was Air Commodore Chilton, who had been Toni Ragg's assistant at Bomber Command and then at Air Ministry with Mackworth. He and his wife Bunny had become good friends with my Bunny and me. On hearing that I was in Ceylon, he sent a staff car to take me to his official residence – a palace on the mountain at Kandy, where I spent the next day with them.

From Ceylon we flew direct to Changi (Singapore). The runways at some of the other stations on our itinerary would be too small for the Lancastrian, so at Singapore we changed to a Dakota to visit Saigon, Bangkok, Rangoon, Calcutta and Delhi. We nearly always slept under mosquito nets, of course, but in addition we always had a loaded pistol under the pillow. At the entrance to any tent in which I was sleeping, I always arranged a tripwire that would cause anyone entering to fall over and wake me – hopefully in time for me to shoot any intruder. In the aftermath of war, none of these places had yet recovered to normal.

I was particularly interested in Saigon because my uncle had lived there when he was Postmaster General of Indo-China. The main currency there was cigarettes – much better than dollars, because they were in even shorter supply. With a couple of packets of cigarettes, I bought Bunny a pearl necklace which was later valued at several hundred pounds. In Bangkok I bought a zircon that I had set in a gold ring in Delhi. My main memory of Bangkok, where I stayed in the main hotel, was, on asking for a shower bath, the appearance of two girls carrying buckets of water that they gently poured over me. In Rangoon, it was of masses of rats running all over the streets.

Our tour of duty with Dickson came to an end in Delhi, where Toni Ragg (by then Air Vice-Marshal) arranged that, instead of me returning to England as a passenger in one of the transport aircraft, I should fly an Expeditor aircraft due to be ferried back to the UK. Flying this, with the other group captain and the two wing commanders as passengers, I hopped from airfield to airfield along the Persian Gulf to Lydda. There, having taken a trip to have a swim in the surf at Tel Aviv, I was in a taxi returning when we met an angry mob of Arabs who tried to block our way and were stoning us. Luckily, although we had a couple of windows broken, we managed to get away without injury. It was my first experience of the tension in that area (which continues to this day).

From there, I stopped at several airfields in North Africa, then Malta, Naples, Rome, Marseilles and Paris, where I spent a very enjoyable evening with Pliny Holt's brother Frank, who was the US Air Attaché. On arrival back in England, I – like most others with "Acting" ranks – had to revert to my peacetime rank of Wing Commander and was posted to 47 Group HQ (based at Milton Earnest Hall, near Bedford) as training officer.

While I was away, after leaving Oakington, Bunny and Pam had again gone to live with the Measures at Blackburn Hall. When I was posted to Milton Earnest, we moved to Riseley, as paying guests at the Rectory occupied by the local vicar – the Reverend Poulson and his wife. She was the sister of Bob Wade-Geary, who had originally rented Blackburn Hall to the Measures. Poulson also ran a small school into which we put our daughter, Pam. One of the other pupils was a little boy, named William Ward, who used to arrive each morning on his pony, having ridden across from Melchbourne, where his father farmed the land of a wealthy landowner.

[15 year later, that little boy on the pony was married to Pam at nearby Bletsoe Church, and 52 years later, Bunny died in the room that I had used as an office at Milton Earnest Hall – which by then had become a Nursing Home.]

Apart from the arrival of our second daughter, Patricia, little of interest happened while I was on the staff there. I managed to do some flying – mainly on Yorks, with which the group was being re-equipped, and a Messenger, which had the facility of being able to take off from the lawn at the back of the Hall and land in a few yards. Our AOC, David Atcherley, was a particularly interesting person with whom I had an excellent relationship. He and his identical twin brother Dick were both famous characters.

Surprisingly, David was a bachelor. This puzzled people and whether he was gay was often the subject of discussion. To put an end to speculation, one of the more vivacious wives volunteered to get a definite answer. She reported back – so I was told – that he most definitely was not queer. The trouble was that he got too excited too quickly, so that everything was over before it had started. I felt rather sorry for him. I have wondered more recently whether that could also have been the problem in Ted Heath's case.

David's brother Dick had been one of the Schneider Trophy team. When he had been serving in Egypt, he used to challenge other pilots to fly in the front cockpit of a dual-control trainer aircraft with him in the rear one. Having climbed up to 10,000 feet, he would then trim the aircraft into a vertical dive and both had to put both hands on the fuselage outside the cockpit. Whichever one took their hands off first to pull it out of the dive paid for the drinks. After two aircraft had been damaged by them pulling up slightly too late, the practice was stopped.

On another occasion, he had arranged for the seat to be taken out of a light training aircraft and a small slit to be cut in the bottom of the cockpit so that, kneeling down in the cockpit, he could fly the aircraft by looking at the ground through the slit. To people on the ground, the aircraft would appear to be unoccupied by any pilot. Two days before the AOC's parade and inspection at a nearby airfield, he reported sick on some pretence that would ensure him being retained in hospital for three days. With the connivance of one of the orderlies in the sick quarters (who was doubtless well rewarded), he slipped out to the airfield, took off in the prepared aircraft and, as the parade was all assembled and the AOC was just beginning his inspection, he dived down straight at him in what appeared to be an unmanned aircraft completely out of control. On repeating the attack, he saw the whole parade break up, with everyone running for cover; so he flew back, landed, and was back in bed in the hospital almost before the seat had been replaced in the aircraft. Needless to say, the orderly could certify that Dick had been in bed throughout that period, and with communications much less efficient in those days, the culprit was never found.

Dick's brother David was similarly enterprising. But, much as I admired David and enjoyed serving under him, that did not compensate for the uninteresting job of being a staff officer. Luckily, I had only been posted there to fill in time before going to the Allied Staff College at Bulstrode (Gerrards Cross) for which I had been selected. Also, that summer, I was able to take my two months' post-war leave entitlement.

For that we rented a house, "Sandy Hollow", on the beach at Morgan Porth in North Cornwall, near the farm where Bunny and I had enjoyed many happy holidays before. We invited several friends to join us there, including the Stokes. The day after we arrived, it started raining, and it never really stopped the whole time we were there. Water seeped through onto the ground floor, there was no proper heating and we were worried that little Pat, in her pram, might suffer – as I had – from everything being damp.

Traversing the long stretch of sand in the wind and rain in just swimming trunks to reach the sea was pretty unpleasant, and the return journey even wetter and colder; but the surfing was so good that we usually endured it twice each day. But that holiday was not a great success.

Although I had no regrets at leaving my staff post to go to the Staff College, I was sorry to leave that area where we had so many friends. I never saw David Atcherley again – he was reported missing while flying an aircraft near Cyprus, probably at high altitude, and must have crashed into the sea for reasons that were never clearly established, but were thought probably to have been caused by a faulty oxygen system. (Jack Richards again?)

Bunny found a house to rent at Chorley Wood to which we moved in November. It had little heating and food was still rationed. Bunny had difficulty getting enough for us all, and entertaining our friends was almost impossible.

We had nearly always had a dog. When I was young, down in Evian, we had a St Bernard on whose back I used to ride. In Canada, we had reared a couple of Saint Bernard puppies. So, when we saw an advertisement by a chap named Barrizetti for a three-month-old St Bernard puppy, we could not resist replying to it.

Barrizetti arrived with the puppy (Bulldrummond of St Bury – "Bully") for us to see that Saturday afternoon. Bunny opened the door to him and got quite a fright. The puppy was already enormous – its paws bigger than my hands, and when it put them on Barrizetti's shoulders, his head was higher than that of his owner. It was, without doubt, the most magnificent dog we had ever seen and we paid Barrizetti the £35 he asked for him.

[Three years later, when a posting to London forced me to part with Bully, the best offer I had was £15 – from a butcher who was, during rationing, the only type of person outside a military camp that could feed him the 4 lbs of raw meat he needed each day. His new owner showed him at Crufts, where Bully became a Champion and was then sold for 600 guineas.]

I enjoyed Staff College. It taught me to think more clearly and to write more concisely (although reading this may not give that impression). The course had little to do with aviation or flying an aircraft, but more about organisation, administration, strategy and tactics. It included a visit to Hamburg to see the utter devastation our bombing had produced, and a tour also of Berlin where, at the

Opera House, we saw a stunning performance of *Salome.* There, however, it was the intense concentration of the German audience on the sadistic scenes that left in me the most impression.

Returning via Brussels to attend a lecture from a senior official at the British Embassy, another chap and I took advantage of ten days' leave to go by overnight train to Switzerland and the tiny village of Zermatt, where we enjoyed a week's skiing before returning to England.

The winter of 1946 was extremely cold, with snow lying on the ground around our house at Chorley Wood for many weeks. We enjoyed long spells of clear skies and Pat's pram was often in a sunny position in the front garden, with Bully on guard beside it. Inside our house, it was bitterly cold and fuel rationing forced us to live mainly in the kitchen; but even there the water was often frozen. On the large pond at Bulstrode, the ice was thick enough for us students at the staff college there to play ice hockey on it right through to March.

During the course, to widen our outlook, we had lectures from many senior officers, Cabinet ministers, and civil servants. Some of the politicians were quite awful and obviously unfit to have anything to do with running a country. I thought they ought to have passed some test – apart from having the gift of the gab – before qualifying. It is about the only profession that demands no standard of ability.

We had to practise public speaking and also give lectures on chosen subjects. One subject I chose concerned the potential use of satellites, launched by rockets, for military purposes. The Commandant and most of my audience seemed quite impressed, but one of the instructors (an otherwise quite intelligent Group Captain) criticised me for being so stupid – he insisted that any object put up into the sky was bound to fall back down to earth. I demonstrated centrifugal force with a weight tied to the end of a piece of string and mentioned the earth circling round the sun without falling in. But all to no avail.

"What goes up must fall back," he insisted. He nicknamed me "Rockets", in a rather derogatory tone.

However, I cannot have done too badly at Staff College because, on conclusion of the course, I was promoted to Acting Group Captain and posted to be Deputy Commandant of the Empire Air Navigation School at Shawbury in Shropshire. I was delighted and looked forward greatly to my new task.

I was warned by Chillie, however, that I would find the Commandant there (Air Commodore Jimmy D'Aeth) neither the easiest nor the most pleasant of officers with whom to be closely associated. How right he was!

Chapter 14

EANS Shawbury

My posting to the Empire Air Navigation School as Chief Instructor and Deputy Commandant was dated 9th June 1947, although I reported there a couple of weeks before that for the usual hand-over period from the chap I was due to relieve. I found that I would also be responsible for the Air Traffic Control School at a station further south. It was this latter that emphasised to me the growing world-wide problem of how to prevent collisions in the increasingly congested air lanes.

To escape from some of the tedious business of learning how my predecessor managed things (which I soon decided needed drastic altering), I spent part of each day doing aerobatics in a Spitfire or visiting other stations in a Mosquito. I had also, of course, to become acquainted with the Commandant – Air Commodore Jimmy D'Aeth. Calling on him or his wife was known as "being at D'Aeth's door", which is something not many looked forward to; Bunny and I decided that we liked his wife even less than we liked Jimmy.

For the first time ever, Bunny and I occupied an official married quarter, with batmen to look after us. However, Shawbury had been designed to be commanded by a Group Captain, but now had an Air Commodore as Commandant. So Jimmy occupied the larger quarter designed for a Group Captain and we were in a smaller one – just opposite, on the Officers' Married Patch. I found it interesting that, up to the rank of Group Captain, the regulation furnishing for the bedroom was a double bed – but for all ranks above it was single beds, presumably because by the age they reached Air Commodore they were deemed to be "past it". (Perhaps I should be grateful that, at age 99, I am still only a Group Captain!)

Jimmy had been one of the first Cranwell cadets when the RAF College was formed soon after the First World War. Like some of the other cadets from that era, he had drifted up to a rank for which I considered him to be quite unfit and to have reached that level only because of the "Old Boys' Network" or Masonic connections. I had been warned that Jimmy was quite fond of his drink. With rationing still in force, I guessed that the ample supply of bottles containing alcohol in his married quarter probably came from the officers' mess bar – perhaps "free" for official entertainment on some pretext or other. I soon learned that he was rather religious, and that his wife was very friendly with one of the RAF chaplains, who in turn influenced several of the aircrew (on their regular navigation training flights to Gibraltar) into bringing back certain items that were in short supply in England and cheaper there. Selling such things in England could be quite profitable.

Then, when I tested some of the senior navigators on my staff there, I found that, while their theoretical knowledge was good, their practical ability to navigate an aircraft safely was appallingly inadequate. Also, the school was overstaffed, with many officers engaged on unnecessary tasks just making jobs for themselves. I became pretty critical of the whole set-up. However, with Jimmy there it was difficult for me to introduce many changes, as otherwise he could take that as criticism of himself. But, luckily, he was not due to remain there much longer.

Most RAF postings lasted two years – which, incidentally, meant that few ever had time to learn any job properly. This may have been a relic from the days when the RAF was originally formed partly by naval officers, whose tour of duty in a ship was traditionally limited (? by Nelson) to a couple of years away from their family. Jimmy's two years of duty there were nearly finished. So, rather than run the risk of friction with him, I decided it would be best for me to go away for a couple of months until he departed. With help from Chilton at Air Ministry (who fully shared my uncomplimentary views of Jimmy), I organised that I would fly "Aries II" on a lecture tour and "magnetic investigation flight" to New Zealand and South Africa.

I selected Wing Commander Mike Wyatt, the head of the Experimental Section, to come with me as my co-pilot in Aries. As a preliminary, I arranged for myself and Mike to be thoroughly checked out on our instrument-flying ability at the Central Flying

My co-pilot and me setting out

School at Hullavington. I was awarded a "Master Green" (the highest category) and Mike a "Green". Having a Master Green authorised the pilot to overrule any senior officers regarding the suitability of the weather conditions in which he could fly.

In the interval before we set off, some extra instruments were installed to help us check on the magnetic anomalies that had been reported in one part of Central Africa. In fact, we never had much success with that part of our intended task. More importantly, I had a Bendix Radio Compass fitted (thank God!), so that I could operate it from my pilot's seat and so navigate myself almost anywhere without having to rely on the navigators.

While this was being organised, I heard that Pliny Holt, now a Commander, was temporarily in England. So I flew up to Liverpool in a Lancaster to fetch him to stay with us for a couple of days. I let him fly the Lancaster from the second pilot seat beside me. He was absolutely horrified at the primitive autopilot and other instruments with which RAF aircraft were still equipped. So was I. (Now that we were no longer fighting a war to help the Russians, Jack Richards and his communist comrades in the Ministry of Supply were again doing everything they could – with considerable success – to prevent the RAF becoming more efficient.)

Aries II was a modified Lincoln (which was an improved version of the Lancaster bomber) with long-range tanks (including one in the nose), fitted with the latest British navigational equipment and capable of carrying a crew of about 15. Its forerunner, the original Aries (a modified Lancaster) had been used to break many records. The pilot and co-pilot sat side by side, each with a full set of controls like most big aircraft, with plenty of room behind for the crew to move around or sit at their desks. It was rather satisfying for me to see that the Astrograph, Drift Recorder, Astro Compass and other instruments which had resulted from my work at Farnborough were still in use.

Both Mike and I practised flying the aircraft in a lightly laden condition, and making emergency landings, including with simulated engine failures, until I was satisfied that we were both competent. I appointed Mike to supervise the servicing and loading of the aircraft. We had a sergeant and four excellent mechanics with us to look after the maintenance, and a flight sergeant signaller ("Sparks") for the radio. We also carried a civilian publicity agent to deal with the press. All the rest were navigation specialists, with three graduates from the N* course to take turns doing the navigation – a total crew of 15, including myself.

With the aircraft fully loaded, I took off on 29th September, heading for Malta and flying at about 10,000 feet – our planned cruising altitude for most of the entire flight. Approaching the airfield there (Luca), I reduced power to start our descent. The aircraft immediately began to nose down towards the ground – almost out of control. I heaved back on the control column, but this had insufficient effect. I quickly opened up the engines to cause more airflow over the tailplane and shouted an order to the crew to clamber quickly back towards the tail. I struggled frantically with the controls and just managed to stop the aircraft going into a steeper dive – from which we could never have recovered – and then get it under control again. With most of the crew located nearer the tail, I was able to land the aircraft safely.

There was obviously too much weight in the front of the aircraft – the centre of gravity ("CG") was dangerously wrong. I asked to see the CG calculator. There was none. Every large US aircraft, including the Liberators, always had one. Neither Mike nor the others had ever heard of one. The RAF had excellent pilots – but their standard of knowledge of aviation was abysmal. I wanted the centre of gravity checked at Luca, but there was no equipment there for that purpose. It was not until we eventually reached Melbourne in Australia that I was able to get it properly checked. Avros in England appeared not to have considered the effect of their modifications, which included that large extra fuel tank in the nose, on the vitally important CG. The problem had only manifested itself when the aircraft was fairly heavily laden and flying at reduced engine power. I ordered some of the equipment and baggage to be moved further aft.

The next leg to Habbaniya in Iraq was uneventful. While there, I took the opportunity to have a look at Baghdad. There is no better way of describing it than inserting the article written by Squadron Leader Martingell – the Chief Flying Instructor at Cranwell when I was a cadet there, and to whom I referred in an earlier chapter. He must have written it either during or shortly after the First World War, but it only came to light when Pat found it amongst Peter's mother's papers after she died. It was written in pencil on both sides of a single sheet of foolscap.

Baghdad

In the days of my callow youth, I have sometimes sat and pictured the East, and the picture has always been of sun and temple bells, of waving palms and balmy breeze, of seductive scents and smiling girls with pearly teeth, noble savages, flowering plants, luscious fruit, gay birds, starry nights and deep blue skies. I have sat and dreamed of the romance of it all, and, in my ignorance, I have envied him whose path of life led to those imagined pastures. And now I am in the East and have seen superficially some of the places, the very names of which sounded full of colour and romance: Basrah, whence Sinbad sailed, the heart of the Arabian Nights; and Baghdad, the city of Caliphs, of the prophets of Islam, the capital of the desert Sheiks, the sleepy centre of the legendary East.

And what do I find? Dead Sea fruit and worse. Not only empty, but bitter as gall. The scents of Araby are stinks – foul, sour and revolting. The colours drab and faded, the people dirty in Summer and slimy with mud in Winter. The land a desert, the water foul with rotting garbage, and the towns but a little better than slums. Basrah is nondescript, dirty, dusty, dreary, a few polluted streams or creeks, many date palms, a bank or two, a few shops, a bazaar and then flies, mosquitoes, dust and heat.

But Baghdad is worse, for its disillusionments complete and entire. Of romance there is none, or what there is is so deeply hidden that it passes unseen even to the diligent seeker. Lethargy is the spirit of the people. The streets undrained and filthy. The children with sore eyes and blotchy skins, poorly clad and unwashed. A people pox- and boil-marked. The young men are un-ambitious, content to spend a youth in a blind alley. The finest type – the Kurds – an alien race. Arab and Kurd, Jew and Gentile, Assyrian and American, Christian and Moslem, each distinct and with few interests in common – remnants of a mighty race whose history goes to the dawn of all history, but now merely remnants.

"By the waters of Babylon we sat down and wept", sang the prophet of Israel, and for other reasons may we also weep by Babylon's waters, for the greatness that is past and the hopelessness of the future. This people's eyes are not upwards, they are on the ground. Feed them, from the riches at their feet, flatter them, protect them from their enemies. They will take all and give – what? They are content with things as they are. They do not want our Western ideas. Teach them sanitation and they still prefer muck heaps or the casual Tigris. Give them government buildings, and they use them for private wranglings or spittoons. Give them a shotgun and call them minions of the law and order and it is doubtful they will thief the less. Their merits are not our merits, nor their faults our faults. Of all the maxims of my youth, the one that now rings to me the truest *is that which tells that "East is East and West is West and never the twain shall meet."*

Is this criticism the criticism of one who has eyes which see not and a mind that does not understand? Maybe. Maybe it is that of the American who complained, "What can you make of a people who say 'Well played, Sir!' when they mean 'Atta boy!' It is immature certainly. The desert Sheik, the patient camel, the mutter huts, the lonely desert, the caravans, the pilgrims, may all contain the germs of romance, but it is deeply hidden from the newcomer from the West, and seems far removed from the old tales of the East.

One day, perhaps, I will write a book on the East, on Baghdad of the many stinks, of Baghdad the sordid. It will be an antidote to the flowery tales I used to read; and in writing, should anyone ever read it, I shall be branded as a cynic; whereas I know myself as most romantic.

I shall confess that the book is that of a superficial observer. I have not delved below the surface for the romance that may be there. But, somehow, I feel that it is not worth the trouble.

My own impression of Baghdad – and indeed of that whole area – could not have been more eloquently expressed than on that treasured piece of foolscap.

I decided to fly the next leg to Ceylon by night to test the navigators' ability to use the stars. They had all passed their examinations in advanced theoretical and practical Astronomical Navigation. Also, the weather forecast was that, at 10,000 feet, we should be above cloud soon after leaving Iraq, with the stars visible nearly all the way to Ceylon. However, the weather at Habbaniya was so bad that the station commander there tried to prevent me taking off. Flouting my Master Green authority, I overruled him and took off just after dusk – straight into a violent thunderstorm.

I had often flown through thunderstorms before, but never one so large nor of such continuous intensity. The aircraft was fully laden and far more difficult to handle than the Expeditor I had flown through the tornado in America; also, the much larger wingspan of Aries subjected the airframe to far greater stresses. I climbed up, with large hailstones threatening to break the windscreen or damage the propellers, while I could do no more than try to lessen the effects of violent updrafts and downdrafts and prevent the aircraft from breaking up. Lightning flashes were almost incessant. It was impossible to steer a steady course, or even get an indication of direction from the widely oscillating compass and juddering instruments. All that mattered was to keep the aircraft in the air. It was one of the nastiest, prolonged, experiences in my whole flying career. I felt that I was not really in control.

Usually, in the air, things happen suddenly. But this went on and on and I wondered if it would ever end. It did. One moment we had been in extremely turbulent cloud: the next we were flying in clear air, with the stars shining brightly above and the flashes of lightning receding into the distance behind us.

I gave a great sigh of relief. The white cheeks of Mike regained their colour and I was at last able to steer the course given to me by the navigator. We expected to reach Ceylon in about 12 hours. I had four hours' sleep while Mike took the controls, then we changed places. Meanwhile, the three N* navigators were also taking it in turn to navigate.

Shortly after dawn, Mike and I were both back in our seats, with me flying it. We were at about 10,000 feet and there was – exactly as forecast – a continuous layer of cloud about a couple of thousand feet below. The navigators had been able to use their sextants and the stars for fixing our position throughout the flight.

"Time to start our descent, captain," from the navigator. "About 30 miles to go. Same course. Straight ahead."

Experience had already taught me to rely no more on any navigator (however well qualified) than a modern bungee jumper would rely on damaged elastic rope held together with frayed string. So, to check our position myself, I tried to tune my Radio Compass into the Ceylon beacon frequency to check. There was no response.

"Are you quite sure of our position, navigator?" I asked. "That it is absolutely safe to go down through the cloud?"

"Yes, Captain," from the navigator. "28 miles to go. No high ground ahead."

My Aries crew

I tried tuning the radio compass again to the Ceylon beacon. I had no intention of descending until I had personally confirmed our position. While I was trying to do so, we saw a slight break in the clouds ahead. As we approached closer, we could see a range of mountain peaks pushing up into those clouds.

I called to the navigator to come and look. Peering over my shoulder, he went as white as a sheet. He (and the rest of the crew) realised that, but for me checking, we would all have added to the long list of aviators who have flown into mountains or high ground.

By tuning the radio compass to other stations, I found that we were more than a hundred miles north of Ceylon and out of range of their beacon. Using the radio compass on other beacons, I soon fixed our position, then myself navigated to Ceylon and landed there. Afterwards, I went through the calculations the navigators had made and was able to point out their errors and emphasise the inaccuracies of astronomical navigation.

On the next leg to Singapore, the navigator got his timing wrong by one hour – a miscalculation of the time zone (in relation to GMT) into which we were flying. The flight from there to Darwin was uneventful. I was surprised to find that the town was so small and the buildings mainly made of corrugated iron. I was even more surprised to see, while I was bathing in the nearby Crystal Pool, a large tarantula spider suspended a couple of feet above my head from an overhanging branch of a tree. That gave me quite a fright and tested my powers of underwater swimming as I dived away from it.

From Darwin we flew to Melbourne, where we managed to get the CG of Aries checked. The Royal Australian Air Force Navigation School was located just outside Melbourne. The CO (Group Captain Kingwell) had been on the navigation course at Manston with me before the war and he arranged for me to be treated like a VIP. In consequence, I did a radio broadcast about our flight and was also invited to the Melbourne races, where one of the senior officials entertained me. None of the horses on which I put bets did well – so he took me aside, consulted his notebook, and advised me the horse to bet on for the next race. It won. Later, again consulting his notebook, he gave me another tip. That horse also won. I rather enjoyed being treated as a VIP.

We spent some time with Kingwell and his navigation staff, before flying up to Sydney, where I enjoyed surfing on some of the lovely beaches there. Then up to Brisbane, from where we flew across to Auckland in New Zealand. The thing that impressed me most there was the drinking laws, which resulted in many people rushing to get drunk before the bars closed at 6pm. An old friend, Wing Commander Titch Whitely (another navigation specialist) had joined us in Melbourne for the trip to New Zealand and was with us when we flew down to Christchurch on the South Island, where we spent several days.

One afternoon (mid-November 1947), Titch and I went into Christchurch to do some shopping. I happened to spot half a dozen framed reproduction prints of old English scenes, which I thought would look nice on the rather bare walls of our married quarter at Shawbury. So I bought them. Not wishing to add to the weight in Aries, I paid for them to be shipped to Bunny in England as a

The navigation specialists with Titch on left

The nose full of fuel

Christmas present. That, as I explain later, had a surprising result when they arrived in England.

I did not realise that most of the crew had also been picking up souvenirs – sometimes quite heavy ones – at almost every place we stopped. Unlike me, they stored these in the back of the aircraft or in their baggage, without realising the effect that the cumulative extra weight might have. That only became apparent later.

That same afternoon, while still shopping, Titch and I were upstairs together in Ballantines Stores, in the ladies' lingerie department. I had selected some silk stockings for Bunny and was about to pay for them when I smelt something burning. The girl at the counter said that it was nothing unusual as there was a laundry next door that often caused that. I felt uneasy, but Titch was negotiating for his purchases and did not seem perturbed. The smell of burning got stronger. I suddenly saw a vision of that Zeppelin in flames – just as I had at the Coconut Grove in Boston.

"Titch," I said, "I'm getting out!" and started walking towards the stairs about 20 yards away.

The girl at the counter called to me to say there was no need to worry. But I was panicking.

"Come on, Titch," I shouted. "We can always come back."

He followed me to the top of the stairs. Smoke was now beginning to billow up.

We hurried down the stairs, rushed along to the door and out into the street. We must have been almost the last to get out. We crossed to the other side of the street and turned to look at it. The whole building was now alight. Soon, flames were rising several hundred feet into the sky, just as they had from the Zeppelin, and people were jumping out of the windows of the lingerie department where we had been. Their bodies were lying on the pavement – untouched because it was too hot for anyone to approach them. A tram that the driver had stopped to watch had itself caught fire, but the driver and passengers managed to escape unhurt.

As usual, I had my camera with me. I took a series of photos of the fire. Later, my brother (who was with Crusader Insurance)

Ballantynes Department Store 1947

Ballantynes Store 1947

Ballantynes Store Fire 1947

borrowed them from me and they were published all over the world. The fire, in spite of the efforts of the fire services, still caused a bright glow in the darkened sky that evening. That fire was one of the most tragic in the history of New Zealand. (I was sad to learn of the recent earthquake which caused further extensive damage to that area.)

Looking back, it was my childhood memory of the Zeppelin that had saved our lives.

We flew to Wellington for a couple of days and then back to Melbourne, where we dropped off Titch. The next important place we were scheduled to visit was Cape Town. I had hoped to fly straight there from Australia. For a whole day I studied the winds, the distances, our fuel consumption and the probabilities of us being able to make that long flight. Very reluctantly, I decided that there was insufficient margin of safety to justify subjecting all my crew to that risk. Instead, we would return by the same route to Ceylon and make the hop across the Indian Ocean to Kenya – a flight that I believe had not yet been attempted – and from there to Cape Town.

So we returned to Ceylon (via Darwin and Singapore) and took off for Nairobi in Kenya – a 15-hour flight – in the evening, so that we could use the stars to help us navigate across that large expanse of water, where there were no beacons. About half way across, when I was flying the aircraft and Mike was asleep in the back, the navigator reported a smell of burning. That, for me, was a very nasty moment. A fire is second only to a collision in my list of potential dangers. We all had parachutes, but dropping into the middle of the Indian Ocean – for anyone not relishing the prospect of being eaten by sharks – was not very enticing. There was nowhere I could land – except on the water, providing the fire did not make the aircraft uncontrollable or burn us first. Our only real hope of survival was to get the fire out quickly.

I immediately ordered everyone to switch off everything electrical and to search for the source. I heard the click as the intercom went dead and realised I could no longer communicate with any of my crew. By this time the smell of burning had reached me too. I could not leave the controls and had to rely completely on the others in the back. The smell got worse. But there was nothing

I could do but sit there, controlling the aircraft in the darkened cockpit, and wait. It was a very frightening few minutes and I felt helpless – but knew the others would be doing their best. I also felt very lonely. I looked up at the stars above and then down into the blackness below. All I could do was just wait – and hope.

Then one of the navigators tapped me on the shoulder and shouted:

"Sparks thinks he's found it."

Relief surged through me. I had enough faith in our excellent radio flight sergeant to feel that he was pretty certain to deal with it successfully. I waited anxiously.

Another tap on my shoulder. The excited navigator shouted:

"It's OK, Sir. Short circuit. All isolated. Permission to switch on the intercom?"

Five minutes later, with Mike beside me, we were flying through the night sky as though nothing had happened. The weather at Nairobi was good and we landed without further incident. The height of Eastleigh airfield there was 5,900 feet above sea level. (That, ten years later, was a key point in my first best-selling novel, for which Alfred Hitchcock bought the film rights.)

In Nairobi, I was well looked after by Dicky Richardson, who had been one of my navigation instructors at Manston and was now stationed there. Our visit to the National Park was interesting, but the following day flying from Kenya down to Pretoria was absolutely fascinating. I flew low enough for us to get a full view (denied to travellers on the ground) of some of the enormous herds of various types of magnificent animals, of which I took many photographs.

After a couple of pleasant days in Pretoria, where I again made some radio broadcasts, we continued down this massive, wild area (reputed to harbour the birth of civilisation) to Cape

Clifton Beach - Cape Town

Town. We had good weather most of our time in Africa and the navigators had little chance to lose us. We spent three days in Cape Town, before returning to Pretoria and then proceeding to Bulawayo.

Taking off from Bulawayo, we escaped disaster by a hair-breadth. The airfield was relatively small, and at a height where the thinner air not only caused slower acceleration, but also a greater take-off (and stalling) speed. The 13-hour flight to Khartoum necessitated a full load of fuel. All this I knew and I had made allowances for it. Also, I had taken the precaution of timing our take-off for dawn, when the air is denser before being warmed up by the sun. But what I had not allowed for (because I was unaware of it) was the extra weight of all the accumulated purchases that the crew had added during the last two months. This had not been noticeable when taking off from longer runways, or at sea level, and I had not needed full fuel tanks recently. But at Bulawayo, with a full load of fuel, Aries – without me realising it – was badly overweight.

Halfway through the take-off, but too late to stop, I realised that we were unlikely to get airborne before hitting the hedge. We were approaching the hedge with increasing velocity. I tried to lift the aircraft off the ground without success. In desperation, a few yards short of the hedge I rammed the stick forward to press the nose down, thus compressing the undercarriage. Then immediately I lifted the nose for take-off, hoping that the springs in the undercarriage would help bounce us over the hedge. It did. We cleared the hedge with our wheels skimming the top and I just managed to keep the aircraft from stalling onto the ground on the other side because, luckily, the ground sloped gently downwards. I was so shocked at the narrowness of our escape that it was a few seconds before I could give the order "Wheels up", followed a little later by "Flaps up".

None of the crew behind me realised how close we had been to disaster – they were strapped in their seats and could not see ahead. But Mike beside me was so shaken that he could not at first even move a hand to obey my commands, until I repeated them. I had nightmares about that take-off for several weeks and still look back on it with horror. It was the additional weight of the baggage

Just made it!

that caused the problem. And it was that bounce that saved us from crashing.

We made the flight to Khartoum without further incident; but then, to avoid having to take off again so heavily laden with fuel for the planned further 15-hour flight back to Shawbury, I cut that in half by landing in Malta. On our final leg, flying in cloud at 10,000 feet over northern France, we began picking up so much ice that I had to turn back and then try again at lower level. Flying at low level over the sea approaching the English coast got rid of all the ice and we landed at Shawbury exactly nine weeks after we had left.

Two days later, I had to report to the Assistant Chief of Air Staff (Training) at Air Ministry to give him an account of my flight. Basil Embry was one of our most highly decorated, and finest, officers, who should later have been appointed Chief of the Air Staff (and would have been, but for the opposition of certain civil servants). When I narrated to him the incompetent way in which even our N* navigators performed, pointing out that, but for the radio compass, we would have crashed into a mountain, I was merely confirming what he already knew – that a radical new approach to our navigation problems was needed. He said that the new Commandant, who was to be appointed to Shawbury to replace Jimmy, had been chosen to help achieve that.

305

The timing of my return from our long flight had been pretty good. Not only was the Christmas break due to start, but also Jimmy was on the point of departing.

Shortly before Christmas, a large box containing the pictures I had bought in New Zealand arrived. I had to pay a heavy duty on them because they were being imported from abroad. Then, when we opened the box, we found all the glass had been broken and some of the prints slightly damaged. So I took them to an art gallery in Shrewsbury to be repaired. There I saw a set of identical pictures on the wall at half the price I had paid in New Zealand (where they had been imported from England). Adding in the cost of repairs, they cost me nearly three times the price for which I could have bought them in England. The real irony was, however, that, after I had them hung on the walls of our dining room, we decided that we did not really like them all that much. Later, we gave them to our youngest daughter Wendy. A few years later, tiring of them herself, she gave them back to me. They languish in a cupboard as a reminder of my folly.

I was delighted to learn that the new Commandant was to be Air Commodore Kelly Barnes — the pilot who had force-landed in Iceland and taken his bride there, and had to share the bedroom with Toni Ragg, while I enjoyed that luxurious suite.

Kelly Barnes was one of the finest, and most intelligent, officers who ever served in the RAF. He had been (in 1920) one of the first cadets at Cranwell and knew Jimmy D'Aeth well. He spent the first two days looking into the organisation we had inherited, discussed everything with me, agreed with me about the big changes that were necessary, gave me instructions about the additional things he wanted done, and then departed on two weeks' leave to a cottage with no telephone while I carried them out. He was a leader that I would have followed anywhere. We got on famously together and became great friends.

Two days after he went on leave, Aries caught fire while being refuelled and the aircraft was destroyed. A static electrical spark was blamed. I sent him a telegram to inform him before he read about it in the newspapers. Instead of the criticism I expected, his reply came back:

Ensure replacement has fire extinguisher.

As soon as Jimmy had left, I had instituted an enquiry into the activities of the chaplain and also into the book-keeping concerning the officers' mess bar. When Kelly returned, I reported to him the findings (which were even worse than I had feared), suggesting the culprits should be punished. He considered the matter for a while, then asked his favourite question:

"What is our primary aim, Tubby?"

We had already discussed that and agreed on it. So I replied:

"To enable the RAF to navigate accurately."

He nodded and then asked: "Does pursuing this matter help achieve that aim?"

I had to admit that it did not.

"Then forget it," he ruled. "Let's put all our energy into achieving our aim."

We did.

I delegated most of the running of the station to the highly efficient Wing Commander Andy Anderson. (Some years later, I discovered he was a cousin of my youngest daughter's mother-in-law.) We selected a dozen of the best brains amongst the staff to form a team with us, and arranged first for scientists from the research establishments and industry to lecture us on all the latest developments connected with Navigation. These were followed by lengthy discussions and visits by Kelly or me to anywhere that was likely to add to our knowledge. We also replaced some of the weaker staff with better officers. Everyone had to be ready to answer Kelly's famous question, "What is the aim?", in relation to whatever task they were doing.

One of my wing commanders, in spite of a great deal of assistance from me, could not stand the strain and I sent him off to a nearby farm to help pick potatoes for a month so that he recovered from a near nervous breakdown before being posted away.

Meanwhile, I fitted in quite a lot of flying in various types, including my first jet – a Meteor. I also tested the first British Radio Compass, carried out blind landings in fog, and on Battle of Britain Day gave aerobatic displays in a Spitfire at a couple of stations.

On one occasion, while the Spitfire was upside down, a stinging fluid suddenly splashed into my eyes. It blinded me – at least temporarily. My eyes were hurting so badly that I could not open them. I thought it might be acid and that the only way to get down safely would be by parachute. Instinctively, just by the feel of gravity, I managed to get the aircraft somewhere near upright and made an emergency call to the control tower, asking in what attitude I was flying. The air traffic controller thought I must have been joking to ask such a silly question. But when I told him I was blinded he panicked into helping me.

He then told me, in a continuous running commentary, in what attitude and direction I was flying. With my eyes tightly closed, I managed to keep the Spitfire more or less level, doing a wide circuit round the airfield at a safe height until I had wiped enough of the stinging fluid away to blink open one eye, and a little later the other. I asked for someone to be available to bathe my eyes immediately on landing. With his further help to get into the right position and blinking hard, I managed to make a normal landing. The liquid was found to be brake fluid from a damaged pipe. Although painful, it did no permanent damage to my sight.

About ten months after Kelly had arrived, we had reorganised everything and were making excellent progress. Then he began feeling unwell. I remember helping lift him onto a stretcher at his married quarter to be taken to hospital. He was diagnosed with having leukaemia. He knew there was no cure, and rather than continue lying in bed with constant attention, one night he deliberately brought it to an end. I flew 15 of our senior officers down to his funeral near Benson on 17th December 1948. I had again lost a valued friend and the RAF one of its finest officers.

The Commandant normally held the rank of Air Commodore. But my peace substantive rank was only Wing Commander, with seniority 1st October 1946. To have promoted me to Acting Air Commodore would have meant me being jumped right over all the substantive Group Captains many years older than me, which would have set, in peacetime, an unacceptable precedent. The C-in-C of

Me as Commandant

Pam with puppy!

Training Command (Cochrane) visited Shawbury and instructed me to take over as Commandant, but in my present rank.

I continued the work Kelly had started, and then began extending his ideas outside navigation to the administration of a station. I centralised in a large lecture room a series of displays, each kept up to date daily, by every section to show their precise aim and how well they were achieving it – not in figures, but by clear diagrams or pictorially, so that the information could be gleaned at a glance. For example, the fuel and coal stocks (important during rationing), occupancy of married quarters, vehicle availability, and aircraft serviceability state – everything a station commander needed to know, measured against the ideal. Thus, anyone could immediately see if any section was not achieving the aim – which had to be clearly stated for every section.

The resulting improvement in efficiency was considerable – no section commander wanted to display any failure to meet their task. It also meant that, just by visiting that room each day and glancing around, both Andy and I were fully and easily informed without the need for meetings or inspections.

When Cochrane next visited Shawbury, I showed him, in addition to the navigation analysis displays, this administration display room. It was just like the time I explained the Radio Range to him at Oakington. He had never seen anything like it before and was full of praise (a rare compliment from him) and instructed me to start a similar analysis to cover all other RAF operations. It became known as "Operation Bonehead", and I appointed six of my brightest officers to form the Bonehead team, one of whom was particularly alert – Flight Lieutenant O'Brian Nicholls (about whom more later).

The Russians, who had recently caused the Berlin Airlift (in which some of my aircrews had been involved), were now clearly the only major power with whom we were likely to be confronted and all discussions were based on that premise. The Bonehead analysis of Bomber Operations (which was the first we concentrated on) highlighted what I had known for years – that aiming a bomb by flying an aircraft in a straight line towards the target was no longer practicable. Quite apart from the question of inaccuracy, Russian ground-to-air missiles would eventually make any bomber carrying a heavy bomb a sitting duck. There had to be another solution. Ground-based rockets carrying a nuclear bomb were, of course, the obvious deterrent and were being developed. But I felt, very strongly, that there must also be a solution for bombers too. That was a problem that I decided to concentrate on. Meanwhile, Bonehead was examining the problems facing other types of operations too and it seemed to me that the armed services needed to be completely reorganised with a Rocket Force to protect us against any major threat – leaving the other services to handle minor wars that might break out.

In the spring of 1949, I learned that Cochrane was to become Vice-Chief of Air Staff. Also, that he had arranged for me to be appointed to be Deputy Director of Operational Requirements at the Air Ministry in Richmond House, Whitehall – just opposite the Cenotaph.

Cochrane also ordered me to move Operation Bonehead into the wartime underground offices of Winston Churchill in the building opposite in Whitehall, and to take complete charge of this Top Secret analysis, develop it further, and report on it only direct to him – in addition to my normal duties. I was to select whatever staff I needed to expand it to cover every aspect of our future operational capability – first of the RAF, but to consider rockets as well later.

Meanwhile, my normal duties would include recommending the future requirements for all types of flying and navigational instruments that the RAF would need – and for these to be developed by the Ministry of Supply at RAE Farnborough and by industry.

My future work looked intensely interesting, but I hated the idea of having to go to London every day and only fly a desk round the office. Also, there was another problem – a domestic one – in addition to that of getting rid of Bully, our giant St Bernard, which I have already mentioned.

Back in 1936, when Bunny had been in Egypt with me, the Egyptian guide who accompanied me to the top of the Giza pyramid had, on our descent, drawn some lines in the sand and forecast to Bunny that she would have two children. Bunny was superstitious and she believed him. In the summer of 1948, we had been on holiday down in Cornwall and I remember teasing Bunny about her superstitions. We both rather wanted another child anyway. So I decided to prove that Arab wrong. In consequence, Wendy was due to be born a few days after I was due to take up my new appointment. So I had to leave Bunny at Shawbury and find somewhere for our expanding family to live from where I could commute to London. Loving to be near the sea, I chose Angmering on the South Coast, with an excellent train service from nearby Arundel to London. But it was a little while before Bunny with the new baby could join me there, and when she did she had to go into hospital. Pam, then ten years old, had for the first time, but not the last, to manage everything for me and her two younger sisters. Quite soon, however, we were all reunited in a lovely house on the Ham Manor estate. It was there that the daughter (Annie Gros) of one of my father's school friends at Evian-les-Bains joined us to help look after all three daughters.

Although working very hard, I had decided also to have a go at winning the first post-war annual Gordon-Shephard Memorial Essay Prize on a subject which, that year, particularly suited me – *The effects of recent developments on the future of the RAF.*

I won 1st Prize – not perhaps because of the contents, but because, having detailed all the things that pointed to the RAF needing to be completely reorganised and re-equipped to cope with the developments of satellites, smaller atomic bombs, guided missiles and longer-range rockets, I guessed that the judges would be some nostalgic old deadbeat Air Marshals who were living in the past. So I concluded it by saying that, in spite of all the revolutionary new developments, good old Coastal, Fighter, and Bomber Commands had done such a wonderful job that it would be folly to change anything radically. My guess was correct and I think it was that illogical conclusion that caused the nostalgic old deadbeats to award me that quite prestigious prize.

Before I left Shawbury, I did as much flying as possible, knowing I would get little while serving at Air Ministry. My last flights there included a couple of trips to Gibraltar and Malta in a Lancaster testing the navigational ability (or inability) of some of the graduates, and doing aerobatics (just for the joy of it) in a Meteor 4 at night.

The prospect of mainly sitting at a desk in Whitehall was, however, balanced by the importance and challenge of my new responsibilities.

Chapter 15

The Air Ministry

In May 1949, I began the tedious routine of going from Angmering up to London and back by train every weekday, just like some of the civil servants with whom I now found myself working. I mainly used the line from Arundel to Waterloo that ran almost exactly to time and with the train so little crowded that quite often the only other person in my compartment was the Duke of Norfolk on his visits to the House of Lords.

My job was to establish the requirements for all flying and navigational instruments for future RAF aircraft – which would then be transmitted to the Ministry of Supply, for them to direct RAE Farnborough to develop. In fact, many of the more successful ones were developed and produced by instrument firms on their own.

My office was in Richmond Terrace, overlooking the Cenotaph and Downing Street, with my RAF staff in adjacent offices. Much of the building was occupied by administrative civil servants – mainly of quite a different type from the scientists at RAE who had, in the work in which they were engaged, been pretty intelligent. In all my time at Air Ministry, I never met a single one who ever made a decision on his own. Everything always had to be referred to large committees for two reasons – so that no one could ever be held individually to blame for a wrong decision, and also to increase the number employed. Lengthy papers had to be prepared before any committee meeting and circulated to all concerned and everyone needed at least a couple of weeks to study them first. Trying to achieve anything there was incredibly frustrating.

But I was lucky. I could escape into the "Top Secret" area of the underground offices in the building on the other side of the road, into which no one but my Bonehead team were allowed without my authority. There we were making good progress in analysing, and displaying pictorially, the precise aim (and capability to achieve that aim) of each section of the RAF. From that we analysed the main requirements to overcome the deficiencies (which were mammoth) in order to enable us to be ready to operate efficiently in any future situation then envisaged – primarily, of course, resulting from a confrontation with Russia, but also from events elsewhere.

Thinking deeply about that, I wrote a paper (which I was later told had been considered by the Cabinet) suggesting that, for the benefit of future world peace, and before Russia developed their own atomic bomb, the US and Britain should threaten Moscow immediately with an atomic bomb attack unless Russia disarmed completely and opened up their country to us. Similarly with any other country – like China and Burma – so that the US and Britain would effectively guarantee world peace in the years to come. Later that year, on 29th August 1949, only a day or so after the Chief Scientific Advisor had given a lecture at the Staff College confirming that Russia would need at least another five years to develop one, the Russians detonated their own atomic bomb. By that date it was already becoming too late! The first, and perhaps the last, chance of enduring world peace had probably gone for ever. But I still think it would have been a good policy to have adopted.

The unexpected speed with which the Russians had developed their atomic bomb led me to wonder whether Richards, who had discussed the two main designs (about which he seemed very knowledgeable) with me during his visit to the USA in January 1945, was partly responsible for giving them helpful information. I wrote a highly confidential and critical report about the subversive activities of Richards when he had been Head of the Instrument Department at Farnborough and of his communist beliefs. It recommended that he and all his like-minded pals should be immediately removed from posts where they could do further damage to our national interests. I understood that it had been passed to the appropriate authorities, but I heard nothing more about it.

For my work connected with Bonehead, Cochrane left me to get on with it in any way I liked, with him merely taking a look at progress from time to time. My immediate boss in the Operational Requirements organisation was Air Commodore Harry Satterley –

an ex-sergeant pilot who, as a Flying Officer, had been one of my flying instructors at Cranwell. He was a highly efficient officer and we became very friendly, but he was completely lacking in imagination, incapable of forward thinking and should never have been in that post. Later, he was replaced by an ambitious, much decorated officer, who unfortunately did not even have Satterley's asset of being efficient – but prided himself on giving quick decisions on matters which, unfortunately, he often did not fully understand.

Above them was the Assistant Chief of Air Staff (OR), with whom I had many dealings – Air Vice-Marshal Claude Pelly. He had been a cadet at Cranwell with Kelly Barnes in 1920 and was a pleasant, but rather small, officer, with whom I got on quite well. However, like many of his vintage, who were now filling all the senior posts in the RAF, he had drifted up to that rank without the outstanding qualities really needed. Nevertheless, he was more intelligent than most – but not up to the standard of the few senior officers whom I really admired. I had first met him when he flew himself up to have lunch with Kelly Barnes at Shawbury. My opinion of him was partly influenced by my having waited over an hour on the runway there to greet Pelly, only to find that, in clear weather, he had mistakenly landed at the wrong airfield!

Soon after I arrived at Air Ministry, I found that a new Top Secret development (largely sponsored by Jack Richards, who had been promoted to Head of the Telecommunications Research Establishment at Malvern) was causing great excitement. It was a guided bomb with television in the nose. Vast sums of money were being poured into it. I checked on its design and proposed use. It was almost exactly the same as the one I had tested at Tonapah back in 1944 and would have similar limitations – making it effectively useless.

I sought an interview with Pelly and told him so. He said that the scientists were convinced that it would work.

"But I have actually used one," I insisted.

"You can't have done," he replied. "It has only just been invented. The scientists won't have it ready for tests for at least another six months."

I gave up. That project, after millions of pounds had been spent on it, was finally abandoned for the same reasons as it had been in the USA – which had been fully explained in the report that Stevens and I had written and sent to the Air Ministry (and RAE when Richards had been there) six years previously!

Another thing I found was that everything connected with radar was falling behind schedule, or experiencing unexpected problems. Although a different section from mine covered radar developments, they greatly influenced the navigational requirements for which I was responsible. In consequence, I attended many meetings at the Telecommunications Research Establishment. The reason for all the delays and malfunction of equipment was obvious to me. I accumulated enough evidence to convince me that Richards was again working against British interests and confirmed my worst suspicions – but proving that was difficult. Then, one evening, when several of us were having drinks together, Richards was asked why he was delaying a project that would have increased RAF efficiency, and he blurted out:

"Because I do not think it will benefit the world for the RAF to have it."

That was proof that he was working on the Russian side. Encouraged to do so by several others who also knew of his communist leanings and activities, I decided to try to do something more to prevent it. The Director of Intelligence (who was our main contact with MI5 and MI6) had also been a navigation specialist. So I went to see him and told him all I knew about Richards. A week later, he asked me to go and see him again. He told me in confidence that the security services knew of Richards's communist leanings and kept him under surveillance, like many of his like-minded comrades – including even politicians like Harold Wilson.

I questioned why then, if they knew Richards was a danger, he was allowed to continue in such an important job. The answer was that he, like any civil servant, had worked his way to that elevated position by virtue of his ability, as judged by his peers (some of whom might themselves be communists) under a system in which the political leanings of any individual could not be used as a barrier to promotion.

"My advice to you, Tubby," he concluded, "is just to keep your views to yourself – otherwise you could find you are the loser. Even your life could be in danger. Do not forget that Richards has comrades in even higher positions."

I left that discussion feeling pretty depressed.

The RAF Club in Piccadilly was my usual venue for lunch and the bar there was frequented by some retired senior officers whose conversations were almost all nostalgic, such as: "I say, old boy, do you remember that time back in Poona ...?".

With rare exceptions, they had gone to seed and had little ambition but to prop up the bar and exchange reminiscences – yet most were much younger than my father who, at that time, was just starting out on a new project setting up an antimony mine in Morocco. When I had joined the RAF in the depths of the Depression, it had been the attraction of a pension that had influenced my choice of a career. For the first time I began wondering whether – at whatever rank – I wanted to wait for a pension to enable me to become like that group? Perhaps it would be better to leave while young enough to take up another challenge. Just that little seed of doubt was planted in my mind – that I should retire early from the RAF, rather than wait and then be compelled to do so around age 50.

Meanwhile, in my job I came into contact with a whole mass of senior officers – some of whom had drifted up to a far higher rank than their ability and intelligence justified. A few were brilliant, but the majority knew little about modern aviation and nothing about the likely future developments. Some had never flown a modern aircraft and their promotion had been partly based on their success as a pilot in a dogfight in the First World War. I proposed that every officer of Group Captain or higher rank should take an exam (both practical and theoretical) to determine to what level their ability should require them to be demoted – or retired. Some senior officers backed the idea, but it was not adopted and the Air Ministry remained the location of many deadbeats.

To relieve the tedium of going each day to London, I managed to arrange a little flying in various aircraft – and also arranged to go on a lecture tour on navigation developments to some of the RCAF units in Canada, going by boat each way.

I made a series of very interesting flights in a dual-control Meteor, learning to do aerobatics safely while blind flying – without seeing outside the aircraft at all from take-off to landing – always, of course, with a safety pilot looking out. It was an astonishing experience learning to ignore completely all the sensations to which I was subjected and rely solely on what the instruments were telling me.

In December 1949, I heard that a Meteor 4 at Farnborough had been fitted with modified "fly by wire" controls so that the pilot received no feedback feel from the control surfaces while flying, and decided to try it out. In all other respects, the aircraft appeared absolutely normal. It was around midday and sunny, with the wind from the south so that the short runway was in use. Because of a slight intervening hill, the first part of that runway was not visible from the control tower.

Having taken off and climbed up to a safe height, I tried a few aerobatics and found it easier, for example, to do a roll with those controls, although it was a little strange getting no feed-back through them. After half an hour, I decided to land and made a normal approach, but right into the sun. In the last part of my straight approach, I was keeping a particularly close watch on my airspeed because of the runway being relatively short.

My survival from that flight on 21st December 1949, without any injury, from what happened next was a miracle.

Suddenly, at about 500 feet, the aircraft stalled. I had lost control and we were diving almost vertically down. Had the controls been of the normal type, I would probably have felt the stall approaching and been able to prevent it. All I could do now was try to regain control before hitting the ground. Instinctively, and immediately, I had opened up both engines (full power) to gain more speed. Then, as soon as I judged that I had enough extra speed to regain control, I pulled back on the stick to try to flatten out. I had just achieved that, although still descending, when we hit the ground in line with, but a hundred yards short of, the runway – with a force that shattered the undercarriage, but left the rest of the aircraft (fuselage and wings) skidding along at about 100 mph (and accelerating), with the engines still at full power. I was too dazed to do anything further. Ahead, I saw the row of concrete tank blocks that we had built there in 1940 when threatened by a German invasion, then felt a terrific jolt as we hit them. I saw my starboard engine start its fifty-yard flight into the air. Both wings, the other engine and all the fuselage behind my cockpit were torn off. By sheer luck, the nose cone and cockpit, with me strapped in my seat, happened to go through a gap between the concrete blocks and finally skidded to a standstill at the beginning of the runway.

At first I just sat there in a state of shock. I wondered whether I was dreaming, then checked each limb to see if it was working. I decided it was real. Then, slowly realising (to my amazement) that I was completely unhurt, I pressed the transmit button to tell the control tower, which was out of sight, the good news – but my radio was dead. So I climbed out of the cockpit to survey the scene. I stared in astonishment at the only part of the Meteor left intact – effectively, just the cockpit in which I had been sitting. The rest of the aircraft – fuselage, wings, engines and the fuel tanks – was just crumpled, scattered wreckage back by the concrete blocks, with two wisps of smoke rising into the air from where the engines had finished up.

But why – I wondered – had I stalled that Meteor?

Even though the sun had been directly ahead, I was certain that I had read the figures on my airspeed indicator correctly – I was far too experienced to have made a mistake on that. So I climbed back into the cockpit to examine that instrument. Staring at it, I suddenly realised that it was one of the old type – never used in modern aircraft – calibrated in miles per hour, not knots – but with that indication partly erased! So, when I had read 75, it meant that our speed was less than 70 knots. That was the sole cause of the accident, and I had been amazingly lucky on three counts: my quick reactions that had just – by the skin of my teeth – saved me from being killed on hitting the ground; sheer luck that the nose had gone between the concrete blocks; and those blocks preventing it catching fire by tearing off the engines and the wings with the fuel tanks.

When the ambulance and fire engine crews arrived, they stared at me in disbelief. They were amazed to find me still alive – and could not at first believe that I was unhurt. The last anyone had seen from the control tower was the Meteor diving towards the ground at an angle and height from which they thought recovery was impossible.

The enquiry into the crash exonerated me from any blame. But, since it had resulted in no injury and the reason for it was obvious, the enquiry may not have been very thorough. I never heard an explanation of how that wrong instrument came to be fitted, but felt grateful (as things luckily turned out) for the interesting and unique experience that had resulted. Calculations showed that, if I had been just a tiny fraction of a second later in my reactions, I would certainly have been killed. But it was to those concrete blocks that I had helped erect in the dark days of 1940 that I also owed my survival. That was the only real crash I had in my whole flying career.

But a few nights later, having gone to bed still wondering how that wrong instrument could have been fitted, I woke up in a sweat. I remembered the voice of the Director of Intelligence warning me that "my life might be in danger" and connected that with the puzzle of how that obsolete instrument (in mph) could possibly have been fitted to the Meteor – unless it had been a deliberate attempt to kill me. The next day, I arranged a further meeting with him to discuss that. He had not previously been aware of my crash in the Meteor. He said he would investigate further and see me again as soon as possible.

At the next meeting, he confirmed my fear. He told me that it would be difficult, and unwise to try, to prove that the communists had tried to eliminate me. My suggestion of threatening to smash Russia with nuclear bombs unless they disarmed and let the USA supervise all weapon developments there was certainly known to some highly placed communists – but it was my possession of the damning evidence that I had accumulated over many years about the activities of Richards that he thought was the key. He advised me to be particularly wary of again giving the communists any reason for another such attempt and careful not ever to publicise anything about Richards', or any of his communist pals', subversive activities. On that basis, he felt confident that a second attempt on my life was unlikely.

[Therein lies the main reason why I did not publish these memoirs long ago.]

Although I hated being at the Air Ministry, my job there was quite interesting. Also, Bonehead was progressing well. I invited several scientists to come and discuss particular problems. I remember, for example, Barnes Wallis (of bouncing bomb Dambuster fame) coming up twice to discuss with me, and advise us on, the aerodynamics of low-flying aircraft and missiles.

The main problem confronting Bomber Command – the only really offensive arm we had – remained that of delivering a bomb accurately. And, as I mentioned earlier, the procedure of aiming it by the aircraft having to fly straight towards the target was now too dangerous for a high-flying aircraft; it was too easy a target for ground-to-air missiles. Nor could such tactics be safely used at low level with an atomic bomb. Furthermore, hoping to aim the bomb by aiming the aircraft was unlikely to achieve the necessary accuracy – even if the pilot could see the target. In consequence, Britain had no real deterrent to prevent a Russian attack.

I have always believed that every problem has a simple solution – if only it can be found. So each night, before going to sleep, I gave my subconscious mind that problem to solve. This, incidentally, is a process I have used many times in my life – frequently with success.

One night, at the usual time for any bright ideas to emerge (around 2am), I woke up with the answer and wrote it on the pad that I always kept by my bedside for that purpose. In the morning, I had no recollection of having done so. I noticed the writing on my pad, but had no idea what it was about. I studied it – feeling a bit confused. Then suddenly it all came back to me. I immediately wrote it out in more detail and then, over the next week, having consulted an expert at Farnborough about the potential accuracy of certain instruments, but particularly gyros, I refined the idea and prepared a Top Secret paper proposing "The Vielle Bombing System". This followed an earlier Top Secret paper I had written on bombing policy, suggesting that flying at low level was the only safe policy for bomber aircraft and recommending the immediate development of a low-level bomber.

Harry Satterley did not really understand my "Vielle Bombing System", but passed it to Claude Pelly, who then discussed it with me in more detail. He undertook to pass it to the head scientist at the Ministry of Supply for comment. Two weeks later, the reply from Scott-Hall arrived saying – in quite polite language – that it was complete nonsense and could never work. That was, of course, not an unusual reply to any proposal that did not originate from within his own organisation, but it convinced Pelly. He advised me to just forget it and get on with my usual job. I toyed with the idea of selling my system to a firm in the aviation industry. In a way, I regret not having done so.

I took my proposal down to my Bonehead team to get – in particular – the opinion of O'Brian Nichols. He was quite ecstatic. He thought it was the obvious solution – with very far-reaching implications. It meant that we could have a method of attacking Russia against which there was (and I believe still is) no reliable method of defence – in other words, an effective deterrent to prevent them attacking, or threatening, Britain.

I then discussed my proposals with Harry Pritchard. They excited him. I think he must then have spoken to Scott-Hall, because two days later another letter arrived from Scott-Hall withdrawing his earlier letter and substituting another saying that my proposed new Bombing System had considerable merit and should be subjected to urgent further investigation. I considered taking out patents in my own name, but I linked my ideas with those of Dr Adams, who had given me advice on the gyro accuracy, and left that for the authorities to handle. The patents became the property of the Air Ministry and were made Top Secret.

A few mornings later, I found some more scribbling on the pad beside my bed. That caused me to write a further Top Secret paper proposing the low-level bomber and my bombing system in combination. Those two papers altered the whole conception of bombing and started the developments that led (as more accurate navigation methods became available) to the Cruise Missiles in use today. They also threw into question whether we needed to proceed with the proposed V-bomber programme. My system

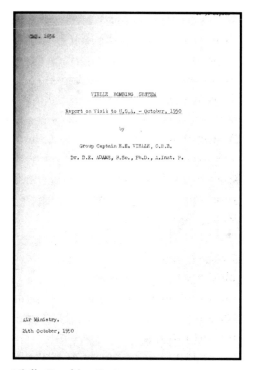

Vielle Bombing System

eliminated the need for the bomber to be flying at high level in order to avoid being damaged by the blast from the atomic bomb they had launched.

My proposals reached Cochrane, who by then was Vice-Chief of the Air Staff. He invited me to dinner at his luxurious London apartment, where we discussed the far-reaching implications of my ideas. He thought it would be best to get the co-operation of America in developing my Bombing System.

Another morning, I again woke up to find some more scribbling on the pad beside my bed. These were simpler to understand – just *"Alverez – Eagle antenna – install sideways along fuselage"*. The idea was so obvious that I should have thought of it years earlier. It was the final piece in a large jigsaw and became known as "Blue Shadow". That sideways-looking fixed narrow radar beam enabled the crew to see on a map, with an accuracy of a few yards, the exact position

of the aircraft in most areas of Europe when flying at any level –
although not over the sea or desert, where there were no radar
responses from known surface irregularities. Furthermore, because
it was not (like earlier systems) radiating ahead of the aircraft, Blue
Shadow rendered the approaching aircraft less likely to be detected.

Because Cochrane was now interested, Harry Satterley and
Claude Pelly were beginning to understand the importance of my
proposals. But, so far as they and some of the scientists at the
Ministry of Supply were concerned, I was a damn nuisance – they
might have to alter many of their ideas and change some of the
plans already in place.

With the enthusiastic backing of the highly intelligent Chief of Air
Staff (Slessor) and his Vice-Chief (Cochrane), it was quickly arranged
with the US authorities for me to present my ideas to a high-level
gathering in Washington DC, at which our Ambassador and the top
brass and scientists of the USAF and USN would be present.

I wanted to take Harry Pritchard with me, but he had just been
appointed to go to the Southern Hemisphere in charge of the atomic
bomb tests there, so I took Dr Adams instead. He was good with
the calculations of gyro accuracies, but, unfortunately, turned out
to be a very poor public speaker. To get a bit of rest and have time
to prepare myself, I elected to travel by sea and found myself on
the maiden voyage of the *Canberra*. On board, I ran into Bob and
Nancy Cameron (who had looked after Bunny in 1940), who were
just returning to Canada from a spell in England.

The gathering in Washington was tremendous fun. An audience
of even more important VIPs than I had expected confronted me.
But I knew my subject well and had no difficulty in putting my ideas
across. Slessor and several others congratulated me and I went off
with Dave Adams to celebrate. I learnt the next day that the USAF
high command had decided immediately to provide whatever help
was required to prove the practicability of my Bombing System (with
their priority being the low-level version). They decided to centralise
the task of assisting me via the C-in-C of their Strategic Air Command –
the famous General Curtis LeMay.

A Dakota and crew were put at my disposal to fly me first to the research establishment at Wright Field to explain the system to the top scientists there, and then continue on to the HQ of Strategic Air Command at Omaha. There, in the big underground operations control room, I gave another presentation to Curt LeMay (one of the most impressive personalities I ever met) and his senior staff. He asked some pretty searching questions. But I had all the answers ready. Finally, he sat back for a while and then said:

"Right, Vielle. I buy it. Let's go. What d'you want? Aircraft? Scientists? Equipment?" Then, turning to his Chief of Staff, he ordered: "See this guy gets everything he wants. Top priority and Top Secret. Appoint two senior colonels to act as liaison officers directly to help Vielle and keep me informed."

He then congratulated me, shook me by the hand, wished me good luck with the project, and left.

After a day there with his staff, I flew on to Albuquerque and Los Angeles to discuss certain instrument developments with experts I knew there, and then to New York to see Vlad Reichel, to get his advice on the gyro design and probable accuracies. The flight from Los Angeles to New York took 17 hours. I then returned to England in a BOAC Stratocruiser in a similar flight time.

On my arrival back at the Air Ministry, Satterley told me that Cochrane had given me the option of remaining in my present post, running Bonehead as well and leaving others to develop my bombing system, or of going to Farnborough again to take charge of the development myself. I was reluctant to hand over control of Bonehead – but the compensation of not having to come up to London every day was too great.

On 8th December 1950, I was again posted to the Special Duties List for service at the civilian-controlled RAE, reporting direct to the VCAS and having authority to demand, with top priority, anything I needed from the RAF, and – via the two liaison officers – from the USAF. I doubt whether any officer had ever been given such sweeping powers before.

My task was urgently to prove and develop the "Vielle Bombing System", which was given the Codename "Red Cheeks". My promotion to full peacetime Group Captain was gazetted three weeks later – on 1st January 1951.

Chapter 16

Red Cheeks

Perring

Jacques

On my arrival at RAE Farnborough, the Chief Superintendent (W. G. A. Perring), who knew me quite well, greeted me enthusiastically and assured me of his full co-operation in progressing the Red Cheeks project, and invited me to go to him personally if at any time I needed his help. He had decided that I should be located in the Instrument Department, the head of which was now Jaques, who had been deputy to Jack Richards back in 1940. Perring said Jaques had been instructed to give me his full co-operation.

Jaques also knew me well and had even been a guest at our house in Washington. I regarded him as a mediocre civil servant who had drifted up to a level beyond his real ability. Right from the start it was obvious that he regarded me as a damn nuisance, intruding into his territory and without him having any control over me or Red Cheeks. I never had proof that he was a communist, but his close

327

association with Richards, and his obstructionism, did sometimes make me wonder.

He was unable to provide me with a decent office, but put a third desk into a room already occupied by two Wing Commanders. One of these was Rod Harman (my former assistant in Washington), who had been located there specifically to try to speed up the introduction of a new type of H2S into the service. Then, when I presented Jaques with the names of the three main scientists on his staff who I particularly wanted in my Red Cheeks team, he unhelpfully made two of them unavailable. However, I got one of them and we formed a team which included about half a dozen other scientists from his department.

On 8th December 1950, the day my posting to Farnborough had become effective, I had flown to the USA to plan that side of my programme, which initially included the supply of a B29 Bomber and several small target aircraft to be used as the test bombs. I had returned shortly before Christmas and by 1st January had the English side planned too.

Meanwhile, Bunny had discovered a lovely old house, perched on the top of a hill, with a panoramic view of the countryside, which we were able to rent furnished from an Army major serving elsewhere. Sheephatch House, Tilford (just south of Farnham) became our home for the next fifteen months – and we also returned to it some years later.

The whole of 1951 was a year of great excitement and activity for me, and we achieved more in that period than would normally (at RAE) have taken several years. I made four more trips to the USA, both to test parts of the system and to co-ordinate progress. Everywhere, except from Jaques and Jack Richards, I had wonderful co-operation.

The C-in-C Bomber Command, Air Chief Marshal Sir Hugh Pugh Lloyd, was particularly enthusiastic and himself piloted a Vampire around prearranged tracks in England at very low level to get experience of the new tactics that Red Cheeks would facilitate. His deputy (Air Vice-Marshal George Harvey) attended the main Red

Cheeks meetings to assist me and appointed to my team one of their best crews, captained by Flight Lieutenant Owen, to fly the American B29 that would be our main aircraft for the initial tests.

In principle, my bombing system was relatively simple. An aircraft, preferably flying at low level, would release the bomb while flying over some predetermined point which was easy to find or see – such as a prominent building or river junction – within, say, 10 miles of the intended target. The bomb (with small aerodynamic controls) would then be jet- or rocket-propelled and controlled by an autopilot guided (to begin with) by a fairly crude pre-set internal gyro navigation system, to direct itself the remaining distance to the target, while the aircraft flew out of the explosion zone. The distance from the target would depend on the accuracy of the navigation system available. At that time, with relatively simple gyros, adequate accuracy for a release point up to around 20 miles from the target was envisaged. With more accurate navigation systems, and increased propulsion, the bomb could be launched at greater distances from the target – even from ships or from the ground. The sideways-looking radar ("Blue Shadow" in the UK) would help enormously to ensure the accuracy of the aircraft release point. A contour-following device to aid the aircraft low fly safely, on which I later personally obtained a patent, completed the system.

It was a method of attack against which there was, and I believe still is, no reliable defence. It would have given Britain and the USA a deterrent against Russia way ahead of anything the Russians had yet developed – although I had little doubt that Richards and his pals were keeping them informed of its details.

The design of the aerodynamic bomb, and its propulsion, was merely a matter of combining technologies that were already proven and was not part of my responsibility at that stage. My job was to prove the principle of the system and the accuracy that would result – which could be done most easily by tests at around 10,000 feet.

I arranged that the Americans would supply the aerodynamic "bombs" to be used in the tests and went down to White Sands (where the first Atomic Bomb had been developed) to examine the suitability of a small target aircraft they had designed there. It had full aerodynamic controls and, by eliminating the engine (and propeller), it provided a good substitute for a bomb, with adequate space inside for our test instruments. Fitted with a parachute set to open a little above ground level and an inflatable bag underneath to soften its landing, we thought we could use each one for several drops. An American scientist joined my team to supervise that aspect of our work.

The key instrument would be the gyro-controlled guidance system inside. For the short time of flight envisaged, no great accuracy was necessary; a relatively cheap and easy to manufacture gyro system was envisaged. On this, the suggestions from Vlad Reichel were of great help. At my request, he became one of the main advisors on that part of the project.

By early May, everything was ready for our first test of the "bomb". The RAF Experimental Establishment at Boscombe Down had fully equipped ranges for observing falling bombs and was the obvious place to carry out the trials. It was commanded by Air Commodore MacDonald, who had been Commandant at the Allied Staff College when I was a pupil there and he knew me well. Everyone at Boscombe Down was co-operative and the Commandant enthusiastic.

The weather that May was good and the early mornings produced clear blue skies – ideal weather for the bomb tests. But the scientists from Farnborough never started work before 8 o'clock – nor did Boscombe Down; so, by the time we were ready to start, it was at least 0930, by which time the clouds had built up and the test had to be abandoned. After two mornings of that, I decreed that we would plan to start the test at dawn. Can you imagine? Asking civil servants to start work before 0800 hours? To leave their homes in the dark to get down to Boscombe by dawn? I had quite a rebellion to quell. But I insisted. It proved so successful that it was soon adopted by Boscombe Down as a routine to speed up much of their other work too. And the staff found that finishing work at midday more than compensated for the early rise.

Red Cheeks Team with Commandant of Boscombe Down

I watched the first "bomb" being attached to the B29 and then motored out to the range to supervise the test and observe the result. To my dismay, that first bomb came tumbling down out of control. The pilot (Owen) had reported feeling a bump immediately after release and we later found that the scientist who did the final check had omitted to notice that the elevators had been pre-set incorrectly upwards. That had caused the bomb, immediately after release, to climb back steeply and hit the underside of the B29. Luckily, no serious damage was done to the aircraft; but we had a slight delay getting another bomb ready.

The next series of tests went almost perfectly and proved that part of the system.

Meanwhile, the sideways-looking radar antenna project ("Blue Shadow") had been given both to the Telecommunications Research Establishment at Malvern (run by Jack Richards) to develop, and also to the Americans. By August, I was able to test a fully developed sideways-looking antenna in a B29 in America. That too worked perfectly. The "Blue Shadow" one developed in England under Jack Richards' direction was not available for another year – and then broke down!

By indicating continuously the accurate position of the aircraft, that radar system enabled the exact direction and distance to the intended target to be pre-set either by hand, or automatically into the bomb autopilot at the point of release – in any weather and from any level, including a high-speed aircraft flying just above the ground. I had also invented, and satisfactorily tested, a "Razsight" (range and azimuth sight) that could be used – as an alternative to the radar – if the target was visible to the attacking aircraft crew.

By September, I had proved the principle, and potential accuracy, of every component of the Red Cheeks system and went to the USA to discuss further plans. The only remaining step was to develop the bomb itself, with some form of added propulsion, which could be dropped from a low-flying aircraft and cruise to the target. That merely involved modifying some of the Guided Missiles I had tested at Tonapah during the war. If it carried an atomic bomb, it would need extra propulsion to climb to a height over the target to get maximum results from the detonation.

[Later, the navigational accuracy was gradually increased over the years until – with the satellite navigation system in use today (even in cars) – it is to within a few feet. So now the only limit to the distance from which the original Red Cheeks bomb could be launched to hit its target with perfect accuracy was the propulsion system.]

The main part of my job was virtually finished and my American friends were delighted with the results. They then went full speed ahead independently with the development of the low-level version – the "Cruise Missile".

When I returned to Farnborough in October, I found a rather tense atmosphere. The Air Ministry (and even some senior civil servants in the Ministry of Supply) had questioned why – if a single Group Captain could have achieved so much in such a short time – so many other developments were lagging so far behind schedule.

In particular, I found Jaques was being particularly awkward and obstructive. I only learned much later that one suggestion being put forward – by one of the senior civil servants at the Ministry – was

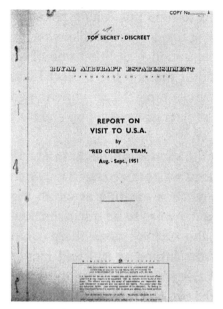

My Red Cheeks report

Professor A.A. Hall

that I should be promoted to Acting Air Commodore to take over from Jaques as Head of the Instrument Department. Without me realising it, I had become a threat to him. The friction between us had increased markedly, but without me fully realising the cause.

Meanwhile, the Chief Superintendent of RAE (Perring), who had been such a help to me, had suddenly died. His replacement was A. A. Hall – the clever young ambitious Professor, with strong communist sympathies, who had been one of the scientists who had joined RAE from being at a university at the outbreak of war. He had then worked in a separate department from me, and had not been one of those living in the staff mess, so we did not know each other well.

The implications of Britain now having communists as Chief Superintendents of both RAE and Malvern (our two key research establishments) did not at first hit me and I failed to realise the effect this could have on Red Cheeks.

I did realise, however, that, on coming in freshly, the new Chief Superintendent Hall found that the authority given to an RAF officer concerning a development designed to help put Britain ahead of Russia in the Cold War was also leading to questions challenging the efficiency of at least part of his organisation – and that one of his department heads wanted to get rid of me and the project I was running. The success of the Red Cheeks project had undermined Jacques' future, and the sooner the project was wound up and I left RAE the better for him.

In mid-December, this festering situation was brought to a head in a way that I later became convinced was pre-arranged between Richards and Hall. Richards was to chair a meeting at which the operational aspects of bombing by radar were to be discussed. Red Cheeks was clearly involved and I should have been there – but Richards specifically excluded me from attending it. I told Jaques that I definitely should be there and asked him to arrange it. He lost his temper and said that I already had too much authority and that he was running that department, etc, and refused.

I discussed the situation with Rod Harman and the other Wing Commander – both were highly efficient officers and both were increasingly frustrated by Richards' and Jaques' obstructionisms. They both felt that the time had come for me to see Arnold Hall to seek better co-operation from Jaques.

I did so – but without realising that Hall would automatically back Richards. He indicated that the increasing friction between Jaques and me meant that one of us had to go. That, I later learned, became a matter of principle of whether a civilian or an RAF officer should head a department in a civilian establishment – whatever the relative merits of the individuals concerned. But underlying it all was the determination of Richards and Hall to best serve their communist masters by getting Red Cheeks cancelled.

The Christmas holidays intervened and then, in early January, Cochrane sent for me and told me to take some leave while it was being sorted out. I was later told that the controversy over what degree of control the RAF could exercise in a civilian establishment had been referred right up to the Prime Minister himself. Churchill had ruled that the Chief Superintendent must have ultimate control and that if he wanted civil servants to be in charge of a project without interference from an RAF officer, then he had that as a right.

I then learned that, at Hall's insistence, probably backed by Richards and by Sir Ben Lockspicer, the Red Cheeks project in England was being cancelled. Why the Air Ministry allowed this to happen still remains a mystery to me.

However, two years later, the high-level version of Red Cheeks (for the V-bombers) was resuscitated as "Blue Steel". Meanwhile, my friends in the USA had continued fast with the development and production of the low-level version of Red Cheeks, which became known as the Cruise Missile.

So Jack Richards and his communist pals had achieved his aim of yet again preventing the RAF from becoming more efficient. High-flying aircraft, such as the V-bombers, were increasingly vulnerable "sitting ducks" to ground-to-air missiles.

Later, I have little doubt that Richards, Hall and their communist comrades helped influence Harold Wilson also to cancel the low-flying bomber – the TSR2 – which had been designed to use Red Cheeks. If Wilson was not acting on instructions from his masters in Moscow, then why did he take the extraordinary step of having all the plans destroyed? In that connection I remain convinced that Hugh Gaitskell was murdered so that the Russian puppet Wilson could take his place.

However, although Jack Richards managed also to delay Blue Shadow (the sideways-looking radar antenna) for a year, he was not able to cancel it completely – but merely make sure it was unreliable and that the English version often failed.

I received much sympathy from my US colleagues when Red Cheeks in England was cancelled. One suggestion was that I should join an instrument firm in the USA, but again – after discussing it with Vlad Reichel – I decided against it. But I resolved that if I had any other bright ideas then I would sell them to industry. However, after I retired, I took out a further patent which made low-flying and the Cruise Missile more reliable. That was immediately categorised "Secret".

I never received any thanks, or reward, while I was in the RAF (nor afterwards) for any of the inventions I made after the war. The official reply to my request for recognition was that I had been merely "carrying out my normal duties".

The little seed, already planted, that I should leave the RAF while still young enough to start a new career, was beginning to grow firmer roots.

I then learnt that Cochrane, at the request of the C-in-C of Bomber Command, had arranged for me to take over command of a particular station in Bomber Command.

My posting to command RAF Upwood, near Huntingdon, was dated 8th April 1952. The station was mainly equipped with the Lincoln bombers of Nos 7, 148, and 214 Squadrons, but additionally housed the Radar Reconnaissance Flight – a unit which I later discovered was involved in secret work of which I had previously been unaware. In retrospect, it seems that my invention of the sideways-looking "Blue Shadow" was partly responsible for that posting.

Patent No. 871926

ℰlizabeth the Second by the Grace of God of the United Kingdom of Great Britain and Northern Ireland and of Her other Realms and Territories Queen, Head of the Commonwealth, Defender of the Faith : To all to whom these presents shall come greeting :

WHEREAS Eugene Emile Vielle, a British Subject, of Ch. de Tattes Fontaine, Vandoeuvres, Geneva, Switzerland

(hereinafter referred to as the said applicant) hath prayed that a patent may be granted unto him for the sole use and advantage of an invention for Improvements in or relating to aircraft navigational apparatus

AND WHEREAS the said applicant (hereinafter together with his executors, administrators, and assigns, or any of them referred to as the patentee) hath declared that there is no lawful ground of objection to the grant of a patent unto him :

AND WHEREAS the complete specification has particularly described the invention :

AND WHEREAS We, being willing to encourage all inventions which may be for the public good, are graciously pleased to condescend to his request :

KNOW YE, THEREFORE, that We, of our especial grace, certain knowledge, and mere motion do by these presents, for Us, our heirs and successors, give and grant unto the said patentee our especial licence, full power, sole privilege, and authority, that the said patentee by himself, his agents, or licensees, and no others, may subject to the conditions and provisions prescribed by any statute or order for the time being in force at all times hereafter during the term of years herein mentioned, make, use, exercise and vend the said invention within our United Kingdom of Great Britain and Northern Ireland, and the Isle of Man, and that the said patentee shall have and enjoy the whole profit and advantage from time to time accruing by reason of the said invention during the term of sixteen years from the date hereunder written of these presents : AND to the end that the said patentee may have and enjoy the sole use and exercise and the full benefit of the said invention, We do by these presents for Us, our heirs and successors, strictly command all our subjects whatsoever within our United Kingdom of Great Britain and Northern Ireland, and the Isle of Man, that they do not at any time during the continuance of the said term either directly or indirectly make use of or put in practice the said invention, nor in anywise imitate the same, without the consent, licence or agreement of the said patentee in writing under his hand and seal, on pain of incurring such penalties as may be justly inflicted on such offenders for their contempt of this our Royal command, and of being answerable to the patentee according to law for his damages thereby occasioned :

PROVIDED ALWAYS that these letters patent shall be revocable on any of the grounds from time to time by law prescribed as grounds for revoking letters patent granted by Us, and the same may be revoked and made void accordingly : PROVIDED ALSO that nothing herein contained shall prevent the granting of licences in such manner and for such considerations as they may by law be granted : A N D lastly, We do by these presents for Us, our heirs and successors, grant unto the said patentee that these our letters patent shall be construed in the most beneficial sense for the advantage of the said patentee.

IN WITNESS whereof We have caused these our letters to be made patent

as of the   twelfth   day of   December

one thousand nine hundred and   fifty-eight   and to be sealed

Comptroller-General of Patents,
Designs, and Trade Marks.

A patent I took out later

Chapter 17

Upwood

About two weeks before I was due to take up my appointment at Upwood, I received a message that the C-in-C Bomber Command wished to see me. I already knew Hugh Pugh, as he was called, quite well from my Red Cheeks activities. He had become famous as the C-in-C Malta, where, with very limited aircraft (one of which had been flown by David Beaty, who later "ghosted" my first novel), he had withstood the German onslaughts and earned Malta the George Cross.

"Tubby," he said, "I've appointed you to clean up Upwood. Also, you have the Radar Recce Flight there."

"May I ask, Sir, what in particular you want cleaned up?"

He shook his head. "I'll leave you to judge that for yourself. I don't think it will take you long."

"And the Radar Recce Flight?" I asked.

"Their work is Top Secret. The CO is Squadron Leader Instrell. He has my authority to discuss it with you, and I want you to supervise everything they are doing. You are never to discuss that with anyone else but me personally – not even with your AOC, and certainly with no one else on your staff. Understood?"

"Yes, Sir," I replied, then added: "May I ask what their task is?"

He smiled. "What the name says – Radar Reconnaissance. Instrell will tell you all you need to know about it."

I then went to see his deputy, George Harvey. He briefed me on the operational aims of the three Lancaster squadrons at Upwood, and, as I departed, he said:

"Your second in command there is Derek Dowding – he's your Wing Commander Flying. Be careful how you handle him, Tubby. Don't forget his father is a Marshal of the RAF."

I thought at the time that was rather a strange remark, and had cause to remember it later.

A week before my posting date, I went up to stay at the George Hotel in Huntingdon to be briefed by the Group Captain from whom

I was taking over. I had met him only once before and did not like him one bit. By the end of the takeover, I liked him even less. He was kind enough, however, to throw a cocktail party to welcome me. The only officer there I knew well was Wing Commander Ken Greenwood – a pilot who had transferred to the Engineer branch and had served with me in the BAC in Washington.

Quite early on at the cocktail party, I heard a crash behind me and looked round to find that the Station Commander's wife had fallen to the ground and had broken the glass she had been holding. I rushed to her aid and helped her up. She seemed unhurt. A short time afterwards, while I was again chatting to Ken, there was another crash. She had fallen again. I was about to rush to her aid, when Ken laid a restraining hand on my arm:

"Don't worry," he said, "she always does that!"

That was my first indication of what the C-in-C had intended to convey. But there were many others that emerged during my takeover. The most serious to my mind was that one of the Flight Lieutenants was in police custody, having been caught soliciting in the men's lavatory in a nearby town. Also, the rather effeminate Flight Lieutenant PA to the station commander struck me as being quite unsuitable for that job. And I was certainly not at all impressed with The Hon. Derek Dowding; he seemed very nervous at meeting me. I then learned that one of the wives ran a lesbian club ... and so it went on. But it was not all bad – there were some fine officers there too.

One of the first things I did after taking over was to ring the personnel officer at Group HQ to demand a really first class PA to replace the drip I had inherited. Then, a little later, I rang the Special Police Branch at Air Ministry, requesting that a suitable officer from that branch should visit me to discuss a confidential matter. Wing Commander Brown arrived two days later and I voiced my suspicions to him. He asked me to arrange a dance in the officers' mess and send out invitations to him and certain members of his staff, including two particular WAAF officers. I did so.

The morning after that dance, he came to my office and confirmed most of my suspicions. During the following weeks, over a dozen officers, including some Squadron Leaders, were posted away – some forced into retirement.

Meanwhile, a new PA had arrived – a highly efficient dour Scot named Jock Ireland. He and his wife became wonderful friends to me and all my family until their deaths 45 years later. With his helpful advice, I was able to clean up all the administrative side of the station as my C-in-C had ordered.

Squadron Leader Instrell preferred to talk to me only in the confines of the closely guarded building in which the Radar Reconnaissance Flight was housed. There he showed me the most recent radar pictures, taken from the air, of parts of Russia. He and his staff were analysing them to detect items of military interest. By a special process, they were able to enhance the pictures to show up details that otherwise might have gone unnoticed. I knew, of course, that the USAF pilot, Gary Powers, had been shot down while flying a reconnaissance plane over Russia, but had not known that the RAF was also involved in flying spy missions. (Later, when satellites became available, photographic pictures from space made these unnecessary.)

I immediately realised that planes equipped with Blue Shadow could produce far more detailed pictures and later guessed that was partly why Hugh Pugh had wanted me there. There were further interesting developments during my time at Upwood and I met some of the pilots and aircrew involved in flights over Russia.

The routine work of the three Lincoln squadrons was, like most of Bomber Command, practising mass raids in exactly the same way they had fought the last war. It was rather like my brother, right up to the outbreak of the 1939 war, being in a cavalry regiment waiting to face the heavily armoured advancing German tanks. Great fun, but quite irrelevant to modern warfare. I took part, as pilot, in some of the night practice raids on places like Heligoland and other targets, where we were able to drop bombs on a remote target. On one such mass raid, I saw a bomb, released from an aircraft above me, flash down past me between my starboard inner engine and the cockpit. A foot or two either side, or a split second later, and it would have exploded and wrecked the Lincoln I was flying. These exercises were complete nonsense – particularly now the Russians had the atomic bomb and the ability to deliver it. But what else could Bomber Command do to occupy everyone and keep the aircrews in practice?

One thing was to do the flying for a company making films of wartime episodes. With the approval of my AOC, a chap named Aubrey-Baring came to see me to plan the making of a film at Upwood in which some of my aircraft and crews would participate. Dirk Bogarde was playing the main part, with a gorgeous leading lady. They had freedom to do more or less as they liked on the airfield for a month. Pam on her pony, with me on the horse that I kept in the bomb dump, used frequently to ride on the airfield in the evenings and so got to know most of the cast quite well.

I had a communications aircraft – an Oxford – in which I did a fair amount of flying, mainly visiting friends at other stations or flying to Bassingbourne to borrow a Meteor in which to do aerobatics or to practise flying a Canberra in preparation for a special one which was due to arrive at Upwood for me shortly.

Dinah Sheridan and cast with us at Upwood

Enjoying Dinah Sheridan's company with C in C!

Pam and me enjoying a ride

Almost exactly a year after I had first tested the first sideways-looking Eagle radar antenna in the USA, I flew down to RRE Malvern to collect a Canberra fitted with the British version known as Blue Shadow. I took Instrell with me and he carried out the first test of it on the way back. He was amazed at the clarity of the pictures it produced.

During the next few days I carried out a series of quite long flights, with Instrell operating that radar, around England and Scotland, testing its suitability for reconnaissance over Russia and for general navigational purposes. Part of the time we were flying at high altitude – above 50,000 feet – but we also tested it at low level.

We then demonstrated it – for navigational use, but with no mention of its reconnaissance potential – to my AOC (Air Vice-Marshal Brook) and others.

One afternoon, I suggested to my Wing Commander Flying – Derek Dowding – that he should also fly the Canberra. I said I would teach him the following morning so that he could then do so. That evening, he was found wandering round the camp in a dazed condition and taken to Sick Quarters. Our doctor, a super chap who later became a Harley Street specialist, came to see me the next morning to say that Derek had suffered a complete nervous breakdown. I asked him to look into his medical history, while I sent for his flying logbook. Together, we decided that Derek was quite unsuited to be in any post involving piloting an aircraft himself. He had been categorised as LMF during the war and it was his fear of flying that had caused his collapse. It seemed that it was only the influence of his father that had enabled him to stay in the RAF and reach his present rank.

The following day, I had a surprise visit from his parents, Lord and Lady Dowding – obviously to put pressure on me to hush it up. I took that as an insult to my integrity.

I got our doctor to report the situation to the Chief Medical Officer at HQ and I rang George Harvey to say that I needed a really first class Wing Commander to replace Derek. George did not appear unduly surprised. A couple of weeks later, Don Smith (DSO, DFC, and

Canberra

Reporting to AOC

a former junior tennis champion at Wimbledon) was posted in as my deputy – an excellent choice. He and his bubbly wife Irene became our friends for life.

Soon after Don arrived, there happened to be a ball at the Officers' Mess, to which the AOC and his wife were invited. The party was in full swing and Don's wife, Betty, was dancing with the AOC when the elastic in her knickers broke and they fell round her ankles. She quickly stepped out of them and picked them up. Seeing her embarrassment at having nowhere to hide them, the AOC grabbed them and stuffed them into his pocket. The dance continued, followed by others and also drinks.

It was not until she undressed to go to bed that night that Betty had cause to remember the incident. She phoned up my wife, told her of the incident and asked her advice. She felt in quite a quandary – should she ring up the AOC and remind him that he had her knickers in his pocket, or just leave it to chance? They decided that any telephone conversation might only make matters worse – particularly if the AOC's wife happened to overhear it.

The AOC had also forgotten about the flimsy things in his pocket and it was not until the following morning that his wife, while preparing his clothes for pressing, had discovered them. That, as he sadly recounted to me next time we met, resulted in one of the biggest challenges he had encountered in his married life.

"It's not part of your normal duty, Tubby," he said, "to check the elastic in the knickers of all your officers' wives. But next time you invite me to a party with them, I'd be grateful if you would!"

I had already arranged for the Blue Shadow Canberra to be fitted with long-range wing tanks. I also undertook my instrument flying tests to renew my Master Green status to make sure I was in good shape for flying it in difficult conditions, and planned longer test flights of this new equipment.

On 15th August, with Instrell and another navigator, I took off for Gibraltar to have morning coffee with Chilton, who was the AOC there, then to Malta for lunch, intending to be back at Upwood for a late tea. Unfortunately, we were delayed for three hours while refuelling at Malta by the inefficiency there. That was not surprising (because the AOC there was Jimmy D'Aeth); but then, over northern France, we started running into some of the thickest and highest clouds I have ever encountered. I climbed up as high as possible – up to 53,000 feet – but even then we were still sometimes in wispy cloud. I had always believed that clouds never reached that height. As we approached England, the clouds seemed even denser beneath us. And thanks (I am convinced) to the communist Jack Richards, our Blue Shadow radar (on which we relied to navigate) developed a fault and ceased to function.

I have mentioned the date because that is the night that Lynton and Lynmouth were washed out by some of the biggest storms ever known in England. We crossed the south coast flying well above 50,000 feet, but were still sometimes in cloud. Beneath us was a black mass so dense that, yet again, I found that even the lightning flashes were dulled. The sun had set and the prospect of descending was like standing naked on the diving board above a swimming pool filled with ink in which hungry barracuda were darting around looking for a meal.

But the Canberra is one of the loveliest aircraft to handle that I ever flew. We made our descent down to Upwood through those massive storms with surprisingly little difficulty – a very different experience from flying the heavily laden, cumbersome Aries in that thunderstorm over Iraq. I found our airfield and we landed with just enough time for me to change into mess kit for dinner.

It was during those high-altitude flights in the Canberra on the trip to Gibraltar and Malta that, for the first time in my life, I began to wonder what effect the rays from the sun were having on me. I had always loved sunbathing and taken every opportunity to strip off to enjoy the beneficial effects. But sitting up at 50,000 feet, with nothing to filter its vastly more brilliant intensity of rays, was quite a different matter. At those heights there is insufficient air to diffuse the light, and even at midday the sky appears dark. The glaring sunlight casts sharp shadows, so that it is difficult to see anything on which it is not directly shining. And the reflection from anything on which its rays fall is brilliant enough to make dark glasses a necessity – thus making it even more difficult to distinguish anything in the shade. The intensity of the sun on my head and face made me fear that the radiation was harming me. [After I had carried out more research on it, that became the main theme, fifteen years later, of my second novel – also a best seller. More recently – in 2001 – I saw that the subject was back in the news again and that my fears had been fully justified.]

At those heights, also, was the problem of the low air pressure outside the aircraft. Without a pressurised cabin, at heights above about 35,000 feet the gases (like oxygen and nitrogen) which are always present in our blood start boiling out – bursting the blood vessels and quickly causing death. All there was between me and the sky to keep our pressure safe was the large transparent plastic cockpit canopy. I was pretty confident that adequate tests had been carried out to make sure it would not develop a crack – but if the cabin had lost all pressure we might not have had time to descend to a safer level before our arteries popped. But, for me anyway, that slight risk was counterbalanced by the minimised chance of colliding with another aircraft up at that level.

Flying at really low level was more fun, of course. But sitting up there, right outside the normal world, my thoughts could wander freely. It was up there, with no danger of collisions, and little else to think about, that I began wondering how I could find a solution to that collision problem for aircraft flying at more congested levels. That seemed to me to be the most important issue facing future aviation.

I also pondered on the advance in the design of aircraft. The Avro 504 (designed in 1912 and first produced in 1913) on which I learnt to fly had only three things in the cockpit which I could operate – apart, of course, from the switch to stop the engine. These were: the throttle with my left hand, the stick with my right, and the rudder bar with my feet. Nothing else!

The Canberra, less than forty years later, had (in addition) so many other things over which the pilot had control that it needed a lengthy list of items to be checked to make sure nothing had been missed – before take-off, after take-off, while cruising, before landing and after landing. Even with a checklist, there was plenty of room for errors. Everything was so much more complicated that I always used the checklists very carefully.

Back at Upwood, the analysis of the radar pictures that we brought back from the Gibraltar/Malta flights confirmed the enormous superiority of the sideways-looking antennae for aerial reconnaissance. Other flights that we made confirmed its suitability also for use at both high and low level.

With the team of officers I now had at Upwood, the whole station was running very smoothly. In consequence, I had more time to go flying and took every opportunity to do so. In this I was encouraged by my AOC (Brook) and Hugh Pugh – both of whom I taught to fly the Canberra. It did not have dual control or a seat for a second pilot, so I would do the take-off with them standing beside me, with me explaining exactly what I was doing, and then at about 10,000 feet I would trim the aircraft to fly level, quickly get out of my seat to change places, with me holding the stick to maintain stability, until they were in position to take over. Then, still at 10,000 feet, we would go through the landing drill (slow down, wheels down, half flap, etc) to let them get the feel of it and then pretend to land, but do a dummy overshoot and go round again with all the correct procedures. When they were happy, I would continue standing beside them and talk them down to a landing back at Upwood.

AOC, C-in-C and me at Upwood

Both Brook and Hugh Pugh (and their staffs) were some of the finest officers with whom I was ever privileged to serve. Brook and I formed an excellent friendship. Together with an honorary member of the mess, Colonel Darrell Moore (formerly of the Ghurkas), we used to go pigeon and pheasant shooting whenever possible on the Lord Ramsey estate. [Lord Ramsey and Darrell had been prisoners of war in Japan together and had promised Darrell one of his farms if they survived.]

All Canberras, except the one allocated to me for the Blue Shadow trials, were concentrated in No 2 Group, commanded by Dermot Boyle (then an Air Vice-Marshal, but later Chief of the Air Staff). Another version of the Canberra, fitted with a new type of Rolls-Royce jet engine – the Avon, with tremendous power – had been developed and it would have been logical for it to be allocated to 2 Group for testing. But the C-in-C decided that it would be sent to me at Upwood to do the tests. Rolls-Royce required the engines to do 600 hours of flying – to be completed on it as soon as possible. That, on past experience and allowing for bad weather, would need at least about six months and probably up to a year to complete.

Together with Don Smith, I suggested a new approach to the problem, but without telling anyone at HQ. To prevent any interruptions due to weather (it was December), we would have a Met officer always available to advise the Canberra where in the British Isles, if there was any doubt about Upwood, would be the clearest weather to land and refuel. Also, there would always be a team of mechanics, trained to refuel it quickly and do any necessary maintenance, plus spare pilots that I had trained to fly the Canberra, at standby in a Lincoln to fly to wherever the Canberra was going to land – day or night – to await its arrival. That way, I reckoned that the whole 600 hours flying could be completed in about a month.

The plan worked perfectly, with the refuelling crew and fresh pilot always available wherever the Canberra had to land. It is interesting that Kinloss, on the coast near Inverness in Scotland, became, after Upwood, our most used airfield.

350

About two weeks after the Canberra with the new Avon engines arrived, the C-in-C rang me up one morning to ask me how the trials were going. I apologised for the slow progress and said that, with the bad weather we were experiencing, it might take another couple of weeks to complete the full 600 hours, but that we were doing our best.

He assumed I must be joking and was pretty cross. He did not actually roar down the phone and call me a bloody fool, but that was implied by his tone of voice.

[That reminded me of another occasion when a Wing Commander rang HQ asking to speak to the duty officer. He then roared down the phone, calling him a bloody incompetent fool for some stupid action he had taken. But the operator, by mistake, had connected the Wing Commander not to the duty officer but to the C-in-C. After a few seconds listening to the tirade, the C-in-C had shouted:

"Do you know who you are speaking to? This is the Commander-in-Chief!"

The startled Wing Commander, in as stern a voice as he could muster, replied:

"And do you know who this is?"

"No," replied the C-in-C.

"Thank God!" murmured the Wing Commander, quickly putting the phone down.]

In my case, however, it was a different matter. When I had convinced him that what I had told him was true, he told me to expect him within a couple of hours – an informal visit, no guard of honour. As usual, he arrived in his Devon, piloting it himself, and gave me a wave from the cockpit before getting out. Also, as usual whenever he visited any station, he went straight to the Operations Room, where Don and I explained the organisation we had set up to keep the Canberra in the air for all but about 3 hours in every 24.

He was full of praise. Nothing like that had ever been done before. He suggested, however, that I should give the crews a break over the Christmas holidays. The 600 hours, with the Avon engine having performed perfectly, were completed in just over the month –

an achievement that everyone had thought impossible. Rolls-Royce were so delighted that the Board of Directors invited me, Don and some of the pilots to a celebratory lunch, at which the Chairman presented RAF Upwood with a large silver cup.

During the Christmas holiday, to get away from all the festivities and to give me a break, we had rented a furnished cottage on the edge of Dartmoor. One morning that I luckily happened not to have gone for my usual walk, I was in the sitting room with Bunny and Pam while the two younger girls were in bed with a slight cold. We suddenly heard screams. I rushed to the door just as Pat burst into the sitting room with her nightdress in flames. I grabbed her, threw her on the sofa, beat out the flames with my hands and told her to stop screaming – which amazingly she did. Meanwhile, Pam had rushed out and come back with a bucket of water. Wendy was crying by the door and Bunny was in complete panic. I started lifting bits of the burnt clothing off Pat's chest, but realised that I might be damaging the raw flesh underneath. It was a third-degree burn, but had luckily not hurt her face or eyes.

We had no phone there, so we sent Pam to a nearby house to phone for a doctor, who luckily arrived soon afterwards, tended the burns and left a layer of gauze impregnated with penicillin on them. What had happened, we discovered, was that Pat had spilt some orange juice down the front of her nightdress and then stood in front of an electric fire to dry it. The up-current of hot air had drawn her nightdress into the fire – with the obvious result.

That episode left its mark on me far more than anything I ever did flying. Luckily, one of my Wing Commanders at Upwood was married to the Carreras girl whose father was a close friend of McIndoe – the famous surgeon who operated on many RAF officers who had received burns during the war. She arranged for McIndoe to see Pat and he brilliantly grafted skin from her thigh to help repair the damage.

During that winter, several Canberras in 2 Group had crashed into the ground in the vicinity of their own airfields, killing the occupants. All had happened either at night or in relatively bad weather. One suggestion was that this must be due to failure of some of the blind flying instruments. It so happened that the Canberra was one of the first aircraft to have an electrically powered artificial horizon instrument in the blind flying panel. Previously, the gyro on which it depended had been air-driven. So this was thought perhaps to be the main culprit. But that, to my mind, did not make sense. The other instruments should have been adequate to prevent a well-trained pilot from losing control. If, indeed, the artificial horizon had suddenly failed, then it might have contributed to temporarily confusing the pilot, but should not have caused those crashes. Some thought that the electric switches for the fuel tanks might have been incorrectly used. But the cause of those crashes was a mystery that 2 Group had failed to solve.

One day in February (1953), O'Brian Nichols (who had been in my Bonehead team, and was now in a Canberra squadron in 2 Group) flew down to have lunch with me in order to get my opinion on the reliability of the artificial horizon. I rang one of my old friends in the instrument department at RAE to get more information about

AOC 2 Group (later CAS) in our Sergeants Mess

it. Yes, of course any instrument could fail, he advised me, but the exhaustive tests on the new one in the Canberras had convinced him that it had far less than a one in a million chance of doing so. But O'Brian departed unconvinced. He said all the pilots in his squadron were beginning to distrust that instrument.

Two mornings later, I read in the paper that O'Brian Nichols had been killed flying a Canberra the previous evening. I felt very sad – yet another good friend lost and in a way I felt somehow I might have prevented it.

That same morning, I had a call from the C-in-C.

"Tubby," he said, "there's been yet another Canberra crash and 2 Group don't know the reason. I want you to do a thorough investigation yourself. Let your deputy run Upwood. You are to devote your full time finding the cause of these accidents and preventing any more. Start immediately. Top priority. Both AOCs have instructions to give any assistance you need. I've appointed Pete Brothers from my staff here to help you. Understood?"

I asked Bassingbourne for one of their most experienced Canberra pilots – not to do any flying, but to help my investigations. It so happened that a splendid young Squadron Leader named Lowe (who later became an Air Marshal) had recently damaged his wrist and was off flying and so could be easily spared. He helped enormously and was largely responsible for completely rewriting the Handling Notes for the Canberra while we were together.

The first thing I did was to investigate the O'Brian Nichols crash. He appeared to have been doing a normal night approach to land on the runway, but decided to abort the landing and go round again. He was heard to have opened up the engines to full power to do so, but shortly afterwards had transmitted a call "Instruments gone" and subsequently dived straight ahead into the ground.

I felt sure that the instrument had NOT failed, but that something had caused O'Brian to think that it had, and that had influenced him to put the nose down and dive. There was no dual control (at that time) in a Canberra. So I decided that one of the things I must do was to try to replicate the exact conditions that O'Brian had experienced –

but at a safe height. First, however, I flew a Canberra down to Boscombe Down and Farnborough with Lowe, to see whether any of the test pilots (most of whom were old acquaintances) had any ideas or suggestions. They had none.

The runway at Farnborough was a very long one. So, with Lowe standing beside to warn me if anything was going wrong, I decided to act as though I was doing a blind take-off. I lined up, then put my head in a position where I was unable to see out, but could concentrate on the instruments. Using only the instruments, but flying very accurately by them, I did the take-off, but constantly asked Lowe whether I was climbing too steeply – because that was the feeling I got. He said no, it was a perfect take-off and climb.

Up at a safe height – around 10,000 feet – I then went through the full procedure of approaching to land, aborting and opening up to go round again and climb away, concentrating hard on the instruments. Lowe said it was perfect. But again, on opening up the engines, I had the sensation that I was climbing far too steeply and my memory flashed back to my early training at Cranwell.

I then also recalled my experience, some years previously, of testing the amount of "G" I could withstand before blacking out. Bill Stewart (the young doctor who had been at RAE with me in 1939 and had become head of the Institute of Aviation Medicine at Farnborough) had tested me in the centrifuge there. (My build, incidentally, can withstand much more "G" than taller pilots.) At the end of the test, with the centrifuge rapidly decelerating, I had experienced awful sensations of tumbling head over heels forwards.

That gave me the answer. The powerful acceleration of the Canberra gave the pilot (if he had no outside reference) the opposite to that – the overpowering impression that he was looping upwards, thus causing him to push the stick forward. Doing that caused even greater acceleration, more feeling of looping, resulting in the pilot putting it into a vertical dive. If he trusted his instruments, he could resist that sensation. But if he did not trust that electrically driven artificial horizon, and failed immediately to cross-check on the other indicators, then the physical sensation would cause him to dive.

This I was easily able to demonstrate. I got other pilots to fly the Canberra with me standing beside them. I pretended to have a switch that would cut the electricity to the instrument. Then, at a safe height of around 10,000 feet, I would instruct them to put their head inside, fly solely by instruments, and go through the approach and landing procedure. I would then put my hand behind the dashboard and tell them I had switched off the artificial horizon. On opening up the engines to full power for an overshoot, every single pilot I tested pushed the stick forward, most of them into an alarming dive. Only one pilot I tested would not have crashed into the ground had the test been at normal approach levels.

The problem was solved. I demonstrated it to the C-in-C, my AOC, and a host of other senior officers. In consequence, all Canberra pilots were trained to realise that danger. It was introduced into training throughout the RAF and I never heard of a similar accident again. Hugh Pugh and many others congratulated me. But the AOC of the Canberra Group (who later became CAS) never forgave me for pointing out what he himself should have discovered two years earlier.

Shortly after that, Hugh Pugh retired and Air Marshal Mills replaced him as C-in-C Bomber Command. What a difference! I had never met Mills before. He announced (through his PA) his intention to visit Upwood. I had the Operations Room specially spruced up and all three squadrons alerted. I waited with Don Smith and a Guard of Honour on the tarmac to welcome him. The Devon arrived and we could see him in one of the back seats reading a newspaper. We waited for several minutes while he finished reading it before he got out. He gave just a cursory glance round the Guard of Honour, and then told me that the first thing he wanted to inspect was the church. I was dumbfounded. I couldn't even remember where the church was!

I turned to Don. "Lead the way to the church in your car, Don, and we'll follow."

Don gave a grimace. He didn't know either, but grabbed an airman who did to guide him. The whole visit was a complete fiasco.

Mills never visited the Operations Room and was clearly not the slightest bit interested in anything to do with flying or the three squadrons we had there. I formed such a low opinion of him that I would not have wanted him on my station even as a Flight Lieutenant. It was the first and last time I ever saw Mills, thank God. But I read in the papers that after his retirement as an Air Chief Marshal he had been appointed Black Rod.

During his visit, he never mentioned the Radar Recce Flight – one of the units that Hugh Pugh always visited. I was not sure that Mills even knew of its existence. I found that very strange, but thought it best not to mention the unit to him. In fact, Instrell had been kept very busy with many new pictures of Russia arriving to be examined.

All the personnel employed in the Radar Recce Flight had been carefully vetted by a special security branch of Air Ministry and cleared for top secret work. But another separate branch kept the records of anyone suspected of having communist leanings and visited stations regularly to check where they were employed. Jock Ireland handled that for me. On one such visit, Jock reported to me, with considerable concern, that one of the airmen on that second list (of potential communist sympathisers) was employed in the Radar Recce Flight. It appeared that the two branches of Air Ministry had not co-ordinated their work. I never found out how serious that mistake became, but that airman was posted to some remote station pretty quickly.

Soon after Mills had taken over from Hugh Pugh, I learnt that – to help my future career – I was to be appointed Head of Plans and Deputy Senior Air Staff Officer at Middle East Air Force HQ based at Ismailia, in the Canal Zone, Egypt. It was considered one of the most important staff jobs for a Group Captain – and a stepping-stone for promotion to much higher rank. (Both my predecessors in that post reached Air Chief Marshal, with one then becoming Governor of New Zealand.) I protested that I did not want that job, but was told that my name was on a shortlist for higher promotion, but that, lacking the requisite experience in staff posts, I had no option.

I learnt that there were no available married quarters at Ismailia and that I could not take my family with me. Some other officers had paid for their wives to go and live in Cyprus – less than a couple of hours flying away from the HQ. So, yet again, the Air Ministry was going to separate me from my family – in peacetime – for perhaps a couple of years. Also, it would not be to a flying job, but sitting at a desk in an encampment guarded against the hostile owners of the uninteresting desert surrounding it. I did not relish the prospect.

That little seed about leaving the RAF had now not only grown roots, but was beginning to push shoots up through the ground. I thought I could probably get a job as an airline pilot, or test pilot with some firm – but, to do anything, I would first need permission to retire from the RAF. And that, I gathered, would not be forthcoming.

So I had no choice but to make the best of it. Brook (my AOC) was both sympathetic and helpful. He suggested I should make a trip out to the Middle East to survey the scene and told me to arrange a training flight to Cyprus and Egypt for a Lincoln that I would fly myself. I learned that he too would be leaving the Group soon to become Vice-Chief of Air Staff. I was delighted to learn that such a good friend, to whom I could turn if I needed help or advice, would soon be in such an influential position.

I flew the Lincoln non-stop to Egypt, taking Jock Ireland with me, where I had a brief discussion with Jack Davis – the highly regarded and very efficient staff officer that I would be replacing – and with Griffiths, who had served with me at Milton Ernest. The advice from Griffiths, who had moved his wife to Cyprus, was that I would be wise to do the same – he just loved it there and was able to fly there most Friday afternoons and return to the HQ early Monday mornings. He offered to help me find suitable accommodation there, recommending Kyrenia as the best area.

Both Jack Davies and Griffiths, however, gave me a most disturbing account of the situation within the HQ. It was run by a C-in-C who was incapable of ever making a decision, with his senior staff all at loggerheads and playing politics, none with any real job to do, and most of the junior ones thoroughly discontented – altogether a most unhappy set-up. Above all, Jack Davies warned me that my immediate boss – the SASO, of Jimmy d'Aeth's vintage – was one of the most foul-mouthed guttersnipes who had ever been commissioned into the RAF. Their descriptions, as I later discovered for myself, did not exaggerate the situation at HQ Middle East one little bit.

After those dispiriting discussions at Ismailia, I flew across to Cyprus, landing at Nicosia, where I hired an open Morris Minor for the weekend to survey the scene there. I fell in love with Kyrenia and chose that area in which Bunny and the children should live. With helpful advice from Griffiths and the local dentist there (Campion), I decided to rent what was probably the most luxurious house in Cyprus at that time. It had 8 acres of vineyards, a private sandy beach, a view across to the distant Turkish mountains, was fully furnished and had a Turkish gardener (Izet), whose wife Gemolia was housekeeper/cook. I was unable to view inside because Dirk Bogarde was temporarily living there with his boyfriend and insisted on complete privacy. But he would shortly be leaving and I could rent it from its owner in Scotland.

I flew the Lincoln back to Upwood overnight (11½ hours). When I took off my flying helmet, much of the skin from the top of my head came off with it – too much sunburn in the open Morris – leaving me scarred for life. I then did a deal over the phone with Colonel Laing Anderson, who had retired to near Lismore in Scotland, to rent his house in Kyrenia – at practically no cost on the basis that we would be looking after it for him. We then bought a new Morris Minor in which Bunny and I planned to motor out to Naples – from where boats capable of carrying a small car sailed to Cyprus. Don and Irene Smith agreed to look after the three girls until we had arrived safely and then put them on a plane for us to meet at Nicosia airport. The officers at Upwood gave us a lovely send-off and later presented me with a silver mug that I greatly treasure.

En route to Cyprus

Although I thought I would have fewer opportunities in future for flying, I took the precaution of undergoing the instrument flying test to renew my Master Green pilot status before leaving.

My effective date of posting to HQ Middle East Air Force was 15th July 1953. That gave us time to enjoy a few days en route – Paris, Geneva, Lake Garda, and Naples by car – then Athens and the Corinth Canal by boat (with the car on board), before disembarking at Limassol. We then had a further week settling into our new house before I was due in the Canal Zone, during which I learned that Brook, shortly before he was due to take up his post as Vice-Chief, had been killed in a flying accident.

Yet another of my close friends had disappeared. I felt very sad.

Chapter 18

Middle East

At Limassol, we were met by the PA to the AOC Cyprus (Air Commodore Tom Bowling), who had very kindly sent him to help us with our baggage and formalities. The PA then led the way in his Land Rover across the dry plains to the AOC's residence in Nicosia for a welcoming meal. At that time, Cyprus was a peaceful island, with the Turks and Greeks living together in reasonable harmony.

Tom was a first class officer, and when he too confirmed the unhappy situation at the HQ in the Canal Zone, I realised it must be pretty bad. He reckoned that the only two sane officers at Ismailia were Tom Prickett and the chap I was relieving, Jack Davies. One point of particular interest to me was that, in spite of opposition from HQ, Bowling had recently, and very sensibly, installed radio beacons so that aircraft could now approach Nicosia airport and land there safely in almost any weather.

Our House in Kyrenia

After lunch, he sent his PA to guide us to the house we had rented and sent a message to Don Smith at Upwood that we had arrived. Since we were not even going to be serving under his command, I felt he was exceedingly helpful. The three girls arrived at Nicosia, Wendy carrying a Teddy Bear bigger than herself, and we spent a week together in our new home before I had to depart to Ismailia.

The British garrison in the Canal Zone comprised three main areas – Fayid (the main army HQ), Ismailia (the operational half of the RAF HQ), and Abu Sueir (the Administrative staff of the RAF HQ). All these HQs were vastly overblown remnants of the last war, and their location there was strongly opposed by the Egyptian government. Because of that, and strong local opposition, all the encampments were enclosed in barbed-wire fences, beyond which no English personnel could venture without an armed escort. Some sailing, however, was permitted on the Great Salt Lake through which ships passed along the Suez Canal.

In consequence, the officers serving in the two halves of the RAF HQ rarely met, and living in either was like being in a prison camp. Several of the officers had been PoWs during the war and the similarity of conditions did not help their full recovery. Most of the Air Commodores and Air Marshals had their wives with them there – which, with few others having that privilege, alone was a considerable source of friction. There were quite a few WRAF personnel stationed there too, but the accommodation was pretty awful for everyone. With practically no important work, and little else of interest to occupy anyone, it was a splendid incubator for backbiting and intrigue, and a hotbed of discontent. Add to that a very poor bunch of mainly incompetent senior officers, and I found myself in an organisation so aimless and unhappy that I regretted not having already resigned from the RAF.

The only thing I could look forward to was flying across to Cyprus and spending very happy weekends in our lovely house in the glorious setting of Kyrenia. In Egypt, I would drive on the right in my staff car to the airfield, and in Cyprus I would get out of the aircraft and drive on the left – all because Henry Ford didn't ride a horse and preferred to steer his car with his right hand and give hand signals with his left!

Early morning breakfast picnics at the top of Mount Hilarian, with the smell of a wood fire and of frying eggs and bacon, followed by swimming in the wonderfully clear water at the Club by the Castle in Kyrenia, will always remain as some of my happiest memories.

As Head of Plans, I, together with my Army opposite number Brigadier Williams (a distant cousin of John Northey) and a senior Navy Captain, formed the planning team of advisors to the three C-in-Cs, and sat in at all their meetings. I soon incurred the wrath of the Army C-in-C (General Sir Cameron Nicholson – "Camiknicks") for criticising his ambitious plan to build an enormous new Army HQ in Cyprus. Then, acting on orders from "Cocky" Spencer (the Senior Air Staff Officer, to whom I was deputy) to oppose a proposal being put forward by "Dolly" Gray (the AOA located in Abu Sueir), our C-in-C ruled that I was wrong to have opposed his pal Dolly's suggestion. Cocky then did not back me up – in spite of me obeying the orders he had given me. So I did not get off to a very good start.

Air Marshal Pike (a splendid officer who knew me well and later became CAS) was the head of Plans at Air Ministry and arrived to do a brief tour of the Middle East. I accompanied him to Jerusalem, Amman, and Baghdad before going to Cyprus, where we entertained him in our house. While visiting Nicosia, I managed to borrow a Meteor to practise aerobatics and, in fact, seized every opportunity to fly throughout my tour in the Middle East. I kept my hand in flying various types (partly flying to Cyprus and back) and renewed my Master Green instrument flying category by tests each year. Very few other officers there did any flying. Few of the senior ones displayed any interest whatsoever in flying, or in any other aspect of aviation – nor in the likely future role of the armed services. The whole overblown aimless organisation was basically administrative, not operational.

When we learned that our incompetent C-in-C was soon to be retired and replaced, we hoped that some dynamic Air Marshal would replace him. To our dismay, we learned that it would be little Claude Pelly – promoted to Air Marshal – on whose staff

I had served at Air Ministry. Camiknicks had meanwhile been replaced as Army C-in-C by a very powerful, impressive but rather dim-witted character (General Sir Charles Keitley – the twit who, together with Harold Macmillan, had sent a thousand Polish officers to their deaths at Russian hands), against whom Pelly would appear insignificant.

Furthermore, Keitley had as his deputy one of the most brilliant Generals – Dick Hull – who later became Chairman of the Chiefs of Staff. The local Army GOC, Frankie Festing, was also one of the most admired and glamorous Army commanders I ever met. By comparison, our RAF C-in-C had only the foul-mouthed Cocky Spencer, or later the quite inadequate Stephenson (who replaced Cocky and appeared frightened of flying) to back him up.

Prior to each weekly meeting of the Cs-in-C, I had a briefing session with Pelly, at which the AOA and SASO were present. Claude Pelly and I would then motor down to the Army HQ at Fayid. Having agreed his brief, Pelly would confirm to me his determination to stand firm on certain points against Keitley.

At the meeting, Keitley would boom out: "That's the policy we must adopt!" and then, turning to Pelly, boom out again: "I know, Claude, that you agree?"

And little Pelly, avoiding my eyes, would meekly murmur his agreement. I found it quite embarrassing.

In September, I flew a Devon, via Benina and Idris, with three passengers, to a meeting in Malta. The SASO, who never piloted himself, elected to fly there by airline, although there was plenty of room for him in the Devon. In March (1954), a team of

Turkish border

Planners arrived from Air Ministry, with whom I and Brigadier Williams flew down to Aquaba on the Persian Gulf and then on to Amman and Jerusalem. Amongst the group was my friend Peter le Cheminant, who (although junior to me) had been one of my instructors at Staff College and later, having retired as an Air Marshal, became Governor of Guernsey. In Jerusalem, we visited the Mount of Olives and other places of interest. As usual, I had my camera with me and took many photos. In the middle of Jerusalem, I was attacked by a group of angry Arabs to prevent me taking pictures of their fortifications – I had not until then realised the sensitivity of the situation between Arabs and Jews.

The next day, we returned to Amman for discussions with Glubb Pasha (the famous British advisor to the King of Jordan), who later entertained Peter le Cheminant and me to dinner at his home – a great honour and a very interesting evening. The next day, we were entertained by one of the Arab leaders in his tent to a meal of sheep's eyes, and later had a swim in the Dead Sea – if being buoyed up in that salty water can be called a "swim". There we met a Naval Lieutenant who had served there a couple of years and had almost

Turkish border

"gone native". The bluebottle flies in that area were horrific: they covered the bread as soon as a sandwich came out of its wrapper and we did our utmost to keep them off. But that Lieutenant was no longer concerned with them and, to our amazement, merely blew off just enough flies for each mouthful, leaving the rest of the bread covered with bluebottles.

We visited Jericho and then made a reconnaissance flight over northern Iraq and the Turkish border. I had never imagined such rugged country. We spent the next night in Baghdad, before visiting Nicosia and swimming in Kyrenia, where Bunny and I entertained them at our house.

Around that time, Jock Ireland (who had been my PA at Upwood) arrived to serve with me again, locating his wife in Kyrenia as I had done. Bunny had helped find a flat overlooking the harbour for them and I flew Jock across with me whenever possible.

As I mentioned, the Egyptians (quite rightly now the British Empire was being dismantled) wanted all British troops out of their country. There was, in fact, no reason for us being there – except to provide somewhere to locate the vastly overblown numbers of senior Army and RAF officers and their enormous staffs. The tiny amount of real work could have been done more efficiently by just a small group located anywhere in that area – Cyprus being the obvious place. The British government, under pressure from President Nasser of Egypt and the US Government, finally agreed to negotiate an Anglo-Egyptian agreement for us to move out.

As Head Planner for the RAF Middle East, I was appointed to represent the RAF in the team, led by an army general from England, whose task was to negotiate the terms of that agreement. The meetings took place in the vacant Palace of the deposed King Farouk, near the Gaza Pyramids. For these meetings I moved to Cairo, where our Air Attache and his wife very kindly accommodated me in their official residence. Our main team included several civil servants from England whose ability can be judged by their arrival in black suits, bowler hats and with furled umbrellas for these discussions in the Sahara Desert. They knew nothing of the Arab negotiating customs of always demanding three or four times what they expect to eventually get. These idiots sometimes even accepted the Arabs' opening bids. President Nasser (who I quite admired) and his foreign minister Fawzi were so much cleverer than our team that they got almost everything they wanted. I got to know Nasser quite well and he afterwards sent me a Christmas card.

During my time at Farouk's Palace, I took the opportunity to walk the short distance across the desert to the Great Pyramid. There, I was approached by the Arab guide who had guided me to the top and had prophesised that I would revisit there. (They always forecast that to everyone in case you ever do – so that they can then say they were right and demand a tip for their correct prophesy.) I recognised him and he remembered Bunny. I told him his forecast had been wrong about the number of children she would have – but gave him a tip nevertheless.

One of the troubles brewing up in Africa was the Mau Mau atrocities. Our AOC in Kenya was Air Commodore Beisiegel – a fine officer, about whom I wrote earlier. He got little support from Pelly and, like me, was pretty disgusted with the whole RAF Middle East organisation – so disillusioned that he retired from the RAF.

Tom Prickett told me confidentially that there was a rather serious situation arising at our HQ in Iraq. I was senior to Tom and he wanted me to investigate for myself, so that perhaps I could do something about it. The AOC there, Hawtrey (brother of the actor), had been a close friend of our AOA – Dolly Gray.

The deputy to Hawtrey was Group Captain Doggy Oliver, CB, DSO, DFC – one of our finest officers, who was a friend of both Tom and myself. Tom had learnt from Doggy that Hawtrey (well known to be "gay") had fallen in love with one of the airmen serving in their HQ and, in consequence, his lover was influencing Hawtrey in so much of what he did officially – that it was becoming detrimental to both discipline and efficiency.

I found some excuse to fly out to the HQ in Iraq. I was met on landing by Hawtrey, who forbade me to see Doggy. I understood that he was putting in an adverse report on Doggy for disloyalty. I managed to see Doggy for a few minutes later that evening, when he confirmed to me what Tom had told me. Other things I had noticed tended to confirm the veracity of that report.

On my return, I hinted to Claude Pelly that there seemed to be a bit of friction at the Iraq HQ, but was very careful what I said, because I knew that he and Hawtrey had been cadets at Cranwell together in 1920. Nothing, so far as I knew, was ever done about that situation – except that Doggy Oliver never got promoted.

That was the sort of unhappy situation that prevailed throughout the RAF Middle East HQ under the command of Claude. It was no better than the mess he had inherited from his predecessor.

For a month in 1954, I was able to arrange for Bunny and our three girls to come and stay with me at Ismailia in a married quarter hut that had become vacant. I took the opportunity to take the girls sailing in a dinghy on the Great Salt Lake and then Pam and I also motored down, in a convoy with armed guards, to a rest camp that the RAF Regiment had set up on the beach beside the Red Sea, about thirty miles south of Suez. We had a tent about 20 yards from the water and swam inside the reef most of the day, using our snorkels to view the magnificently coloured fish, while a guard armed with a rifle watched out for sharks from a tower erected nearby.

On the second day, using our snorkels, Pam and I swam out to the reef. There we found a whole line of barracuda looking over the top of the reef, and so beat a hasty retreat. Later, armed with a spear gun, and much nearer the shore in about five feet of very clear water, I shot a fish about nine inches long that, naturally, was then flapping violently on the end of the spear. I remember seeing a large eye – a good 1½ inches in diameter - flash past my head as the spear was torn from my grasp and both Pam and I were buffeted sideways in water which had become churned up with sand. I grabbed Pam and rushed for the shore a few yards away. The injured fish, flapping on the end of the spear, must have attracted the shark and we were very lucky to have escaped unhurt. The guard had been concentrating on something he had seen much further out nearer the reef and had not noticed the one that had come so swiftly towards us.

Meanwhile, Air Vice-Marshal Gil Saye (with whom I had been friendly 20 years previously) had replaced Dolly Gray. I also knew his deputy (Jock Melvin) well as a sharp ex-Halton boy who had won a place at Cranwell and joined my squadron there three terms behind me. He had specialised in Signals and should have transferred to the Technical Branch, but reckoned that promotion would be quicker if he remained in the GD (flying) branch, and pretended still to be a pilot – a pretence which I happened to uncover.

Taking several other officers (who had their wives in Cyprus) as passengers with me, including Jock Ireland and Melvin, I was flying to Cyprus for the weekend. Believing him to be a pilot, I sat Melvin in the second pilot's seat beside me. The weather was pretty bad and we were in thick cloud approaching Cyprus, with low cloud over Nicosia. But, thanks to the radio beacon that Tom Bowling had installed, I knew exactly what I was doing and that we could land with perfect safety. As we descended below the level of Mount Trudos, Melvin became agitated; and then, as I went even lower in thick cloud on the approach to the airfield, he became hysterical and started screaming. I ordered him to shut up, but he continued – making it very difficult for me to concentrate on flying accurately. At about 200 feet – exactly as I expected – we came out of the cloud with the runway straight ahead and he collapsed in tears – a despicable example by a Group Captain to the other passengers, who all had complete confidence in my flying ability.

Because of that incident, Melvin, while professing to be my friend, hated my guts and thereafter did everything possible to undermine me.

As a result of the Anglo-Egyptian agreement being signed, I had to plan the move of the HQ to Nicosia in Cyprus, which was pretty simple, compared with moving the Navigation School to Canada during the war. But the problem of finding suitable accommodation for the senior officers to live in was not my job – that was the responsibility of Gil Saye and his deputy, Melvin. Most of the more senior officers – including both the Cs-in-C – wanted houses in Kyrenia, but the officers who had brought out their wives privately were already occupying all the better ones – with me in the most palatial one of all.

You can imagine the feelings of a C-in-C facing the prospect of having to live in a tumbledown shack with a corrugated iron roof well back from the coast – which is where Pelly ended up – while I was in our lovely house with its private beach! First, they tried to get me posted to Aden, but the Air Ministry refused to agree. Then, to curry favour with Saye and the C-in-C, Jock Melvin and his army opposite number started trying to get us out of our house by other means.

I received a letter from Laing Anderson in Scotland (from whom we were renting the house) saying that he had been approached by the War Office with a proposal to requisition his house for occupation by one of the Cs-in-C moving to Cyprus. I immediately drafted a letter from Bunny to the Secretary of State for War complaining that, behind her back, the Army was trying to evict her from her home by underhand methods.

That really set the cat amongst the pigeons. Keitley received a severe rocket from the War Office for allowing such a thing to take place under his command. He was livid with me – but could not take any action against me, as the letter was from my wife. Saye and Melvin bore the brunt of the blame and never forgave me. They both became very antagonistic towards me.

The HQ moved from the Canal Zone to Nicosia on 1st December 1954. Willie Tait (who had been at Cranwell a couple of years after me) had replaced Tom Prickett as Group Captain Ops, and when I flew him across to Cyprus in a Pembroke I believe that was the last RAF flight ever from Ismailia.

For the first time, all the officers of both parts of the HQ were now together, so that I now saw Saye and Melvin frequently, not only at work but also at the swimming club in Kyrenia. I realised that the sprightly young Squadron Leader that Saye had been when I knew him at the beginning of the war had now developed into a rather unhealthy Air Vice-Marshal with a high blood pressure. (That, I later understood, was the cause of his death, when he collapsed a couple of years later while inspecting a parade.) I also realised that Melvin resented my having found out that he was frightened of flying and yet was still masquerading as a pilot – just as Dowding had done. The atmosphere in the HQ was not conducive to good comradeship – or to efficiency.

Soon after we arrived in Cyprus, the tension between Greece and Turkey had resulted in the Greek General Grivas starting to stir up the Greeks in Cyprus to take over the Island from the Turks. There was no logical reason for this – Cyprus had belonged to Turkey since 1571, until, in 1878, the Ottoman Empire placed it under British Administration and in 1914 Britain annexed it. But in 1955 Grivas started widespread terrorism throughout Cyprus via the Eoka movement to try to achieve union with Greece.

Our living conditions changed dramatically. Even picking up Pam from the convent in Nicosia where she was at school became too dangerous. Rounding the main square, with me driving our open Morris, we narrowly missed being stoned, and at least one RAF officer was shot. With help from our Turkish gardener, I had managed to expose an Eoka plot and get four culprits captured; as a result, my name was near the top of their list of people to be bumped off and my movements were restricted.

But little Claude Pelly, and the dim-witted Keitley, hadn't a clue what to do, except to arrange armed guards for us when travelling. They could have nipped the trouble in the bud if they had taken resolute action.

Luckily for us, Kyrenia was mainly Turkish – as were our loyal cook and gardener. Even so, Pam and I always kept loaded Colt pistols beside us on the dinner table, and two fierce dogs outside to give warning. One evening, after Pat and Wendy had gone to bed, we were disturbed at dinner by Pat shouting down to us that there were two men in our garden. Pam and I rushed upstairs to our separate balconies, each with pistol ready, and I saw two men running towards our house.

"Halt! Hands up or I fire!" I shouted.

They did so.

"Advance slowly towards me!" I ordered.

Glancing anxiously at Pam, who also had her pistol aimed at them, they appeared quite frightened and hesitated before doing so.

"Who are you?" I demanded.

"We are guards from General Keitley's residence," one stammered out; which, on further questioning, appeared to be the case. They had been playing some game and had strayed onto our land.

I ordered them to get the hell off my property, and I have little doubt that they told the General about the incident. But living under the constant threat of attack, and having to move about only with an armed escort, was not pleasant.

Then came the preliminary indication, originating, I assume, from Anthony Eden, that we might have to prepare plans for the invasion of Egypt. I took the Christmas card that I had received from President Nasser with me to show Pelly. I told him that, having been part of the team that had successfully negotiated the Anglo-Egyptian Agreement with the President of Egypt, I was not now prepared to be responsible for planning a breach of that agreement and following a policy with which I heartily disagreed. I expressed my strong opinion that the proposed policy would be such a disastrous step (although I was confident that we could plan for a Suez invasion to succeed) that I would prefer to be relieved of my post – even if it meant my resignation from the RAF. In fairness to Pelly, I believe he agreed with my views, but when I suggested that both he and Keitley should offer their resignations if they disagreed with the policy, he thought that was going a bit too far.

[In fact, the Suez invasion proved to be one of the most serious international blunders ever made by Britain.]

Around that time, the tension between me and Gil Saye, aided by Melvin, reached a climax. As a result, I wrote a letter that I wanted sent to the Air Council which would ensure that I was posted away from that command. At my final interview with him, Pelly did his utmost to persuade me to withdraw that letter. But I refused, knowing that it probably meant the end of my RAF career – but which also might, however, facilitate me getting early retirement.

My posting to Air Ministry as Deputy Director of Operational Training came through shortly afterwards – effective 21st November 1955. I was delighted to learn that I would be leaving that unhappy and rudderless HQ – even the dismal prospect of only having to fly a desk round an office in Whitehall again was better.

Out of spite, Gil Saye tried to get me sent home by air, thus leaving Bunny to fend for herself. But the regulations gave me the option of taking my family with me by boat. The movements' officer on his staff, who liked Saye no more than I did, arranged for us to travel on a Norwegian cargo ship, on which we would be the only passengers.

We boarded that ship at Famagusta and enjoyed a wonderful cruise lasting over three weeks. We had gone first to Beirut, then Alexandria in Egypt, followed by a few days in Kavalla in northern Greece. From there we went to Crete to take on a cargo of grapes, which took four days to load – giving us plenty of time for sightseeing and fishing – before sailing right past the white cliffs of Dover to Hamburg, where we spent a couple of days. On finally reaching England, having returned from an overseas posting, I was then entitled to a month's leave. For once, the RAF had treated me quite well.

But that did not alter my decision, finally made during the voyage back, to leave the RAF at the earliest moment that I could find a way of arranging it.

Two little things stand out in my memory concerning our youngest daughter Wendy, who was then about six years old. When swimming in Kyrenia, I had tried to teach her to let out her breath to sink onto the sand in about four feet of water. After the third unsuccessful attempt, she said: "I can't do it, Daddy, I sink up!"

Then, on the voyage home, I was up on deck when she came up to tell me that lunch was ready.

"Daddy," she announced, "the gong has gone."

I looked at her and asked: "Where has it gone?"

She seemed very puzzled for a moment and then replied:

"I don't know, Daddy, but it's wented."

Chapter 19

Bunkers Hill

I could, of course, have just continued in the RAF until at least aged 50 and retired with a good pension. Thus, there was no great urgency to abandon that security. But having decided to retire, I wanted to do so as soon as possible. I was faced with two separate problems – how to make enough money to live comfortably, and how to persuade the RAF to let me go. The latter might depend on the solution I found to the former. So I gave priority to that and in best Staff College tradition I wrote an "Appreciation of the Situation". The Aim was "To make money", and I compiled a list of the main ways I could think of which might achieve that aim.

Two obvious ones were:

a. Run a brothel – which is how the family of a former Air Minister was reputed to have become so wealthy.

b. Smuggling drugs or other things – which was a growing industry.

However, Bunny was rather opposed to either of these, so I reluctantly had to discard them. Next on the list were:

c. Write a best-selling novel, and hope for a film.

d. Invent something that was badly needed.

Bunny approved of both of these, so I decided to try to do them simultaneously.

Meanwhile, since I had no other income, I would have to continue in the RAF until one or other of them succeeded. (In fact, both did.)

The immediate problem was where to live while I was at the Air Ministry. We chose the Guildford/Godalming area because we had been happy there before and it had a good train service to London. Pam, who had now left school, wanted to live on a farm and I also thought it would be wise to learn how to live off the land. By chance, we found a 30-acre farm named Bunkers Hill, with a small recently constructed house, fully furnished, for rent on the outskirts of Godalming. We rented it and moved in. What followed became – in spite of me having to go most weekdays to the Air Ministry in Whitehall – one of the most interesting and enjoyable periods of my life.

My job at Air Ministry was so simple that I used my office mainly as a place where I could sleep most of the day sitting at my desk (like many others did in Whitehall), without much fear of interruption; but I normally set aside one day a week to go flying. Apart from one or two things of particular interest to me, I delegated practically everything to my well-qualified staff. Our main problem was my immediate boss – a quick-witted and amusing officer – Teddy Donaldson – who had no interest in anything that did not affect him personally. He was the pilot who had been chosen to fly the Meteor that broke the world speed record, and he was also a lightweight boxing champion. Whether he was born dim or – more likely – his brain had been affected (like so many boxers) by the frequent buffeting, the result was that I found it difficult ever to discuss much of importance with him. Although he was brilliant at piloting a fighter aircraft, his knowledge of aviation or international affairs was very limited. He was divorced from his wife (who had then married O'Brian Nicholls – who had been a member of my Bonehead team, but was later killed flying the Canberra), and his main affection seemed to be his Siamese cat, which he took everywhere with him – including to his office near mine in Whitehall, where he expected his staff to look after it.

Immediately above him was "Paddy" – Air Vice-Marshal the Earl of Bandon – a splendid officer. But he was more often on the phone to members of the Royal Family arranging shooting parties, than reading files prepared by the civil servants. A few months after I arrived, George Harvey, with whom I had an excellent relationship from his days as SASO Bomber Command, replaced Paddy Bandon.

One incident concerning Paddy occurred when, having studied a file prepared by some civil servant recommending something to the Under Secretary of State, he decided it was utter nonsense. As his comment, he was going to write *"Balls"*, but out of consideration for the girl secretaries, he instead wrote *"Round objects"*. Two days later, the file came back with a handwritten request from the Under Secretary:

376

"Who is Mr Round and why does he object?"

It was not easy, while serving at the Air Ministry, to fit in much flying; but, using the excuse that to be in charge of operational training I ought to have experience of flying most of the types with which the RAF was now equipped, I managed to keep my hand in.

The first time I flew a helicopter – a Whirlwind – I found it vastly different from the Autogyro that I had flown 18 years previously – and much more complicated. That was true also of many of the new types that had recently come into service. The actual flying – controlling the aircraft – was simpler, because of the better instruments to assist the pilot, particularly when flying in cloud. But there were so many additional gadgets that the pilot had to operate, and the speeds so much greater, that pilots and aircrew needed more careful training, and to be better technically qualified, than hitherto.

By 1956, a dual-control Canberra had come into general use for training, so I used one in which to pass my annual test for renewal of my Master Green instrument rating. Then, in August, I flew a Hunter 6 through the sound barrier – something I was determined to do before retiring. I took off from Boscombe Down, noting that I was doing 160 knots still on the runway just before lift-off (faster than I had ever been on land before) and, having climbed to 45,000 feet, I headed for the South coast. (Supersonic speeds were banned over land because of the sonic boom frightening people and animals.) Over the English Channel, I put the Hunter into a gentle dive and was soon flying at well over the speed of sound. To my surprise, I felt nothing unusual at all and found it just as manoeuvrable as at slower speeds. I then did a loop and slow roll, thoroughly enjoying myself.

It was a beautiful day, with no clouds. Under those conditions there is no clear horizon at those heights and the dark sky just gradually fuses into light mist below, with no reference point visible to the pilot. From the cockpit of the Hunter, the pilot gets no view of either the aircraft nose or of the swept-back wings.

I had turned back towards Boscombe, flying straight and level at normal cruising speed, when I experienced what I afterwards learned was a panic attack. I suddenly felt I was balanced on a pin, and that I would fall off if I moved an eyeball or even blinked. I sat there rigid, sweating – petrified that I would fall off. I was incapable of moving a single muscle – not, at first, even my eyes. They happened to be looking towards the empty sky ahead, where there was nothing on which they could focus.

I had once before – as I explained earlier – been unable to overcome (with my eyes open) my instinctive reactions when flying towards the Grand Canyon. But this was different and much worse.

I had frozen completely and could not even have pressed the transmit button on which my finger was resting. I do not know how long this lasted, but I later worked out that it must have been more than a couple of minutes – perhaps as much as ten. There was no noise, no sense of speed, no indication that I was even in an aircraft – just me, up in space, balanced dangerously on a pinhead, with the least movement liable to cause me to fall off. Some instinct had been triggered which had taken away my ability to move even an eyelid.

I tried to reason with myself, knowing that I had somehow to get myself out of this situation. Finally, I persuaded myself to pretend that I was flying a Link Trainer on the ground and so get my eyes inside the cockpit. I managed, very slowly, to redirect them towards the instrument panel and then slowly forced my right hand off the control stick to about three inches away. Concentrating to overcome my instincts and still pretending I was in a Link Trainer on the ground, I then forced my hand to bang the stick sideways.

That caused the aircraft to roll to the left onto its back. The panic attack disappeared instantly. I felt absolutely normal. I was so relieved that I carried out a few more aerobatics to celebrate.

I then decided to experiment to see whether the same thing would happen again, and, as before, I turned the aircraft towards Boscombe (using the instrument panel) and started flying straight and level. I then looked out at the sky ahead. Everything seemed normal.

Then, suddenly, without any warning, I had another identical panic attack. I could not move a muscle. Again, I was balanced on that pin out in space from which I would fall if I upset the balance. I began sweating with fear – absolutely petrified. This time, however, I knew what to do. But it took enormous willpower and many seconds to move my eyes back into the cockpit, get my hand off the stick and then bang it sideways. Immediately I did so, I was again right back to normal.

By this time I was very near Boscombe, so I made my descent and landed. I asked some of the test pilots stationed there whether they had ever experienced similar reactions. None had. So I arranged to fly the same aircraft again that afternoon. And I experienced exactly the same panic attacks every time I began flying straight and level at high altitudes and looking outside at nothing on which I could focus my eyes. When flying lower, where I could focus my eyes on the ground, or even on a cloud, I had no problem.

After landing, I motored straight to Farnborough to see my old friend Bill Stewart – now the head of the Institute of Aviation Medicine – and related my experiences to him. He was intensely interested.

"Thank God, Tubby, that you found that out and came to see me. It explains two mysteries which have been worrying everyone here – why we have had pilots flying the Hunter continue on a straight course out to sea until they ran out of fuel and then crashed; and why some of the young Hunter pilots have asked to be taken off flying. They obviously dared not give any explanation, for fear of being accused of LMF. Only someone like you, with your wide background and experience, could explain the panic you felt."

The following week, I again flew the Hunter at Boscombe Down to experiment further. The panic attack only occurred when there was nothing outside the aircraft on which I could focus my eyes. My experience led to all pilots being warned and saved further crashes from that cause.

Some 40 years later, an airline pilot was reported in the *Daily Telegraph* to have had a similar experience; so I contacted their aviation editor, who did a feature article about my experience of a panic attack and how I got out of the difficulty. One subsequent letter asked that airline pilots should always tell the passengers to strap themselves in before taking my remedial action. Also, the *Telegraph's* Dr le Fanu explained that similar panic attacks to the ones I had experienced were quite well known amongst Eskimos fishing in their kayaks when the sea was dead calm and a haze obscured the horizon.

Most of the time (when not asleep) in my office, and in the train, I was scratching my head about the two things that might enable me to get out of the RAF – an invention, and a good story for a book.

As I have mentioned before, I regarded the danger of collisions to be the most serious problem facing all aviation. I had already developed some ideas on the way that complex problem might be solved. I felt that – as was the case with my bombing system – there must be a simple solution to it, but that it was unlikely that boffins on the ground would find one. It needed practical experience of flying, plus some deep thinking, to solve it. I chose that to be the subject of my proposed invention.

As a first step, I studied the available evidence on ship collisions. To my astonishment, I found that on average there had been in the recent period up to 1956 around four hundred collisions each year. A typical example was one that had recently occurred in perfect weather out in the middle of the ocean between two ships, with no others within a hundred miles. At dawn each ship ("X" and "Y") had observed the other, hull down on the horizon, heading on a converging course to cross each other's path some considerable distance ahead. After a couple of hours, ship X realised they could be on a collision course with ship Y – so altered course slightly. But ship Y had come to the same conclusion and had also altered course. [It is almost impossible to detect, either by radar or by observation from a distance, when a ship makes a slight alteration to its course.] Neither X nor Y realised what the other was doing. This happened several times subsequently during the day, until finally – towards dusk – the two ships had collided.

That was the most astonishing example I found, but similar cases were occurring at sea with amazing frequency – in spite of the complex shipping regulations that had been designed to prevent them.

I had reason to sympathise with the ships' captains because, quite frequently when walking along Piccadilly, I had nearly collided with someone approaching from the opposite direction as a result of each of us moving sideways to avoid the other and ending up face to face. We could stop and apologise to each other – but aircraft cannot do that.

Then one day, when I was walking down Piccadilly near the RAF Club, I saw a man with a white stick approaching me. I knew he would just walk straight on – so I had no difficulty avoiding him. As usual, I went to bed thinking about the collision problem. I must have woken up during the night, because on the pad by my bed I found, the next morning, a scribbled note: *"Only one must take avoiding action."*

That, I realised, had to be the basis of any anti-collision system.

In that connection, I was later amused by the following transcript of the ACTUAL radio conversation between a US Naval ship and the Canadians, off the coast of Newfoundland, released by the Chief of Naval Operations on 10th October 1995:

Canadians: *Please divert your course 15 degrees South, to avoid a collision.*

Americans: *Recommend you divert your course 15 degrees to the North, to avoid a collision.*

Canadians: *Negative. You will have to divert your course 15 degrees to the South to avoid a collision.*

Americans: *This is the Captain of a US Navy ship. I say again, divert YOUR course.*

Canadians: *Negative. I say again, you will have to divert your course.*

Americans: *THIS IS THE AIRCRAFT CARRIER USS LINCOLN, THE SECOND LARGEST SHIP IN THE UNITED STATES ATLANTIC FLEET. WE ARE ACCOMPANIED BY THREE DESTROYERS, THREE CRUISERS AND NUMEROUS SUPPORT VESSELS. I DEMAND THAT YOU CHANGE YOUR COURSE 15 DEGREES NORTH. I SAY AGAIN, THAT'S 15 DEGREES NORTH, OR COUNTER-MEASURES WILL BE TAKEN TO ENSURE THE SAFETY OF THIS SHIP.*

Canadians: *We are a lighthouse. Your call.*

My study of ship collisions indicated that many could have been avoided by that simple rule of only one taking avoiding action. Avoiding collisions between aircraft was much simpler than ships on the water – because an aircraft could change height, if flying with its wings level with the ground, almost instantaneously. Furthermore, providing both aircraft were flying with their wings level, they could pass each other safely with only a slight difference between their heights – as I had already experienced. And the most important factor was that, unless the aircraft were (or were going to be) at the same height, there was no danger of collision. So height was the key.

From my own experience, I reckoned it might take a pilot of a large aircraft up to 30 seconds to recognise a warning and get the plane flying straight and level; then another 30 seconds to climb or dive to a different level, as indicated by the warning device. So the device would need to detect any other aircraft that was (or would be) at the same height within about 60 seconds. With altimeters being inaccurate (due to having been set according to the different atmospheric pressures, depending on where the Captain had last adjusted it), my device would need a standard sealed capsule in all aircraft for measuring height relative only to other aircraft.

That capsule would vary the frequency of a radio transmitter and receiver (but with greater power in the forward direction). Only aircraft flying at a similar height (or going to be within 60 seconds) would come into radio contact. Then a comparison of the radio frequencies would indicate their relative heights and the device would instruct just one of them (usually the lower one) to descend.

The pilot, on first getting a warning of another aircraft at a similar height, would have 30 seconds to get the plane flying straight and level first. That could, of course, all be done automatically through the autopilot.

In principle, it was quite simple, although the gadgetry would be complicated.

That was the basis of the system, but there were many refinements – for example, small aircraft would only carry a tiny responder, while airliners would have the full equipment. About the time I had worked out the basic principles of the system, two airliners collided over the Grand Canyon – adding urgency to the need for such a system.

As I have already mentioned, my application to the Air Ministry for an award for my inventions of Red Cheeks and Blue Shadow had been refused on the basis that, "It was part of my duty". I was not prepared to stand any more of that nonsense. I got my father, who was a resident of Switzerland, to patent each part of my invention in his name. In principle, on paper, I had completed the whole system.

Meanwhile, regarding the other part of my plan to make money, I joined the Smiths Book Club that automatically sent me, on loan, two bestseller books each week. I studied these to try to decide what made them successful. The key thing was obviously to have a good story. So most nights, before going to sleep, I told my subconscious mind to come up with one, but it failed to do so – until it was triggered by something I considered my duty at Air Ministry.

There, it was part of my job to decide the sort of training exercises in which Bomber Command should be engaged. I had myself flown the new V-Bombers – the Valiant and the Vulcan – that were specifically designed to carry the Atomic Bomb, and I had attended a brief course on the British design of that weapon. To get maximum effect – as at Hiroshima – the bomb was set to explode well above ground level. Also, to fuse it before being dropped, a red button in the aircraft had to be pressed to activate a final bit being inserted into the bomb to make it "live". One danger, even if the bomb had not been made live, was that of the aircraft carrying it crashing – thus causing atomic material to be spread over a large area without the bomb itself detonating.

Walking back to my office after lunch at the RAF Club on another afternoon, I happened to meet my old friend Wilf Oulton. He told me that he had just learned that he was to go to Christmas Island to take charge of the Hydrogen Bomb test there. (He afterwards wrote his book, Christmas Cracker, based on those experiences.) The chief thing worrying him was if, after the red button had been pressed to make the bomb "live", the bomb "hung up" – ie it failed to release itself from the bomb rack. That was not an uncommon occurrence with ordinary bombs – but in that case the aircraft could still land safely with the bomb attached. But with an atomic bomb pre-set to explode at around 5,000 feet, that would create quite a problem.

That night I came up with an answer and the next day suggested to Wilf a simple mechanical solution. A handle with a bicycle chain which, if all else failed, could be used physically to mechanically unscrew the large metal pins holding either the bomb or the whole bomb rack itself, and so release it from the aircraft.

A few days later, after I had time to think more about that problem and its potential implications, both my immediate bosses were away and I represented the Assistant Chief of Staff (Training) at the weekly meeting of the Vice-Chief of Air Staff, Ivelaw-Chapman – one of our finest officers, whom I greatly admired. Amongst the items on the agenda for that meeting were three that I remember.

The first was to approve plans for the next series of Atomic Bombs, involving the expenditure of several hundred millions of pounds. None of the others present had a clue about that subject and it was passed immediately without any discussion.

The second was whether WAAF knickers should be mentioned in a list of items to be included in AMOs (Air Ministry Orders). That was a subject everyone understood – and that discussion lasted half an hour.

The third concerned placing an aircraft at the entrance to an RAF station, which only took 20 minutes' discussion.

At the end of the meeting, Ivelaw-Chapman asked whether anyone had any other points they wished to raise.

"Yes, Sir," I replied. "What procedures are to be followed if the captain of one of our V-Bombers discovers that they have a problem with the Atomic Bomb they are carrying? Or, for example, even with the undercarriage, which might mean them crashing on landing? Would they not be ordered to jettison the bomb before landing?"

The Air Marshals all stared at me in astonishment. They understood WAAFs' knickers, but anything to do with modern aviation or practical flying was completely beyond most of them. Ivelaw-Chapman finally said:

"Vielle, that is a very good question."

Then, turning to the others, he asked if anyone had thought of that before or had any answers. No one spoke.

"This is to be kept secret," Ivelaw-Chapman then ordered: "No one is to mention it outside this office. But I want you, Vielle, to lay on a training exercise with a dummy atomic bomb – pretending it is a real one – with only the aircraft crew, the Station Commander and the C-in-C of Bomber Command being aware of it. And let's see what happens."

I did so. And the result was sheer unadulterated panic – at several offices in Whitehall.

Bomber Command, when alerted to the crisis, ordered the crew to jettison the bomb in the sea; but where would it be safe to do so? The Admiralty were asked to designate an area free of shipping where it would do least damage. The Navy chose a location up towards the Arctic Circle. The crew of the aircraft were ordered to proceed there and drop the bomb. Refuelling aircraft were alerted and got airborne to ensure the bomber would have adequate fuel to remain at a safe height and then return.

On approaching the designated area, the V-Bomber Captain reported detecting ships ahead on his radar and later confirmed that below him he could see the lights of the Russian fishing fleet "looking like a village of stars".

At that stage, the panic became so extreme that Ivelaw-Chapman called off the exercise and instead ordered that proper plans for such an emergency were to be prepared.

A few mornings later, I woke up to find on the pad beside my bed: "*Book. Fused bomb set to go off at ? height. Can't defuse it. Can't drop it – Russian fishing fleet. Only answer: land at airfield above that height.*"

So, I had the story for my first book. I began writing it on the train to and from London. Gradually, it began taking shape, but I realised that it would be a long job completing it.

Meanwhile, the farm was becoming more interesting every day. I had decided to see whether it was possible to feed the family and make enough profit to pay for the other essentials of life and so become self-sufficient. With Pam's full time help, we set out to do so.

Close to the house, which stood towards the bottom of a hill, there was already a small pond fed by a stream from higher up and a Nissen hut 50 yards away that had been used for pigs and cattle. So, to get the farming project started, I borrowed £200 from Barclays Bank in Godalming. My first purchase was a gander and three geese from a farmer about three-quarters of a mile away. Having no method of transporting them, I decided to walk them home, driving them along with a lengthy stick, just like in the pictures I remembered in the children's books when I was young. That was a real pleasure and when I saw them splash happily into our pond I felt a new life was beginning for us.

The next addition was six pigs – also brought to Bunkers Hill on foot along a pathway through the woods. Then a dairy cow – then another. Quite soon we added chickens, Aylesbury ducks, baby chicks, and turkeys. Then, using an old incubator that we had purchased cheaply, we started hatching out bigger flocks. I expanded the pond by hand, and built another for the ducks with an island in the middle to prevent the foxes getting at them at night. I used to get up at 5 o'clock to milk the cows and help Pam feed the other animals, and helped her each evening as soon as I returned from sleeping at the Air Ministry. Bunny made the butter, we salted our own hams and, after getting them smoked, we had hams and sides of bacon hanging round the dining room walls – just as farmers had done a century ago.

We also had a small vegetable patch – enough for ourselves. Bunny sold much of the other produce to the local hotels – particularly the ducks, turkeys, young chickens and eggs – to help pay for the food for the remainder. We had well over a hundred ducks and hatched out about 20 goslings – the most delightful of all the young animals. I frequently shot rabbits and sometimes a hare, pheasant, partridge or pigeon, to vary our diet. Whenever friends visited us, I would offer them a choice of meat for lunch and then pluck and degut the duck (or whatever) that Bunny would

Bunkers Hill

Bunkers Hill

then cook on our Rayburn. It was a wonderfully happy, interesting and healthy existence.

I remember Pam waking me up in the middle of the night, saying that Marigold (her favourite cow, whose horns she used to polish daily) was calving, but the calf had got stuck and would I quickly come and help. I grabbed an instruction manual and a piece of rope that I had been told always to have ready and rushed up to the barn with a torch to read the instructions. Pam was stroking the cow and crying. The calf was half out, but clearly stuck. As I arrived, Marigold looked round at me and gave a terrific bellow. The calf shot out and a moment later Marigold started licking it dry. It was a wonderful sight, watching the calf eventually struggle to its feet, falling over many times at first, and then quite quickly finding the exact place to get its first breakfast, while Marigold chewed contentedly on the hay that Pam had offered her.

The calf was the first of several Hereford crosses that we reared, fattened up, and Pam – by herself – took to market. She became quite an expert at dealing in cattle.

At haymaking time, several of my staff, and other friends, came down to help. I had no machinery – so everything had to be done by hand. I had arranged for a couple of large barrels of cider to be ready for everyone to quench their thirst and the whole operation was a huge success.

I realised that my book was unlikely to be completed for some time, but my anti-collision system was reaching the stage where I felt we could begin thinking about exploiting it. I decided to devote all my energies to that end and gave up wasting any more time flying. I made my last flight ever as a pilot in early 1957 in one of the V-Bombers – a Vulcan. About that same time, I learned that Jock Melvin – the little rat that had pretended still to be a pilot and screamed when flying to Cyprus beside me, had (as a result of arrangements originating in my office) undergone a flying test at Manby. The result was that Melvin had to resign his commission immediately. Soon afterwards, his only son was lost in a tragic accident at sea. I had occasion to recall that 30 years later when another nasty chap who tried to blackmail me also lost his son in a tragic accident.

By the spring of that year, my father had taken out enough patents to enable us to discuss the anti-collision system with potential commercial partners. It would need scientists and engineers to do the detailed design of the actual bits and it was a question of whether to sell my ideas outright to one of the big firms or develop it further first.

A retired RAF Group Captain Engineer Specialist named Joe Poole (much older than me, whom I had known during the war) was working with my father on one of my father's inventions, and tried to help us. He and my father let the fact that we had a new invention be known to one or two friends, including a solicitor in London. The solicitor mentioned it to an Irish entrepreneur, who, shortly afterwards, on the death of his father, became the Lord Dunsany. The recent collision of the two airliners over the Grand Canyon had stimulated interest everywhere in finding a solution and Dunsany, in turn, introduced us to two young financiers – the brothers Gerald and Kenneth Shipman, who had recently set up an instrument and electronics firm that was looking for new projects to develop.

The father of the two brothers had recently died, leaving them (but mainly to Gerald, the elder) the quite considerable fortune that his foresight had generated. He had been a member of the Jewish community in Germany and deemed it prudent to escape from there shortly before the Munich Crisis in 1938. He came to London and, I believe, scraped a living by playing an instrument in an orchestra. He foresaw the war and started buying up old bicycles, which at that time cost practically nothing, and stored them in an empty warehouse. When the war started, petrol rationing was imposed, the bicycle makers were switched to making more vital war equipment and the value of his stored bicycles made him his first fortune. He had then used that to make a much bigger fortune by advancing money to the former owners of property (mainly in London) that the German bombing had destroyed. He would offer to buy the bomb hole for half the current value in cash to help them cover their immediate needs, with the other half to be paid if we won the war – a splendid gamble which came off.

First, I was thoroughly investigated by Dunsany and his solicitor. Then, for a few days I was grilled by the senior scientist from the Shipmans' new instrument firm, who was finally satisfied both on the whole system and on our patent position. The fact that everyone agreed on the urgent need for such a system gave it a good chance of success.

As a result, the Shipmans offered me double the salary of an Air Marshal (minimum period three years) to leave the RAF in return for a half share in my anti-collision system and my help in exploiting it. They would provide the staff, facilities and necessary finance.

When my good friend Jock Ireland heard that I was proposing to leave the RAF, he came rushing round to my office in great concern for my future. I showed him the terms of my proposed agreement with the Shipmans. He agreed with me that it was an offer and opportunity that I would be stupid to refuse. My problem now was how to get the Air Ministry to let me retire. He helped me draft a letter that might do the trick.

The letter said that my father was managing director of a company exploiting an antimony mine in Morocco and owned two other companies developing new inventions, and was now well over 75 years old – all of which was true. Furthermore, he had recently taken out patents on an anti-collision system for aircraft for which he urgently needed my full-time help to exploit and thus benefit aviation. If I left the RAF now, I could take over all these interests and thus enjoy a future career; whereas, if I continued in the RAF, those opportunities might be lost to my family and me forever. So I wanted to retire immediately.

When the letter reached George Harvey, he sent for me to discuss the matter. He knew only too well the frustrations I had experienced with my Red Cheeks project – and also my opposition to the Suez Invasion. When I mentioned the old deadbeats propping up the bar at the RAF Club and my fear of joining their ranks, he agreed that, if I so wished, I now deserved to be allowed to start a new career. He undertook to do his utmost to get my application approved. In fact, it was due to his assistance that, in August, he was able to tell me that I was being granted special leave to do whatever was necessary to help my father until my retirement was officially gazetted. I started work with the Shipmans immediately. My retirement came through three months later on 14th November 1957, 25 years after I went to Cranwell.

It was a big decision to leave the security of the RAF, with all the perks that went with it – security of income, bigger pension, medical care, marriage allowance, free accommodation (or extra allowances), office with secretary and a staff to carry out my orders, travel, long paid holidays, help in studying any desired subject, sports facilities, social life, etc. But I decided to take a chance on my own ability to do better outside the service, where I hoped my efforts would be better rewarded and not stifled by incompetent seniors.

One of my saddest memories was the astonishing deaths of so many of the officers under whom I had served or friends who would have influenced my career. At school my best friend Dudley Ashton had died of tuberculosis; then, shortly after leaving Cranwell, Henry Molyneux had been killed. Then, while I was at Cardington, A. A. B. Thomson had walked into the propeller. In Washington, Mansell had died the evening after I had spent the afternoon with him discussing instrument flying. Tommy Thurlow, David Waghorn, David Atcherley, followed by – the biggest blow of all – Kelly Barnes, and then Brook, just as he was about to become VCAS. The death of the Chief Superintendent at Farnborough had opened the way for Jack Richards and his communist comrades to delay the adoption of Red Cheeks and Blue Shadow.

I looked back at what I had achieved. Having learnt to fly in a pre-First World War type of aircraft designed in 1912 (just nine years after the Wright Brothers' first ever powered flight) and produced in 1913, I had piloted over 150 different types of aircraft – right through to supersonic speeds. Apart from the air collision at night in Canada, no pilot flying under my orders had ever been badly injured or crashed. My inventions had not only saved lives, but also influenced the future of offensive operations and reconnaissance.

In 1939, I had qualified as a weather forecaster and had been elected a Fellow of the Royal Meteorological Society (FRMetS).

During the war, I was elected an Associate Fellow of the Royal Aeronautical Society (AFRAeS) and an Associate Fellow of the Institute of Aerospace Society of the USA (AFIAS); then a Fellow of the Royal Institute of Navigation (FRIN) and a Fellow of the British Interplanetary Society (FBIS).

I had enjoyed a wonderful life in the RAF. I loved flying and had survived, by the narrowest of margins and amazing luck, more than the proverbial nine lives of a cat. My inventions had saved many lives; so had the results of my flying experiences. My bombing system, the Cruise Missile and sideways-looking radar antenna had changed strategic policy – and military aircraft design – for the USA as well as the UK. I saw no future challenge by just continuing in the RAF. I loved giving orders, but hated having to obey those with which I disagreed. But I was now walking away from financial security in a big organisation to face the challenge of an adventurous new life on my own.

Chapter 20

The Avel Corporation

On the advice of the Shipmans' solicitors and accountant, and because the patent applications had been made there, my father arranged for his old friend Maurice Merkt in Geneva to set up a new Swiss company, the Avel Corportation SA, Geneva (abbreviated from "Aviation Vielle") to hold the patents for my anti-collision system. That company then licensed a new company in England, "Vielle Shipman Ltd", to develop the system. That was in 1957, when I was 43 years old.

Our London office was in 60 Park Lane (which was part of the Shipmans' property empire) where a couple of rooms on the top floor, which was the main centre for their various business enterprises, were set aside for me and my secretary. (What a difference that was from the sparsely furnished Air Ministry!) Their chauffeur-driven Rolls-Royce was available for my use when needed. Kenneth and I usually lunched together – frequently at the Ritz, where he was already well known.

For the first few months, I spent most of my time with four of their scientists at their electronics firm at Twickenham (where the Shipmans also owned film studios), working on the detailed design of the anti-collision system and taking out more patents. I also had to visit Geneva occasionally, sometimes with our accountant, Edward Surman.

I had become so busy, and so often away, that I decided – much as I hated leaving it – that we would have to give up our farming enterprise and not be restricted by regular milking or feeding times. So we sold off all the livestock and moved into a furnished house on the outskirts of Farnham – Hope Cottage – that was more suitable for entertaining the type of business visitors with whom I was now associating. That also freed Bunny to join me on trips away. Overall, our farm accounts showed a total profit during the two years of £200. That enabled me to repay the original overdraft – but not repay all the hard work we had all put into it. But the immense

393

amount of enjoyment and lovely food we had derived from it had made it worth a fortune to us.

One of the first things I did was to buy a Mercedes 190 SL – the first in a long line of Mercedes that I have always (until recently) owned since that first glamorous sports car. Its performance was not all that exciting and the brakes were not up to the job, but it was a sheer delight to drive – or in which enviously to be seen.

About that time, I read in the paper that Claude Pelly had been knighted and promoted to Air Chief Marshal and was now a member of the Air Council. I decided that it would be fun to let him know that I too – in a quite different way – had also been promoted. So I rang him up to congratulate him and invited him to have lunch with me at a restaurant in Piccadilly. He welcomed the proposal, but mentioned that, in London, he did not have a staff car in which to get there. So I said I would pick him up. When he saw the Rolls, with the chauffeur, Claude's eyes almost popped out of his head.

At the Ritz, the doorman gave me his customary greeting, the barman my usual drink, with an enquiry after my family's health, and the headwaiter: "I reserved your favourite table by the window, Group Captain." That was all quite enough to stagger little Claude. But when he learnt that I was chairman and managing director of Swiss and English companies exploiting an anti-collision system that I had invented, he was even more impressed – and, to give him his due, was clearly pleased. He began apologising for what had happened, and the way I had been treated, in Cyprus – but I told him it was probably all for the best.

At the next table, it so happened that Group Captain Dudley Saward (who had been in my term at Cranwell, but had retired soon after the war to go into industry) was entertaining a batch of business people. Towards the end of lunch, Dudley came over to say 'hello' and I introduced him to Claude, whom he had never met. I later explained to Claude that Saward was now head of a large American company in England, but did not mention that my salary was already double that of an Air Marshal – and Dudley's probably three times more than mine. I felt that I had already made my point with Claude.

[I found it interesting, looking back through the records, that Dudley and I were the only ones of our term in the Cranwell entrance exam to achieve 100% in the personality test. So far as I know, we were also the only ones to retire voluntarily to go into business.]

My main interest, of course, was now the anti-collision system. But since leaving the farm I also had more time to spend on writing my first novel. I had already nearly completed the first draft, but it would involve very much more work before it would be ready to go to any publisher.

Hope Cottage, in a line of houses on the outskirts of Farnham, was not the ideal venue to induce relaxation and encourage writing. So, when Sheephatch House became available for rent, we moved into it for the second time. There, in complete quiet and contemplating the lovely view, I found writing much easier and started making notes for a second book. My main efforts were, however, concentrated on the anti-collision system.

After a few months' hard work, the scientists and I were satisfied with the design of the whole system and had applied for enough patents to cover it. So Kenneth, Gerald and I decided that the time had come to enlist the help of some powerful organisations to get it properly exploited. We started with the insurance companies – we felt they would be the most eager to assist in reducing the risk of collisions.

Lord Dunsany, who I had arranged to be one of our directors on the board of Vielle Shipman, arranged a gathering of about a dozen of the most powerful men in that industry, including the Chairmen or Managing Directors of several of our biggest insurance companies. I gave them a presentation of our new system and the reduction in the dangers of collisions that would result from the adoption of it.

At the end of my talk, they were unanimous in praise of my invention. They agreed that, as airline passengers, they would greatly welcome its adoption. But, as members of the insurance industry, they were not the slightest bit interested. If the risks of collision were reduced, then the premiums would also be reduced and they would not make any greater profit. The greater the risk, the larger the premiums and the bigger the potential profits – it was, to them, simply an actuarial calculation. So, while congratulating me and wishing us success, they made it quite clear that no insurance companies would be prepared to back my invention in any way.

This, to us, was an astonishing setback. But, on reflection, it should not have surprised me. That is how all businesses are run – and I was at the beginning of a learning curve. I eventually realised that no business organisation – nor government – would ever do anything unless the individuals concerned expected personally to gain from it. Whatever the wider benefits might be, they were not interested. That was so completely different from serving in the RAF that it took me quite a while to appreciate it. Everyone in the Services was trained, and undertook, to give even their lives to benefit others.

I was absolutely confident, however, that I would get the enthusiastic backing of another organisation, headed by a retired Group Captain whom I knew. So I arranged a similar presentation to him and his staff of the Civil Aviation Accident Investigation Branch. Their sole purpose was to prevent flying accidents – including collisions. They did so by investigating in detail every accident (or near miss) that occurred, with a view to proposing methods to be adopted to prevent any reoccurrence – and so increase safety.

My presentation went well and I was able to explain to this audience exactly how the system worked in much more detail. They were full of praise and agreed that if it was adopted it would certainly reduce, even perhaps eliminate, the risk of air collisions. One great advantage of my proposed system was that, by putting a tiny responder beacon on any high ground near airports, it would also reduce the risk of aircraft flying into them – which had been the cause of some civilian air accidents.

But, although he pretended to be enthusiastic, I sensed that the head of that organisation was not going to do anything to help get the system adopted. I learned the reason later, when I invited a couple of his staff to have drinks with me.

"Don't be a bloody fool, Tubby," one of them said, "you've got to realise that the more accidents there are, the more important the Accident Investigation Branch becomes. We've just put in for an increase in staff and we are not going to back anything that reduces the number of accidents."

That, to me, was another real eye-opener. But the logic was there.

Every RAF or civilian pilot (and other members of aircrew or cabin crew) who heard of my new system had been enthusiastic. So I then approached the Guild of Air Pilots. They were wholeheartedly in favour and promised every bit of help they could give. But they were not as influential as those with business interests, and, beyond encouraging us to persevere, the Guild could not really assist.

I tried the aircraft manufacturers. They too were full of praise, but pointed out that every piece of extra equipment in their aircraft meant extra weight and maintenance. So, unless all aircraft were forced by the authorities to fit an anti-collision system, they would be against its adoption. Furthermore, they were not the slightest bit concerned with collisions – that was a matter for the operators. If there were more collisions, then they would have to make more aircraft (and more profit) by selling replacements for those lost.

Who, then, could we find to back the full development of the system? The Civil Aviation Authority in the UK expressed great interest, but was not in the business of actually developing, or sponsoring, anything. The FAA (Federal Aviation Authority) in the USA might be a more progressive organisation, but they were unlikely to back a tiny English or Swiss company.

So we approached some of the airline companies. They said they would welcome such a system, but that they were merely in the business of operating the aircraft. They encouraged us to go ahead with all speed and wished us luck, but until such time as all other airlines were similarly equipped, they would not become interested. As had been the case with navigation systems and landing aids, getting international agreement to have airliners operated by so many different countries all to adopt the same system had, in the past, proved extremely difficult – sometimes impossible. The NIH factor (Not Invented Here) was a formidable obstacle in getting each country to agree to any one system.

Our best hope seemed to be to get one of the big international organisations, with subsidiary companies in most of the important countries, to take on the job of getting the system fully developed, tested and adopted. We had already talked to Sperry in England; but, like most subsidiary companies, they could do nothing without it going through their parent company, which was in New York. We decided, however, to explore possibilities in Europe before trying America.

With the help of various contacts in the aircraft instrument industry, we arranged for me to give a presentation of the system to some of the main European companies that we thought might be interested in exploiting the system. At the suggestion of the managing director of Sperry in England (who had served in the RAF during the war and was an old friend of mine), we included the Sperry office in Paris.

By that time, the Shipmans and I had also set up another company – "Shipelle Ltd" – to exploit other new inventions as well. My wartime experience at Farnborough and in Washington helped us judge their likely success. Many inventors had great difficulty in getting their ideas developed and, knowing the Shipmans were interested, several of these had approached them for help. I had also taken out several patents myself – including, for example, one for an electric toothbrush ("Operation Molar") which was beaten to the post by one from Boots.

Although extremely interesting, the job of bringing new inventions to market and profitability is one of the most difficult operations one can ever envisage. Also, because few people welcome change, there is an inbred opposition to the adoption of new ideas. We found it frustrating.

One of the inventions, which had been brought to us by an Italian named Grillet, was for an attachment to the carburettor of cars to increase performance and conserve fuel. To test it, he had already modified his own Rolls – with apparently good results – so I decided to fit one to my Morris Minor (but not to my lovely Mercedes) and to test that on my tour of Europe.

I set off in the Morris, with Bunny, first for Paris (to the Sperry subsidiary there), then Eindhoven in Holland (Philips) and so on via Germany and Italy to several of the main international instrument companies. Everywhere we went I was royally entertained, congratulated on my invention – which generated great interest – but always met the obstacle that all countries would have to adopt the system, and all aircraft carry at least a tiny responder beacon, for the system to be fully efficient. Getting international agreement would be a formidable task, particularly as some companies in the USA were believed to be trying to develop their own different types of anti-collision systems.

We returned to England having made virtually no progress, except that the gadget on the car had worked well. Even so, Grillet, in spite of our help, never managed to make a commercial success of it.

Soon after returning from my European trip, I learned that Marcus (an old friend from my Washington days and now a director of Bendix in New York) was in London. I invited him and two other officials from his company, to our offices in Park Lane, where I gave them a presentation of my system.

He was enthusiastic and invited us to offer it to the Bendix research establishment at Baltimore in the USA, where their scientists had been trying for years to develop an anti-collision system without much success. We agreed to do so. Kenneth and I booked our passage on the *Queen Mary*.

Then came a bombshell. Our patent agent advised us that they had discovered the Kollsman Instrument Company of New York had already been granted a patent for the standard pressure capsule on which my system was based. Without that, our patent coverage would be greatly weakened. Unless we first obtained a licence from Kollsman, we could not proceed. Panic!

As I mentioned earlier, during the war Tommy Thurlow and I had done the original tests on a new Kollsman compass – and we had spent many an evening with the managing director of Kollsman – a delightful chap named Victor Carbonara. So I made a phone call to

New York to see whether he was still there. He was, and I made an appointment to see him the afternoon of the day we were due to dock there.

Victor greeted us warmly. He remembered the patent, but Kollsman had never made much use of it and he offered to assign it to me as a gift in recognition of the help I had given him fifteen years ago. Two hours later, having spent most of the time reminiscing, I left with the document assigning that vitally important Kollsman patent to the Avel Corporation Geneva. Panic over! As is so often the case, it is not what you know – but who are your friends.

We spent over a month at Baltimore trying to arrange a deal with Bendix. But the scientist in charge of their own efforts to develop an anti-collision system (which I judged never to have had any hope of success) felt his own position was being undermined and made any agreement impossible. While there, however, I made contact with many old friends, including Vlad Reichel and Chick Hayward, who was now a full Admiral and Vice-Chief of the US Navy.

After visiting several other organisations, we finally decided that Sperry (where I had cordial relations with many of the senior people) was probably the most likely, as well as the most suitable, firm to commercialise my system. Even there, however, we ran into opposition from the scientists who had been trying to develop their own ideas and, of course, the NIH factor was ever present. Also, we should really have had a far more experienced businessman (and lawyer) to negotiate a deal with the legal sharks employed by such firms.

Sperry could find no technical reason why the system would not work – and finally agreed that it could be the complete solution to the collision problem. But the biggest hurdle would be to get international agreement that all aircraft would be fitted with the system. Without universal adoption, no system could be a complete safeguard, and too many instrument firms (even governments) already had vested interests in other systems that they were trying to develop.

We returned to England without a signed agreement on the understanding that (with co-operation from the Sperry UK branch) we would develop the system still further and then return to New York with their top UK scientist to help Sperry there make a presentation of it to the Federal Aviation Authority (FAA) in Washington. If the FAA then agreed to provide the necessary funds and to back it internationally, then Sperrys would sign an agreement with us and take over its future development. That, it seemed to us, was our only real hope of success.

I had not enjoyed being parted from Bunny during the several weeks we had spent in the USA and decided to take her with me (at the company's expense) on any future visit. Meanwhile, in England, I found that I had to put in very long hours to cope with all the work. I was often woken by phone calls in the early morning from Geneva, which was one hour ahead, and with calls until after midnight from New York (five hours behind). It took me an hour each way motoring to and from the office. I realised that I had unintentionally joined in the "rat race".

At first it was exhilarating, exciting and stimulating. But gradually I began asking myself what in life would give me most enjoyment. I began longing for peace and quiet in the countryside, with Bunny and my family, where I could escape from the rat race (like I imagine many other businessmen do). I wanted quietly to develop new ideas. I prayed that my first book would be successful. I had written the outline story for a second novel and had ideas for a third.

After a few weeks' work with the scientists and patent agents, I was ready to return to the USA for the FAA presentation. Bunny accompanied me (at company expense) on the famous French liner Libertie, in which we witnessed an incident which I think is worth recounting.

There were not many other passengers travelling first class and the luxurious dining room was far from full. At the next table to us were a couple of ladies from Midwest USA who seemed a bit unaccustomed to such surroundings. Our impression was that they had won some prize which had enabled them to venture beyond the boundaries of the USA, or even perhaps their own state, for the first time.

One night it happened to be our wedding anniversary – so Bunny and I decided to celebrate. We arrived at our table well before the two ladies and had a lengthy discussion with the Maitre d'hôtel concerning the appropriate food for such an important occasion. With few other tables occupied, several of his minions as well as the sommelier and his deputy, in all their regalia, stood around, nodding with approval as we made our choices.

Then it was the turn of the sommelier, hovering with what was reputed to be one of the most famous wine lists anywhere. Having chosen the white wine to go with the fish, we came to the red wine to go with the meat. I decided to seek his advice.

"We are celebrating a very important anniversary," I informed him, "and I would like something special."

He drew himself up to his full height, beaming broadly.

"In that case, Monsieur, I would recommend one of the only four bottles remaining of one of the most famous Bordeaux wines this century."

Travelling on an expense account, I was not concerned with the price, and did not even look at the wine list. I just nodded.

With great ceremony, the dust-encrusted bottle was produced. I cannot remember now, but I think it was probably a vintage Chateau Latour. With tremendous ceremony and loving care, with the Maitre d'hôtel and several other waiters looking on approvingly, the sommelier decanted it over a candle. In due course, he then took a small sip to taste it.

Beaming like Father Christmas, he poured a sample into my glass for my approval. It was, without doubt, the most delicious wine I had ever tasted. Bunny agreed, and all the happy staff were almost clapping their hands with delight.

A little later, the two ladies arrived and ordered their meal. When the sommelier presented them with the wine list, the elder one turned to me, asking:

"Mister Veel, what wine am you drinkin' tonight?"

"It's a very special one," I replied.

"Is it nice?" she asked.

I nodded. "It is absolutely delicious."

She turned to the sommelier. "That's what we'll have then. Bring us a bottle."

The ceremony was repeated. With the sommelier in all his regalia, the Maître d'hôtel and several of his minions all watching, she took a sip of the sample he poured for her to taste. All expected her to be quite excited by it.

"It's a bit sour!" was her comment. "Bring me some sugar."

The scene was like a Bateman drawing. Everyone stared at her in disbelief. Complete silence reigned for several seconds. She seemed oblivious and began chewing bits off a bread roll. The Maître d'hôtel had clearly suffered one of the greatest shocks of his life. The sommelier simply did not believe what he had heard. He leant forward, saying: "I beg your pardon, Madame?"

With her mouth now half full, she repeated her order: "I said, bring me some sugar."

The Maitre d'hôtel turned to one of the startled minions and ordered him to get some sugar. When it was placed on her table, she took some into the spoon and stirred it into the wine. Then, leaving the spoon still in the wine glass, she tasted it again.

Turning to me she said: "Quite right, Mister Veel. That's a nice wine – that."

We wondered whether she got a shock when she saw the bill!

Discussing that incident with Buuny afterwards, I maintained that if those ladies got greater enjoyment from drinking their wine that way— rather than the customary French way of drinking bottled grape juice – then why should it logically have prevented them from doing so. Why should tradition overrule pleasure?

When we arrived in New York, our old friend Vlad Reichel met us and entertained us, before I went to see the Sperry people. We then stayed at a luxury hotel in Garden City, as also did the head scientist from Sperry UK, who had flown over to help prepare for the Washington meeting with the FAA. I was to give the main presentation, with the backing of the Sperry scientists, in a few days' time.

That presentation went extremely well. It resulted in the FAA putting up one million dollars to fund the development of my system to the stage of an air demonstration. At that stage, Sperry took over the further commercialisation of my invention and my task had been completed.

We returned to England believing that a very profitable agreement with Sperry would soon be signed, but we had not reckoned with the cutthroat lawyers of American big businesses, and in the end I was only rewarded with a relatively small sum. However, I have the satisfaction of believing that the developments resulting from my invention were partly responsible for the increased safety of air travel.

Kenneth and I were great friends and a couple of years later, when he wanted a company in Switzerland for other purposes, I made him a gift of the Avel Corporation. Although I did not see much of him until shortly before his death a few years ago, I still miss his tremendous sense of humour and his zest for life, and shall always be grateful to him and Gerald for having helped me start a new life after leaving the RAF.

Chapter 21

Books

As I mentioned earlier, my experience at the Air Ministry concerning the problem of where to jettison a malfunctioning atomic bomb had given me the story for my first book. Also, my earlier high flying in a Canberra had generated ideas for another one.

I had completed a full draft of the first under the title *Hell's Atoms* and later a skeleton of the second that later became *Star-raker*. But I was so busy and preoccupied with the anti-collision system that I realised it would take me a long time to complete even the first. Also, I had developed ideas for a third, based on the use of the bombing system I had invented to frustrate the potential threat from Russia, which seemed very real at that time.

I also realised that, although I had little difficulty in writing the action parts and all the flying bits, I was not good at bringing out the characters of the people involved. Also, ever since that incident when I had been a baby, I had had a complex about criticism. So I decided that it might be wise to employ a "ghost" to rewrite them for me and publish them under a pen name.

I happened to mention this to my old friend Terry McComb, who suggested that I should contact the ex-Squadron Leader who he had nominated to be my second pilot on that Liberator trip to Ceylon at the end of the war, and had married my WAAF equipment officer. He was now with BOAC, and had recently managed to get one of his books published.

We were then living at Sheephatch House and I invited David Beaty to come and see me there. We chatted happily about old times and his ambition to become a successful author. He felt that the publication of his first novel, *Call Me Captain* by "Paul Stanton", might be the first step in that direction. That, by coincidence, had been the basis of the film of which the flying part had been filmed at Upwood when I was there.

I asked his advice about finding a ghost writer and gave him a brief outline of my proposed novel. He became wildly enthusiastic and pleaded with me to let him rewrite it. So I typed out a very simply worded letter of agreement between us that he would rewrite my story, each of us paying our own expenses; he would deal with the literary aspects, I would deal with the financial ones, and we would share the copyright and all proceeds 50/50. We both signed it and (two years later) my solicitor said it was as clear and binding agreement as any he had ever seen – better even than a complicated legal agreement drawn up by solicitors.

Because I did not want the novel to appear under my name (which proved to be a grave mistake), I left him to select a suitable pen name for us both. I visited him and Betty at their house in Kent to discuss further details of the story, but then did not hear from him for well over a year – not until about the time that we had decided to sell out the anti-collision system to Sperrys in New York.

Then, in the spring of 1960, I received a very cordial phone call from David saying that he had finished the book, submitted it to his literary agents, Curtis Brown in London, and was sending me a copy to read.

I found that he had copied all the flying parts almost exactly from my draft, but had brought out the characters in more detail. Apart from the very beginning, however, the first one third of the book was quite awful and almost irrelevant – I guessed he had copied it from some other story he had begun to write. The remainder was better and the overall story was exciting. I found a serious technical error, also that an important issue had been missed out, and I had several suggestions for minor improvements. So I jumped into my Mercedes and rushed across to see him, expecting a welcome for any constructive comments.

To my surprise, he resented any suggestion that it was not perfect, and, although admitting he had missed out an important point, he refused to make any amendments to the draft he had submitted to the agents. It was my first (but not my last) experience of coming up against the "Prima Donna" complex. So, instead of discussing the matter further, we adjourned to his lovely garden and reminisced about our flight to Ceylon together and our subsequent flying experiences.

About a month after that visit, I received an excited phone call from him.

"John Bull has offered us £400 for the serial rights," he said. "They serialised my earlier book and want to do the same with this one. But it also must be under the same pen name – Paul Stanton – as the other one. Otherwise they probably won't take it. So I've changed the name to *Village of Stars by Paul Stanton*."

I too was so excited that, beyond protesting that I thought the name *Hell's Atoms* was far better, I merely suggested that we should have dinner together at the Ritz to celebrate. His news, to me, was a very pleasant, opportune and welcome surprise.

About a week later he rang me up again – this time so excited he could hardly speak.

"*Readers Digest* have offered us £35,000, plus additional royalties, to condense it. May I accept?"

I had difficulty believing my ears. When I recovered from the shock (that sum was nearer to about £½m in today's money), I agreed that we should.

The next week I had another phone call. This time David was even more excited.

"20th Century Fox have offered £75,000 for the film rights. But Curtis Brown have advised us not to accept. They think they can get more."

When I had recovered from that shock. I meekly suggested that it might be better to accept that offer than run the risk of losing it. But he said he had faith in Curtis Brown knowing their business and that it was best to leave it to them.

Two days later, I had another call from David:

"Tubby," he screamed, "Alfred Hitchcock at Paramount has offered £100,000 for the film and television rights. Curtis Brown recommend we accept. I think we should. Do you agree?"

By this time I had succumbed to that sort of numb feeling that I had once experienced when I was involved in a train crash in the middle of the night, thrown out of my bunk and knocked unconscious. As I recovered on this occasion, I had no difficulty agreeing with David. Then, on the back of an envelope, I started doing some calculations of the royalties on the basis that the book itself now seemed likely also to be successful.

That led to me consulting Edward Surman (our Vielle Shipman accountant).

"Before you sign any agreements for lump sums or royalties," he advised me, "you must first have established residence outside the UK. Otherwise you may have to pay tax of up to 92% on all the money you receive. Since you're already working as managing director of the Avel Corporation, Geneva, why don't you simply move down there?"

At one week's notice, in May 1960, that is exactly what Bunny and I did. With help from my father, we managed to rush through all the formalities of becoming Swiss residents, and lived for a while in a private hotel on the Lake until we found a small furnished house to rent at Vendoeuvres (a small village near Geneva). We arranged for Pam to stay (in a caravan) with the Measures at Blackburn Hall and the two younger girls to become boarders at their school.

But, even before we had moved to Switzerland, a crisis had arisen. David rang me up, in a frantic state and almost screaming, to say that we would lose all the offered contracts unless I wrote him a letter giving him sole ownership of the copyright. His excuse was that otherwise he could not use the Paul Stanton penname he had used on his earlier book. He assured me that it would not affect my entitlement to 50% of the proceeds.

I trusted David. One learns to trust your second pilot. So I began writing him the letter he had requested. But Bunny (who was always much wiser than me) said: "Tubby, don't send any letter until you have the advice of a solicitor. Too much is involved."

So, the next morning, instead of posting that letter, I sought the advice of the friendly Bank Manager in Godalming who had lent me the £200 for the farm. He arranged for me to see his friend the solicitor whose office was just opposite. That solicitor, after I had shown him my original agreement with David and explained the situation, said:

"It's the oldest trick in the game. And I'll bet this chap Beaty will be on to you saying that you will lose the contract unless you send that letter immediately. That contract you drew up and he signed is as solid as a rock, but had you posted that letter you would not have got a penny."

The next day David, not having received the letter, was on the phone screaming at me, conveying exactly the message my solicitor had forecast. When I told him that I had consulted a solicitor who had advised me against sending any such letter, he cursed me for not trusting him and slammed the phone down.

We later discovered that David had already signed contracts as Paul Stanton, with all the money to be paid to him. It took my solicitor several weeks to get it all sorted out with David's solicitor. Needless to say, David and I were never again on speaking terms.

Village of Stars became a worldwide best seller and was translated into over 20 languages. In Germany it did particularly well, because the publisher there first promoted it by selling a limited edition without the last chapter – on the basis that whoever came up with an ending most similar to mine won a big prize. I do not think David was pleased by the review in the USA that concluded:

"Brilliant story ruined by bad writing."

David later had it republished as one of his "David Beaty" novels. In addition to that, I found out later that he was also receiving other payments that he was not sharing with me.

David was very stupid to have ruined our friendship and co-operation, as I had several other stories he could have rewritten for me. Instead, I advertised in *The Times* for a ghost writer for my next book.

I had several replies to that advertisement. I finally selected a budding author, Donald Payne, who had already enjoyed some success. We formed a friendship that endures to this day and he rewrote four of my stories. The first, *Star-raker*, was also a worldwide best seller and was condensed by *Readers Digest* (but that organisation insisted that we changed the final chapter to make it a happy ending). If both *Star-raker* and *Village of Stars* HAD been published under the same name – such as my own – the future of any further books would have been greatly enhanced. But at the time, as was the case with David Beaty, I preferred not to have my name publicised. I let Donald Payne arrange the pseudonym and he used two of his Christian names – "Donald Gordon" – in which we each still have a 50/50 interest.

By that time we were living in the village near Geneva and were wondering where we should make our permanent new home. We had a request from Pliny Holt's brother to see his daughter, who was attending a finishing school at Gstaad. We stayed the night at the Hotel Maurice there, and the next morning we decided to take the chair lift up the Eggli Mountain, where, leaving Bunny at the café, I wandered into the surrounding hills alone.

Sitting on the grass, with a wonderful view of the Alps to the south and the smaller mountains surrounding that area, I was suddenly overcome by a strange sensation of complete peace and a silence that I had never before experienced. Compared with the rat race I had been in, it was a completely different world. I decided that that was the sort of area and surroundings in which I would like to spend the rest of my life. Perhaps I was subconsciously influenced by its proximity to where my father, and his mother, had been born.

We later travelled extensively in Europe, but that area (Gstaad/Chateau d'Oex and the hills above Montreux) became our main home and was where, following that second success, I wrote the outline of three other novels that Donald then rewrote for me. All were based on my own experiences – with a bit of imagination added – which his further ideas and professional writing considerably enhanced.

At that time (the early 1960s) I – like many other people – was deeply concerned about the Russian threat. There was no defence against any strategic missile armed with a nuclear warhead that the Russians might decide to launch against us – only a deterrent. Our high-flying bombers were too vulnerable to the Russian ground defences realistically to provide that. For years I had advocated the low-flying bomber, using my bombing system (Red Cheeks, Blue Steel or Cruise Missile) as the weapon most likely to provide the deterrent we needed to preserve peace.

View of our chalet -Gstaad

View from our chalet

Gstaad

Near Gstaad

The Olden-Gstaad

Chateaux Chillon

Bernese Oberland

411

My third novel, *Flight of the Bat*, which was published in 1963 as a Donald Gordon, was based on that theme. It was translated into several languages and did quite well. A film company was going to make a film of it, and had bought an option to do so, but the contract was badly handled by the agent and the deal fell through. Many people correctly assumed the aircraft I was writing about was the TSR2 – the low-level bomber that the communist sympathiser Harold Wilson cancelled and had all the plans destroyed to please his Russian masters.

My next story, *Golden Oyster*, was based on Ed Link's attempt (in which I was involved) to find and retrieve the Rommel Treasure from the bottom of the Mediterranean Sea. The background to that, and the invention of the "Snorkel", is dealt with in a later chapter. That novel also had the distinction of being published in a country behind the Iron Curtain.

Our last Donald Gordon novel, *Leap in the Dark*, was published in 1970. Like *Star-raker*, it was based on my own flying experiences. Although Donald Payne had flown as a pilot during the war, we had some difficulty agreeing some of the technical details I wanted to include. Nevertheless, with the supersonic Concorde now on the horizon, our novel attracted considerable interest and did quite well in several countries.

About four years earlier, I had decided, having more spare time and some successful novels behind me, also to try writing a book completely on my own. I had several potential stories in skeleton form from which to choose. But an incident while I was crossing the English Channel gave me another idea.

In 1965, as a Fellow of the Royal Institute of Navigation, I had been invited to attend a lecture in London on the subject of Continental Drift, to be given by one of the scientists with whom I had worked at RAE early in the war – Professor Blackett (as he was then). Approaching England on the cross-channel ferry, we were delayed by fog from entering Dover harbour and the ship was stationary. I was on deck and looking down at the water. I noticed, with increasing interest, that a whole series of bubbles were coming to the surface. In due course, I began wondering where they were all coming from.

The government, at that time, were considering proposals for a cross-channel link – either a bridge or tunnel – from Dover to Calais. (Those plans were later cancelled. The tunnel project was only resurrected, in slightly different form, in the 1980s). So, like most frequent cross-channel travellers, I was naturally interested in anything that would make it easier to get "across the pond". It was very frustrating being delayed in fog just a little distance from Dover, and I began considering what difference a bridge, or tunnel, would make to me – and whether one would ever be built.

We had stayed the previous night at the Hotel Maurice in Calais, where they had, on the wall in the small bar, a century-old humorous picture of the tunnel being built. It showed one section starting from each side, but failing to meet in the middle – missing each other by several yards. This reminded me that, nearly a hundred years before, the building of a tunnel had actually been started – but abandoned after a couple of miles or so from each side had been dug out. Quite possibly, I thought, those bubbles might be coming up from the English part of that original tunnel – particularly as we were probably just in the area above it.

The lecture, at the Royal Geographical Society building, was fascinating. Blackett explained that he now had proof of "Continental Drift" – a theory that had been under discussion for several years. By measuring the magnetism found in rocks along lengthy stretches of the coastlines on either side of the Atlantic, and then comparing them, scientists now knew that they had once been attached. Furthermore, they could now measure the speed at which America and Europe/Africa were continuing to move apart.

Thinking about the implications of that, I wondered whether France and England were moving in relation to each other and what affect that might have on a cross-channel tunnel. I obtained copies of the detailed plans for both the proposed bridge and the tunnel, and studied them. One thing stood out quite clearly. A road bridge, with a railway attached underneath (as was proposed) would have enormous advantages – from every point of view – over a tunnel. It seemed to me quite crazy even to contemplate building a tunnel which could only carry trains, with all the enormous disadvantages such as cost, fire hazard, maintenance, and security. Furthermore, if France was moving in relation to England, then the tunnel represented a far greater hazard than a bridge that could be built to be flexible – and, if it was broken by any sudden earth movement, offered a better chance of survival to anyone using it than being in a tunnel. The only argument against a bridge was that a ship might run into one of the artificial islands supporting it. But the danger of a fire in the tunnel was potentially far more serious and much more frightening.

I then consulted one of the top geologists at London University. From him I learnt that three fault lines run down the English Channel and that there had been a very minor earthquake a few years previously which had moved the English coast a fraction of an inch sideways in relation to France. Even as a schoolboy I had learnt that the North of Scotland was known to be sliding along the Southern part, although that was obvious from just looking at a map. From that geologist I also learnt that Calais was now already some 20 kilometres sideways in relation to Dover from its original position some millions of years ago.

So, with the plans for a tunnel being frequently discussed in the media, I decided to write a book warning against the danger presented by these land movements to a tunnel that would stretch at least 22 miles under the water. I myself had already gone through a frightening experience of being stuck in a car on a stationary train in the Simplon tunnel through the Alps, with our terrified children screaming. That had been alarming enough – without the additional threat of it also becoming flooded.

So, in 1967, I wrote *No Subway*, with help from my youngest daughter (whose suggestion it was that we should kill off one of the characters in the final chapter), and had it published under my own name. The story hit the headlines in *The Times*, and I was interviewed on television and radio. The book sold well in England and France and we nearly clinched getting it made into a film; but it was of too little interest to people in other countries.

Later, returning to the theme of the Cold War and the Russian threat, I wrote *The Shadow of Kuril*. I considered it, in many ways, to be the best story of all. It was about tracking an enemy submarine under the Arctic icecap. It proved a mammoth task even making sure that I had the technical details right – such as the phases of the moon and the angle at which the submarines would view it through holes in the ice, etc. It took nine drafts, each of around 500 pages, before I was satisfied that everything was accurate. I should then really have done a further draft to bring out better the characters of the people involved. That, I believe, would have made it another bestseller, but I was already past the date agreed with my publisher and I stupidly let it go without those improvements.

In consequence, *The Shadow of Kuril* did not do as well as I had hoped – mainly, as an American publisher told me, because the characters were too weak.

I had written several other stories in skeleton form, but had become too involved with managing investments (for myself and others) to be able to concentrate on writing. I had submitted a synopsis to Curtis Brown (my literary agents) for comment and received such an enthusiastic letter encouraging me to write it (or get it written) that I encouraged Don Stokes to have a go at it – but without success.

That was about our fellow cadet at Cranwell, Jeudwine, who had been a prisoner of war in Japan, together with his great friend who had married the girl whose hand they had both sought. Jeudwine made a miraculous escape from an assassination attempt and later served in Bomber Command. His friend was recaptured and believed killed. Jeudwine married his friend's widow and had, by the end of the war, a couple of children.

His great friend had not, in fact, been killed, and was one of the ex-PoWs that my aircraft had brought back to Oakington. He was the one who had asked me if I knew Jeudwine. A couple of days later, Jeudwine had been killed flying into the side of one of the hangars

415

on his airfield. I guessed, of course, that it was the only possible solution to this tragic situation – suicide.

Using a little imagination, I had turned that into a story for a novel that I named *The Ghost of Salembou.* The synopsis that Curtis Brown enthusiastically encouraged me to turn into a novel is still waiting … and I have several other half-written stories. When I have finished these memoirs, I may again turn my attention to them. Meanwhile, my bookcase already has 85 different editions of my books, published in various languages. Great fun!

Chapter 22

The Rommel Treasure

I first heard about Ed Link in the 1930s. He became famous as the inventor of the first aircraft flight simulator – the Link Trainer – which was used by most Air Forces for training their pilots to fly, using only their instruments, in bad weather or at night. I first met him in 1941, when I was entrusted with carrying out the service trials of another of his inventions – the Link Celestial Navigation Trainer – at Port Albert in Canada. The following year, when I was stationed in Washington, we cemented a friendship that lasted until his death 40 years later.

As I mentioned earlier, I believe that I might have lost the sight of my left eye, but for his timely warning that I needed immediate medical attention. Then, in 1942, he and his wife Marion invited Bunny, Pam and me to spend a couple of weeks with them and their two young boys on Perch Island – their island in the St Lawrence River near Gananoque, on which they had a log cabin. They kept their yacht (*Python*) anchored nearby in the river. They also had two canoes and a mooring for the amphibian in which Ed commuted daily to his main factory in Binghampton, in New York State.

Ed Link's Amphibian - Perch Island

Ed's yacth

Shortly after we joined Marion there, Ed arrived back one evening with a new type of fly fishing rod. It was made of a material that appeared to be metal; but was much thinner and lighter than the split cane ones we normally used, and he was very excited about it. He suggested I should try it, but warned me to take great care of it, as it was experimental and the only one yet constructed. So, the following morning, after he had taken off to fly to Binghampton, I went out to fish with it.

I paddled the canoe out into the middle of the river, where the bottom, varying between about six to twelve feet below, was covered in long reeds that were swaying in the current of about three knots, and I began fishing. The lightweight birch bark canoe had no anchor, so, from time to time, as it was carried downstream, I had to paddle back to keep near Perch Island.

Fishing with that new rod was sheer delight. When I was about a hundred yards from Perch Island, I felt a sharp tug on the line from what must have been quite a large fish, and immediately cast again towards the same spot. But my hand must have been wet and the rod slipped from my grip into the water and sank quickly into the reeds. Had I dived in after it (which I thought of doing), the canoe would have drifted away and I might never have been able to retrieve it. Instead, using the paddle, I tried to keep the canoe over the spot where I had last seen the rod, meanwhile trying to fix that position in my mind by noting which trees and other objects on both banks were in line.

But an hour later, when I returned with a makeshift anchor for the canoe and started diving, hanging onto the reeds to prevent drifting downstream, and not finding the rod, I began to doubt the accuracy of my navigational fix. When Ed returned that evening and learned what had happened, he was devastated. I felt awful.

[It is interesting, however, that my loss of that rod set in motion a chain of events that completely changed Ed's later life

Near Perch Island

Near Perch Island

and resulted in developments – many recorded in *The National Geographic Magazine* and elsewhere – that helped advance science and revolutionised underwater exploration. It may also have been responsible, later, for the tragic death of his son.]

We went out together in the canoe and Ed started diving down, trying to find it. He made a glass-fronted head mask to see better, but could only stay underwater for about a minute without coming up for air. He tried with a rubber tube in his mouth with me in the canoe holding the open end, but the tube had to be at least ten feet long and he found he was breathing in the air he had expelled. So he made a bigger mask covering his whole head, with a narrow rigid tube about a foot long sticking up from it to let him take further breaths near the surface with his head continuously in the water, while searching between the reeds. Holding on to a rope from the canoe with one hand and using a pole with the other to move the reeds aside, while I paddled the canoe backwards and forwards over the area, proved a better method. But sometimes the water would get into the tube, so he designed a valve (using a ping-pong ball as a lever) to close the tube if it went below the water level. That, I believe, was the first "Snorkel". (The scuba was developed later, I believe, mainly in France by Jacques-Yves Cousteau.)

Although we never found the rod, that incident led to Ed becoming interested in underwater exploration. He spent much of his energy after the war developing equipment to facilitate that field of activity. First, he designed his motor yacht – *Sea Diver* – specifically to facilitate underwater exploration. It had a glass panel in one part of the bottom for viewing the water below and carried a small amphibious aircraft. His successes with that hit the headlines and were the subject of many articles.

One of Ed's successes was finding Columbus's flagship, the *Santa Maria*, from which he gave me something I still treasure – one of the "pieces of eight" that he retrieved from that ship. His pioneering exploits in that field are well documented both in books (such as *Sea Diver* and *Windows in the Sea* by Marion Link, *Life* and *The National Geographic*).

Sea Diver - Beginning of record breaking dive in capsule

View of Villefranche from Sea Diver

My own involvement was very minor. But my eldest daughter and I did the research in England for his underwater exploration of Port Royal – the pirate's city in Jamaica that was swallowed up by the sea in the 1692 earthquake and is now 60 feet down – and then for Caesarea off Israel.

In August 1962, he had invited us down to be his guests on *Sea Diver* while he carried out his record-breaking deep dive off Cap-Ferrat. I, while talking to him from the deck of Sea Diver during his descent and during his sojourn down at depth, was probably the first person ever to discover the effect of heliox (the mixture of oxygen and helium that he was breathing) on speech. Luckily, we were both familiar with the Morse code – to which (to his astonishment, for he had no way of realising the effect that breathing mixture was having on his voice) I had to persuade him to resort.

Lord Kilbraken, a writer and photographer, was with us at Villefranche to handle publicity. Jacques-Yves Cousteau, who had ratted on a joint programme that he had originally agreed with Ed, was jealously sniffing around to gain any knowledge that might be of benefit for his own projects. Cousteau's sole aim appeared to be self-aggrandisement. Ed's was scientific research for the benefit of mankind. The US Navy, whose Sixth Fleet were in that area of the Mediterranean, did everything possible to help Ed.

Following Ed's epic dive, his team proved (on 7th September) that it was possible for a diver to do underwater exploration down at 200 feet – even emerging from the capsule to use a "pinger" and magnetometer to detect, through mud or sand, artefacts and metal buried in the sediment on the bottom of the sea.

Lord Kilbraken duly reported this in publications that reached most countries – including Germany. That resulted in a German solicitor contacting Lord Kilbraken to inform him that he had details of exactly where the Italian ship carrying the "Rommel Treasure" to North Africa had been sunk. He said that it was in about 200 feet of water and now that Ed Link had proved it possible to dive to that depth, he wanted an agreement with Ed Link to disclose that location and so get a share of the resulting proceeds.

Kilbraken told Ed Link. Ed asked me to look into it for him. I did so.

The story given to me (which later evidence indicated was substantially correct) was that Rommel, advancing on Egypt during the war, had requested substantial sums of gold and jewellery to be put at his disposal to help induce various Egyptian and Libyan officials to come over to the German side. Six large ammunition boxes containing gold and other valuables had been loaded, together with six German soldiers to guard them, onto an Italian ship that headed for Tripoli. But, en route, that ship had been sunk by Allied action. The captain and the six German guards, who were the only ones who knew anything about the contents, had transferred the ammunition boxes to a lifeboat. Somewhat overloaded, the lifeboat struggled on, with the captain charting their position, until it sank in a storm. There were only two survivors, one of whom managed to retain that chart.

After the war, this survivor went to a German solicitor, told him the story and gave him the chart for safe custody. The location where the lifeboat had gone to the bottom with the six ammunition boxes had a depth of water slightly less than 200 feet – far beyond the depth that anyone had so far managed to retrieve anything from the ocean floor. On learning that Ed Link had achieved that depth from the articles that Kilbraken had written – which had been publicised worldwide – the German solicitor (and presumably his client) wanted, at last, to cash in on the valuable knowledge in their possession.

The evidence that Kilbraken presented to me was convincing – and there was no reason why the German solicitor should have made it up. So I helped draw up an agreement with the German solicitor, which Ed finally approved, and we then had an exciting examination of the chart. To our great delight, the position proved to be outside the territorial waters of any country – otherwise ownership could have been claimed by others. Ed reckoned he and his team on *Sea Diver* could both find and then salvage the ammunition boxes and the treasure therein.

But that led to the problem of what to do with it once the treasure was aboard *Sea Diver*? Ed obviously did not want to have any government lay claim to it or be involved in disputes about ownership. Above all, he wanted not to have to pay enormous taxes on it, or have the Mafia (who were already known to be keeping an eye on his activities) trying to hijack it.

Ed gave me the problem of solving all those administrative and transportation angles, in exchange for 10% of the final profit, while

423

he concentrated on planning to find and retrieve the loot from the bottom of the sea and getting it aboard *Sea Diver*.

I first rechecked that the location of the treasure was outside the territorial waters of any country, then I examined the import regulations of the countries bordering the Mediterranean. The only place that did not tax the import of gold was Beirut – but that was far too dangerous an area to contemplate. All other countries would claim large chunks of tax if it entered their territory – some would confiscate the lot.

I sought advice from my friends in Geneva. It became obvious that a Swiss bank would be by far the best final destination for any gold and valuables that we retrieved.

So I recommended to Ed that he should go ahead with the attempt on that broad basis. He and Marion came to stay with us in Switzerland to discuss details. They agreed with me that everything – from beginning to end – must be done legally and with the approval of the Swiss authorities. At a meeting in Geneva, advised by my father's old friends, Maurice Merkt and Eduarde Pictet, we set up a Liechtenstein company, "l'Etablissement pour l'Exploration Sous-Marine", with me as managing director and sole authority, with the sum of $50,000 – a gift to me from Ed that I then put into the company to use as working capital.

Merkt made the formal arrangements with the Swiss authorities to a levy (as tax) of 4% of value of any gold or other valuables we imported into Switzerland. The main remaining problem was how to get the loot safely into Switzerland without taking it into any other country first. There seemed only two ways of doing so – either to sail Sea Diver via the Bay of Biscay and the English Channel to Holland and then down the Rhine to Basle (which we decided to abandon, because it gave the Mafia too long and too much opportunity to hijack it en route), or to fly it direct to a Swiss airport – preferably Geneva. That, however, would involve transferring the treasure to a seaplane, flying boat or amphibian while *Sea Diver* was at sea outside territorial waters, and landing at Geneva either on the lake or at the airport.

I then thought of a third way — which plan we finally adopted. I arranged with BEA that they would, at short notice, taxi an aircraft to the sea end of the Gibraltar runway, where the treasure could be loaded, within a couple of minutes, onto the aircraft directly from *Sea Diver* without it touching the ground. That aircraft would then fly direct to Geneva. The Governor of Gibraltar at that time was General Keitley, whose co-operation, if required, I was confident I could arrange.

I would have liked to join the party on *Sea Diver* and help salvage the treasure, which, at that time, was reckoned by the German solicitor to be worth over £22,000,000. But Ed insisted that I should remain in Switzerland to control the arrangements for getting it safely to Geneva. So, with his help, I set up a special long-wave radio set in the top floor in our chalet at Gstaad, with which I could communicate directly with him in Sea Diver in the Mediterranean. We arranged a series of codes by which he could inform me of progress and arrange the rendezvous on the Gibraltar runway.

In fact, Ed did locate the six ammunition boxes in which the gold and other valuables were reputed to be stored. But, on that trip he was unable to overcome the problem of raising them in the strong current and shifting sand. We planned another trip, with more elaborate equipment, to do so. However, he became involved in even more urgent projects, triggered by the tragic loss of the nuclear-powered submarine *USS Thresher*, and his subsequent work with the US Navy delayed our second attempt. We then learnt that another organisation had pounced on the Rommel treasure and carried away the loot. I regretted that, but Ed was far more concerned with the wonderful things he was doing to advance science than what was (for him) merely getting a little more cash.

Meanwhile, giving an entirely false position for its location nearer the Libyan coast, and adding a bit of imagination, I wrote the skeleton story based on our attempt to find the Rommel Treasure and entitled it "*The Golden Oyster*". Donald Payne, after we had motored down from Geneva and then gone by boat to Tripoli to get the right atmosphere, rewrote it and we published it jointly under the penname Donald Gordon. It hit the bestseller lists in several countries.

After that, I saw Ed fairly regularly. His exploits, particularly in connection with salvage operations for lost submarines, and an atomic bomb, made him world famous. Then he became interested in railway engines and I helped him arrange a reconstruction of Stephenson's "Rocket". I also arranged his 29-day tour of England and Scotland in 1981. The night before he left to return to the USA, we all stayed at The Elms at Abberley. In the morning, we were standing outside the front door of that hotel. Bunny and I were saying goodbye to him and his wife Marion. We were very sad to see them go.

Then a strange thing occurred. As I shook hands with Ed, a sort of electric shock went up my arm. We stood there, looking into each other's eyes, clasping hands for quite a long time. Something told me that I would never see him again. I had never experienced any sensation like that before – nor have I since. About three weeks later (7th September 1981) the message came from Marion that he had died.

I was terribly sad. But he had left me many, many happy memories. Also, by having helped me set up "Sous-Marine" with that $50,000 gift, he had – unwittingly and by sheer chance – started me on a path that completely changed my life, as well as that of my daughter Pat and grandson Robin, and taken me into the world of finance – with which (now in my 100th year) I am still actively engaged.

It always amazes me how one small and apparently trivial incident can have big repercussions over many decades. Ed – thank you, yet again! But I am sorry we failed to raise the Rommel Treasure!

Chapter 23

Financial

The first time I can remember handling money was when my mother gave me tuppence to buy my sister some sweets for her birthday present – probably in 1917, when I was four years old. I remember walking from 39 Carson Road in West Dulwich, where we happened to be visiting my Auntie Flo and Grandma (just round the corner from where we lived in Dalmore Road), up to the shops about a hundred yards away. Armed with a small paper bag full of sweets, I started on my way back.

The temptation to taste one was so great that I could not resist it. It was so nice, I tried another. By the time I ended my journey back, there were, alas, none left. It was some time before my mother entrusted me with any more money.

My experience of finance was next augmented by discovering a silver threepenny bit in my Christmas pudding and my consequent excitement, each Christmas Day, of hoping to find another. One birthday, also, my father gave me a sixpenny bit – a vast fortune to me. Much later, as a schoolboy at Dulwich College in 1930, I had an allowance of £50 per year – but I rarely spent any of that, and I believe it went into War Bonds (one of the biggest rackets ever organised by the Government to swindle its loyal citizens). Then, just after I left school in 1931, my father lost all his money as a result of the Great Depression. The fear of starvation, which helped motivate me, was something that is difficult to imagine today in England.

Winning the Prize Cadetship to Cranwell meant that I should have enough to live on, theoretically, for the rest of my life – but with a very good chance that I would shorten that by being killed in a flying accident, even without a war. Married as a junior officer in the RAF, with no entitlement to any marriage allowance or extra benefits, I was always desperately short of money. In 1935, however, I did invest £25 in the new Blackpool Tower project, which did me little good. After I reached the rank of Squadron Leader in 1939, which entitled me to marriage allowance, things were better; but we RAF officers were still very poorly paid compared with, for example, officers in the American services or people with equivalent responsibilities in industry. Nevertheless, we enjoyed life immensely.

When I left the RAF in 1957 and had enough money to start investing, my old friend "Baldy" (Wing Commander Piggot, of the Equipment Branch from Cardington days) introduced me to Benny Myers – a school friend of his who had become a partner in a stockbroker firm - J. M. Finn & Co in London. On his advice, I invested a little of my precious capital in a company named South African Breweries, but a week later he rang me up to advise me to sell them immediately as their price was falling. That was my first real experience of investing on the stock market, and it did not inspire confidence.

But I gradually managed to do better with my investments. Kevin O'Hanlon, who had taken over from Benny Myers, put me into some property shares (eg Capital and Counties, and Land Securities) that did quite well. When I moved to Switzerland in 1960 and had rather more substantial sums to invest, I was advised to put most of it into one of the big five Swiss banks and let them invest it for me. I chose one of the biggest banks in Geneva.

I soon found that the investments made by the bank were losing me money faster than I was making it from writing. I could not allow that situation to continue. So I gave up writing for a couple of years to devote all my time to studying finance and the stock markets. Applying the teachings of the RAF Staff College, my experience with "Bonehead", and studying all the factors that normally influenced share price movements, I evolved a method of presenting all the relevant data in a pictorial form that was easy to understand and permitted quick comparisons between individual shares. It was somewhat similar to the Bonehead displays I had organised in Churchill's underground offices in Whitehall, and I used the same Cardex system for presenting the consolidated data.

That system of having all the data presented in pictorial form was the basis of my future success. Nobody else, to the best of my knowledge, had ever used such a way of investing. Over the years, my daughter Pat and I refined it. It had nothing to do with the "technical analysis" chartist method of investing, although reference to that often forewarned us to what other investors were likely to do.

I was once asked to give a talk about my method to the staff at one of the stockbrokers I used. To demonstrate the advantages of my pictorial displays of judging shares, I presented each person there with a page of statistics concerning the dimensions of the limbs and body of a famous actress and asked them to assess how attractive she appeared. From those figures they simply could not visualise her. But a single glance at a picture of her gave them an instant answer. It was exactly the same with the pictures I used for depicting the relative potential value of company shares.

After our attempt to raise the Rommel Treasure had failed, Ed Link gave me the Lichtenstein Company (Sous Marine, which was still worth nearly $50,000), on the basis that I should invest it only in shares of Canadian companies. He pointed out that Canada was a young, growing country that had surplus minerals and oil, a small but growing population in a vast area, stable government, few race problems, and everything necessary for future prosperity. Furthermore, since few people troubled to invest in Canadian shares because the nearby big American stock market received so much more publicity, there was much less competition there with which to contend.

I was advised to use the Lausanne branch of a Canadian stockbroker firm for information on Canadian shares. That led to my friendship with Jean-Claude Blanc, who was one of the most charming Swiss gentleman, with a lovely, vivacious wife, that it has ever been my privilege to meet during the many years I have been resident in that country. He, and his staff, helped me enormously, and we remain great friends to this day.

Taking the advice that Ed had given me and using the pictorial presentation of relative share values I had developed, I had the good luck to nearly treble the value of "Sous-Marine" during the first year of investing. The next year was also successful – it so happened that

I had hit a good period to start and my system seemed to work quite well. I told Ed about it and thanked him profusely for having given me such good advice. He, of course, was delighted and mentioned my progress to a friend of his who lived in Switzerland and was married to a Swiss lady, with whom Bunny became friendly.

In consequence, I received a request from this chap to take over the management of a proportion of his investments from the Swiss bank that had – as in my case – been losing him money. I was extremely reluctant to accept such responsibility, but was finally persuaded to do so by the offer of 20% of any profits and an assurance that if, perchance, I lost it all – the relatively small sum involved would not be disastrous for the owner.

That led to other people with money to invest in Switzerland seeking my help and increased my work which, together with my own investments, continued to prosper in a moderate fashion. One of my problems was that writing books and managing investments did not mix. Writing required absolute quiet, dreaming oneself into imaginary situations and talking to fictitious characters for long periods, with any interruption being a great hindrance. Investing involved frequent phone calls and urgent action.

One of the people I met was Robin Mackness, a young British chap (rather less than half my age). He and his lovely wife Liz were living in Lausanne. Robin had the distinction of having been the first person seriously to introduce the concept of duvets into Britain, virtually completely unknown in the early 1960s. He had spotted the virtues and advantages of duvets over blankets, a talent that he kept shrouded in mystery (but it apparently had something to do with Norway and Norwegians). Suffice to say that 85% of the British population now use them in preference to sheets and blankets, whereas virtually nobody used them when he started his Slumberdown Company in Edinburgh in 1963, shortly after coming down from Cambridge.

Robin had also been a founding shareholder of a very successful merchant bank in Edinburgh, and when I first met him, it was flatteringly clear to me from his early questions that he appeared to have a nose for a good opportunity. We started working together in the delightful surrounds of that part of Alpine Switzerland, and the results started coming in.

Robin's objectives were a little different to mine, in that, rather than restricting himself to managing the investments of friends, he was keen to establish a formal company to do the same thing, perhaps in a more structured way. He secured the backing of one of the Big Three Swiss banks, and his venture proved to be very successful. I do know that he made some substantial financial returns out of it. I was delighted for him, and we became close friends – a friendship that lasts to this day.

Robin has lived a life of blistering adventure, and he has written about many of these adventures. One of them. *"Oradour, Massacre* and *Aftermath"*, tells the story of the frightful German massacre at Oradour-sur-Glane in South West France in 1944, never previously explained. As always with wartime mysteries, there was endless controversy about this story, which included Robin learning that he was on a French hit list, since they disapproved and were offended by his explanations and findings. The book was the third publication by the then fledgling Bloomsbury Publishing, and with their help it became a bestseller for over a month. It is currently being made into a film.

Our differing client approaches meant that, while we co-operated together, we actually worked separately. I had my own banking connections in Switzerland and Robin had developed his. The paranoia with which Swiss Banks guard their secrecy meant that co-operation in that department would not have been appropriate. However, we spent a great deal of time in the most scenic places, with our two wives, and many decisions were taken at high altitude and with much enjoyment.

In my situation, I realised that the cost of keeping our two children at expensive schools, plus all our own expenses for living and travel, meant that looking after the money we already had made, and trying to invest it (and the other money entrusted to me) wisely, was probably more important than writing further books. So I decided to make investment my top priority and main occupation.

My own investments, which were on quite a modest scale, were progressing satisfactorily until Bunny, in 1972, decided that she wanted to return to England to be near our daughters and particularly to our eldest, Pam. I was dead against it. Jock Ireland and others warned us against it, but I gave in to Bunny's wishes. I feared it would prove a disaster, particularly as it would cause the collapse of the investment organisation that I was successfully building up in Switzerland. I knew also that I would be out of touch, and unable to work properly, during the move.

That move turned out to be, as I had feared, a complete disaster. The house we had arranged to rent in Pertenhall (near Bedford) became unavailable. I had, for over two months, nowhere to work or receive regular investment information. I was borrowed in Swiss Francs, but largely invested in English and Canadian shares, and the Swiss franc (having been 12 SFr to £1 Sterling) appreciated to nearly three times that value, while the UK and Canadian stock market collapsed. That "scissored" the overall value of my assets to a fraction of their former value. Meanwhile, Bunny and Pam had committed me to start building a bungalow (which I never wanted) on some ground at Keysoe that I had bought in Pam's name some years previously.

One afternoon, sitting forlornly in the garden of a rather depressing house we had rented in Carlton, I dismally weighed up our situation. It was pretty awful. The value of my own investments had fallen to a total of no more than £32,000. Our only other asset (apart from our clothes and tiny RAF pension) was our sports Mercedes in the old wooden shed that served as a garage. Then, that afternoon, as I sat there looking across at it lovingly but rather sadly, one of the oak beams holding up the dilapidated building suddenly fell sideways and dented the side of our car. I stared in disbelief. That was the last straw. I wondered whether we could even afford to have the dent removed. Then, two days later, driving away from that dismal house, a large tree was blown down as we were passing it. Luckily, it just missed us – cutting off the road behind us in a symbolic way.

And that, as it happened, turned out to be the nadir of our fortunes.

We returned to Switzerland, living as cheaply as possible, and I started investing again. I had encouraged Pat to start taking an interest in investing in shares and taught her the method I had developed for assessing their relative values. With her help, and advice also from Ron Douglas at Richardsons in London, and hard work, we together, over the next 12 years, gradually turned that £32,000 into well over £7 million – an achievement that staggered everyone who knew about it.

Pat formed her own investment company in England, where she had her own clients. Together, our reputation as fund managers had grown to an extent that we were looking after quite large investment sums for various friends and clients.

One reason for our success was my experience as a pilot. That gave me an enormous advantage denied to anyone without that background. My flying training and subsequent experience – which I applied to investing – was far, far more valuable than any degree in economics or any number of years working in a bank or stockbroker firm.

That similarity between surviving as a pilot and investing successfully needs explanation.

Taking off in a military aircraft is very similar to buying shares. Once you are airborne, you only have one option – to get down again safely, perhaps by parachute, but hopefully having accomplished your mission. Similarly, once you have bought a share – you really only have one option, and that is to sell it. As with the pilot, you need continuously (every minute) to ask yourself – is it safe to go on? In other words – if you had not already bought that share – would you now buy that share under the new circumstance now pertaining? Unless the answer is an emphatic and enthusiastic "Yes" – then you must sell immediately. An instant decision – no dithering – parachute, or it may be too late.

Similarly, before taking off in an aircraft, I always studied the weather conditions (economic background), checked that the aircraft was properly maintained (annual reports, etc) and that the tanks had adequate fuel (cash). In the cockpit, I had a checklist to complete and then, just before take-off, test the engines and controls and give a final glance at the sky to check the weather before committing myself to the take-off (ie buy the share).

Once airborne, I had only one option – I had to descend, by one means or another, to the surface of the earth. I might have decided to abandon the intended flight and land back immediately, but as long as I continued flying I would be listening to the noise from the engines and keeping a close eye on all my instruments, so that I could take immediate action if anything was not going as planned – also watching like a hawk the oil pressures, the fuel gauges and the weather – the three things most likely to cause alarm. In an emergency I could try to make a forced landing, or even eject and take to my parachute; but I was always ready instantly to make that decision if necessary.

Compared with the training, and experience, of a deskbound economist ("on the one hand, on the other …") or even a bank manager, I had that great advantage.

My criterion for buying any share was that – for one reason or another – I was convinced that it would double (or at least go up 50%) in the next six months from its existing price under the conditions pertaining on that day. Every day after buying it, I would again access it on those criteria and, unless the answer remained a positive "Buy", then I would sell it immediately.

On that basis, there could never be any such thing as a "hold". Every day, each share was either a "buy" or it was a "sell". Furthermore, as soon as the big institutions started buying shares in any company we held – that was usually a warning to start thinking of selling, because they had become only potential sellers.

In my original studies of the stock markets, I had drawn historic charts of all the factors I considered important (going back to when statistics first began). These proved invaluable in helping judge the main market moves. On several occasions I sold out every share in my portfolio and then waited until my criteria were again met. It was hard work, but very satisfying – and profitable.

By 1985, at age 72, with over £7m worth of assets in my bank, I felt that I now had enough capital (without further income) to meet all our financial needs for the rest of my life. In consequence, my interest in the stock market began to wane. At that stage, also, Bunny's health was beginning to deteriorate and I more or less retired – but relied on Pat and an assistant whom we employed to keep up to date the master pictures which would warn if markets were getting too high.

The stock market crash of 1987 occurred while I was out of touch, travelling slowly across France trying to get Bunny (whose deteriorating health was now a serious handicap) back to England. By the time I was properly in touch again, the value of my assets had diminished by nearly £3 million – but that left me (so I thought) still more than enough to last my lifetime.

So I ceased worrying about making more money – particularly after Bunny died in 1990 and I had only myself to look after. I thought I had plenty to carry me through the few years I then expected to continue living. My father had died at 82 and I saw no reason why I should live much longer than that.

Instead, I helped finance two projects which I thought would help the world – while giving me a good return on the money I provided.

The first was a method (originally developed at the University of Vancouver) of keeping food and flowers fresh for long periods. This has since been adopted successfully worldwide, but the commercial side was badly handled and, instead of me reaping the benefits, I did not even recoup the outlay that my correct vision had cost me.

The second was The Green Cone – a dustbin for food waste, each of which, when fed with the regular amounts usually produced by a couple of people, made it almost completely disappear, with attention only needed annually. It was tested in many parts of the world and proved to be extremely successful in disposing of food waste – without any smell or contamination. But getting enough authorities to adopt it proved impossible – they preferred to employ more people and contaminate the planet. Perhaps its successor, the Green Johanna, will have better luck.

Meanwhile, without much effort on my part, my other investments were adequate to enable me to live to the standard to which I had become accustomed and enjoyed – until 9 years ago when, in 2004, a stupid mistake by a clerk in the US patent office led to the sudden collapse of a share in which I was heavily invested. Numerous other shareholders were also badly affected – with several bankruptcies and loss of homes resulting.

Now, however, I am working hard to become a millionaire again before I reach my 101st birthday.

Also, the "Ghost of Salembou" is beckoning to me to write that dramatic story.

Chapter 24

My Home

Looking back, I realise that I have never lived anywhere that I could really call "my home".

The first house in which I remember living was in Dalmore Road, West Dulwich, London, SE21, during the First World war (1914-1918). Soon after that war ended, we moved to 81 Alleyn Park, also in Dulwich. Then, a couple of years later, we moved up the road, to the big house at number 17. We usually spent our summer holidays at my father's family home near Evian-les-Bains, on Lake Geneva. Then, in 1928, we moved to 35 Cator Road in Beckenham, Kent. Three years later, we were back near Dulwich at 47 Lancaster Road, from where I joined the RAF.

When asked – for example, by other boys at school – where my home was, I did not know how to answer and began envying those who really had one.

The RAF (and particularly the Fleet Air Arm of the Royal Navy) had moved me around so much that Bunny and I had lived in 57 different apartments or houses in five different countries during my RAF career. In 1960, on finding ourselves with both the freedom and enough money to make our home wherever we liked, we never settled in any house long enough for it to really become more than a temporary base – although we spent more time in the Gstaad and Chateau d'Oex area of Switzerland (which became my official residence for the next 50 years) than anywhere else.

We had previously tried living in Italy and stayed a few weeks in Capri (near where Gracie Fields lived), but the hordes of trippers ruled that out. We had also spent three months touring the entire coastline of Spain and Portugal without finding anywhere that really appealed to us. We visited the Scandinavian countries and other parts of Europe (including Yugoslavia), and then, on returning to Switzerland, we rented a lovely apartment with a panoramic view of Lake Geneva and the Alps, which we thought might become our permanent home.

But, after the owner insisted on us paying the rent for six months in advance, we found that it was her habit always to play the piano non-stop for two hours immediately below our bedroom, starting at midnight, so forcing the occupants to leave and forfeit their deposit. We then decided to go back to live in Gstaad – which area, together with Chateau d'Oex, was our main base. Then, as we got older, we lived much of each year in hotels, with spells on the French Riviera in the winter and Scotland – fishing – in the summer. Bunny would have preferred living nearer to our daughters and their growing families, and we took every opportunity to visit them.

On Bunny's 80th birthday, having had dinner with Pam to celebrate it, we were walking back to where we were staying, when she suddenly stopped.

"I'm 80 now!" she said sadly, "I must get a stick and walk slowly."

"Don't be so bloody silly," I replied. "That's just a number. It's all in the mind. Try walking faster."

She shook her head. "I remember Mummy ..."

From that night onwards, her health slowly began to deteriorate. She had previously been very fit – although, without her knowing it, she had a crumpled aorta, for which reason I always carried in my pocket a note from her doctor warning that, if she suddenly collapsed, that might be the reason. To begin with, I was able to look after her myself, but then arranged a carer for her until she finally had to go into a nursing home. We chose one near where our eldest daughter lived, where we could all easily visit her. When I was away, I normally phoned her at least once a day.

On one Monday in August 1990, I was down in Switzerland and planning to return to England and see Bunny in the nursing home that weekend. I had phoned her that evening and we had our usual jovial chat; but then, soon after midnight, I woke up in a sweat with the extraordinary feeling that something was wrong. I felt an overwhelming urge to get back quickly to see my darling Bunny. I rang her at breakfast time to say that I was cancelling my plans and would start motoring back to England the next day. She was very surprised and saw no reason for me to do so – but I had the feeling that I must.

438

I arrived back in the area fairly late in the evening and had planned to go straight to see her, but she preferred that I should delay my visit until the next day. I spent two hours with her that morning. She seemed in better health than she had been for a long time and we were joking and laughing about various things in our lives which had amused us. That evening, at 7 o'clock, I had another half hour on the phone with her – again, a very happy one. At 9pm I was going to bed when the phone rang. It was our doctor. He said that Bunny was dead.

For a while I just sat on the bed in a state of shock. Then, slowly and sadly, I took out the pills from the drawer of my bedside table and laid them out on the top. I knew (because I had once before by mistake taken a slight overdose) that four of the beta blockers would make me unconscious, and that a dozen, together with the other pills I had ready, would finish the job. Swallowing those would be easy. A glass of whiskey would help. I would do it in the garage with the door closed, sitting in the car with the windows open and the engine running. That would make doubly sure.

However, as always before any take-off, I decided first to go through a checklist.

One thing was certain. Life without Bunny held no attraction whatsoever. Everything that I had done since I was 15 years old and had first fallen in love with her had either been with, or for, her, and my decision was irrevocable.

Second on the checklist were the children. Since, already in my 70s, I seemed unlikely to live very much longer anyway, would it really make much difference if I departed immediately? With Pam, probably not, and financially it might even help her. Similarly with the youngest, Wendy. But Pat, who had been working closely with me, might still welcome my help.

The only other item on the checklist was Bunny herself and what she would have wished. She, I thought, would have approved my decision. But there was one thing she would have wanted me to do first – to destroy all the intimate letters which we had always exchanged when separated. We often took pleasure in rereading some of these together and one packet of them was locked in a drawer down in our apartment in Switzerland. I finally decided that, for her sake, I must destroy them first.

Reluctantly, around midnight, I put those pills back for future use, took a sleeping tablet and went to bed.

For fear of breaking down completely in public, I could not face attending Bunny's funeral. Our wise old friend Jock Ireland had guessed my ultimate intention and, thinking that her funeral might be the day I had chosen, he stayed close beside me all that day so that he could prevent it.

Instead, the following evening, I picked one of Bunny's favourite red roses and walked quietly up through the fields to place it on her grave, where I sobbed my heart out in a private and final farewell.

The sad task of sorting out Bunny's things in England took much longer than I had expected, and by the time I had also dealt with them in Switzerland – and then realised that I would be leaving many of my own affairs for others to sort out – the urge to use those pills began diminishing. Everyone was being so kind and helpful that it became postponed – and I finally decided that perhaps Bunny would not have wished me to do so anyway.

I was, however, extremely lonely and, about four years after Bunny died, my doctor advised me that I was unwise to continue motoring long distances on my own. So I advertised in the Officers' Pensions Society Magazine ("*The Pennant*") for a companion. I had many replies and interesting meetings that led to me gaining a partner – the widow (23 years younger than me) of a retired Army officer.

My recollections now of that association have become very fuzzy. In recent years I have found that my memory of things that happened in my childhood has gained enormously in clarity, and amazingly in detail. But most things that have happened as I have grown older – and particularly since Bunny died – have become increasingly difficult to recall. I believe that is normal, but in my case it may have been aggravated by a mini-stroke that we think I may have experienced a few years ago.

One incident I do remember, however, is walking up the pavement of Evening Hill near Sandbanks and suddenly stopping to look back towards the harbour entrance to see the reason for the shrill warning blasting out from the siren of the ferry. A second later, a car coming up the hill too fast skidded and crashed onto the pavement, brushing my arm, at the exact location where I would have been, but for me having been stopped by that siren. My amazingly good luck still seems to be operating well.

So, while recent events in my life have gradually, but now increasingly, become rather a blurred muddle, the damage done to the RAF, and to England, by the efforts of that communist Jack Richards and his pals becomes clearer every day. Had they not deliberately prevented our military aircraft becoming properly equipped, I believe the war would have ended much earlier and I wonder who now is working against the best interests of our country? The news, and recent developments, do little to justify complacency.

The only other main event in my recent life that I can now remember clearly is that in November 2010 my partner had a terrible accident which left her brain damaged and I, in my 98th year, unexpectedly and suddenly, was forced to leave the luxury apartment which I had helped purchase, and fend for myself on my own.

I had heard of "Care Homes" and had always dreaded the idea of perhaps, one day, having to become resident in one. Two of my daughters, however, insisted that there was no alternative. After six weeks of struggling alone to look after myself and do the shopping and cooking, I had to agree.

On 22nd December 2010, with ice and snow everywhere, Pat brought me here to Chantry Court, where she had arranged for me to rent this apartment. I had gout (which prevented me walking much), a painful eye infection, a pulse rate which was varying dangerously between 160 and 33 per minute, and I also had some lumps of skin cancer which urgently needed removing.

The awful weather continued, there were delays at the local surgery in me seeing a doctor, my medical records had not yet arrived, and over the Christmas holiday I was the only one here, except for a skeleton staff. And when I did finally see a doctor, she was obviously too inexperienced to understand my situation. Furthermore, she made her opinion very clear that anyone entering a "care home" was obviously expecting to die soon and that it was not, therefore, worth her spending any of her valuable time trying to discover the cause or delay it. Prescriptions for masses of pills to reduce the pain seemed to be her only remedy for almost any problem.

Then, as the other residents and staff began returning, the weather started improving, a different doctor had visited me and I became accustomed to my new surroundings, I realised that this establishment was more like a happy rejuvenation centre which was run as a luxury hotel – furthermore, it was being managed by someone who had the experience of running one of the best private hotels in the British Isles.

Living here is even better, in many respects, than in the expensive and highly regarded hotels that Bunny and I had become accustomed to using in Europe. I also find it an ideal place for an author to write without fear of distractions.

My gout appears now to have been cured, my heart problems eliminated by a pacemaker, the cancers removed and my eyesight is excellent – all due to the good advice and arrangements made for me by the splendid staff here (and particularly the advice from "Alan", which directly contradicted that of the first two doctors that I saw, and so saved my life). My comfortable suite of rooms here is equipped with everything I need; it has views over several miles of the Wiltshire countryside, and is completely quiet. I can call immediate assistance by pressing a button or phoning, and there is always a receptionist downstairs to whom I can go to seek advice or have a chat. Many of the other residents have similar backgrounds and interests to mine, which has resulted in me forming several new friendships. All are younger than I am – some considerably so – and several appear perfectly fit, but are here to enjoy the excellent facilities.

This establishment is utterly different from my original conception of a "care home". They label it as "A retirement village with care" or "Independent living with a network of support" – but I could not care less what labels they put on it.

Now I have reached my 100th birthday and have been here over 2 years. For the first time in my life – after all my wanderings – I feel that I am at last residing somewhere that I can genuinely refer to as "My Home".